POLITICAL
EMOTIONS

POLITICAL EMOTIONS

Why Love Matters for Justice

Martha C. Nussbaum

The Belknap Press of Harvard University Press

Cambridge, Massachusetts
London, England

First Harvard University Press paperback edition, 2015
First Printing

Library of Congress Cataloging-in-Publication Data

Nussbaum, Martha Craven, 1947–
    Political emotions : why love matters for justice / Martha C. Nussbaum.
        pages cm
    Includes bibliographical references and index.
    ISBN 978-0-674-72465-5 (hardcover : alk. paper)
    ISBN 978-0-674-50380-9 (pbk.)
1. Political science—Philosophy.   2. Emotions—Political aspects.
3. Emotions (Philosophy).   4. Political psychology.   I. Title.
    JA71.N88 2013
    320.01'9—dc23
                                                            2013010890

In memory of Terence Moore,

1953–2004

Contents

This day of torment, of craziness, of foolishness—
only love can make it end in happiness and joy.

—W. A. Mozart and Lorenzo Da Ponte,
Le Nozze di Figaro (1786)

A Problem in the History of Liberalism

Lo, body and soul—this land,
My own Manhattan with spires, and the sparkling and hurrying
    tides, and the ships,
The varied and ample land, the South and the North in the light,
    Ohio's shores and flashing Missouri,
And ever the far-spreading prairies cover'd with grass and corn.

Lo, the most excellent sun so calm and haughty,
The violet and purple morn with just-felt breezes,
The gentle soft-born measureless light,
The miracle spreading bathing all, the fulfill'd noon,
The coming eve delicious, the welcome night and the stars,
Over my cities shining all, enveloping man and land.

—Walt Whitman, "When Lilacs Last in the Dooryard Bloom'd"

My Bengal of Gold,
I love you.
Forever your skies,
Your air, set my heart in tune
As if it were a flute.

—Rabindranath Tagore, *"Amar Shonar Bangla,"*
now the national anthem of Bangladesh

ALL SOCIETIES ARE FULL OF EMOTIONS. Liberal democracies are no exception. The story of any day or week in the life of even a relatively stable democracy would include a host of emotions—anger, fear, sympathy, disgust, envy, guilt, grief, many forms of love. Some of these episodes of emotion have little to do with political principles or the public culture, but others are different: they take as their object the nation, the nation's goals, its institutions and leaders, its geography, and one's fellow citizens seen as fellow inhabitants of a common public space. Often, as in my two epigraphs, emotions directed at the geographical features of a nation are ways of channeling emotions toward its key commitments—to inclusiveness, equality, the relief of misery, the end of slavery. Whitman's lyric is part of a poem mourning the death of Abraham Lincoln, and it expresses the combination of passionate love, pride, and deep grief that the speaker feels at the current state of his nation. *"Amar Shonar Bangla"* expressed Tagore's capacious humanism, his aspiration toward an inclusive "religion of humanity" that would link all castes and religions in his society. Sung as the national anthem of a poor nation, it expresses both pride and love at the beauty of the land and (in subsequent verses) sadness at the work that remains to be done.

Such public emotions, frequently intense, have large-scale consequences for the nation's progress toward its goals. They can give the pursuit of those goals new vigor and depth, but they can also derail that pursuit, introducing or reinforcing divisions, hierarchies, and forms of neglect or obtuseness.

Sometimes people suppose that only fascist or aggressive societies are intensely emotional and that only such societies need to focus on the cultivation of emotions. Those beliefs are both mistaken and dangerous. They are mistaken, because all societies need to think about the stability of their political culture over time and the security of cherished values in times of stress. All societies, then, need to think about compassion for loss, anger at injustice, the limiting of envy and disgust in favor of inclusive sympathy. Ceding the terrain of emotion-shaping to antiliberal forces gives them a huge advantage in the people's hearts and risks making people think of liberal values as tepid and boring. One reason Abraham Lincoln, Martin Luther King Jr., Mahatma Gandhi, and Jawaharlal Nehru were such great political leaders for their liberal societies is that they understood the need to touch citizens' hearts and to inspire, deliberately, strong emotions directed at the common work before them. All political principles, the good as well as the bad, need emotional support to ensure their stability over time, and all decent societies need to guard against division and hierarchy by cultivating appropriate sentiments of sympathy and love.

In the type of liberal society that aspires to justice and equal opportunity for all, there are two tasks for the political cultivation of emotion. One is to engender and sustain strong commitment to worthy projects that require effort and sacrifice—such as social redistribution, the full inclusion of previously excluded or marginalized groups, the protection of the environment, foreign aid, and the national defense. Most people tend toward narrowness of sympathy. They can easily become immured in narcissistic projects and forget about the needs of those outside their narrow circle. Emotions directed at the nation and its goals are frequently of great help in getting people to think larger thoughts and recommit themselves to a larger common good.

The other related task for the cultivation of public emotion is to keep at bay forces that lurk in all societies and, ultimately, in all of us: tendencies to protect the fragile self by denigrating and subordinating others. (It is this tendency that, following Kant, I shall call "radical evil," though my understanding of it will be rather different from Kant's.) Disgust and envy, the desire to inflict shame upon others—all of these are present in all societies, and, very likely, in every individual human life. Unchecked, they can inflict great damage. The damage they do is particularly great when they are relied upon as guides in the process of lawmaking and social formation (when, for example, the disgust that people feel for a group of other people is used as a valid reason for treating those people in a discriminatory way). But even when a society has avoided falling into that trap, these forces lurk in society and need to be counteracted energetically by an education that cultivates the ability to see full and equal humanity in another person, perhaps one of humanity's most difficult and fragile achievements. An important part of that education is performed by the public political culture, which represents the nation and its people in a particular way. It can include or exclude, cement hierarchies or dismantle them—as Lincoln's Gettysburg Address, with its breathtaking fiction that the United States has always been dedicated to racial equality, so stirringly does.

Great democratic leaders, in many times and places, have understood the importance of cultivating appropriate emotions (and discouraging those that obstruct society's progress toward its goals). Liberal political philosophy, however, has, on the whole, said little about the topic. John Locke, defending religious toleration, acknowledged a problem of wide-spread animosity between members of different religions in the England of his time; he urged people to take up attitudes of "charity, bounty, and liberality" and recommended that churches advise their members of "the duties of peace and good-will towards all men, as well towards the erroneous as the orthodox."[1] Locke made no attempt, however, to delve into the psychological origins of intolerance. He thus gave little guidance about the nature of the bad attitudes and how they might be combated. Nor did he recommend any official public steps to shape psychological attitudes. The cultivation of good attitudes is left to individuals and to churches. Given that it was precisely in churches that the bad attitudes festered, Locke leaves his own project in a fragile and uncertain posi-tion. In his view, however, the liberal state should confine itself to pro-tecting people's rights to property and other political goods, when and if others assail them. In terms of his own argument, which grounds religious toleration in equal natural rights, this is intervention one step too late.

Locke's silence about the psychology of the decent society is common in subsequent liberal political philosophy in the Western tradition—in part, no doubt, because liberal political philosophers sensed that pre-scribing any particular type of emotional cultivation might easily involve limits on free speech and other steps incompatible with liberal ideas of freedom and autonomy. Such was explicitly the view of Immanuel Kant. Kant delved deeper into human psychology than did Locke. In *Religion within the Limits of Mere Reason,*[2] he argues that bad behavior in society is not a mere artifact of current social conditions: it has its roots in uni-versal human nature, which contains tendencies to abuse other people (to treat them not as ends in themselves, but as instruments). He called these tendencies "radical evil." These bad tendencies lead people to en-gage in envious and competitive striving as soon as they find themselves with others in society. Kant felt that individuals have an ethical duty to join some group that will strengthen the good tendencies they have (ten-dencies to treat other people well), so that those tendencies will have a greater chance of winning out over the bad. He believes that a church of the right sort would be such a support structure for social morality, and he even argued that all people therefore have an ethical duty to join a church. Kant concluded, nonetheless, that the liberal state itself was highly limited in its war against radical evil. Like Locke, Kant seems to feel that the state's primary job is the legal protection of the rights of all citizens. When it comes to taking psychological steps to ensure its own stability and efficacy, such a state finds its hands tied in virtue of its very commitment to freedoms of speech and association. At the most, Kant argues, government might give financial subsidies to scholars who work on the form of "rational religion" that Kant favored, a religion that would teach human equality and urge obedience to the moral law.

Kant was both drawing from and reacting against his great predecessor Jean-Jacques Rousseau, who is the primary source for Kant's view of radical evil.[3] In *On the Social Contract*,[4] Rousseau argued that a good society, in order to remain stable and to motivate projects involving sacrifice (such as national defense), needs a "civil religion," consisting of "sentiments of sociability, without which it is impossible to be a good citizen or a faithful subject." Around this public creed—a kind of moralized Deism fortified with patriotic beliefs and sentiments—the state will create ceremonies and rituals, engendering strong bonds of civic love connected to duties to other citizens and to the country as a whole. Rousseau believes that the "civil religion" will solve problems of both stability and altruistic motivation in the society he envisages. It will achieve that goal, however, he argues, only if it is coercively enforced in a way that removes key freedoms of speech and religious expression. The state should punish not only conduct harmful to others but also nonconforming belief and speech, using means that include banishment and even capital punishment. For Kant, this price was just too high: no decent state should use coercion in these ways, removing key areas of autonomy. He does not think to question the belief (which he appears to share with Rousseau) that a "civil religion" will be efficacious only if it is coercively imposed.

Here lies the challenge this book takes up: how can a decent society do more for stability and motivation than Locke and Kant did, without becoming illiberal and dictatorial in the manner of Rousseau? The challenge becomes even more difficult when one adds that my conception of the decent society is a form of "political liberalism," one in which political principles should not be built upon any comprehensive doctrine of the meaning and purpose of life, religious or secular, and in which the idea of equal respect for persons gives rise to a careful abstemiousness about government endorsement of any particular religious or comprehensive ethical view.[5] Such a liberal view needs not only to watch out for dictatorial imposition, but also to beware of too much energetic endorsement, or endorsement of the wrong type, lest it create in-groups and out-groups, casting some as second-class citizens. Since emotions, in my view, are not just impulses, but contain appraisals that have an evaluative content, it will be a challenge to make sure that the content of the endorsed emotions is not that of one particular comprehensive doctrine, as opposed to others.

My solution to this problem is to imagine ways in which emotions can support the basic principles of the political culture of an aspiring yet imperfect society, an area of life in which it can be hoped that all citizens overlap, if they endorse basic norms of equal respect: the area of what Rawls has called the "overlapping consensus."[6] Thus, it would be sectarian in an objectionable way for government to engender strong emotions directed toward the religious holidays of one particular sect, but it is not objectionable to celebrate the birthday of Martin Luther King Jr. as a profoundly emotional public holiday that affirms principles of racial equality to which our nation has committed itself, and that rededicates the nation to the pursuit of that goal. The idea will be to think this way across the range of the "capabilities" that provide the core of the political conception: How can a public culture of emotion reinforce attachment to all of those norms? On the negative side, a decent society can reasonably inhibit the formation of emotions of disgust toward groups of fellow citizens, since that sort of repudiating and the related formation of hierarchies are subversive of shared principles of equal respect for human dignity. More generally, society may inculcate distaste and anger directed at the violation of people's basic political entitlements. Basically, it should be no more objectionable to ask people to feel attached to good political principles than it is to ask them to believe them, and every society with a working conception of justice educates its citizens to think that this conception is correct. Antiracism is not given equal time with racism in the public schools. The careful neutrality that a liberal state observes—and should observe—in matters of religion and comprehensive doctrine does not extend to the fundamentals of its own conception of justice (such as the equal worth of all citizens, the importance of certain fundamental rights, and the badness of various forms of discrimination and hierarchy). We might say that a liberal state asks citizens who have different overall conceptions of the meaning and purpose of life to overlap and agree in a shared political space, the space of fundamental principles and constitutional ideals. But then, if those principles are to be efficacious, the state must also encourage love and devotion to those ideals.

If this devotion is to remain compatible with liberal freedom, it will be crucial to encourage a robustly critical political culture to defend the freedoms of speech and association. Both the principles themselves and the emotions they prompt must be continually scrutinized and criticized, and dissenting voices play a valuable role in keeping the conception truly liberal, and accountable to citizens. Room must also be made for subversion and humor: making fun of the grandiose pretensions of patriotic emotion is one of the best ways of keeping it down to earth, in tune with the needs of heterogeneous women and men. There will clearly be tensions along the way: not every way of poking fun at cherished ideals is respectful of the equal worth of all citizens. (Imagine racist jokes about Martin Luther King Jr.) But the space for subversion and dissent should remain as large as is consistent with civic order and stability, and that space will be a major topic throughout.

One way of addressing several of these worries at once is for the state to give ample space for artists to offer their own different visions of key political values. Whitman and Tagore are much more valuable as free poets than they would be as hired acolytes of a political elite, Soviet-style. Of course, government often must and does decide to pick one artistic creation over another—preferring, for example, Maya Lin's design for the Vietnam War Memorial, with its winding black wall full of names, evoking the equal worth of countless unknown individual lives lost, to other more jingoistic conceptions; preferring the contributions of Frank Gehry, Anish Kapoor, and Jaume Plensa for Chicago's Millennium Park to other submitted designs. During the Depression, as we'll also discuss later, Franklin Delano Roosevelt hired artists and gave them considerable freedom—but also exercised careful selectivity in choosing photographic images of poverty to put before the American public. The tension between selection and artistic freedom is real, but there are good ways of addressing it.

The issue of emotional support for a decent public political culture has not been entirely neglected by liberal thinkers. John Stuart Mill (1806–1873), for whom the cultivation of emotion was such an important theme, imagined a "religion of humanity" that could be taught in society as a substitute for existing religious doctrines, and providing the basis for policies involving personal sacrifice and comprehensive altruism.[7] In a very similar way, the Indian poet, educator, and philosopher Rabindranath Tagore (1861–1941) imagined a "religion of man" that would inspire people to promote the improvement of living conditions for all the world's inhabitants. Both thought of their respective "religions" as doctrines and practices that could be embodied in a system of shared education and in works of art. Tagore devoted much of his life to creating a school and university that embodied his principles and to composing roughly two thousand songs that influence public emotion even in the present day. (He is the only poet/composer to write songs that became the national anthems of two nations, India and Bangladesh.) The similarity between Mill's and Tagore's ideas is not surprising, since both were heavily influenced by French philosopher Auguste Comte (1798–1857), whose idea of a "religion of humanity," which would include public rituals and other emotion-laden symbols, had enormous influence in the nineteenth and early twentieth centuries. Both Mill and Tagore find fault with Comte's intrusive and rule-ridden implementation of his scheme, and both insist on the importance of liberty and individuality.

The topic of political emotion was given a fascinating treatment in the twentieth century's greatest work of political philosophy, John Rawls's *A Theory of Justice* (1971).[8] Rawls's well-ordered society asks a lot of its citizens, since inequalities of wealth and income will be permitted only when they improve the situation of the worst-off. The commitment to equal liberty, which Rawls's principles prioritize, is also one that human beings tend to honor unevenly. Even though Rawls is imagining a society that begins de novo, without bad hierarchical attitudes left over from earlier histories of exclusion, he is still placing large demands on human beings, and he therefore astutely realizes that he needs to think about how such a society will bring up citizens who will support its institutions over time, ensuring stability. Stability, moreover, has to be secured "for the right reasons"[9]—in other words, not by mere habit or grudging acceptance, but because of a real endorsement of the principles and institutions of the society. Indeed, since showing that the just society can be stable is a necessary part of its justification, the question of emotion is integral to the arguments justifying the principles of justice.

Rawls imagines how emotions arising initially within the family can ultimately develop into emotions directed at the principles of the just society. His compelling and insightful account, in this respect ahead of its time, employs a sophisticated conception of emotions similar to the one I shall be using here, according to which emotions involve cognitive appraisals.[10] Rawls later bracketed this section of the book for rethinking, along with other material in *A Theory of Justice* that he thought too closely linked to his own particular (Kantian) comprehensive ethical doctrine. In *Political Liberalism,* he no longer seems to endorse all the details of that particular account. But he insists that he is leaving a space for a needed account of a "reasonable moral psychology."[11] In effect, the present book aims to fill that space, with reference to an account of a decent society that differs from Rawls's in philosophical detail, but not in underlying spirit—although its focus is on societies aspiring to justice, rather than on the achieved well-ordered society. This difference will affect the precise shape of my normative proposals, since I need to grapple with issues of exclusion and stigma that the well-ordered society can be taken to have resolved. Nonetheless, I shall argue that the tendency toward stigmatizing and excluding others is present in human nature itself, and is not an artifact of a defective history; Rawls did not take a stand on this issue, but said that his account was compatible with this sort of pessimistic psychology, as well as more optimistic account. Certainly, in any case, Rawls's project and mine, though distinct, are closely related, since Rawls is proposing a society of human beings, not angels, and he knows well that human beings do not automatically pursue the common good. Thus, even though in his well-ordered society problems of exclusion and hierarchy have been overcome, they have been overcome by human beings who still have the underlying tendencies that produce those problems. *Even here,* stability requires grappling with the complexities of real human psychology.

Rawls's account impressively understands the emotions and their power. Its requirement that such emotions support the society's principles and institutions not merely as a useful modus vivendi, but in a way that involves an enthusiastic endorsement of its basic ideas of justice, is, moreover, a reasonable requirement to impose. A society that is held together only by adherence to a temporary compromise, viewed as instrumentally useful, is not likely to remain stable for long. Thus it is not surprising that the emotions Rawls imagines are directed at principles rather than at particulars: if society is to be stable for the right reasons, its basic principles must somehow be embraced with enthusiasm.

It is plausible to think, however, that the moral sentiments on which Rawls relies cannot be transparently rationalistic—simply an embrace of abstract principles presented as such—if they are really to do the job he assigns to them. In his brief schematic account Rawls does not say (although he definitely does not deny) that an essential motivational role, in connection with the love of just institutions, may need to be played by more indirect appeals to the emotions, using symbols, memories, poetry, narrative, or music, which lead the mind toward the principles and in which the principles themselves are at times embedded. I believe that he should grant this, and I will attempt to show that such a role for the particular is fully compatible, ultimately, with the embrace of principle he has in mind. Real people are sometimes moved by the love of just principles presented just as such, abstractly; but the human mind is quirky and particularistic, more easily able to conceive a strong attachment if these high principles are connected to a particular set of perceptions, memories, and symbols that have deep roots in the personality and in people's sense of their own history. Such an account could easily go astray, achieving stability for the wrong reasons (for example, in order to assert the superiority of a particular historical or linguistic tradition). If the sources of memory are securely tethered to political ideals, however, such problems can be transcended, and the symbols may acquire a motivational power that bare abstractions could not possess. Even in the well-ordered society this would appear to be true, since its citizens are still human beings, with limited human imaginations, but in imperfect societies aspiring to justice the need for particular narrative and symbol becomes even more compelling.

Another way of putting this point, to which I shall often return, is that all the major emotions are "eudaimonistic," meaning that they appraise the world from the person's own viewpoint and the viewpoint, therefore, of that person's evolving conception of a worthwhile life.[12] We grieve for people we care about, not for total strangers. We fear damages that threaten ourselves and those we care about, not earthquakes on Mars. Eudaimonism is not egoism: we may hold that other people have intrinsic value. But the ones who will stir deep emotions in us are the ones to whom we are somehow connected through our imagining of a valuable life, what I shall henceforth call our "circle of concern." If distant people and abstract principles are to get a grip on our emotions, therefore, these emotions must somehow position them within our circle of concern, creating a sense of "our" life in which these people and events matter as parts of our "us," our own flourishing. For this movement to take place, symbols and poetry are crucial.

Consider the two epigraphs to this chapter. Whitman has been imagining Lincoln's coffin traversing the nation that he loved. He now asks what he should give his dead president, what pictures he can "hang on the walls,/To adorn the burial-house of him I love?" The answer is word pictures of the beauty of America. This stanza is one of those pictures. It depicts the beauty of Manhattan and then, radiating out from Manhattan, other regions of America—the physical beauty, and the beauty of human activity. Images of natural beauty are always heart-rending for their link to mortality and the passage of time. Here, they are more profoundly heart-rending for their link to Whitman's imagined ritual of mourning for Lincoln—and, of course, their implied link to all that Lincoln stood for, a nation of free activity and the equality of all Americans beneath the sun. These thoughts merge in an almost unbearable crystallization of love and grief. (For some reason, I find the line "Lo, the most excellent sun so calm and haughty" the most excruciating line in English poetry, and I weep whenever I read it—the idea of the sun's majesty, eternity, and radiance juxtaposed to the image of Lincoln, immobile, in a little dark box.)

What Whitman is striving to create is a public ritual of mourning expressing renewed dedication to the unfinished task of realizing America's best ideals, a "public poetry" that will put flesh on the bones of liberty and equality. Here the reader is asked to imagine a particular person who symbolizes the difficult struggle for equality and justice—the "large sweet soul who has gone"—and the poem cannily connects that morally symbolic person to already loved features of the land and the varied people who inhabit it. The poem prompts emotions that sustain and inspire the difficult pursuit of justice. (Indeed, they also contain the idea of justice inside themselves, as the flesh/bones metaphor suggests.) It would not do this effectively if it did not deploy imagery that is somewhat mysterious, that strikes deep into the personality, summoning thoughts about mortality and longing, loss and intense beauty. Participating emotionally in Whitman's poem, readers are summoned to throw their full hearts into the search for an America that does not yet exist, but which might become reality.

Tagore's poem (which, unfortunately, we must study in translation)[13] was initially written without reference to the nation of Bangladesh, but a great deal of his thought has an unstated political relevance. As we know from his own discussion, his poem *"Jana Gana Mana,"* which later became the national anthem of India, was inspired by a desire *not* to honor the British monarch on his visit to India. Invited to contribute to a celebrating of empire, Tagore wrote that song in order to insist, instead, that all Indians owe obedience to a higher power, the moral law. It is in that sense a highly Kantian document, closely connected to his "religion of man." *"Amar Shonar Bangla"* (1906) is more indirect, but equally political. Close in its poetic strategies to Whitman's lyric, it is a poem of ecstatic and highly erotic delight in the natural beauty of Bengal. The speaker imagines his nation as a delicious inviting lover, seductive and thrilling. The song was inspired by the music of a Baul singer—a member of a community of itinerant singers (combining Vaishnava Hindus with Sufi Muslims)[14] known for their ecstatic and emotional view of religion, their poetic celebration of physical love, and their unconventional sexual practices. As we shall see in Chapter 4, Tagore made the Bauls central to his conception of the "religion of man." The music of *"Amar*

Shonar Bangla," the association of both words and music with Bauls, and the words themselves, all reinforce an image of the speaker—a representative inhabitant of Bengal—as a person whose sexuality is playful and joyful, not aggressive, the sort of sexuality exemplified by the figure of Krishna in many classic works of Indian visual art, as well as in Jay-adeva's great erotic lyric *Gitagovinda* (twelfth century). (By casting the representative Bengali as androgynous, Tagore also gestures toward the social and political empowerment of women, a lifelong passion of his, as Chapter 4 will describe in greater detail.) Tagore imagines a type of sexuality that he elsewhere positions against British imperialism and the sort of aggressive nationalism in India that apes it.

What is the point of all this? The poem was written in 1906, shortly after the British decision to partition Bengal into two for administrative reasons. This division, corresponding roughly to the later division between the state of West Bengal in India and the nation of Bangladesh (the former East Pakistan), aimed at separating Hindus from Muslims, as well as expressing the usual British policy of "divide and rule," weakening a subject people by division. Tagore appeals to his readers to imagine the beauty of the undivided Bengal—undivided geographically and undivided by religious animosity—to love her, to feel deep grief when sorrow befalls her. He certainly kindles a spirit of resistance to empire in his reader, but it is a compassionate and nonwarlike nationalism, neither the violent nationalism that he imputes to European traditions in his writings on the topic, nor the Hindu-first sort of nationalism that he criticized throughout his life.[15] His use of the syncretistic Baul tradition strongly emphasizes religious amity and inclusiveness. The song's aim is to cultivate the spirit that could sustain this new Indian nationalism—a spirit of love, inclusiveness, fairness, and human self-cultivation.

The music Tagore wrote to go with *"Amar Shonar Bangla"* is similarly sensuous, a slow, measured erotic dance. Several good versions exist on YouTube, and invariably these combine beautiful images of the land with images of women and men dancing seductively—showing how citizens of the nation understand the spirit of the piece. Tagore and Whitman are first cousins, clearly, though Tagore makes a contribution that is multidimensional, in that he was not only a Nobel Prize–winning poet, but also a composer and choreographer of world class distinction.

What does it mean to make a song such as *"Amar Shonar Bangla"* the national anthem of a nation? Bangladesh, today, laments a history of imperialism that divided India from Pakistan and "East Pakistan" from the Bengal to which it is culturally united. But it also celebrates the independence of a young Bengali nation, a pluralistic democracy. The song asks all citizens to assume in body and voice a compassionate spirit of love and concern for the fate of this land and its people, and to do so in a spirit that retains gentleness, play, and wonder.

Like Whitman's poem, Tagore's is culturally specific, drawing on imagery that has deep Bengali roots. Part of what makes each successful is this particularity. It makes no sense to suppose that strong motivation can be generated by art, music, and rhetoric that are a common coin of all nations, a sort of Esperanto of the heart. Wisely, neither poet attempts this. Tagore's songs will not move an American, at least not until after years of immersion in Indian, and especially Bengali, cultures. Even then, the Baul tradition and its music may continue to seem weird and inaccessible. Whitman's poetry travels a little better, but still its memories and images are haunting primarily to Americans, steeped in the sights and sounds of that nation and remembering the Civil War as a major national event. Both poets' choices suggest that any successful construction of political emotion must draw on the materials of the history and geography of the nation in question. Martin Luther King Jr. drew a great deal from Gandhi, but he was perceptive enough to understand that Gandhi's ideas had to undergo a total cultural makeover if they were ever to move Americans.

Both poets, however, are also culturally radical, asking people to discard some cherished ways of thinking about social relations (involving hierarchies of religion, caste, and gender). They cleverly hold their intended audience through sufficient rootedness in culture and history: indeed, it is rather remarkable that figures as radical as Whitman and Tagore should be so widely and intensely loved and accepted. But then they challenge their cultures to be the best they can be, and far better than they have been before. Thus a kind of political love that has its roots in specific traditions can also be aspirational and even radical. "I am he," writes Whitman, "who tauntingly compels men, women, nations, / Crying, Leap from your seats and contend for your lives!"[16]

Both poets suggest by their choices that the problems of their troubled societies need to be confronted in a spirit of love, through works that tap deeply into the roots of people's anxious confrontation with their mortality and finitude. That, in essence, will be the contention of this book. What type or types of love, conveyed through what media and institutions, will be a long, and ultimately an open-ended, inquiry. The inquiry will expand to take on a family of interrelated emotions, such as compassion, grief, fear, anger, hope, and the inhibiting of disgust and shame—and, with these, the spirit of a certain sort of comedy, taking amused delight in human idiosyncrasy. Several different, though interrelated, types of love are rightly involved in the process, suited to different occasions and problems. Lincoln's Gettysburg Address was appropriate to its solemn occasion, and a Tagore song would not have been able to convey what Lincoln's rhetoric conveys. Yet love is at the heart of the Gettysburg Address as well, and I shall argue that all of the core emotions that sustain a decent society have their roots in, or are forms of, love—by which I mean intense attachments to things outside the control of our will. My examples already suggest what I shall be arguing: that the principle-dependent emotions envisaged by Rawls, if not complemented and infused by love of this sort, will remain too calm and will lie too near the surface of the mind to do the job he has in mind—which requires access to the quirky, fraught, in some sense erotic relationship we all have, in a variety of forms (both comic and tragic), to the meaning of our lives. Love, I shall argue, is what gives respect for humanity its life, making it more than a shell. If love is needed even in Rawls's well-ordered society—and I believe it is—it is needed all the more urgently in real, imperfect societies that aspire to justice.

It is a propitious time to write on this topic, because cognitive psychologists during the past several decades have produced a wide range of excellent research on particular emotions, which, supplemented by the work of primatologists, anthropologists, neuroscientists, and psychoanalysts, gives us a lot of empirical data that are extremely useful to a normative philosophical project such as this one. Such empirical findings do not answer our normative questions, but they do help us to understand what may be impossible and what possible, what pervasive human tendencies may be harmful or helpful—in short, what material we have to work with and how susceptible to "work" it may be.

Part of justifying a normative political project is showing that it can be reasonably stable. Emotions are of interest in part because of our questions about stability. But then we need to ask what forms of public emotion can themselves be stable over time, not placing too great a strain upon our human resources. We need, I shall argue, to investigate, and to cherish, whatever helps us to see the uneven and often unlovely destiny of human beings in the world with humor, tenderness, and delight, rather than with absolutist rage for an impossible sort of perfection. A primary source of political difficulty is the ubiquitous human wish to surmount the helplessness that is so large a part of human life—to rise, we might say, above the messiness of the "merely human." Many forms of public emotion feed fantasies of invulnerability, and those emotions are pernicious. The project I envisage will succeed only if it finds ways to make the human lovable, inhibiting disgust and shame.

No such project could succeed if it did not tie the question of public emotions to a definite set of normative goals. I envisage throughout a type of liberalism that is not morally "neutral," that has a certain definite moral content, prominently including equal respect for persons, a commitment to equal liberties of speech, association, and conscience, and a set of fundamental social and economic entitlements. These commitments will limit the ways in which public emotions can be cultivated. The society I imagine must grapple with Rousseau's problem within the commitments of a Lockean/Kantian state. One might think that the idea of a sustaining "civil religion" cannot be achieved within these constraints, or can't be achieved in an interesting and engaging way. But let's see.

The focus of the project is on society's political culture, not the informal institutions of civil society. This is not to say that civil society does not pervasively shape citizens' emotions; but this is not what I am investigating here. The idea of the political, however, is understood in an inclusive way, as comprising all those institutions that influence people's life chances pervasively and over the entire course of their lives (John Rawls's notion of the "basic structure"). The political thus includes the family, although the dealings of government with family are limited by the already mentioned commitments to adult freedom of speech and association. Within the general area of political culture, the project will investigate political rhetoric, public ceremonies and rituals, songs, symbols, poetry, art and architecture, the design of public parks and monuments, and public sports. It will also consider the shaping of emotions in public education. Finally, it is possible to create institutions that embody the insights conveyed in a particular type of emotional experience, and the book, while not focusing on this part of the project, acknowledges its importance.

The primary unit of analysis is the nation,[17] on account of its pivotal importance in setting life conditions for all on a basis of equal respect, and as the largest unit we know until now that is decently accountable to people's voices and capable of expressing their desire to give themselves laws of their own choosing. Global concern will be an important issue: we rightly assess a public culture in part by seeing what sentiments toward other nations and peoples it encourages. I shall, however, be agreeing with Giuseppe Mazzini and other nineteenth-century nationalists that the nation is a necessary "fulcrum" for the leveraging of global concern, in a world in which the most intransigent obstacle to concern for others is egoistic immersion in personal and local projects. Another reason for the focus on the nation is the need for historical particularity in all good proposals for the formation of political emotions.

As my pairing of Whitman with Tagore indicates, my project will focus on the United States and India, two extremely different nations that are both, in their own ways, successful liberal democracies, held together by political ideals rather than a sense of ethnic homogeneity. Both contain large inequalities and must therefore motivate redistributive projects, as well as projects involving larger global concern. Both also contain deep divisions involving religion, race, caste, and gender. They need, therefore, to inhibit the inner forces that turn these divisions into baneful hierarchies or even occasions for violence.[18]

In writing on the emotions in *Upheavals of Thought,*[19] I defended the view that emotions necessarily involve cognitive appraisals, forms of value-laden perception and/or thought directed at an object or objects.

As we'll see, the cognitive psychologists whose work on emotions such as compassion and disgust will be central to my analysis hold a similar thesis, to which the work of anthropologists on the role of social norms in emotions gives additional strong support.

Part I of the book introduces the problem of political emotions through three historical chapters.

The time of the French Revolution saw fervent questioning about social unity and the value of "fraternity." If absolute monarchy and submission to royal authority were not going to be sources of cohesion for the more egalitarian societies of the future, what next? Philosophers such as Rousseau and the German thinker Johann Gottfried Herder vigorously debated the shape that a new patriotism might take. In Chapter 2, I end with consideration of their proposals, but I begin with a very different contribution: that of the opera *The Marriage of Figaro* (1786), by W. A. Mozart and Lorenzo Da Ponte. Based on a play of the same name by Beaumarchais that is generally seen as one of the major precursors of the Revolution, the opera addresses the transition from feudalism to democracy in a way that focuses centrally on the construction of sentiments. Beaumarchais suggested that the problem of the old order is institutional, and in a way quite simple: we dethrone feudal authority and usher in, through a change in political institutions, a new society of equality. I argue that the opera (not just its insightful libretto, but a musical expression of ideas that in key ways goes beyond the libretto) should be regarded as a formative philosophical text in the unfolding debate about new forms of public culture. Its vision is very different from that of Beaumarchais. Focusing as it does on sentiments and on the role of women, the opera has usually been understood to be merely domestic rather than political. I argue that it is not only political, but also correct: the new order cannot be stable without revolutionary changes in the heart, which include the adoption of new norms of male and female gender roles, and a new conception of the citizen that breaks decisively with the male norms of the ancien régime. Although the ideas I find in the opera seem in some ways light-years ahead of their time, they were in fact in the air during this time of ferment: the political vision of the opera bears a close resemblance to Herder's ideas about a "purified patriotism" in the 1790s, as I'll show, and both are antecedents of a type of liberalism later developed by John Stuart Mill and Rabindranath Tagore, in which political principles protect spaces for individual expression, play, and craziness. It should be emphasized that I am treating the opera as a philosophical text, part of a conversation that includes Rousseau, Herder, and, later, Mill and Tagore. I am not, then, proposing that modern democracies use the opera as a device to kindle public emotion of the right sort. Although it may surely do so in people who love it, it is insufficiently inclusive today to implement its own values on a wide scale. (So much is also true of the writings of philosophers.)

The nineteenth century continued the debate about political emotions, and this time the debate was global in nature. Central was Auguste Comte, with his idea of a "religion of humanity" that could motivate altruism and provide stability for demanding political principles. Comte's ideas were enormously influential in virtually every corner of the world. In Europe he had a large influence on the thought of his friend and collaborator Mill, who devoted an entire book to Comte and who contributed to the articulation of the "religion of humanity." Comte was also a major figure for Indian intellectuals and a primary source for Rabindranath Tagore's idea of a "religion of man." Chapters 3 and 4 examine the history of these rich ideas. I support the contention of both Tagore and Mill that the public cultivation of emotion needs to be scrutinized by a vigorously critical public culture, strongly committed to the protection of dissenting speech. Their proposals remain valuable sources—although both, and especially Mill, have a naïve faith in human progress, rooted in an incomplete psychology, that we cannot endorse today.

Before turning to the present day, we need a sketch of where we are heading, a normative account of a decent society worth aspiring to and sustaining. Part II begins by proposing such a sketch in Chapter 5. The account has a lot in common with the aspirations defended in my "capabilities" approach—but also with Mill's normative proposals, with Rawls's theory, with the New Deal, with many aspects of European social democracies, and with the aspirations of the Indian constitution. Many aspects of the envisaged goal, though certainly not all, are also part of the public culture of the United States, even today. I don't argue here that these norms are the best way to envisage a minimally just society; instead, I stipulate a set of very general norms. I then ask: If we should want to get and keep political principles and institutions of roughly that type, showing equal respect to all and guaranteeing key areas of both liberty and material support, what should we do to cultivate emotions that support and sustain such principles and institutions?

At this point I introduce the idea of "political liberalism," which imposes additional constraints on the public cultivation of emotion, requiring us to depart from the openly antireligious humanism of Comte and Mill. I also grant that the task of creating public emotions has two aspects, the motivational and the institutional, which need to work closely together. In other words, government may attempt to influence citizens' psychology directly (for example, through political rhetoric, songs, symbols, and the content and pedagogy of public education), or it may devise institutions that represent the insights of a valuable type of emotion—as a decent tax system, for example, could represent the insights of a duly balanced and appropriately impartial compassion. This book focuses on the motivational, but it is important to bear in mind that it is always in dialogue with the institutional.

Part II continues by surveying the resources at our disposal and the psychological problems obstructing our path. It is illuminating to begin with our animal nature, and Chapter 6 surveys relevant aspects of what we currently know about the emotional tendencies and capacities of the animals closest to us in intelligence and form of life, such as chimps, bonobos, elephants, and dogs. The human world contains some capacities that these creatures lack, but it also contains problems and deformities from which their lives are free. Reflecting on these differences, with a focus on compassion, takes us back to the helplessness of human infancy, which contains the roots of much later difficulty, as well as the seeds of some valuable resources. Chapter 7 addresses those early roots of emotion, examining the development of the capacity of concern for others and its relationship to the capacity for imaginative play. These two capacities unfold in tandem, nourishing each other, and a decent society can find many ways to encourage their blossoming.

Part III turns to contemporary reality and recent history, still focusing on the United States and India. Chapter 8 addresses the topic of patriotic emotion, or love of country, arguing that, despite its many dangers, a decent public culture cannot survive and flourish without its cultivation in some suitable form. Studying appeals to ideas of the nation, and love of the nation, in the political rhetoric of Abraham Lincoln, Martin Luther King Jr., Mohandas Gandhi, and Jawaharlal Nehru—as well as Whitman and Tagore—I develop an account of a humane and aspirational patriotism, fortified against the dangers that Herder identified in the aggressive and warlike forms of patriotism he saw around him. I investigate the different types of love that constitute it.

Chapter 9 then turns once again to the emotion of compassion, so crucial for motivating and sustaining altruistic action and egalitarian institutions, and to the related idea of tragic spectatorship. As they mature, citizens must learn, in effect, to be both tragic and comic spectators of the varied predicaments of life. The tragic perspective gives insight into shared vulnerabilities; the comic perspective (or a comic perspective of a particular sort) embraces the unevenness of human existence with flexibility and mercy, rather than hatred. (Hatred of self is all too often projected outward onto vulnerable others, so attitudes to self are a key element of a good public psychology, however slippery and difficult to access.) Beginning with some lasting insights of the ancient Greek tragic and comic poets, I ask how large modern democracies might attempt, indeed have attempted, something analogous.

Chapter 10 investigates three emotions that pose special problems for compassionate citizenship: fear, envy, and shame. Analyzing each of these and separating their constructive contributions from the negative roles that they all too frequently play, I then identify some strategies in modern societies that combat these problems, and some that make them worse. Chapter 11 draws the argument to a close.

At the end of *The Marriage of Figaro,* the Countess sets the tone for the new regime by saying yes to a plea for sympathy. "I am nicer, and I say yes." A compassionate and generous attitude toward the frailties of human beings—prominently including oneself—is a linchpin of the public culture I am recommending here, closely linked to the comic spirit. The type of love embodied by the Countess's generous "yes" involves flexibility, the willingness to give love and understanding priority over rigid norms. It requires pursuing admirable goals in such a way as to embrace women and men as they are, rather than hating what is imperfect. Her "yes" is a key to the type of political love that lies at the heart of this book.

Because this is a long book, it is important to head off misreading by placing some especially important issues up front, so that they cannot be missed.

1. *The account of political emotions assumes a set of normative commitments.* All political conceptions, from the monarchical and the fascist to the libertarian, have a place for emotions in the public culture, supporting the stability of their characteristic principles. But specific strategies depend on specific goals. The account in this book stipulates a general set of political principles, described in some detail in Chapter 5, which are similar to (though more general than) those for which I have argued in other books, and similar, as well, to the goals of the New Deal, of the political conceptions of J. S. Mill and John Rawls, and of many European social democracies. They overlap considerably with the goals of American political culture, even today. I do not argue for this normative account here, although I do explain it. What I am asking is how such principles might be rendered stable through emotions. People who embrace different political norms can still learn a great deal from this account, although they will need to imagine how it would have to be altered in order to support the norms that they themselves favor.

2. *The account is framed by an acceptance of "political liberalism."* As Chapter 5 will further discuss, the normative ideal is a set of principles that do not "establish" a particular religious or secular "comprehensive doctrine" (to use Rawls's phrase), and which can, at least potentially, become the object of an "overlapping consensus" among a variety of comprehensive doctrines held by citizens, so long as they are prepared to respect one another as equal citizens.[20] This allegiance to political liberalism makes my account depart from the sort of "civil religion" recommended by Rousseau and from the "religion of humanity" recommended by Auguste Comte and J. S. Mill. All these thinkers offered their accounts of civic emotion as replacements for existing religions, which they thought society should denigrate and marginalize.

3. *Emotions: generic and specific.* I will be giving an account of how emotions such as compassion, fear, envy, and shame work in the context of a particular normative conception. These same generic emotions will also play a role in other types of political culture: in monarchical, fascist, or libertarian regimes, for example. To that extent, the emotions are an all-purpose tool kit. (Disgust may be an exception; I argue that "projective disgust" has no useful role in a liberal society, although "primary disgust" at wastes and decay still proves useful.) At the level of the species, however, the liberal society I imagine uses a distinctive set of emotions. Thus, both liberal and illiberal views use shame to motivate, but they use different types of shame. A liberal society asks people to be ashamed of excessive greed and selfishness, but it does not ask them to blush for their skin color or their physical impairments.

Emotions are also general and specific in a different sense: a specific compassion for soldiers fallen in the Civil War may lead on to, and in a larger sense contain, a compassionate embrace of the deepest principles of the nation. (It is in this way that my project complements, rather than displaces, Rawls's.)

4. *Ideal and actual.* My question is how to render political principles and institutions stable, and thus the inquiry presupposes that basically good institutions exist, or can be rather shortly realized, albeit in a form that will require ongoing work to improve and perfect. Still, since we are dealing with real societies and real people, the focus is on the urgent aspiration to an ideal of justice, rather than justice already achieved. The

historical examples deal with the real, not the ideal, and thus with people who are trying to implement a normative vision that is not yet actual in all respects. (This is true even for Lincoln, who claims to be defending what has existed for a long time, for he recharacterizes the nation to such a degree that he is justly described as refounding it.) To that extent, one might always ask whether there could not be nonemotional factors that would prevent the society I describe from coming into being (economic factors, for example). I believe the society I described is not only possible, but in many respects actual, and that something close to the whole of it has existed in some places and times. So while I believe that there are no such impediments, that question lies outside the present project.

PART ONE

History

CHAPTER TWO

Equality and Love: Rousseau, Herder, Mozart

I have no idea what those two Italian ladies were singing about. Truth is, I don't want to know. Some things are better left unsaid. I'd like to think they were singing about something so beautiful it can't be expressed in words, and it makes your heart ache because of it . . . , and for the briefest of moments, every last man in Shawshank felt free.

—Red (played by Morgan Freeman), in *The Shawshank Redemption*,
of the "*Canzonetta sull'aria*" from Act III of
The Marriage of Figaro

My great *peace woman* has only a single name: she is called *universal justice, humaneness, active reason*. . . .Her function, in accordance with her name and her nature, is to inculcate *dispositions of peace.*

—Johann Gottfried Herder, *Letters for the
Advancement of Humanity* (1793–1797)

I. "Happy in That Way"

The ancien régime sings in a loud and authoritarian voice, saying, "No, no, no, no, no, no." So, just before the end of Mozart's *The Marriage of Figaro,* the Count, as yet secure in his status, rejects the urgings of the other characters to mercy and sympathy as they kneel, one by one, before him. To Almaviva, revenge for insulted honor is all-important ("the only thing that consoles my heart and makes me rejoice").[1] To display kindness to the imploring, as they humbly kneel, is a noble prerogative, not a general human virtue. He can give it, or he can withhold it. If he chooses the latter course, putting slighted honor ahead of generous condescension, nobody can say he is wrong. That's how the ancien régime operates, animated by a morality of status, shame, and kingly prerogative.

But suddenly the Countess, removing her disguise as Susanna, reveals herself—revealing, at the same time, the stratagem that has trapped her husband in both error and hypocrisy. (Having boasted of ending the *droit du seigneur,* he has all the while been scheming to enjoy it.) Everyone present exclaims in hushed voices that they don't know what is going to happen next: "Oh heavens, what do I see! Madness! A hallucination! I don't know what to believe!" The strings, coursing up and down with rapid modulations, express immense agitation and uncertainty. In retrospect, it is the uncertainty of transition between two political regimes.

And now the Count, kneeling before the Countess, sings in a voice newly softened by confusion a phrase of a type—lyrical and legato, hushed, almost gentle—that we have never heard from this man before: "Excuse me, Countess, excuse me, excuse me." There is a long pause.[2]

The Countess then sings softly out of the silence: "I am nicer, and I say yes" *("più docile io sono, e dico di sì").*[3] The musical phrase arcs gently upward and then bends down as if, almost, to touch the kneeling husband. And now, in hushed and solemn tones, the entire assembled company repeats the Countess's musical phrase, this time to the words "Ah, all of us will be happy in that way" *("tutti contenti saremo così").* The choral version of the phrase is reminiscent of the solemn simplicity of a chorale (which, in this Catholic musical universe, denotes a sudden absence of hierarchy).[4] A hesitant orchestral interlude follows.

The group now bursts out, a sudden eruption of dizzy elation:[5] "This day of torment, of craziness, of foolishness—only love can make it end in happiness and joy." Love, it seems, is the key not only to the personal happiness of the central characters, but to the happiness of all, of the whole community, as they sing: "Let us all rush off to celebrate" *("corriam tutti a festeggiar").*

By any account, *The Marriage of Figaro* is a key text in the history of liberalism for the way in which it imagines the replacement of the ancien régime by a new order of fraternity and equality. But usually people who turn to Figaro's story focus on the Beaumarchais play and ignore the opera by Mozart and Da Ponte. The opera, however, is, far more than the play, the philosophical text that thinkers about the future of liberal democracy should ponder. The opera, not the play, is worthy to stand comparison with the greatest eighteenth-century philosophical interventions on the topic of fraternity, particularly those of Rousseau and Herder—because, unlike the play, but like Rousseau and Herder, it gives a central place to the cultivation of emotions that are required to make fraternity more than a nice word. To study the opera as a philosophical statement in dialogue with Rousseau and Herder, however, it will prove insufficient merely to study the libretto—for the key insights are attained far more precisely in the music than they are in Da Ponte's witty but sometimes superficial libretto.

The usual story about Mozart's *Le Nozze di Figaro* (1786) is that it is a cop-out. Taking the radical Beaumarchais drama of 1778, whose essential point and emphasis are political, a denunciation of the ancien régime and the hierarchies it imposes, Mozart and his librettist Lorenzo Da Ponte have fashioned an innocuous drama of personal love, defanging the text by omitting, for example, Figaro's long fifth-act monologue denouncing feudal hierarchy, and instead substituting a more extensive treatment of women and their private desires. The Beaumarchais play, which is usually understood to be a major harbinger of the French Revolution, was refused production for many years, and even in 1784, when it was allowed production in France, becoming wildly popular, it remained controversial.[6] Mozart and Da Ponte, by contrast, decided (so the story goes) to escape controversy. The relatively progressive Joseph II had forbidden the Beaumarchais play to be performed in theaters within his realm. Da Ponte, however, persuaded the emperor that an acceptable opera could be written on the basis of the play.[7] In the process, however, says the received story,[8] he and Mozart, despite producing a wonderful love drama, sold out the radicalism of the original.

I shall argue, by contrast, that the opera is as political and as radical as the play, and more deeply so, for it investigates the human sentiments that are the necessary foundation for a public culture of liberty, equality, and fraternity. This construction of sentiment is accomplished more clearly in Mozart's music than in the libretto, so my argument will require going into considerable musical detail.[9] Mozart agrees (in effect)[10] with Rousseau in understanding that a political culture requires a new shaping of human attitudes in the realm of love, but he disagrees with Rousseau about the specific shape of the new attitudes. Whereas Rousseau emphasizes the need for civic homogeneity and solidarity, a patriotic love based on manly honor and the willingness to die for the nation, Mozart envisages the new public love as something gentler, more reciprocal, more feminine—"nicer," to use the Countess's everyday word—connected more to Rousseauian horror of warlike exploits than to Rousseauian ideas of valor. In the process, Mozart also eschews Rousseauian homogeneity, emphasizing that the new fraternity must protect spaces for the free play of mischief, craziness, humor, and individuality—all of which are connected, in the opera, to the women's world. It thus opens up a vision of political emotion that will be revived in the nineteenth century by John Stuart Mill, and in the early twentieth by Rabindranath Tagore.[11]

II. The Ancien Régime and the Male Voice

According to the received view, Beaumarchais dramatizes the opposition between an ancien régime, based on hierarchy and subordination (personified by the Count), and a new democratic politics, based on equality and liberty (personified by Figaro). The key moment of the Beaumarchais play is thus Figaro's Act V monologue, in which he denounces the Count's hereditary privilege. Mozart, omitting this political speech, has depoliticized the opera, turning the conflict between the Count and Figaro into a merely personal competition over a woman.

This view contains a tacit premise: that the contrast that should hold our interest, as political thinkers, is the opposition between the Count and Figaro. It is because Mozart does not locate the center of the political conflict here that his version is felt not to be political at all, but merely domestic. Let us, however, keep an open mind, not assuming that Figaro represents the new citizenship (as the Count so clearly represents the old).

If we do keep an open mind, we are likely to notice very soon that Figaro and the Count are quite similar, both musically and thematically. What do they sing about when they are alone? Outraged honor, the desire for revenge, the pleasure of domination. The energies that drive these two men are not alien, but deeply akin. (Indeed, the two roles are set in such a way that one and the same singer might, in principle, sing either role, and their musical idioms are so alike that it is easy to confuse them.)[12] Figaro's initial aria, *"Se vuol ballare"*, follows his discovery that the Count has plans to sleep with Susanna. But if we simply look at what Figaro says in the aria, we would not discover that any such creature as Susanna ever existed. All his thoughts are about his rivalry with the Count, and his insistent negatives *(non sarà, non sarà)* anticipate the Count's peremptory negations at the opera's end (as well as those in the Count's Act III aria). What energizes Figaro? The thought of paying the Count back in kind, teaching him to dance in Figaro's dancing school.[13]

Similarly, two acts later, the Count imagines Susanna, his own future property, being possessed by Figaro *(ei posseder dovrà),* whom the Count sees as "a base *thing*" *(un vile oggetto),* a mere object.[14] This thought torments him—not because he is filled with any love or even any particularly intense desire for Susanna, but because the idea of being bested by a mere "thing" is intolerable. To this competitive loss he, like Figaro, has to say no: "Ah no, I am not willing to allow you to enjoy this happiness in peace. Brazen one,[15] you were not born to give me torment, and perhaps even to laugh at my unhappiness." Figaro, not Susanna, is the person whom he addresses in the second person. Like Figaro, his head is filled with the picture of another man laughing at him, insulting his honor, putting him to shame. In return for that tormenting picture, to which he (like Figaro) says no, he proposes (like Figaro) to substitute the image of a tamed enemy dancing to his tune, in this case the picture of Figaro forced to marry Marcellina and separated forever from Susanna, whom the Count can then enjoy: "Now only the hope of revenge consoles my heart and make me rejoice."[16] Figaro's *"Se vuol ballare"* is closely based upon the Beaumarchais text; this aria of the Count's, however, is a complete innovation of Da Ponte, since Beaumarchais gives us only what forms the recitative before the aria, not the aria's extended development of sentiments of humiliation and reactive rage.

Musically as well as textually, the Count's aria is a cousin of Figaro's: full of an ill-governed fury that bursts out as the voice reaches the words *felice un servo mio,* and then again at *ah non lasciarti in pace;* anger, in the music, is complemented by sneering irony (the downturning phrase accompanying *un vile oggetto*). The libretto gives us some indication of the kinship between the two men, but the expressive range of the music goes much further to emphasize their rhythmic and accentual similarity, as both express attitudes that range from snide contempt to furious rage.[17] What emotions are absent? Love, wonder, delight—even grief and longing.

According to the conventional political reading of Beaumarchais, Figaro becomes, by Act V, the apostle of a new type of citizenship, free from hierarchy. Mozart's Figaro makes no such progress. As Michael Steinberg aptly notes, throughout the opera (or, at least, until late in Act IV) Figaro dances, musically, to the Count's tune: "He hasn't found a musical idiom of his own; his political and emotional vocabulary suggests a similarly unfortunate mimetic duplication of the Count's"[18]— both in *Non più andrai,* at the end of Act I (where he reenacts "the authority with which [the Count] has just dispatched Cherubino to serve in one of his regiments, forming his phrases from the relevant military march"),[19] and even at the opening of Act IV, when, waiting to catch Susanna in infidelity, he sings once again of slighted honor, asking all males to "open your eyes" to the way in which women function as agents of humiliation. Again, it is men, not women, far less a particular woman, whom he addresses in the second person.

Now maybe this means that Mozart has failed to understand the opposition between Figaro and the Count that Beaumarchais has depicted. But let's not pass judgment so quickly. Perhaps, instead, Mozart sees something that Beaumarchais does not see: that the ancien régime has formed men in a certain way, making them utterly preoccupied with rank, status, and shame, and that both high and low partake of this social shaping. What one does not wish to lose, the other wishes to enjoy. For neither, given their obsession, does any space open out in the world for reciprocity or, indeed, for love.

The suspicion that Mozart is deliberately subjecting the male morality of status to critical scrutiny is confirmed when we see what Mozart puts in the mouths of two males who have little to do with the plot. Perhaps, someone might argue, the sentiments of Figaro and the Count are not to be read as serious political thought: after all, the plot requires them to compete in this way. We have seen that, even so, Da Ponte constructs a parallel that is not so plain in the original text, and that Mozart takes this similarity much further by giving the two men a similar expressive musical range. Nonetheless, someone might still argue that Mozart and Da Ponte are simply amplifying the suggestions of the Beaumarchais plot. This, however, cannot be said of the treatment of Bartolo and Basilio, whose roles in the story line are minimal. Each sings an aria—Bartolo in Act I, Basilio in Act IV (though both are typically cut in performance)—which supply crucial commentary on the morality of maleness. Neither of these arias is based on anything in Beaumarchais's text.

Bartolo is an emotional first cousin of Figaro and the Count. Vocally distinguishable, since he is a basso, he nonetheless sings from the same expressive palate: similar outbursts of rage, tempered by a type of sneering already known to us from Figaro's *"Se vuol ballare"*. Textually, his role appears to be to offer a general theory of what Figaro and the Count both exemplify: "Revenge, oh revenge! It is a pleasure reserved for the wise. To forget humiliations and outrages is baseness, is utter lowness."[20] So life is more or less utterly occupied by competition for status and the avoidance of shame between males, and the smart thing to do is to play that game to the hilt. The recommended attitude not only causes outrage and humiliation to eclipse love and longing (Bartolo, like Figaro and the Count, has no thought at all for Rosina, whom he has lost to the Count through Figaro's scheming), but also precludes any kind of mercy or reconciliation. It is this attitude that leads to the Count's six consecutive *nos* at the opera's end.

Bartolo also shows us something else pertinent to citizenship, for he is very interested in reason and law. His attitude is that the law is an instrument of male revenge, and someone who knows the law will be ahead of someone who does not, because he can find the little weaknesses and loopholes that will allow him to defeat his enemy. At this point the aria becomes rapid, joyful, with a kind of sneering playfulness, a patter song of legal one-upmanship: "If I have to search through the whole legal code, if I have to read all the statutes, with an equivocation, with a synonym, I will find some obstacle there. All Seville will know Bartolo! The rascal Figaro will be defeated!"[21] (Here the music, once again, goes well beyond the text, expressing the sly joy of legal cleverness dragooned into the service of humiliation.) The aria ends as foursquare and martial as it began (though with a little sneer accompanying the words *il birbo Figaro*). Bartolo announces that he will be known to all: "All Seville will know Bartolo"—showing us that he takes his practical identity to be utterly encompassed in his revenge project. His joy at the thought is unqualified—despite the fact that the revenge in question would never return Rosina to him. She is simply not on his mind at all.

At the opening of Act IV, another minor character has his say, and it both inverts and ultimately reinforces the morality of Bartolo. Basilio, a music master, is a less powerful character than Bartolo, and it was he who, in the predecessor play *The Barber of Seville,* discoursed enthusiastically on the crushing humiliation that gossip and slander can offer someone who wants to defeat an enemy. Da Ponte portrays him throughout as both spiteful and weak, lacking the resources to compete on an equal footing with the nobles, lacking the cleverness to compete on an equal footing with Figaro. His Act IV aria offers advice to men who are in this weakened position.[22] He begins by telling the audience that it is always risky to enter a competition with the *grandi:* they almost always win. So, what should one do? A story from his youth offers guidance. He used to be impulsive, and didn't listen to reason; then, however, Lady Prudence made her appearance before him, and handed him the skin of an ass. He had no idea what it was for, but when, shortly after that, a thunderstorm began, he covered himself in that ass's skin. When the storm abated he looked up and found a terrible beast before him, almost touching him with its mouth. He could never have defended himself from a terrible death. But the disgusting smell of the ass's skin scared the beast away. "Thus fate taught me that shame, danger, disgrace, and death can be escaped under an ass's skin."[23]

This aria offers advice diametrically opposed to the advice in Bartolo's, which told us to use reason and law to hound the person who has caused one's humiliation. It's obvious, however, that the difference is slight. Both men see the world in the same way, as a zero-sum game for honor and status. The only difference is that Basilio is aware that some are bound to be losers, and he wants to give advice about damage control to those losers. If you are perceived as smelly and low anyway, use that spoiled identity to protect yourself from yet further outrage. Sung in a sneering, reedy tenor, the aria, like Bartolo's, complements Figaro and the Count from the other direction. It shares with them a view of what the world is really about. If women figure in the aria at all, it is only in the way Basilio confesses to a kind of "fire" and "craziness" in his youth—a false direction soon put right by the counsels of Lady Prudence. The ancien régime does not like low-class people who allow their fire free rein.

III. Females: Fraternity, Equality, Liberty

The females of the opera inhabit a musical and textual world that is from the beginning depicted as utterly unlike that of the men. First of all, it contains friendship. Susanna and the Countess might have seen each other as rivals: after all, the Count is trying to seduce Susanna. However, the thought does not occur to them. They understand that they share a common set of purposes, and that the desired outcome for both is that the two men, Figaro and the Count, become loving and faithful husbands focused on affection and pleasure, rather than revenge and jealousy. (The Count is as dominated by jealousy as is Figaro, despite his apparent lack of love for his wife.) Like the two men, the two women share a musical idiom—so much so that they can be mistaken for each other even by the men who ostensibly love them (until, interestingly, Figaro does at least recognize Susanna by her voice, "the voice that I love").

Unlike the men, however, the women use their similarity not for mutual combat but for cooperation, and, in particular, for the complex masquerade that ends up revealing the Count's hypocrisy. When we focus on their teamwork, we notice as well that there is absolutely nothing like teamwork and reciprocity among the men. The women's partnership, moreover, despite their class difference, appears to be quite unhierarchical, as they benefit each other with genuine mutual friendliness. (Susanna, for example, is surprised that it is she—presumably not all that well educated—who is to write the letter to the Count suggesting the rendezvous: "I should write? But madame . . ." The Countess will have nothing of her deference: "Write, I say, and I will take the consequences.") One way we see their reciprocity is in the nature of their jokes, for here there are no sneering put-downs, no snide spitefulness, only mutual solidarity and the equal love of a good scheme.

Once again, all this is in the libretto, but the music takes the suggestion of reciprocity and equality much further.[24] As the Countess dictates the letter and Susanna writes it down, the women take inspiration from each other's musical phrases, exchanging ideas with a sinuous capacity for response and a heightened awareness of the other's pitch, rhythm, and even timbre. They begin by exchanging phrases, as in a conversation. As the duet continues, however, their reciprocity becomes more intimate and more complex as they wind around each other, ultimately achieving closely knit harmony. Their musical partnership expresses a kind of friendly attunement that is, we might say, an image of mutual respect, but also a reciprocal affection that is deeper than respect. Neither runs roughshod over the utterance of the other, and yet each contributes something distinctive of her own, which in turn is recognized by the other and carried forward.[25]

This duet has acquired fame in American popular culture because of its use in the film version of Stephen King's *The Shawshank Redemption*, when the convict who has become the prison's librarian (played by Tim Robbins) figures out a way to play it for all the prisoners over the PA system, and, locking the door, stops the prison hierarchy from interfering until the duet is done. The men of Shawshank certainly are not fans of classical music, but they hear something in this music and stop in their tracks, transfixed by a promise of happiness. As Red (Morgan Freeman) expresses it, looking back:

> I have no idea what those two Italian ladies were singing about. Truth is, I don't want to know. Some things are better left unsaid. I'd like to think they were singing about something so beautiful, it can't be expressed in words, and it makes your heart ache because of it . . . , and for the briefest of moments, every last man in Shawshank felt free.

What do the prisoners hear in the duet? Freedom, they say. But why, and how? First, they cannot help hearing an absence of hierarchy in the evenly matched voices, and a partnership based on responsiveness rather than dictatorial power. This, in the context of Shawshank, is already freedom. But as the voices soar out over the squalor of the prison yard, I think there is more to be heard in it: the idea of a kind of internal freedom, a freedom of the spirit that consists precisely in not caring about hierarchy, neither seeking to avoid being controlled by others nor seeking to control them. Suppose we imagine Tim Robbins playing the Count's *Vedrò mentr'io sospiro*, or Bartolo's *La vendetta*. Well, those two powerful men express, in their own way, an idea of freedom: freedom as power to dominate, escaping the shame of being dominated. But we know that the men of Shawshank would not have been transfixed by that image of freedom: after all, it is what they live every day. The promise of the duet is not simply a promise of freedom as reversal, freedom as getting your turn to humiliate the one who has humiliated you. It is a freedom that takes us beyond that anxious and always unsettled picture of what liberty, for men, might consist in.[26] It is freedom as being happy to have an equal beside you, freedom as not caring who is above or beneath. That's a freedom that does take the mind far away from Shawshank and from the American society of which that institution is an apt mirror.

In other words, this music has invented democratic reciprocity. Whatever the faults of the film—which is in many ways sentimental—this moment contains a correct insight into Mozart's politics and into the politics of equality more generally. You don't get the right kind of liberty, the idea is, without also having this type of fraternity and this type of equality. To shoot for liberty without fraternity, as Beaumarchais's Figaro does, is simply to turn the hierarchy upside down, not to replace it with something fundamentally different. If there is to be a new regime, if there is ever to be something like a politics of equal respect in this world, the suggestion is, it must start by singing like those two women, and this means becoming a fundamentally different type of man.[27]

To put it a different way: the male world of *Figaro* is its own prison, as each man goes through life dominated by the anxiety of rank, and what those prisoners heard in the duet was the promise of a world without that tension, a world in which one would then really be free to engage in the pursuit of happiness.[28] The new regime, as it never has been realized in any nation in the world.[29]

IV. Educating a Man

The heading of Section III referred to "females," but Section II spoke of "the male voice," and it is the male voice, not maleness itself, that the opera associates with the endless and exhausting fight against the "lowness" of shame. There is, however, a male in the opera who does not sing in a male voice: the teenage boy Cherubino, performed by a female mezzo-soprano. This already seems significant, and Cherubino's education, it shortly emerges, is the focal point of the opera's depiction of the new egalitarian citizenship.

Cherubino is usually treated superficially, as a running joke throughout the opera, and this is, more or less, the way Beaumarchais treats him. His adolescent preoccupation with women and sex is indeed the source of much of the plot, as he turns up repeatedly in places where he should not be, to the consternation of the possessive males around him. In many productions he is treated as a person with no sentiments, but only very intense bodily desires. Let us, however, pay closer attention to what he says and what he does.

Cherubino is clearly, in crucial ways, masculine. He is tall (Susanna has to ask him to kneel down so that she can put on his bonnet), goodlooking (Figaro and the Count are both jealous of him), and sexually active (with his teenage girlfriend Barbarina)—indeed, very likely, the only male who is actually having sex with anyone during the time span of the opera.[30] On the other hand, the fact that he is sung by a female voice forces us to pay attention to the ways in which that voice, and the sentiments it expresses, differs from all the male voices in the opera. So, what does Cherubino talk about?

He talks about love. He is the only male in the opera who has the slightest interest in that emotion. Certainly, the breathlessness of *"Non so più"* expresses the promiscuous quality, as well as the confusion, of adolescent infatuation: "Every woman makes me blush, every woman makes my heart leap." Still, even when he is reporting his state of sexual obsession, he is talking about love: "I talk about love when I'm awake, I talk about love in my dreams, I talk about it to the water, to the shadow, to the mountains, to the flowers, to the grass, to the fountains, to the echo, to the air, to the winds."[31] He shows, here, a romantic and poetic conception of what he is after that is quite unlike the ideas of all the other males in the opera, who all see sex as a means of asserting domination over a key piece of property in the male world. The musical idiom, breathless and yet tender, is utterly unlike the tense accents of the adult males.[32] Indeed, it is the musical idiom, far more than the Beaumarchais-inspired text, that makes us see that Cherubino's sensibility is poetic and romantic, rather than simply energetic.[33]

When we reach the Countess's chamber, Cherubino's difference from other males becomes even more evident. Deeply infatuated with the Countess, he has decided to make her a present. What sort of present? What naturally occurs to him is to write a poem, set it to music, and sing it himself. Thus, accompanying himself on the guitar, Cherubino becomes the only leading character in the opera who sings a solo, that is, whose solo singing represents singing.[34] Growing up in a world of sentiment and musicality, he naturally gives his passion a musical shape.[35]

The content of that passion (in the beautiful aria *"Voi che sapete"*) is remarkable for its utter difference from the arias of all the other males.[36] Cherubino simply talks about his feeling of love, and about its beautiful female object. He has nothing to say about other men, and he seems utterly impervious to all questions of honor, shame, and competition. Furthermore, he is eager to learn something, and to learn it from women: "You who know what sort of thing love is, women, tell me whether that is what I have in my heart." All the other men want to teach rather than to learn; what they are eager to teach is a lesson in competitive one-upmanship, and they want to teach it to other males. (Figaro imagines himself as the dancing master running a school that will teach the Count to dance to his tune; Bartolo is eager to show "all Seville" that he can defeat Figaro; the Count is eager to show Figaro that his "cause" is not, as Figaro believes, "won," but, rather, lost.) Moreover, Cherubino, unlike all the other males, is utterly vulnerable, and he makes no attempt to conceal his vulnerability, which is emotional more than bodily: "I feel my soul in flames, and then it turns to ice in a moment." He describes an intense longing that leaves him no peace. And most remarkably, he locates what he is pursuing in a place outside of his own ego: "I seek a good that is outside myself" *(ricerco un bene fuori di me)*. Hearing these words, we realize that no other male in the opera *does* seek a good outside himself: all are preoccupied with winning a competitive victory, or shielding the ego from shame. His love is infused with intense wonder at the sheer beauty of its object: wonder drives his curiosity and makes it splendid rather than mechanical.

The music of the aria would tell us all this without the words, and indeed it communicates, well beyond the words, the young man's delicacy, vulnerability, and sheer kindness. It is hardly by accident that people who have utterly no idea what Cherubino is saying should have found in this aria (as in the duet between Susanna and the Countess) an image of emotional integrity.[37] Here if anywhere, Mozart's music moves well beyond Da Ponte's text.

How did Cherubino get to be this way, a way that promises real reciprocity in passion? He was brought up by women and kept a stranger to the men's world. Indeed, we've already seen that the prospect of military service utterly confuses and appalls him. In the scene, at the end of Act I, in which Figaro tells him what to expect when he goes off to the army *("Non più andrai"),* Figaro's joke to Cherubino is that he has lived in the women's world of sentiment, music, tenderness, and delicacy—and now, suddenly, he will have to enter a world of drunken men (they swear by Bacchus) with inflexible necks *(collo dritto),* tough faces *(muso franco),* long mustaches *(gran mustacchi),* and "lots of honor" *(molto onor).* Now, in Act II, we see more fully how much the young man will have to unlearn in order to enter this male world: in particular, lovely, sensuous music. "What a beautiful voice," says the Countess when Cherubino finishes his aria—drawing attention, again, to the fact that this singing represents real singing. Figaro has already told Cherubino, however, that the world of male honor knows nothing of beautiful music. Its only music is "the concerto of trumpets, of shells and cannons, whose shots, on all pitches, make your ears whistle."[38] The aria itself, with its boringly foursquare military rhythm, now, in retrospect, contrasts sadly with the grace and elegance of Cherubino's composition.

By singing so beautifully, Cherubino shows himself to be a candidate for fraternity, equality, and the female type of liberty. But before he can be finally confirmed as lovable with good reason, one thing more must happen to him: he must put on women's clothes. The plot requires the disguise, but Mozart connects this moment to the deeper sentiments of the heart.

It has often been sensed that Susanna's tender aria "Come, kneel down" *("Venite, inginocchiatevi")* is a pivotal moment in the opera, that something profound is going on when Susanna first perfects Cherubino's female disguise, then takes a look at him and sings, "If women fall in love with him, they certainly have their good reasons" *("se l'amano le femmine, han certo il lor perchè").*[39] The music is perhaps the most sensuous and tender in the opera, as Susanna, asking him to turn around, adjusts his collar and his hands, shows him how to walk like a woman—and then notices how the guise complements the young man's mischievous eyes and graceful bearing: *che furba guardatura, che vezzo, che figura!* What Mozart slyly suggests, by making this aria so riveting, and, at the same time, so playful, is that here, in an intimate moment of tenderness, the seeds of overthrow for the ancien régime are decisively sown.

To begin with, the aria concerns kneeling. There is lots of kneeling in this opera, and in every other place (until the very final moments) kneeling is a symbol of feudal hierarchy: exalted status on the one side, obedience on the other. In the women's democratic world, however, kneeling is just kneeling. You kneel in front of your dressmaker so that she can fix your bonnet and collar. Kneeling has no symbolism; it is just a useful action. Hierarchy is simply out the window, irrelevant, a nonissue. The music itself expresses this thought: instead of the thumping accents of the quest for honor, we hear little trill-like bursts from the violins, playful jumpings, like muffled outbursts of laughter, that not only betray no hierarchy, but positively subvert the whole idea.[40] Bit by bit, the woman's costume is assembled, the woman's walk learned—until at the end Susanna surveys, with wonder and amazement, the result she has produced. "Admire [*mirate,* 'wonder at'] the little devil, admire how beautiful he is. What mischievous looks [*che furba guardatura*], what charm, what allure. If women love him, they certainly have their good reasons." Cherubino is alluring, it seems, precisely because, while manly and drawn to women, he is not drawn to controlling them or using them as pawns in games with other men. Instead of domination, there are charm and grace; instead of plots to conceal shame or avenge insult, there are "mischievous looks" as he joins the women in their love of jokes and gossip.[41]

All of this is in the libretto—after a fashion. We can, however, imagine musical settings of the text that would have signaled irony, skepticism, or bitterness (certainly an emotion that we could imagine Susanna feeling at this time). Instead, the music expresses both tender sensuousness and, with the playful movements of the strings, laughter, suggesting that these two attitudes go well together, and that both are key parts of the woman's world. We are now led to recall a feature of the overture whose significance we might have missed before: the same type of muffled laughter from the violins is present there, suggesting that subversive play is a major theme of the opera as a whole.

This reading of the aria is shortly confirmed by the duet *"Aprite, presto, aprite,"* as Susanna and Cherubino plot together about getting him safely out of his compromising hiding place. The two sing, extremely rapidly, in hushed conspiratorial voices that show a rare degree of attunement—foreshadowing the more developed duet between Susanna and the Countess in Act III. Cherubino shows that he has now, in effect, become a woman: a co-conspirator, a voice of fraternity and equality, and therefore, as if we didn't know it already, a person internally free from the bonds of status.

As we look at Cherubino, we realize afresh how unradical Figaro's apparent radicalism is. It's not just that he takes over from the ancien régime its proprietary attitude to women; it's something more global than that. Figaro simply sees the world the way the Count sees it: in terms of the quest for honor and the avoidance of shame. He doesn't understand reciprocity, and he really doesn't understand humor. (His idea of a joke is a mean-spirited put-down.)[42] If the new world has citizens like that, its commitment to equality and fraternity will be bound to be problematic. New hierarchies will be thrown up to replace the old, like ramparts defending the male ego. Could there, however, be citizens who simply like to laugh and to sing?

In her fascinating reflections on eighteenth-century pornography, Lynn Hunt has argued that the pornographic idea of the interchangeability of bodies is closely linked to the revolutionary call for democratic equality.[43] Legal theorist Lior Barshack argues that the new subjectivity created by Mozart's operas is just this hedonistic idea of sexual freedom.[44] No doubt such ideas were prominent in the eighteenth century, as people (meaning men) tried to make sense of the new world they inhabited.

If I am right, however, Mozart sees the world rather differently, and more radically. The objectification of bodies as interchangeable physical units is itself, the opera suggests, just one aspect of the ancien régime, which invented and depends upon the idea that some classes of people, including, prominently, women, are just *oggetti,* and thus can be used at will in one's quest for personal gratification. Seeing bodies as interchangeable is, indeed, a clever route to what the ancien régime wanted all along: male control and invulnerability. What would be truly opposed to the ancien régime would be not the democratization of bodies as interchangeable machines— but love. As Cherubino understands, this means seeking a good outside oneself, which is a scary idea. It is, nonetheless, an idea that Figaro must learn before he can be the kind of citizen Mozart (not Beaumarchais) demands—and learn it he does, as in the recitative before his still-defensive aria in Act IV, when he acknowledges both longing and pain. Saying, "O Susanna, what suffering you cost me," he, like Cherubino, seeks a good outside himself.

What's suggested here, then, is that democratic reciprocity needs love. Why? Why wouldn't respect be enough? Well, respect is unstable unless love can be reinvented in a way that does not make people obsess all the time about hierarchy and status. That private obsession, unchallenged, threatens to disrupt the public culture of equality. But, more deeply, the public culture needs to be nourished and sustained by something that lies deep in the human heart and taps its most powerful sentiments, including both passion and humor. Without these, the public culture remains wafer-thin and passionless, without the ability to motivate people to make any sacrifice of their personal self-interest for the sake of the common good.

V. Cherubino, Rousseau, Herder

Now that we have a general idea of what Mozart is attempting, we may make our impressions more precise by comparing the opera's insights about citizenship in the new era to those of two of Mozart's philosophical contemporaries, Jean-Jacques Rousseau and Johann Gottfried Herder. Both share with Mozart the view that a new political culture needs to be sustained by new sentiments, and both also share with him the view that these sentiments must include not only the calm sentiments of respect and civic friendship, but also, sustaining and infusing these, something more like love, directed at the nation and its moral goals. Here, however, the resemblance ends.

In the important final section of *On the Social Contract,* entitled "On Civil Religion," Rousseau makes it clear that intense lovelike bonds of patriotic sentiment are needed to bring citizens together, rendering egalitarian institutions stable over time.[45] Early in human history, he observes, people "had no kings but the gods," and needed to believe that their leaders were indeed gods. Both paganism and feudalism were sustained by some such fiction. "A lengthy alteration of feelings and ideas is necessary before men can be resolved to accept a fellow man as a master, in the hope that things will turn out well for having done so" (220). These new sentiments must have the intensity of the religious sentiments they replace, or they will not succeed in holding the new political order together.

Christianity looks at first blush as if it might be that "civil religion," since it does teach brotherhood of all human beings (224). On further inspection, however, Christianity has a number of fatal flaws from the point of view of the political order. First, it teaches people to hope for a salvation that is otherworldly and spiritual, rather than political; thus "it leaves laws with only the force the laws derive from themselves, without adding any other force to them" (224). Second, Christianity turns people's thoughts inward, as each is urged to examine his own heart; this teaching produces indifference to political events. Third and finally, Christianity teaches nonviolence and even martyrdom, thus teaching people to be slaves. "Its spirit is too favorable to tyranny for tyranny not to take advantage of it at all times" (225). Christian emperors, Rousseau argues, ruined the Roman Empire: "when the cross expelled the eagle, all Roman valor disappeared" (225).

The civil religion we need must inculcate "sentiments of sociability, without which it is impossible to be a good citizen or a faithful subject" (226). These sentiments are based on some quasi-religious dogmas, including "the sanctity of the social contract and the laws" (226). But what are the sentiments themselves like? It is clear that they involve an intense love of the nation and its laws. They also involve a type of fraternity grounded in unanimity and homogeneity: the person who dissents from the "civil religion" is to be banished "for being unsociable, for being incapable of sincerely loving the laws and justice" (226). Civic love, then, is incompatible with active critical thought about the political order, and with a sense of the separateness of the individual from the group. The test for sincerity is unanimity.[46] Furthermore, one thing that citizens must be unanimous about is the willingness to die for the nation—presumably without thinking critically about the plan for war, and whenever the sovereign body of citizens so decrees. The sentiment of civil love has, then, a strong commitment to the suspension of both individuality and reasoning. Indeed, we might say, more generally, that the person-to-person dimension is missing, since the approved sentiments of communal bonding do not lead to or rest upon any sentiments directed at individuals, even sentiments of concern and respect.[47]

Notice, then, that despite Rousseau's intense hatred of the feudal order, he has not been able to think his way very far beyond it, in thinking about the emotions. Civic love, like feudal love, is obedient, hierarchical. (Even if it is "the general will," not an individual, that is sovereign, the general will nonetheless bears to the wayward individual a strongly hierarchical relationship.) There is no room for the sort of reciprocity exemplified by Mozart's women, a reciprocity based on plotting, joking, a sense of the free space within which people can live and be themselves. Moreover, despite Rousseau's attempt, in Book IV of *Emile,* to substitute the egalitarian sentiment of *pitié* for sentiments based upon feudal inequality, that experiment remains deeply unrealized in his idea of the civil religion, since the civil religion counters the allegedly excessive meekness of Christianity by relying, it would seem, on the very ideas of manly courage, assertiveness, and honor that sustained the ancien régime. There is a shift, in that the object of civic shame, civic anger, and civic assertiveness is now the nation, seen as embodiment of the general will. The sentiments themselves, however, feel very much the same, as the nation seeks to establish itself in the world's hierarchy of nations. It's still true, in this new world as in the old, that "to forget shame and insult is baseness, complete lowness of status."

Mozart, by contrast, proposes a radical alteration of the very content of civic love. No longer must love revolve in any way around ideas of hierarchy and status. Instead, it must be aspirational: like Cherubino, it must "seek a good outside myself."

To sustain truly egalitarian institutions, moreover, this aspirational love must remain vulnerable to criticism, ultimately to the fact that each individual has a quirky mind that is not exactly the same as any other. (Indeed, although I speak of "civic love," it is crucial to the new conception that there is a family of types of love that play roles, interwoven, sharing some features but differing in other respects, as do the people these loves connect.) Rather than Rousseau's homogeneity, the Mozartian regime seeks real-life heterogeneity, gives it space to unfold, and takes delight in its oddness. The fondness of the women's world for plotting, joking, every subversion of tradition and obedience, is the sign of something that ultimately becomes crucial to the Enlightenment, in its Kantian and especially Millian forms: the idea of the mind of the individual as containing an untouched free space, a funny unevenness that is both erotic and precious. What the women's world knows is that those "mischievous looks" are precisely what make Cherubino worth loving (so, if women love him, they "certainly have their good reasons"). They know too that the aspirational nature of his love is deeply interwoven with his capacity for subversion. Civic love, then, has a downward movement as well: it can aspire in a healthy way only if it is also capable of poking fun at itself, noticing the everyday messiness and heterogeneity of real people.

How do we imagine this civic love expressing itself? We connect Rousseau's love with solemn public ceremonies, with anthems, with the drumbeat of the call to arms. Mozart's love, by contrast, is expressed through many different types of artistic and musical performance, but, crucially, through comedy, including comedy that pokes fun at the call to arms (as in "*Non più andrai*") and points out some of the unpleasant realities of what passes in some quarters for warlike glory: "instead of the fandango, a march through the mud *[il fango]*."

At this point, we notice that Mozart has an eighteenth-century ally:[48] Johann Gottfried Herder, whose *Letters for the Advancement of Humanity* (1793–1797) develops a remarkably similar conception of a reformed patriotism that would need to be inculcated if the world is ever to become a world of peace. Herder begins by making the point that if patriotism is an attitude toward an entity called "fatherland," it had better figure out what is valuable in the relationship of a child to its father.[49] If we ask this question seriously, he argues, we will see that we want this love to contain aspiration to genuine merit, but also a love of peace, since we all remember with greatest longing and love the peaceful times of our childhood. Moreover, what delighted us in those peaceful times was *"games of youth"*: so, the new patriotism must at the same time be something playful. Above all, it would never involve blood lust and revenge: *"Fatherlands against fatherlands* in a combat of blood *[Blutkampf]* is the worst barbarism in the human language."

Later in the collection, Herder returns to this theme, making it clear that he conceives of the animating spirit of the new patriotism as less paternal than feminine, and requiring a profound gender transformation on the part of males. Here he alludes to what he has managed to learn about Native American Iroquois customs, which, he argues, involve casting one of the potentially warring tribes in the role of "the woman," and then requiring all the others to listen to what "she" says:[50]

> Hence if at some time the *men* around her are at blows with each other and the war threatens to become severe, then the *woman* should have the power to address them and say to them: "You men, what are you doing that you belabor each other about with blows in this way? Just remember that your wives and children are bound to die if you do not stop. Do you, then, want to be responsible for your own annihilation from the face of the earth?" And the *men* should then pay heed to the *woman* and obey her. (401)

By dressing the (members of the) chosen nation in women's skirts and women's jewelry, they express the thought that "from now on they should no longer occupy themselves with weapons" (401). Herder now notes that the members of the Iroquois nation address one another as "sister-children" and "fellow female playmates."[51]

Now to Europe. Herder observes that at one time feudal hierarchy played, after a fashion, the role of this "woman," making people keep the peace. Now that we have rejected feudalism, however, we have to put the women's clothes on all of us, in effect, and this means inculcating in all citizens "dispositions of peace." His "great *peace woman*" (whom he equates with "universal justice, humaneness, active reason") will seek to produce seven (emotional) "dispositions" in the citizens of the future. First is a "horror of war": citizens should learn that any war not limited to self-defense is mad and ignoble, causing endless practical pain and deep moral degeneration. Second, they will learn "reduced respect for heroic glory." They should "unite to blow away the false sparkle that dances around a *Marius, Sulla, Attila, Genghis Khan, Tamerlane,*" until citizens have no more awe for these mythic "heroes" than they do for common thugs. Herder does not say how this "blowing away" should be accomplished, but comedy is clearly a useful technique. Third, the peace woman will teach a "horror of false statecraft." It's not enough to unmask warlike heroics: we must also teach disobedience and disrespect to the sort of political authority that likes to whip up war to advance its own power interests. To produce this result we must teach active critical citizenship: "The universal voice-vote must be victorious over the value of mere *state rank* and of its *emblems,* even over the most seductive tricks of vanity, even over early-imbibed prejudices" (406). Of course, this critical spirit must be taught in conjunction with an admiration for and aspiration to what is really fine.

Fourth, peace will teach patriotism, but a patriotic love that is "purified" of "dross," above all purified of the need to define the lovable qualities of one's nation in terms of competition with other nations, and even war against them. "Every nation must learn to feel that it becomes great, beautiful, noble, rich, well ordered, active, and happy, not in the eyes of others, not in the mouth of posterity, but only in itself, in its own self" (406). The fifth, closely related disposition is that of "feelings of justice towards other nations." The sixth is a disposition to fair principles for trade relations, involving a ban on monopoly of the seas and a determination to make sure that poorer nations are not sacrificed to the greedy interests of the richer. Finally, citizens will learn to delight in useful activity: "the *maize stalk* in the *Indian woman's* hand is itself a weapon against the sword." All of these, concludes Herder, are the principles "of the great peace goddess *Reason* from whose language no one can in the end escape" (408).

Herder and Mozart are in harmony. Each sees the need to feminize the culture of male one-upmanship if civic love is to be productive of true happiness. The Countess, we might say, is Herder's great peace woman Reason, whose gentleness and whose refusal to focus on insulted pride show a way in which "all" can be happy. Cherubino, her pupil, has learned from her a horror of war, a horror of false statecraft, and a love of mischievous subversion of the countless ways in which men try to make the world a world of war. Herder emphasizes the negative side more than does Mozart: the decent society must teach appropriate fear and even horror, not just appropriate love. And he rightly emphasizes the fact that critical reason plays a crucial role in the new approach. In that sense he is echoing Kant's call for an approach to world peace that rests on the Enlightenment value of a critical public culture. But in essence he and Mozart are on the same page. The adult men are led, in the end, to put on those long skirts and think about daily life in a reasonable way, rather than a way informed solely by the insatiable greed of honor run amok. What we have at the end of the opera is something that would appall Rousseau, a world of craziness, foolishness, joking, idiosyncratic individuality—and, inseparably, a world of peace. The new temper may not be sufficient for peace, since external dangers can always threaten. It does appear, however, to be necessary.

VI. Transcending the Everyday?

What, then, happens at the opera's close? Temporarily, at least, the male world yields before the female world, asking for pardon. And then there is a pause. As Steinberg nicely says, "[F]rom Mozart to Mahler, the rest, the musical pause, the moment of silence is the indicator of a first-person musical voice taking stock of itself. Music stops to think."[52] What, in this silence, might the Countess be thinking before she says yes?

If she has any sense—and we know that she has a great deal—she will be thinking, "What on earth does this promise of renewed love really mean? Has this man, who has behaved badly for years, really become a new person just because our joke succeeded and he is publicly embarrassed?" And when, like the sensible woman she is, she gives herself the answer "Surely not," then she must think again, asking herself, "But then, shall I accept him as he is, with his arrogance, his status-consciousness, his anxiety-driven infidelities? Shall I agree to live with just the hope or promise, and the occasional reality, of reciprocal love, rather than its assured stability?"

When, then, after that pause, she answers, "I am nicer, and I say yes," with that downward-leaning phrase, she is saying yes to the imperfection in all their lives, accepting the fact that love between these men and these women, if frequently real, will always be uneven and far from blissful; that people will never get the entirety of what they long for; that even if men are capable of learning from women—and Steinberg has nicely shown how Figaro learns from Susanna a newly tender musical idiom[53]—nonetheless we hardly have reason to expect these achievements to be stable, given the pressures culture and upbringing exert on human development. Indeed, it seems far more likely that Cherubino will be corrupted by the male world around him than that the other men will drop their quest for honor and status and learn to sing like Cherubino. Even in the best of cultures, the aversion to shame and the narcissistic desire for control are profound human desires; they are unlikely to go away, yielding a world in which all lovers get everything they want. (And wouldn't the image of such a world itself be a narcissistic fantasy that might inhibit the real perception of another individual reality?)

So, when she says that "yes," she is agreeing to love, and even trust, in a world of inconstancy and imperfection—an affirmation requiring more courage than any of the battlefield exploits mentioned by Figaro in *"Non più andrai"*.

What she agrees to here is also what the ensemble agrees to. The new public world is a world of happiness *in that way*. What that seems to mean is that all present say yes to a world that seeks and aims at reciprocity, respect, and attunement without being starry-eyed about perfection, a world in which people commit themselves to liberty, fraternity, and equality while understanding that these transcendent ideals are to be attained not by exiting from the real world into a pristine world, but rather by pursuing them in this one, in episodes of love and craziness. The new regime will fail if it demands perfection. It will succeed only on the basis of a realistic conception of men and women, and what they are capable of. But sustaining the hope of fraternity without being starry-eyed (and therefore, in due course, disillusioned and cynical) requires something like an unjaundiced trust in the possibility of love (at least sometimes and for a while), and, perhaps above all, a sense of humor about the world as it is.[54]

These ideas of trust, acceptance, and reconciliation are not in the text, but only in the music.[55] As has long been felt by interpreters, Mozart's sensibility is, at the very least, more determinate than his librettist's, and possibly at odds with it, if we locate in the libretto leanings toward a kind of detached cynicism that Da Ponte at times exhibits.[56] But Mozart's music is not in some unattainable heaven; it is in the middle of our world, and in the bodies of those who sing it. It reshapes the world by reshaping breath itself.

In *The Musical Representation: Meaning, Ontology, and Emotion*, Charles O. Nussbaum gives us the best picture we have in philosophy to date of the experience of musical listening, the nature of the virtual space it creates and the mental representations it evokes. At the end of the book, he adds a chapter that is in many ways underdetermined by the book's overall argument, in which he argues that the great interest we take in (Western, tonal) music derives from our horror of the merely contingent, our desire for an experience of transcendence and unity that is akin to religious experience. This chapter contains fascinating material on quite a few philosophers, including Kant, Hegel, Schopenhauer, Nietzsche, and Sartre—all of whom supply arguments that harmonize with Nussbaum's contentions in a variety of ways. It also contains material on mystical experience that convinces one that the religion/music parallel Nussbaum investigates is real, and illuminating for at least some music.

And yet. Why should we be so inclined to suppose that music offers one particular type of good to human life, rather than many types of good? C. Nussbaum is far too subtle to claim such a thing outright,[57] but in his insistence on this one function of music, he at least suggests the primacy and centrality of this type of good. Like philosophy, however, and continuous with it, music would appear to assume different argumentative positions, seeing the world from different and contrasting points of view, in such a way that Steinberg's metaphor of "listening to reason" appears more apt than C. Nussbaum's idea of a single type of experience. (Indeed, religion itself contains many types of experience—including the mystical impression of transcendence, but including, as well, the passion for earthly justice and the acceptance of an imperfection in earthly striving.)[58]

I have proposed a reading of Mozart's opera according to which it offers a different sort of happiness, a happiness that is comic, uneven, uncertain, wary of grandiose claims of transcendence. Indeed, the music itself laughs up its sleeve at pretensions of that sort (as in those little muffled bursts of laughter in the overture and in *"Venite, inginocchiatevi"*).[59] C. Nussbaum may well respond that opera, that impure mixed art form, which relies on real bodies and real sights, is not the musical medium that his argument (based on music's disembodied and invisible nature) addresses. Even the human voice itself appears an anomaly within C. Nussbaum's conception of a musical art without bounded spatiotemporal existence. All musical instruments refer in some way to the human body, but the voice, alone among the instruments, is a part of the body, and always expresses bodily frailty as well as potentiality.[60]

Just as there is a love that seeks transcendence and a love that repudiates that aspiration as immature and a precursor of disillusionment, so too, I think, there are both sorts of music. It is no accident that Beethoven is on the cover of C. Nussbaum's book,[61] and a major source of his musical examples. But the yearning for the transcendent that is indeed embodied in Beethoven's version of the Enlightenment is first cousin to cynicism: realizing that the ideal political harmony embodied in the Ninth Symphony and *Fidelio* doesn't really exist, one might well make a sour face at the real world.[62]

If, however, one follows Mozart's version of Enlightenment politics, one will still see that the world as it is needs a great deal of work, and one will not stop aspiring to get that work done, making the world of the male voice somewhat more like the world of the female voice, with its commitment to fraternity, equality, and liberty. One will not stop seeking to educate young men to love music rather than the concerto of shells and cannons. One will, however, at the same time embrace real people— even men!—as they are, and one won't stop loving them because they are (no doubt like oneself)[63] a mess. That, suggests the pause within the music, is a more hopeful direction, if not the only possible direction, for a workable conception of democratic political love.

CHAPTER THREE

Religions of Humanity I:
Auguste Comte, J. S. Mill

I have said that the soul is not more than the body,
And I have said that the body is not more than the soul, . . .
And whoever walks a furlong without sympathy walks to his own
    funeral drest in his shroud, . . .
And I say to any man or woman, Let your soul stand cool and
    composed before a million universes.

—Walt Whitman, *Song of Myself*

I. Toward a Liberal Civil Religion:
Beyond Rousseau and Herder

In the aftermath of the French Revolution, as self-governing republics began (though with many backslidings) to emerge across Europe, the search for new forms of fraternity became almost an obsession. Under the ancien régime, the emotions of citizens had been led along the all-too-familiar path that *Figaro* brilliantly depicts: honor for some, shame for others, genuine reciprocity nowhere. This old emotion culture evidently could not sustain a self-governing republic, but what might replace it?

The end of the eighteenth century left Europeans with two distinct and in some ways sharply opposed models of the new civic emotion culture: Rousseau's and Herder's. Both thinkers share the project of forging a "civil religion" that will hold a nation together, render it stable, and motivate its ambitious projects. Both understand that competition, ego-

ism, and the love of hierarchy are major obstacles to the success of republican self-government. At this point, however, they diverge. Convinced that homogeneity in sentiments is essential for civic order and
stability, Rousseau makes his "civil religion" mandatory, punishing dissenters and nonparticipants.[1] His solution was therefore rejected by
Kant and other thoughtful liberals (although philosopher Johann Gottlieb Fichte went even further in Rousseau's direction, proposing to take
children away from their families at am early age and to instill civic values in national boarding schools).[2] Herder, by contrast (like Mozart),
stresses the importance of exactly those qualities, using the image of a
feminine politics to express the idea that the new regime must depart
radically from an earlier culture of masculinity. In keeping with its emphasis on play, humor, and heterogeneity, the new culture would not be
coercively imposed, and it would carefully preserve space both for dissent and for different human experiments. Herder, however, says little
about implementation, beyond the fact that the new attitudes are to be encouraged by public rhetoric and the attitudes of leaders.[3]

Nineteenth-century political thought soon became obsessed with the
question of civic emotion. As time went on, it was understood that the
new "civil religion" had not one but two opponents. The honor-based
emotion culture of the ancien régime was one, but a new capitalist culture of greed and egoism was another. Observing the rise of selfish acquisitiveness and the apparent weakness of any sense of a common good,
thinkers of many types tried to imagine a "civil religion" that would extend sympathy beyond the local group, producing cohesive support for
political ideals involving redistribution and an assault on poverty. Increasingly, they took egoism and narcissism to be their primary targets.
Italian revolutionary, philosopher, and patriot Giuseppe Mazzini (1805–
1872) argued that the goal of the new emotion culture should be support
for equal human dignity, equal political and civil liberty, and a democratic idea of equal entitlement:

> We cannot wish the children of God to be equal before God, and to
> be unequal before men. We cannot wish our immortal spirit to ab-
> jure on earth that gift of liberty which is the source of good and evil
> in our actions, and whose exercise makes man virtuous or criminal

in the eyes of God. We cannot wish the brow that is raised to heaven
to fall prostrate in the dust before any created being; the soul that
aspires to heaven to rot in ignorance of its rights, its power, and its
noble origin. We cannot admit that instead of loving one another
like brethren, men may be divided, hostile, selfish, jealous, city of
city, nation of nation.[4]

How, though, could this new fraternal sentiment be engineered? The
problem of instituting democracy in Europe, Mazzini argues, is at its
root not a legal problem but a problem of hearts and minds. The necessary sentiments should be produced by a reform of education. (This reform will happen all the more effectively, he adds, probably referring to
Comte's proposals, if we could create a pan-European "philosophical—I
might say religious—association," which would take charge of directing
education in all countries.)[5] Fraternal sentiment must, in the beginning,
be organized at the national level. Unmediated cosmopolitan sympathy
for all human beings—"the brotherhood of all, love for all"[6]—is an unrealistic goal at the present time, so immersed are people in egoistic projects and local loyalties. The nation—the democratic nation committed
to equal human dignity—is a necessary intermediary between the ego
and the whole of humanity: we can already see that the nation can be the
object of intense emotions that have motivational efficacy. By building
the right sort of patriotism, then, people concerned with universal love
may hope to produce the basis for truly international fraternity. Mazzini
compares patriotism to a ladder on which we can mount to the cosmopolitan ideal, and also to a fulcrum on which we can leverage universal
sentiment. The fully equal rights of people in all countries must in the
end be the object of our aspiration, but we will best promote this end—
here Mazzini agrees with Kant—if we focus on the formation of an international organization of free and equal peoples, each democratically organized, each animated by patriotism, and all moved by the maxim
"The progress of each for the advantage of all."[7] National sentiment, then,
will be not only a transitional instrument of universal brotherhood, but
also an ongoing principle of its organization.

Such ideas were enormously influential, as national and democratic
movements arose all over the world. It was widely agreed that Mazzini

was correct: people are possessed by egoism; the task of building decent and stable democracies depends on combating their narcissism, extending sympathy. It was widely agreed, too, that this new public emotion culture must both sustain democracy and assist the aspirations of democratic nations to global justice and peace. Of all such proposals, by far the most influential were those of Auguste Comte (1798–1857). A renowned philosopher and social scientist (indeed, he might be called the founder of the very idea of social science), Comte had a worldwide influence that is hard to credit today, so generally neglected are his ideas. Perhaps only Marx, later, attained a wider and deeper influence. Intellectuals from many nations, convinced that human progress required some type of humanistic "civil religion" to counteract the power of egoism and greed, rallied to his call for a new "spiritual power," a "religion of humanity" that could guide nations toward progress through emotions of sympathy and love.

Comte, though rarely studied in philosophy curricula today, was regarded during his lifetime as one of the leading thinkers of the century. Revered by John Stuart Mill as a philosopher of equal rank with Descartes and Leibniz,[8] he had immense intellectual prestige and practical influence all over the world. In Britain, Comtean Positivism claimed such sympathizers as J. S. Mill and George Eliot. In Brazil, the nascent republican movement adopted Comte's motto, "Order and Progress," as the motto of the nation, and the Comtean symbol of a woman holding a child as its new flag. In India, Comte's ideas were so influential, particularly in Bengal, that, as literary historian Jasodhara Bagchi puts it, they were "assimilated into the class subjectivity and common sense of the elite."[9] Because Comte and his European followers were known to be hostile to colonial domination, it seemed subversive rather than submissive to adopt his program—despite the fact that Comte believed in the supremacy of the "white race" and assigned a lead role to the nations of Europe in his scheme of world positivist culture, with France in first place.[10] Tagore's library contained the major works of Comte, and he drew on them throughout his career, particularly in the novel *The Home and the World* (1915) and the much later philosophical book *The Religion of Man* (1930)—not without deep criticism, as we shall see.

Engaging with Comte will prove valuable for our project, since he responds with detailed proposals to the need I have identified—for a public culture based upon love and extended sympathy, which can support the goals of a just society and ensure the stability of its commitments. Comte also follows and develops the promising suggestion of *Figaro,* proposing a reform of gender politics that places the "feminine" spirit at the heart of society. At the same time, he accords great value to the imagination and to the arts as key ingredients in humanity's progress. Comte's arguments in favor of these strategies complement, to some extent, those of Mozart and Herder, promising illumination for our own pursuit of similar ideas.

Comte's enterprise, however, is full of pitfalls, prejudices, and even absurdities, so it must be approached in a critical spirit. Fortunately, two of Comte's most distinguished enthusiasts, Mill and Tagore, do so approach it, and their reactions will help us imagine how we might retain what is insightful in Comte while avoiding what is unappetizing.

II. Comte's Religion of Humanity

Comte might be said to be European philosophy's new Epicurus. Like the ancient Greek thinker, he claims to have proven that the universe is not run by the gods; correct apprehension of the laws of nature will move humankind beyond the era of dependence upon religion. Positivism—the idea that we explain nature by secular laws grounded in perceptual experience—is thus a philosophically grounded replacement for religion. It yields a new approach not only to nature but also to social life. No longer need we explain our dealings with one another in the religious language of godliness and sin; instead, we learn to understand the laws of human social interaction through empirical research. Comte was the founder of empirical social science, perhaps his most lasting contribution to the history of thought.[11]

Comte, however, was no material reductionist, seeking to do away with the language of ethical norms in favor of a language of physical interactions. Nor did he hold the dismissive view of normative ethical argument that characterized the much later "logical positivism" of the twentieth century. Like Epicurus, he seems to have believed that it is one thing to understand how society works, another to reason about how it ought to change and what changes would produce true human well-being. He does hold that morality can be scientific only if it is grounded in a correct apprehension of the way things work in the world, and he does think that human conduct, including the operations of sympathy and love, can be understood in a lawlike way. The preference for extended over narrow sympathy, however, like the other aspects of Comte's normative account of social progress, depends on a normative argument: we are supposed to recognize that a broader sympathy is more advanced, more mature, than the narrow sympathy with family and kin by which most people are animated. One way he makes this point is through a developmental analysis: we recognize that we begin as children with very narrow sympathies, and we see that there is something more mature about the extension of sympathy to a larger group of kin, and something still more mature, more quintessentially human, in the extension of sympathy to friends, spouse, and others whom we select in "relationships of an entirely voluntary nature" (105). Although familial and especially conjugal love play a pivotal role for Comte, as cradles of individual development, the trajectory of human maturity is clear: sympathy extends ever outward, until the unity of the entire species, past and future as well as present, becomes its object. Comte suggests that there is something simply childish and almost bestial in refusing to acknowledge that we are members of a universal kind, and that this fact about us is morally fundamental. Comte believes that we all understand that self-serving moral arguments are bad arguments: once we face head-on the question of how to distribute social goods, he believes, we cannot avoid concluding that a more equitable system is preferable, and that we therefore have reason to cultivate the motives that would produce and sustain it.

Comte's arguments at this point are rather thin, but he is able to rely, no doubt, on widespread acceptance of Kant's profound arguments, which make the universalizability of a principle to all human agents a necessary condition of moral adequacy. (And Kant himself insists that his arguments have their source in a healthy moral understanding that is widely shared.) He repeatedly argues in a Kantian manner, by pointing out that a particular conclusion concerning one's obligations can be avoided only by making oneself a special case; he believes that once this is made clear people will be self-critical enough to refuse this sort of self-serving move.

Unlike Kant, however,[12] Comte believes that the best way to promote due regard for humanity is to focus on the emotions, training people to extend sympathy outward. For this training to succeed, we need two things: order and something like religion. Order is secured by government, which manages the economy (with the assistance of a capitalist class) and provides for bodily security and well-being. Government, however, does not set moral goals. For the ultimate moral purposes of society, we must turn to its spiritual power.

Comte's government protects freedom of speech and freedom of conscience—in the sense that there is no legal penalty for or restraint upon the expression of opinion (Mill, 73-74). This does not mean, however, that Comte has any respect for the *moral* right of individuals to follow their chosen religion and express their chosen ideas. So far as he is concerned, there are right and wrong answers in the moral domain, and those answers are difficult to come by. Only a few very highly trained people, capable of appreciating the arguments of Positivist philosophy, are likely to be able to attain them. Society will, therefore, strongly discourage individual self-expression and dissent, and will encourage a spirit of "moral control" and unanimity (Mill, 75).

Who should exercise this control? Comte argues that the new spiritual power should be entrusted to a small group of specialist philosophers. Trained in positivism, and at leisure so that they need do nothing else but attend to philosophical argumentation, they will understand, and convey, the Positivist conclusion that religion is passé and that people must direct their thoughts to humanity alone. They will then form a council into whose hands society will entrust the spiritual formation of the nation. Comte does not want philosophers to be government functionaries. Following the French tradition of separation of church and state, he argues that participation in government corrupts, and that authentic spirituality must be protected from the influence of the marketplace. The philosophers must therefore be something like tenured academics in a state-run research institute: they will be maintained for life at state expense, but that is the limit of the state's influence upon them. (Mill observes that the whole system is most implausible, since government officials have been characterized in such a contemptuous way that it is impossible to see why Comte thinks they would be capable of recognizing the spiritual authorities, much less supporting them [99].)

Although Comte calls these people philosophers, he does not imagine their function as genuinely philosophical in anything like a Socratic sense, in which philosophy requires continual self-examination and critique. These philosophers will not do what Comte himself did, studying the past critically and coming up with bold new solutions to standing problems. Comte imagines that philosophy has in effect come to a stop with his own contributions. The "philosophers" will simply spend their time examining, internalizing, and implementing the Comtean program. Comte does not think it necessary to mention that this is a rather limited role for a philosopher, nor does he worry that philosophical dissent might compromise unanimity and control. He simply assumes that he has done his job so well that there is no more to be said, and people of reason will simply acquiesce. (He is not the only philosopher to have seen his own contribution as final in this way: both Epicurus in the ancient world and Utilitarian Jeremy Bentham in the modern—though not Mill—do appear to think that they have had the final word on normative matters.)

What Comte is after, then, is not what we (or Kant or Mill) might think of as a philosophical academy, a place of investigative critical argument, dissent, and exploration. It is, instead, a replacement for the pervasive social influence of the Roman Catholic Church and its clergy. The new spiritual guides, understanding Comte's ideas, will propound for the common people a total scheme of thought and practice that organizes their moral lives in its smallest details. To the trivial question of how they are going to displace the actual Catholic Church and its influence, Comte devotes only a side glance. Positivism will install itself the way Newtonian mechanics beat out Aristotle's theories: by the superior ability of its ideas to explain reality. Even if people do not understand all the fine points of Positivism, they will see its superior merit, preferring "the solid study of Laws" to the "fruitless search for Causes," and "submission to demonstrable necessities" to "submission to arbitrary Wills" (441).

The general goal of the new religion will be to extend human sympathy by cultivating the spirit of universal brotherhood. Rather than thinking in terms of private rights of possession, people will learn to pursue a common good with all their hearts, in a spirit of all-embracing humanist love. A linchpin in the cultivation of this love is the imagination: we must become able to see each person's fate in every other's, to picture it vividly as an aspect of our own fate, and to conceive of the whole history of the human kind and its possible future as part of our own sphere of concern, through intense focusing on ideal images of human achievement. In effect, Comte wants to change the way people understand the notion of their own happiness or flourishing: it should not be confined to narrow egocentric projects, but should include the fate of the whole of humanity, past, present, and future.

Imaginative capacities will be developed very early in the family (through a curriculum for early education imparted by the philosophers to mothers!). Throughout life, however, the imagination must continue to be intensified and refined through the agency of art. Comte emphasizes that poetry, music, and visual art must all play a key role in his new ideal. He has a high regard for art in one sense: he sees that it is extremely valuable in creating emotions of the requisite sort and evoking them on suitable occasions. He does not trust artists, however, because he thinks of them as self-serving and unreliable. "The mental and moral versatility which makes them so apt in reflecting the thoughts and feelings of those around them, utterly unfits them for being our guides" (310). So they must be kept under the watchful eye of the philosophers: "Their real vocation is to assist the spiritual power as accessory members" (310). Under the direction of the philosophical council, then, they will assist in the creation of the new positivist religion.

How might Comte's ambitious goal be accomplished? What does it take to create a religion? As Comte sees, it takes a system of education. But it also takes organized modes of worship: "a *cultus*, . . . a set of systematic observance, intended to cultivate and maintain the religious sentiment" (Mill 149–150). A *cultus* must include rituals that organize the day and festivals that demarcate the seasons of the year. Above all, it requires an object of worship. All this Comte provides, imagining an analogue for every motivationally efficacious aspect of Roman Catholic worship. As Mill says, "Here we approach the ludicrous side of the subject" (149).

The object of devotion will be humanity itself. To be imagined and addressed as a deity, however, it must have a singular name: *Le Grand Etre,* the Great Being. The Earth, home of this deity, is now called *Le Grand Fétiche,* "the great adored object." Comte understands the power of ritual to organize emotions, and so he prescribes a multitude of ceremonies, in the most detailed manner. The Christian year, of course, was organized around events in the life of Christ. The new Positivist year will be organized around events in the human life cycle: birth, maturity, marriage, parenthood, aging, death—and also around the stages of human history. Some of these rituals will be "static," stimulating the love of order; others will be "dynamic," stimulating the desire for progress (379). Additional celebrations will focus on the contribution of different classes to the well-being of society. All in all, there are to be eighty-four festivals, thus more than one per week. The arts will be entrusted with the design of these festivals, which will involve appropriate poetry, music, and visual representations. Comte gives the artists a very restricted compass, however, since he himself prescribes so much of the content and even metaphorical structure of these celebrations.

Catholic worship derives a great deal of motivational efficacy from the panoply of saints it recognizes, and from the emotions that are aroused by the stories of their lives and sufferings. Praying to a saint brings the worshipper close to the truths of the religion by providing religious emotion with a conceivable and real human object, rather than a distant abstraction. For this aspect of Catholic practice Comte invents a precise analogue: the lives of noble human beings of the past. Just as Catholic believers are to some degree free to choose which saint to pray to, according to their particular motivational propensities, so too the positivist worshiper will be free to compose a personal form of prayer—just so long as personal prayer occupies enough time. Comte assigns two hours per day to this activity, "divided into three parts: at rising, in the middle of the working hours, and in bed at night" (Mill, 151). He even prescribes the posture of the body: morning prayers will be said kneeling, nighttime prayers in the posture of sleep, so that the influence of prayer will extend into the believer's dreams. Here we may turn to Mill's account—which reveals a comic spirit that one usually does not see in Mill:

This brief abstract gives no idea of the minuteness of M. Comte's prescriptions, and the extraordinary height to which he carries the mania for regulation by which Frenchmen are distinguished among Europeans, and M. Comte among Frenchmen. It is this which throws an irresistible air of ridicule over the whole subject. There is nothing really ridiculous in the devotional practices which M. Comte recommends towards a cherished memory or an ennobling ideal, when they come unprompted from the depths of the individual feeling; but there is something ineffably ludicrous in enjoining that everybody shall practise them three times daily for a period of two hours, not because his feelings require them, but for the premeditated purpose of getting his feelings up. The ludicrous, however, in any of its shapes, is a phaenomenon with which M. Comte seems to have been totally unacquainted. There is nothing in his writings from which it could be inferred that he knew of the existence of such things as wit and humour. . . . [And] there are passages in his writings which, it really seems to us, could have been written by no man who had ever laughed. (153–154)

Mill's example at this point is indeed hilarious. As a replacement for the Catholic gesture in which one makes the sign of the cross over oneself, Comte proposes a gesture in which one touches the *"principaux organes"* of the body, expressing one's devotion to the biological principles through which one is sustained in life. "This *may* be a very appropriate mode of expressing one's devotion to the Grand Etre," Mill concludes. "[B]ut any one who had appreciated its effect on the profane reader, would have thought it judicious to keep it back till a considerably more advanced stage in the propagation of the Positive Religion" (154–155).

After we finish laughing with Mill, however, we ought to step back and ask why these aspects of Comte seem ridiculous, and whether we are right to laugh. Mill is surely hasty in suggesting that it is always inauthentic or absurd to engage in a ritual performance for the purpose of stimulating or arousing certain emotions. Strongly influenced by Romanticism, Mill cannot imagine that a ritual performance of this sort could be other than superficial or even hypocritical. The history of religion, however, shows us that ritual is an extremely powerful device for

the arousal of emotion—in large part because human beings are creatures of habit, and repetition increases the resonance of an image or
thought. Ritual also provides a common ground among participants,
creating areas of shared expression and memory. Denominations that
have tried to emphasize authenticity to the exclusion of repetition usually find themselves reverting to ritual before long in order to hold the
congregation together and increase its commitment. Thus Reform Judaism, animated by an idea of autonomy, for a time eschewed ritual, but
congregants themselves demanded it, and by now a great deal of traditional poetry, music, and performance is back in, albeit in revised form.
The Ethical Culture Society, founded in order to be a kind of positivist
postreligious church, quickly began to take on ritual elements from elsewhere, though without sufficient planning or cohesion to ensure lasting
devotion. Britain's Humanist Society, which attempted to provide pro-
saic analogues for traditional rituals, produced something impoverished
and unappealing.[13]

Comte is on strong ground, then, when he insists on communal rituals and on engendering habits of devotion, and he is wise to call upon
poetry and music for aid, rather than relying on the philosophers to
make up suitable rituals on their own. Nor does there seem to be anything objectionable about the idea that one should perform certain rituals because they will inspire emotions that one wants to cultivate in
oneself. Becoming virtuous is a matter of cultivating appropriate habits,
in emotion as in conduct. The Romantic idea that emotion is not worthy
unless it comes unbidden should be rejected: we can learn to feel appropriately, just as we can learn to act appropriately.

So why do Comte's ideas seem ludicrous? One reason is superficial:
anything that derives its efficacy from habit is bound to seem funny or
odd when presented for the first time—and without the poetic and musical surroundings from which the new religion would ultimately derive a
great deal of its force. Visiting the rituals of an unfamiliar religion, one
typically feels alienation, embarrassment, or even a sense of the absurd.
Laughter is in part, then, just an uneasy reaction to the unfamiliar. But it
also comes, certainly, from the mania for control and homogeneity that
the whole exercise involves, and from a certain contradiction in its purpose. In the name of reason and humanity, Comte treats people like

submissive robots, closing off spaces for rational argument and individual creativity. The Positivist religion shares these problems, to some extent, with its Catholic model, but it is easier to see these defects in something new than in something that is by now familiar and traditional.[14] Whether or not we think it appropriate to laugh at any religion's all-encompassing system of devotions, we may certainly agree with Mill (and Mozart) in thinking that a society respectful of individual differences should be skeptical. For Mill, such mandatory conformity—even if enforced primarily through shame and other social sanctions—will doom society's hope of progress, since progress requires spaces for individual experimentation.

We notice too that Comte gives little scope to real artists. To the extent that Christian devotion seems rich and compelling by comparison to the religion Comte describes, it is because real artists in the Christian tradition have exercised imagination in idiosyncratic ways, producing works of music, poetry, and visual art that are both deeply moving and highly variegated. One suspects that Comte would not be comfortable with the partnership of a J. S. Bach, an El Greco, a Gerard Manley Hopkins—despite the evident Christian piety of all three—because they exercise imagination with personal integrity, trying to discover something of their own; all three would surely be utterly contemptuous of orders coming from the philosophical academy. It's not just control, then, that makes us laugh; it's the combination of control with sameness and of both with smugness, the sense that nothing remains to be learned or discovered.

Another aspect of the comedy of Positivism is its utter indifference to the world's many traditional cultures. Like Roman Catholicism, Positivism is supposed to be a worldwide religion—and yet it is all so very French. Comte does not pause to ask to what extent a religion ought to respect and incorporate elements of each traditional culture, as Roman Catholicism has certainly done very shrewdly.

Both the neglect of culture and the neglect of the individual show up in Comte's utter lack of a sense of humor. Mill is right on target here, and the humorlessness is significant, because it is an aspect of Comte's tendency to treat people like interchangeable machines to be set moving by his orders, rather than as quirky, idiosyncratic entities who might devi-ate from the prescribed course. Humor is contextual and cultural, requiring a sense of intimacy and shared background, so it is impossible for someone who doesn't take cultural difference and individuality seriously to have humor or value it.[15] Humor also typically involves the sense of surprise and an underlying love of defiance and subversion. Thinking of himself as complete and final, not imagining that life has any surprises to offer, Comte has a hard time laughing.

Here we are confronted with an issue that we will need to address repeatedly in what follows. On the one hand, we should take issue with Mill's dismissive attitude toward all uniformity. A common curriculum, including shared works of art (even Mill recommends that everyone read Wordsworth) and some shared ritual performances, seems essential for any new "civil religion" that is going to work, and an intelligent use of habit is an essential part of any program aimed at civic virtue. On the other hand, to work in a way that respects people, the program must itself respect the plurality of cultures and histories. No prescription for one nation can be applied without reinvention to any other. And no prescription for any culture, however efficacious, will prove satisfactory in normative terms unless it respects individual differences and cultivates spaces for improvisation and self-expression. Perhaps Mill is right to suggest that a sense of humor, like the proverbial canary in the mine, will steer us away from the more pernicious forms of homogeneity and control.

So far we have not considered an aspect of Comte's enterprise that appears to bring him very close to Mozart and Herder: his gender politics. Like Mozart and Herder, Comte associates extended sympathy with the influence of the feminine (227–303). Unlike them, however—and also unlike his followers Mill and Tagore—he appears to believe that this association is not simply cultural, but profoundly natural. Women, Comte holds, are fit to become leaders of the religion of sympathy because they are naturally ruled by their emotions, are profoundly sympathetic by nature, and are only somewhat rational. He does not even entertain the idea of making all future citizens learn sympathy and reciprocity—along with rational argument—in roughly similar ways. Instead, he protects a sphere, the family, in which the feminine principle can reign supreme, controlling the early education of all, from birth to puberty (192). Naturally, mothers are not left to their own devices: Comte has a very detailed curriculum for them to follow in their home schooling (192–195). Indeed, Comte trusts them no further than he trusts the artists: they are to be functionaries of the Positivist program, and Comte cannot imagine that their insights could contribute anything new. Moreover, although women are revered—indeed, worshipped—they are not to have any rights as citizens, or any chance to learn philosophy, but are to be confined entirely to the home, in part because their nature is not suited to practical deliberation, in part because, like the philosophers, they are to be kept pure of the taint of political struggle.

Thus Comte's gender proposal ultimately leads in a direction opposed to that of Mozart. Rather than empowering women politically and drawing upon the insights of the women's world—including its sense of fun and subversion—for the construction of a new type of citizenship for all, Comte makes the traditional separation of genders and spheres more rigid, arguing that "Equality in the position of the two sexes is contrary to their nature, and no tendency to it has at any time been exhibited" (275).

What of the pursuit of global justice? Comte's religion is truly international, though it remains organized at the national level. And in the international sphere Comte does not hesitate to give his council of philosophers a quasi-governmental role. Rather like the United Nations, it will preside over debates concerning global policy, including the introduction of a common European currency. Comte envisages a central philosophical/political association that will meet in Paris and will consist of "eight Frenchmen, seven Englishmen, six Germans, five Italians, and four Spaniards. This would be enough to represent fairly the principal divisions of each population" (427). His system would "afterwards extend, in accordance with definite laws, to the rest of the white race, and finally to the other two great races of man" (7). Colonies of Europe get first priority: "four for each American Continent, two for India, two for the Dutch and Spanish possessions in the Indian Ocean" (433). Comte notes, however, that the White race "in all its branches is superior to the other two races" (435), and he holds, as well, that monotheism represents a stage of human development superior to polytheism (435). Last to be incorporated is "the black race," and here Comte gives priority to Haiti, "which had the energy to shake off the iniquitous yoke of slavery," and to Central Africa, "which has never yet been subjected to European influence" (436), since he holds that being treated contemptuously by Europeans makes it harder for formerly enslaved peoples to learn the lessons of Positivism. So his racism is tempered, at least, by a vigorous condemnation of the effects of conquest.

This repellent section of Comte's work also proves instructive for us. If national sentiment is indeed to be the "fulcrum" on which we leverage universal love of humanity, how do we arrange to have national sentiment without chauvinism and racism? One part of the answer is obvious: we must avoid grounding the idea of the nation in a racial or ethnic identity. Even better, we might include antiracism as an element in a national identity. Such things are easier contemplated than realized, however, and the critic of our project will be right to ask whether, when we let the force of emotion assume power, we don't risk giving encouragement to such shameful aspects of human behavior. As we'll see, Tagore has a similar worry.

Comte has so many valuable ideas that the obvious defects of his program give us useful warnings. Mill and Tagore articulate those warnings and try to heed them, while preserving what is most valuable in the Comtean program.

III. Mill's Critique and Replacement

John Stuart Mill is a great admirer of Comte, with large criticisms to make. He admires not only the Positivist account of nature and history, but also the general proposal for a social cultivation of extended sympathy. In *Utilitarianism* (1861), when he faces his own greatest philosophical difficulty (how to move people from individual self-interest to general utility), he appeals to Comte to resolve the problem. In subsequent writings, however, he makes it clear that his conception of how a society should cultivate sympathy is utterly different from Comte's.

Bentham's Utilitarianism is based upon the psychological principle that all people tend to pursue their own maximal happiness; this principle Mill basically accepts, although his conception of happiness is much more variegated than Bentham's, making room for qualitative distinctions and for the intrinsic worth of activities. The normative ethical goal of Bentham's Utilitarianism, however, is the maximization of total or average utility. One might propose that this goal will be reached automatically if we simply leave people free to maximize their own utilities, but such was not the belief of the classical Utilitarian philosophers. They did not think that the present condition of society in their time, in which unfettered capitalism did leave people largely free to pursue self-interest, was a good one. Radical reformers, they understood that privilege makes people indifferent to the pain of others, even vast numbers of others (including the poor, women, and nonhuman animals). Those others, even if numerous, may be so powerless that they are unable to pursue their own happiness effectively, particularly if they lack political equality. So, the Utilitarian philosophers believed that considerable political and social reform would be required before there could be anything like a maximization of total or average utility. For Mill, reforms included considerable redistribution of wealth and income (together with a redefinition of property rights), the extension of the suffrage to women, and extensive legislation against cruel treatment of animals. But what forces in human beings might the Utilitarian rely on to bring about this extension?

Mill believes that moral emotions are the ultimate force behind any moral principle, and that moral emotions are not innate but acquired.[16] In principle, then, it might be arranged that people would learn to identify the general happiness with their own happiness, "when once the general happiness is recognized as the ethical standard" (303). Mill acknowledges, however, that as things are at present, there is a gulf between individual and general happiness, and the person who wants to serve the latter will very likely have to make a sacrifice of the former:

> Though it is only in a very imperfect state of the world's arrangements that any one can best serve the happiness of others by the absolute sacrifice of his own, yet so long as the world is in that imperfect state, I fully acknowledge that the readiness to make such a sacrifice is the highest virtue which can be found in man. (287–288)

In the long run, however, the space between the two needs to be closed. How? By moral progress, prominently including progress in the moral sentiments. Mill believes that to some extent we can simply appeal to people to recognize that society is better organized on a basis of due regard for the happiness of each one: "society between human beings, except in the relation of master and slave, is manifestly impossible on any other footing than that the interests of all are to be consulted. Society between equals can only exist on the understanding that the interests of all are to be regarded equally" (304). Mill recognizes, however, that such statements cut no ice with people who are habituated to regard women and the poor as nonequals, and to regard their own personal happiness as far more important than any other goal. How, then, can we begin to extend sympathy in the way that would be required if we want to effect a stable improvement in the state of society?

What is required, Mill argues, is to draw on a rudimentary sort of fellow feeling that is already general and powerful (303)—the sense of oneself as the member of a group—and to develop that into a genuinely moral sentiment. To some extent this can be achieved by institutional reform, since political improvements, by "leveling those inequalities of legal privilege between individuals or classes, owing to which there are large portions of mankind whose happiness it is still practicable to disregard" (305), will assist the development of suitable moral sentiments. The sentiments, however, must also be addressed more directly.

It is at this point that Mill turns to Comte. The passage is worth quoting at length:

> In an improving state of the human mind, the influences are constantly on the increase, which tend to generate in each individual a feeling of unity with all the rest; which feeling, if perfect, would make him never think of, or desire, any beneficial condition for himself, in the benefits of which they are not included. If we now suppose this feeling of unity to be taught as a religion, and the whole force of education, of institutions, and of opinion, directed, as it once was in the case of religion, to make every person grow up from infancy surrounded on all sides both by the profession and by the practice of it, I think that no one, who can realize this conception, will feel any misgiving about the sufficiency of the ultimate sanction for the Happiness morality. To any ethical student who finds the realization difficult, I recommend . . . the second of M. Comte's two

principal works. . . . I entertain the strongest objections to the system of politics and morals set forth in that treatise; but I think it has superabundantly shown the possibility of giving to the service of humanity, even without the aid of belief in a Providence, both the psychical power and the social efficacy of a religion; making it take hold of human life, and colour all thought, feeling and action in a manner of which the greatest ascendancy ever exercised by any religion may be but a type and foretaste; and of which the danger is, not that it should be insufficient, but that it should be so excessive as to interfere unduly with human freedom and individuality. (305–306)

Here we can see that, despite Mill's strong objections to the Comtean religion, which he registers here, he believes that Comte has shown the practicability of a pervasive cultivation of general sympathy, as a kind of secular religion.

In his posthumously published essay "The Utility of Religion,"[17] Mill returns to this theme and develops it further. The purpose of the essay is to scrutinize the claim that religion ought to be retained on account of its utility, even if we doubt its cognitive warrant. After going through a number of social harms that he believes religion has caused, Mill turns to its supposed benefits. The most conspicuous are three. First, religion broadens sympathy, giving us goals outside ourselves, and ideas and conceptions more beautiful than those we encounter in daily life. "The essence of religion is the strong and earnest direction of the emotions and desires towards an ideal object, recognized as of the highest excellence, and as rightfully paramount over all selfish objects of desire" (109). Second, religion addresses mysteries in life that we cannot understand by experience, thus stimulating imagination (102). Finally, religion offers us consolations, which we will always need, so long as human life is full of suffering (104).

Mill now argues that all these good functions of religion can be promoted by the "religion of humanity," which he describes, in Comtean fashion, as the identification of our emotions with the life of the whole of humankind and our hopes with the hope of progress for humanity. Nationalism shows us that people are capable of rising above narrow self-concern, so it is not impossible "that the love of that larger country, the world, may be nursed into similar strength, both as a source of elevated emotion and as a principle of duty." Following this religion, we will gradually become capable of "large and wise views of the good of the whole."

Mill contends that this new religion is better than theistic religions in four ways: (a) it has a finer object (since the aim is to benefit others, not to achieve immortality for oneself); (b) for that reason, it cultivates motives that are disinterested rather than egoistic; (c) it does not contain morally objectionable elements, such as the punishment of sinners in hell; and, finally, (d) it does not ask people to twist and pervert their intellectual faculties by believing things that are false or even absurd.

Some thoughtful Victorians, thinking about altruism, concluded that belief in an afterlife was essential to link our natural egoism to altruism. No less a philosopher than Mill's Utilitarian successor Henry Sidgwick argued that the "dualism of practical reason" could not be overcome without some hope for life after death. (In consequence, he devoted a good deal of his life to research into communication with the spirit world.)[18] Mill ventures to question this pessimistic idea. The fact that some religions, for example Buddhism, do not promise individual immortality and yet demand extensive altruism make us think it possible, he argues, that in a happier or more developed state of human existence the promise of an afterlife may prove unnecessary. People want immortality because they have never been happy, but if they are happy in this life and get to live a bit longer than at present, then they will be willing to accept life's end, and will see themselves as living on in the lives of those who follow them.

The one place where Mill expresses doubt is with regard to the prospect of being reunited with our loved ones who have died. "That loss, indeed, is neither to be denied nor extenuated. In many cases it is beyond the reach of comparison or estimate; and will always suffice to keep alive, in the more sensitive natures, the imaginative hope of a futurity which, if there is nothing to prove, there is as little in our knowledge and experience to contradict" (120). This poignant passage, which is naturally read as a commentary on his love for his wife, Harriet Taylor Mill, who died in 1858 of tuberculosis (from which Mill himself had previously recovered), reminds us that even the most skeptical and naturalistic of thinkers is still vulnerable to the promises of traditional religion. The religion of humanity will ignore this issue at its peril. Comte does attempt to build personal love into his schema: he tells us that he himself addresses personal prayers to his dead lover, Clothilde, as to an ideal human of the past. One may doubt, however, whether such a formal and institutionalized mode of address really fills the void Mill has identified. The idea that the religion of humanity can and should fully replace existing religion, rather than constituting a public supplement to it (the idea I shall be defending), may therefore be viewed with some skepticism.

Mill's critique of Comte, however, focuses on other problems. He has numerous objections to Comte's account of the role of government, which in his view is far too limited. Government should not simply keep order, but should arrange for the conditions of human equality to be met, something that, in Mill's view, requires substantial redistribution, as well as radical changes in the suffrage—he was the first to introduce a bill for women's suffrage as a member of Parliament.

Furthermore, although this is not discussed in his book on Comte, the entire argument of his *The Subjection of Women,* written at around the same time, constitutes a critique of the sort of naturalistic gender division on which Comte relies. In Mill's view, we have no good evidence for the claim that women's nature and abilities are fundamentally different from those of men, and all the good arguments we do have support giving them equal political and economic rights. Indeed, the whole idea of turning the emotional domain over to women is one that *The Subjection of Women* gives us reason to regard with skepticism, for women's tendencies have been formed in conditions of inequality, and if equal conditions did obtain, there is no reason to think that one sex would be "rational," the other "emotional." Mill agrees not with Comte but with Mozart: women are formed by culture, not immutable nature, and society has treated them extremely badly.

Mill's critique in the Comte book, however, focuses above all on Comte's mania for regulation and control. Even though the norms of Comte's civil religion are not to be coercively enforced by the state (as Rousseau wished), state enforcement is not Mill's only concern. Throughout his career, Mill worries about the stifling effect of the tyranny of majority opinion on individual liberty, and hence on social progress. Here, he objects vigorously to Comte's insistence that people have no *moral* right to express heterodox opinions in ethical matters, and to his related idea that society works best when people are homogeneous in belief and receive their beliefs at second hand from the centralized spiritual authority. *On Liberty* (1839) has already painted a very different picture of the healthy society. According to Mill, the liberty to express dissenting ideas is valuable not only when we are unsure which ideas are correct, but even when we think we have acquired correct ideas. Even the best ideas lose their edge when not subjected to critical argument, and people cease to grasp why they hold them. Moreover, Mill believes that challenging received ideas and thinking for oneself are ways of becoming more complete as a human being; thus docility and submission to authority "will assuredly be more repugnant to mankind, with every step of their progress in the unfettered exercise of their highest faculties" (Mill, 99). His laughter at Comte's prescriptions reflects his love of human heterogeneity and freedom.

Nor does Mill himself ever treat his own intellectual doctrines the way Comte treats his own: as immune to dissenting argument. His lifelong critical confrontation with Benthamism shows a mind that takes nothing on trust, that always looks for the best reasons, and in *Utilitarianism* he also shows himself keenly interested in seeking out anti-Utilitarian arguments and responding to them.

Mill, then, is on the horns of the dilemma that will occupy us throughout our project. He believes that the liberty to differ and argue is essential for the health of society, and yet he also believes that social institutions of the sort he favors (involving greater social equality for women and the poor) cannot be sustained without an extensive cultivation of sympathy that is religionlike in its effects upon character. How, then, does he propose to engender sympathy without undue control?

One part of the answer lies in a distribution of social functions. In his Inaugural Address as rector of St. Andrews University, he makes it clear that the formation of character and of the moral sentiments is by and large the business of the family, not that of the system of public education.[19] His position, however, turns out to be more subtle and complex than that simple statement would indicate: there is, after all, a lot public education can offer without stifling dissent in the manner of Comte.

Where elementary education is concerned, Mill parts ways with other defenders of liberty of thought (for example, William Godwin), holding that compulsory education is fully compatible with the defense of individual liberty.[20] This is so because people should not be free to do as they please when they act for other people who are in their power.[21] Just as "the almost despotic power of husbands over wives" should be limited by law, so too the power of parents over their children should have definite limits. But "[i]t is in the case of children that misapplied notions of liberty are a real obstacle to the fulfillment by the State of its duties" (128). Mill argues that neglect and abuse of the child's mental development is a "moral crime" (128) comparable to abuse and neglect of the child's body. So universal education should be required by law. Mill favors making parents pay for this education if they can, but subsidizing the education of poorer children.

Here, however, for Mill, the specter of Comtean homogeneity rears its head. To say that the state should require education is not to say that this education should be state-administered. Mill worries that state-controlled education would lead to the imposition of definite partisan political views and ideologies.[22] "A general State education is a mere contrivance for molding people to be exactly like one another; and as the mold in which it casts them is that which pleases the predominant power in the government . . . , it establishes a despotism over the mind" (129). He therefore concludes that state-administered education, if it exists at all, should be "one among many competing experiments" (129).

Instead, Mill argues, the requirement of education should be enforced by public examinations, beginning at an early age. First, basic skills of reading and writing will be tested, and, later, the acquisition and retention of knowledge (130). Eventually examinations will test very sophisticated skills, such as the mastery of philosophical arguments. To prevent an "improper influence over opinion," care must be taken to set up the exams without presupposing the truth or falsity of the ideas contained therein wherever "religion, politics, or other disputed topics" are involved. Thus the philosophy exam would ask students to master the arguments of both Locke and Kant, no matter which one he or she prefers; the religion exam would be, similarly, historical rather than requiring any statement of belief (131).

Mill's ideas are naïve and unsupported by empirical study. He seems to think that there is less danger of coercive uniformity in a system of public examinations than in state funding of educational institutions. But this presumes that such institutions could not incorporate robust norms of academic freedom and faculty control, even when state-funded. He also fails to reckon with the many problems involved in a system of means-tested provision of education, which would hardly alter the status quo in which he was raised, with rich parents providing home tutors for their children and poorer children left to attend whatever schools they could afford with their state stipend. The idea that political values of equal worth are expressed by making education free to all does not enter his mind; nor does the idea that equality is further served by requiring all children to attend a state-accredited school (whether public or private), except in very unusual circumstances. Even the idea of competition, much though it resonates with the contemporary vogue for charter schools, needs close scrutiny, and Mill, lacking empirical information, gives it none.

As for examinations, they can be a source of terrible coercion, as the No Child Left Behind Act in the United States has shown. Testing need not be of this simplistic type, but there is certainly a strong tendency for testing to simplify and homogenize, in a way that public schools in and of themselves, especially run at the local level, would not tend to do. About the higher level of testing Mill has some attractive ideas, but, once again, they are not very useful in the absence of study of specific regimes of national testing. In general, Mill should have thought more about structures (academic freedom, local control, faculty autonomy) that protect liberty in privately and publicly funded institutions alike, rather than assuming that the primary danger lies in a particular funding source.

Far more valuable is the set of reflections on university education that Mill presented in his Rector's Address at the University of St. Andrews in Scotland (1867). The lecture is of great interest for its own time, since Mill praises the Scottish system of higher education, with its emphasis on a broad-based liberal arts training, by contrast to the system in England, which is more highly specialized. His remarks about liberal education also resonate across the centuries, because they still offer a powerful rationale for that system, as opposed to one that sees higher education as primarily technical and preprofessional.

It is striking that the question of government-imposed homogeneity is not raised in this lecture. St. Andrews at this time was undoubtedly a public university. Its constitution was subject to acts of Parliament and royal commissions. Finances were mixed: some government grants, but also income from land, bequests, and endowments.[23] (At the time of Mill's address the university was in a precarious financial condition.) It seems implausible that Mill avoids the issue of public education out of politeness, for if he thought it was an issue compromising educational autonomy and quality, he surely would not have agreed to be Lord Rector in the first place. Apparently he thinks that at the university level a tradition of faculty control is sufficiently robust that government dictatorship over content is not a problem.

Mill begins his address by saying that professional education is fine, but it is the job of professional schools, not that of undergraduate university education. The object of a university "is not to make skilful lawyers, or physicians, or engineers, but capable and cultivated human beings. . . . [I]ts province ends where education, ceasing to be general, branches off into department adapted to the individual's destination in life" (3–4). Such an education is essential for the cultivation of informed and responsible citizenship:

> Government and civil society are the most complicated of all subjects accessible to the human mind, and he who would deal competently with them as a thinker, and not as a blind follower of a party, requires not only a general knowledge of the leading facts of life, both moral and material, but an understanding exercised and disciplined in the principles and rules of sound thinking, up to a point which neither the experience of life, nor any one science or branch of knowledge, affords. (8)

Mill accordingly recommends both the study of logic and the study of Plato's dialogues, on the grounds that they cultivate the ability "[t]o question all things; never to turn away from any difficulty, to accept no doctrine either from ourselves or from other people without a rigid scrutiny by negative criticism, letting no fallacy, or incoherence, or confusion of thought, slip by unperceived" (14). The culture of dissent requires not only an absence of Comtean control, but also a deliberate cultivation of the ability to stand up to others with one's own arguments. It is enhanced by other elements of liberal education: the study of history, of comparative law and politics, of economics—all of which give substance to a young citizen's arguments. In a university it is, he believes, inappropriate to indoctrinate people with a single view on normative matters, but highly appropriate to give them facts and arguments that will inform their judgment.

Comte would have said that ethics and politics have come to a stop and that young people may as well simply be told the correct opinions, just as they will be taught the correct doctrines in mathematics and science. Mill, as we have seen, would not reach such a conclusion even if he thought ethics had arrived at final and correct opinions. He plainly does not think this, however. In the Comte book, he strongly asserts that we do not have final doctrines on normative ethical and political issues, and here he repeats that claim: "Politics cannot be learnt once for all, from a text-book, or the instructions of a master. What we require to be taught on that subject, is to be our own teachers. It is a subject on which we have no masters to follow; each must explore for himself, and exercise an independent judgment" (28). We can certainly study the facts "having a direct bearing on the duties of citizenship" (28) and learn how to argue about them with solid arguments; we can also study the different philosophical theories, understanding the arguments for and against each and seeing how far they are in agreement about key ethical conclusions. We can study the history of religion and the different religious conceptions in a nondogmatic way. All these functions are very appropriate to the university curriculum, and all will improve the conduct of public life. Furthermore, the general tone of the university can and should embody certain definite ethical values, such as the idea that there are things in life more important than wealth. Beyond this, however, a university cannot properly venture in the direction of control. Above all, its curriculum will produce citizens who are independent of authority, thoroughly informed, adept in reasoning, and capable of standing up for themselves.

What, though, of sympathy? Mill has said that much of this must be the job of the family; he has also said that social institutions themselves can aid its development, by situating people nearer to one another, so that none seems beneath notice to any. Presumably if he had devoted attention to elementary education, he would think the cultivation of sympathy more appropriate there than in the university.

We know, however, that for Mill the cultivation of appropriate emotion has a more sophisticated aspect that could in principle be built into university curricula: in the *Autobiography* he famously records that his own recovery from depression and his restoration to general social sympathy were greatly assisted by reading poetry, especially the poetry of Wordsworth. Although he does not comment on the specific emotions he found there, it is obvious that Wordsworth makes the cultivation of sympathy, including an active social sympathy concerned with issues of class and poverty, central to the reader's experience. Above all, Wordsworth showed Mill a type of love of humanity that grows from wonder at the beauty of nature. Although Mill does not write much or well about love, his profound love for Harriet Taylor guided the entire spirit of his life, and he discovered this love shortly after his immersion in the poetry of Wordsworth, with its keen invitation to wonder and delight.

In the St. Andrews lecture, then, it is not surprising that Mill devotes considerable attention to the theme of aesthetic education, which he defines as education that refines and cultivates the emotions through the experience of works of art. Mill remarks that this aspect of education is sorely neglected in Victorian England, by contrast with continental Europe (and also with earlier eras in England), on account of an insalubrious combination of the commercial mentality with Puritanism. People in England (but presumably not in Scotland!) learn rigid moral rules without learning sympathy with others, thus becoming rigorous and reliable, but ungenerous (37). They have, moreover, a purely instrumental attitude to virtue, rather than loving it for its own sake. Mill now argues that even at the university level it is worth educating young people "to feel, not only actual wrong or actual meanness, but the absence of noble aims and endeavors, as not merely blameable but also degrading" (37); this can be done by cultivating sympathy with great figures in history or fiction, as well as by the influence of stirring music and visual art.

Mill provides numerous examples of the works he would favor, ranging from Dante's *Divine Comedy* to the poetry of Wordsworth and Shel-
ley, and including Handel's oratorios and the architecture of the Gothic
cathedral. He does not prescribe any specific course of study, but he
makes it clear that the study of these works is appropriate to the university curriculum, and, insofar as works are chosen for their ability to represent some definite moral ideals in a stirring light, this part of the curriculum is not as value-neutral as the others that he has previously
described. It's obvious that the works would still be taught with openness
to different perspectives and dissenting voices. The commitment to critical openness pervades the curriculum. Nonetheless, Mill relies on them
to open and refine the heart—given a decent head start in the family.

The Rector's Address is one of the great documents of higher education, and it is a necessary starting point for any discussion of how universities can contribute to the cultivation of general sympathy. On the whole,
however, Mill's constructive alternative to Comte, though attractive, is
thin. We simply lack information about the import of his ideas for the
practice of early education, and for the many ways in which societies try
to shape emotions in the public domain: festivals, ceremonies, the rhetoric of leaders, the construction of public buildings and parks, the choice
of public songs and poetry. An approach to these topics in Mill's spirit
should follow the lead of the St. Andrews lecture, thinking of ways in
which exposure, while remaining noncoercive, can still be formative—at
least for those who have had a good initial education in the family.

In a future nation for whose traditions Mill (too-faithful employee of
the British East India Company) had unjustified contempt, Comte's
ideas were shortly to be criticized much in Mill's spirit, but by a great
educator and artist who gave substance to notions that in Mill's hands
remained blurry and indistinct.

CHAPTER FOUR

Religions of Humanity II:
Rabindranath Tagore

At a certain bend in the path of evolution man refused to remain a
four-footed creature, and the position, which he made his body to
assume, carried in it a permanent gesture of insubordination.

—Rabindranath Tagore, *Man the Artist* (1932)

I. Comte in Bengal

Comte's ideas were well known to leading Bengali intellectuals at the
turn of the twentieth century, and they helped define people's aspirations for the future of an Indian nation. Two leading thinker/artists, above
all, drew on Comte to articulate utterly different pictures of a national
political culture. Novelist Bankimchandra Chatterjee (1838–1894, often
known as Bankim) was closely linked to an organized Positivist group in
Bengal.[1] He composed numerous prose works that set the development
of Indian society in the context of the Positivist conception of history.
His subsequent influence, however, largely depends on his novel *Anandamath* (1882), which represents Comtean ideas in dramatic form. Pivotal to the novel's appeal is the image of a threatened motherland, which
is deified and worshipped, in a way that shows the influence of Bankim's
understanding of Positivist religion. The threatened goddess is defended
by an extrapolitical order of priests, a "spiritual power" in Comtean
style. The song *"Bande Mataram"* ("Hail Motherland"), which becomes
the rallying point for the priests, teaches a gospel of violent resistance,
founded upon absolute submission to the goddess:

Mother, I bow to thee!
Rich with thy hurrying streams,
Bright with thy orchard gleams,
Cool with thy winds of delight,
Dark fields waving, Mother of might,
Mother free.

Glory of moonlight dreams
Over thy branches and lordly streams,
Clad in thy blossoming trees,
Mother, giver of ease.
Laughing low and sweet!
Mother, I kiss thy feet,
Speaker sweet and low!
Mother, to thee I bow.

Who hath said thou are weak in thy lands,
When the swords flash out in twice seventy million hands
And seventy millions voices roar
Thy dreadful name from shore to shore? . . .

Thou art wisdom, thou art law,
Thou our heart, our soul, our breath,
Thou the love divine, the awe
In our hearts that conquers death.

Bankim was a complicated thinker, and people continue to argue about his intentions and attitudes. It cannot be denied, however, that he was widely understood to sympathize with the priests and their song, or that even in the present time the emotions embedded in that song message continue to resonate throughout India—since the song has become the "national song," put forward by the Hindu Right as an alternative to the official national anthem, *"Jana Gana Mana,"* written by Tagore. At any rate, the novel is read by many as espousing an agenda of submission, conformity, and intense, potentially violent nationalist emotion—with a female figure of devotion at its heart.

II. Tagore: The Tragedy of *Ghare Baire*

Anandamath provided at least some of the inspiration for the *swadeshi* movement that followed the partition of Bengal in 1905, a movement to boycott British goods and buy only Indian products. Rabindranath Tagore (1861–1941), pioneering educator, composer, choreographer, painter, and philosopher, and winner of the Nobel Prize in Literature in 1913, was initially an enthusiast for the movement. During this period Tagore was already well known as a poet and a writer of dramas and short stories, and in 1905 he founded his pathbreaking school at Santiniketan. Tagore found Bankim's nationalist ideas appealing, and he even set the Chatterjee poem *"Bande Mataram"* to music to serve as the movement's anthem. As the movement became increasingly violent, however, terrorizing local people who refused to participate—often for reasons of economic survival—Tagore became disillusioned. In the 1916 novel *Ghare Baire (The Home and the World),* he reflects on his disaffection.[2] Although the novel is now widely admired (as is the 1984 film by Tagore's student Satyajit Ray), and although it was already admired at the time by W. B. Yeats and many of Tagore's friends, it was condemned by radical thinkers. Marxist critic Georg Lukács dismissed it as a "libelous pamphlet" and a "petty bourgeois yarn of the shoddiest kind."[3] Indeed, the novel does pursue an antiradical agenda, condemning a revolutionary nationalist version of "civil religion" that Tagore links to *Anandamath,* in favor of liberal Enlightenment ideas of freedom and dissent—though not without acknowledging that liberalism may turn out to be emotionally problematic.

The novel is narrated in turn by its three leading characters. Sandip, the revolutionary *swadeshi* leader, embodies the Chatterjee/Comte idea of a secular "priesthood" that leads a movement for national independence that places women in the position of goddesses, to be worshipped by the men who take charge of the movement. His slogan is *Bande Mataram*. Nikhil (whose name means "free") is a progressive landlord who exemplifies the spirit of the Enlightenment.[4] He defies custom by giving his wife, Bimala, a first-rate education, hiring a British governess, and encouraging Bimala to be an independent person. Because he wants a marriage based upon choice, rather than submission, he takes the radical step of encouraging his wife to leave the women's quarters and meet other men. Bimala is the primary narrator, and we know from the beginning— since she narrates retrospectively—that a tragedy will ensue.

From the beginning, Sandip and Nikhil differ about the role of imagination and emotion in patriotism. Sandip insists that "there is room for an appeal to the imagination in patriotic work" (36). Nikhil owns that he is "both afraid and ashamed to make use of hypnotic texts of patriotism" (36). Sandip replies that it is not hypnotism but truth: he really does "worship Humanity" (37). Nikhil offers three objections to this new religion. First, the worship of humanity should not lead—as it seems to in this case—to a divisive nationalism that involves deifying one's own nation and pitting it against other nations (one of Herder's central concerns, we recall). Second, any hypnotic stimulus impedes the confrontation with the real truth about one's nation and its current situation. "So long as we are impervious to truth and have to be moved by some hypnotic stimulus, we must know that we lack the capacity for self-government" (42). Third, the sort of uncritical love that Sandip inspires let loose a torrent of violent emotions that include a good deal of anger and hatred. (The nationalist movement soon leads to a violent assault on the innocent British governess, and to both economic and physical violence against poor Muslim traders who cannot survive without the cheaper foreign goods.) "'I am willing,' he said, 'to serve my country; but my worship I reserve for Right which is far greater than my country. To worship my country as a god is to bring a curse upon it'" (29).

What of Bimala? Allowed into the presence of other men suddenly, with no experience of independent choice, she is utterly charmed by Sandip's seductive worship of her as the "Queen Bee," and she quickly takes his side against her husband:

> "I do not care about fine distinctions," I broke out. "I will tell you broadly what I feel. I am only human. I am covetous. I would have good things for my country. If I am obliged, I would snatch them and filch them. I have anger. I would be angry for my country's sake. If necessary, I would smite and slay to avenge her insults. I have my desire to be fascinated, and fascination must be supplied to me in bodily shape by my country. She must have some visible symbol

casting its spell upon my mind. I would make my country a Person, and call her Mother, Goddess, Durga—for whom I would redden the earth with sacrificial offerings. I am human, not divine."

Sandip Babu leapt to his feet with uplifted arms and shouted "Hurrah!"—The next moment he corrected himself and cried: *"Bande Mataram."*

A shadow of pain passed over the face of my husband. He said to me in a very gentle voice: "Neither am I divine: I am human. And therefore I dare not permit the evil which is in me to be exaggerated into an image of my country—never, never!" (38)

Bimala understands acceptance of her humanity to mean endorsement of its more destructive instincts. Nikhil understands acceptance to mean continual restraint of those instincts, in the pursuit of humanity's moral ideals. Sandip scoffs: "Let moral ideals remain merely for those poor anaemic creatures of starved desire whose grasp is weak" (45).

And thus it is that Nikhil, to his wife's regret, "had not been able whole-heartedly to accept the spirit of *Bande Mataram*" (29).

The tragedy of *Ghare Baire* is that Sandip proves correct, at least in the short run: Nikhil's moral ideals are not moving to large groups of people. Sandip's passionate religion destroys the community, pitting Hindus against Muslims. It also destroys the family, since he seduces Bimala. Only too late does she realize her husband's greater strength and insight— but by this time he has already ridden out to his death, determined to stop the religious rioting. As the novel ends, his prognosis is uncertain, but the retrospective narrative makes clear that Bimala has been widowed.

Nor can we simply conclude that Nikhil is correct and Bimala foolish. Nikhil is strangely passive and unerotic. He is easy to approve of, but not so easy to love, and he knows it. He speaks of a "lack of expressiveness in myself," and concludes, "My life has only its dumb depths; but no murmuring rush. I can only receive: not impart movement" (85). Unlike Sandip and Bimala, Nikhil is also humorless. The novel makes Nikhil's moral values—his sympathy for the poor, his enlightened view of women, his respect for Muslims—deeply appealing. But it also shows that Nikhil's own approach to life is insufficient to ensure that his own values prevail and endure.

Comte, then, is right about something (according to Tagore): national ideals require strong emotion, involving symbolism and imagination, for their realization. Strong emotion, here, is linked, as it is by Comte himself, to a politics of submissive deference to the authority of a spiritual elite. In the person of Sandip, this type of authority is shown to be extremely dangerous. But it also appears to win easily over a more bloodless type of humanism.

Is this tragedy necessary? Must political love always be fatally linked to irrational submissiveness, even to sectarianism and hatred? Must high moral ideals be boringly uninspiring, and critical detachment unsexy?

The novel does not show us any way out of the problem it depicts. Its tragic ending, however, sets the agenda for much of Tagore's further thought and work. As a thinker, as an educator, and as a poet, musician, and choreographer, Tagore set out to respond to the challenge he himself had posed—eventually creating a poetic and critical alternative to Comte's religion that corresponds to Mill's "religion of humanity" and develops its key insights further.[5]

Tagore's response involved the composition of more than two thousand songs, two of which became the national anthems of India and Bangladesh. It involved the creation of a school and university that became world-famous exemplars of arts-oriented democratic education. (Although the school has been in existence since 1905, its distinctive features emerged gradually, and the university was founded in 1928.) And it involved, late in his career, a theoretical response to Comte, in the book *The Religion of Man* (1931), based on Tagore's 1930 Hibbert Lectures at Oxford, a book that subsumes the other developments, since it devotes extensive attention to the school and to the role, in the humanism of the future, of a certain type of music and poetry, connected to the critical spirit.[6]

III. Tagore's Religion of Man

From the beginning, Tagore's discussion is framed in terms that lead us to expect large departures from Comte. He insists that what is unique about the human being is a capacity for artistic creativity, the capacity to imagine something other than what is and to move toward a beautiful ideal so imagined. That is what Tagore calls "the surplus in man": un-like all other animals, humans go beyond physical need, living in a world of symbols and imagination, which provides "a surplus far in ex-cess of the requirements of the biological animal" (28).

Thus far, Comte might agree, but Tagore's account of artistic freedom is from the beginning framed in terms of individual self-expression and individual love. For Tagore, the defining moment of becoming human is to discover that one loves an individual other human being: "I have said in a poem of mine that when the child is detached from its mother's womb it finds its mother in a real relationship whose truth is in freedom" (30). The transition from mere biological existence to full human exis-tence is seen in terms of an intense relationship of personal recognition and emotion, suffused with wonder and curiosity; the significance of creativity is inseparable from the freedom of the individual to discard all traditions, all group norms, in favor of a profoundly personal vision. Similarly, in "Man the Artist," Tagore reads even the erect posture of the human body as a gesture of "insubordination"—of freedom to create norms, rather than to be bound by norms from the past. Although the anti-Comtean parts of Tagore's program emerge fully only later in the book, they are evident enough from the beginning. We are led to expect that "Order and Progress," in Tagore's hands, will contain rather less of Order, and more of passionate love.

In many respects, Tagore does set himself in the Comtean tradition. He attaches great importance to the ability to see the human species as a whole, extending into both past and future; he exhorts his reader to be-come invested in imagining an ideal future for the human being, seeing this as his religion. "Religion consists in the endeavor of men to cultivate and express those qualities which are inherent in the nature of Man the eternal, and to have faith in them" (118). His concern with the dangers of personal greed and limited sympathy parallels Comte's. Greed "diverts your mind to that illusion in you which is your separate self" (53). "When greed has for its object material gain then it can have no end. It is like the chasing of the horizon by a lunatic" (132). Tagore often develops this theme by focusing on the new progress in technology, which to him seems to threaten a contraction of human sympathy: "Man is building his cage, fast developing his parasitism on the monster Thing, which he allows to envelop him on all sides" (141). Indeed, Tagore's general account of why we need the new religion is also quite Comtean: we have large tendencies toward egocentrism and greed, and for that reason we fail to realize valuable goals that we could otherwise attain.

Similar to Comte as well is the emphasis on the cultivation of sympathy, which for both thinkers is the core of the new religion. The world of human personality, he writes, is "restricted by the limit of our sympathy and imagination. In the dim twilight of insensitiveness a large part of our world remains to us like a procession of nomadic shadows." Through the imagination, we become "intensely conscious of a life we must live which transcends the individual life and contradicts the biological meaning of the instinct of self-preservation" (38). Like Comte, Tagore insists that sympathy should be promoted through the arts.

Another Comtean feature of the book is its emphasis on the need to form a unified world community. Noting that his own life was shaped by the confluence of three distinct world cultures—Hindu, Muslim, and British—Tagore criticizes the "intense race egotism" (131) of colonialism, and concludes, "Suddenly the walls that separated the different races are seen to have given way, and we find ourselves standing face to face" (134).

Nonetheless, in many respects Tagore's humanism is profoundly critical of Comte's. We can begin with its pluralism. Instead of the hegemony of Europe and the white race, we have a radical assault on all racial and religious distinctions as bases of privilege, a repudiation of tribalism in favor of equal respect for all. "The God of humanity," Tagore writes, "has arrived at the gates of the ruined temple of the tribe." Henceforth, he continues, no people will be able to claim superiority in virtue of imperial power or alleged racial privilege; instead, the future of all peoples must be based upon reciprocity, equal respect, and shared effort toward a common good. "I ask them to claim the right of manhood to be friends of men, and not the right of a particular proud race or nation which may boast of the fatal quality of being the rulers of men" (135). Tagore made this bold statement in England, in the midst of the bitterness surrounding India's independence struggle, and eleven years after he had returned his knighthood to the Crown in protest over General Reginald Dyer's killings of innocent unarmed civilians at Amritsar. He makes it clear that rejection of the racial and political attitudes of the Raj is required for the

humanism of the future. It is not surprising that Tagore strives throughout the work to show respect for the many different cultures and traditions of the world—finding spiritual antecedents in Persian religion, in
Sufi Islam, in English romantic poetry (Wordsworth), and in many other
strands of world history.

Even before we arrive at these revealing statements about globalism,
however, we know that we are in a different world from that of Comtean
certainty and order. *The Religion of Man* is the work of a romantic poet.
Part autobiography, part poetic meditation, it combines arguments with
stories and images in a way that is by turns moving, self-deprecating,
funny, and serene. Tagore depicts himself as a boy who always detested
rules and formulae and who therefore found school excruciating. He had
a good start, in a family that was critical of established religious traditions, which gave him "an atmosphere of freedom—freedom from the
dominance of any creed that had its sanction in the definite authority of
some scripture, or in the teaching of some organized body of worship-
pers" (70). He also possessed a keen sensitivity to nature, and had intense experiences of joy while alone in the early morning:

> Almost every morning in the early hour of the dusk, I would run out
> from my bed in a great hurry to greet the first pink flush of the dawn
> through the shivering branches of the palm trees which stood in a
> line along the garden boundary, while the grass glistened as the
> dew-drops caught the earliest tremor of the morning breeze. The
> sky seemed to bring to me the call of a personal companionship, and
> all my heart—my whole body in fact—used to drink in at a draught
> the overflowing light and peace of those silent hours. (77)

The whole tone of this passage, with its lyricism and its solitary passion,
its wonder at the beauty of nature, is unimaginable in the Comtean
world of organized rituals. And Tagore soon makes plain his skepticism
about all traditional formulas. As the personal narrative continues (and
the very fact that he writes philosophy in this style is itself significant),
he tells us that school, with its rote learning and deadening repetition,
failed to reach the sources of his mind and heart—until poetry came
unbidden into the stultifying world. One day he was poring over a primer,

"dusty and faded, discoloured into irrelevant marks, smudges and gaps" (73–74), until suddenly he came upon a sentence in rhyme, the English of which reads, "It rains, the leaves tremble." Suddenly his mind came alive, and "I recovered my full meaning" (74); the vision of the rain beating rhythmically against the leaves entranced him, and he was once again a person, rather than a machine.

This experience is given a central place in the book, in a chapter entitled "The Vision." So we quickly see that Tagore's religion is the religion of a poet, a view of culture and society based upon the capacities in each human being that are the sources of poetic creation: passionate experiences of wonder and beauty, love of both nature and other particular people, and the desire to make something whole and meaningful out of the isolated fragments of one person's perceptual experience. Its sensibility is both androgynous and antinomian. Nowhere do we find fixed gender roles, and indeed in all of his artistic endeavors Tagore famously cultivated a vibrantly erotic and sensuous persona for both his own idiom as a dancer and poet and for that of the women and men who performed his works. A key element of Comte's religion, its rigid gender distinctions, is repudiated, and a very different spirit, that of keen perceptual sensitivity and intense erotic longing, animates the text throughout.

Tagore's vision also repudiates another fundamental part of Comte's religion, its spirit of control and homogeneity. Clearly Tagore is at best skeptical about tradition and ritual; often he goes further, suggesting that forms handed down by the past are usually dead and inauthentic. Probably he is best read, on balance, as a Millian, who wants the past to be continually challenged and tested, lest it become dead in our hands. His strong emphasis on questioning tradition—a lifelong obsession—is connected to his belief that an excessive reverence for the past is one of the great defects of Indian culture, where "timid orthodoxy, its irrational repressions and its accumulation of dead centuries, dwarfs man through its idolatry of the past" (98). Just as erect posture, for Tagore, represents "insubordination," so all genuine humanity resides in a spirit of wide-awake searching and questioning. Indeed, he convicts Comte's program of feeding a cult of dead habit. What we need, he says, is a "profound feeling of longing and love," but "[t]his is very unlike what we find in the intellectual cult of humanity, which is like a body that has tragically lost itself in the purgatory of shadows" (91). At this point, Tagore, like Mill, turns to Wordsworth: "'We live by admiration, hope, and love,/And ever as these are well and wisely fixed/In dignity of being we ascend'" (91). Even, and especially, toward his own ideas, Tagore urges the reader to cultivate a critical spirit: "The man who questions me has every right to distrust my vision and reject my testimony. . . . I never claim any right to preach" (70). How, one wonders, could this spirit of individualism ever become the spirit of a national religion? Doesn't political love have to have some rituals and prescribed forms?

There is no better evidence of the antinomian and individualistic spirit of Tagore's book than its choice of a central paradigm and source of the new religion: the Bauls of Bengal. Early in the text, Tagore introduces them as "a popular sect of Bengal . . . who have no images, temples, scriptures, or ceremonials, who declare in their songs the divinity of Man, and express for him an intense feeling of love" (6). This love is definitely erotic, and it leads the sect into antinomian erotic practices. So eager is Tagore to have his reader understand this example that he appends to his book an article about the Bauls by Kshiti Mohun Sen, a renowned scholar of Hinduism who left a comfortable professorial life to join Tagore's school and university in Santiniketan. Sen brought with him his young daughter Amita, who later became a leading dancer in Tagore's dance productions in the school, and who contributed writings that illuminate the school's practice of aesthetic education (see section IV).[7]

Sen begins his article by noting that the word *baul* means "madcap," thus referring to the Bauls' refusal to conform to established social usage: "No master I obey, nor injunctions, canons or custom/ . . . And I revel only in the gladness of my own welling love" (177). The cult includes both Hindus and (Sufi) Muslims, and its core idea is to seek liberation from selfishness by the cultivation of an overflowing type of love. Some Bauls are itinerants, some settled householders; they come from all classes and castes, repudiating the salience of these distinctions and seeking simplicity of life (as, indeed, did Tagore's teachers, who lived in simple dwellings). But the Bauls are not ascetics: they reject the idea of renunciation, preferring attachment to humanity. They refuse all rigid formalities, saying only that they "delight in the ever-changing play of life, which cannot be expressed in mere words but of which something may be captured in song, through the ineffable medium of rhythm and tune" (181). Their lives are dedicated to freedom (from both the outward compulsion of society and the inner compulsion of greed), to joy, and to love.[8]

Tagore does not mention the Bauls' unconventional sex lives to his Oxford post-Victorian audience, but it was well known that here too the Bauls defied convention.[9] Also significant is their well-known initiation ritual, in which new members were required to taste all the fluids of the body—thus, apparently, overcoming disgust with one's own bodily nature. These aspects of Baul society remain a subtext and metaphor, but they are there, in the quest for a way of life that embraces this-worldly love and eroticism.

Tagore and Mozart are kindred spirits, insisting that citizenship needs a spirit of play and unpredictable individuality. But what does Tagore really mean by bringing this counterculture into the heart of his prescription for society? How can an ordinary Indian citizen (in the republic of the future to which Tagore points the way) be a Baul? Baul lyrics are important for Tagore's own poems, some of which he cites in the text in order to develop his own ideas of love and freedom. But what can it mean to suggest that organized society, including the political culture of a budding nation, should take its lead from the Bauls? It means, I think, that this society must preserve at its heart, and continually have access to, a kind of fresh joy and delight in the world, in nature, and in people, preferring love and joy to the dead lives of material acquisition that so many adults end up living, and preferring continual questioning and searching to any comforting settled answers. Tagore's prescription is thus very similar to Mill's experimentalism, albeit developed in language that would have seemed strange to Mill.

Modern scholars such as Jeanne Openshaw and Charles Capwell have drawn attention to the way in which Tagore made the message of the Bauls more abstract and spiritual than it really was.[10] But we are dealing with delicacy and metaphorical reference rather than suppression. This was Oxford in 1930, and Tagore knew that he could not get away with too much explicitness. Similarly in his school, he knew that Bengali parents would tolerate only a veiled eroticism. But eroticism it surely was, as Amita Sen's memoir makes clear, and an eroticism that liberated and empowered women. Moreover, as Mimlu Sen's very interesting recent autobiography attests, Baul communities have always contained much diversity. A young middle-class Bengali woman who ran off to join the Bauls, inspired by love of one of their leading singers, she reports that the couple have a monogamous and rather conventional sex life, and that many Bauls have no interest in Tantric practices.[11] So Openshaw misleads when she suggests that a variety of unconventional practices define membership in the group.

Capwell is on solid ground, however, when he says, "For Tagore it was not the doctrinal side of the Bauls that was of interest, but the spontaneous emotional way they could react to and understand the human situation. Such emotion could never be expressed fully in words, so they resorted to song."[12] In one of Tagore's dance-dramas, *Phalguni (Springtime)*, written for students in his school, the Baul character—danced and acted by Tagore himself—is confronted by a skeptical police constable, who represents the spirit of order and homogeneity: "I gather that to answer a question you sing a song?" The Baul replies, "Yes! If we don't, the answer doesn't come out right. If we speak in plain words it is terribly unclear, can't be understood."[13]

The tragedy of *Ghare Baire* came about because Nikhil's liberal ideals were devoid of passion. He never had, or had lost, the fresh delight in the world and in people that might have made him an inspiring leader and a lovable, and loving, husband. He was boring and predictable. Sandip, meanwhile, never had, or at least never tolerated, the "madcap" sense of dissent, critique, and solitary daring: in search of power over others, he cultivated emotions based upon tradition, homogeneity, and submissiveness. What is required for the health of society, Tagore now suggests, is a liberalism that is truly and reciprocally passionate, a life of critique that is also a life of love, play, and madness. Tagore and Mozart are kindred spirits.

IV. Implementing the New Religion:
Santiniketan and Women's Creative Freedom

Still, how could the Baul spirit possibly become the spirit of an entire society? Tagore offers two partial answers: education and popular music. At Santiniketan he founded both a school and a university, the latter

being called *Visva-Bharati,* "All-the-World." *Mutatis mutandis,* the
university was similar to Mill's prescriptions for St. Andrews. It was
based upon the liberal arts, interdisciplinary cooperation, and a continual spirit of critique. But it is to the school that Tagore devotes central emphasis in *The Religion of Man.*[14] He begins by expressing his
lifelong dissatisfaction with the schools he attended: "The inexpensive
power to be happy, which, along with other children, I brought to this
world, was being constantly worn away by friction with the brick-and-
mortar arrangement of life, by monotonously mechanical habits and the
customary code of respectability" (144). In effect, children begin as madcap Bauls, full of love, longing, and joy in the presence of nature. Their
love of play and their questioning spirit need to be strengthened, not
crushed. But schools usually crush all that is disorderly, and Tagore reports that "[t]he non-civilized in me was sensitive; it had the great thirst
for colour, for music, for movement of life" (144). Some books he encountered seemed to capture this antinomian spirit: he praises *Robinson
Crusoe* as "the best book for boys that has ever been written" (145). In his
school, he set out to educate without crushing the spirit of adventure and
love.

The school's pedagogy was primarily Socratic: teachers elicited answers by posing questions, rather than by lecturing. Students even initiated the planning of the day's schedule. Classes were usually held out-
doors, in close proximity to nature's beauty, so that the senses would be
keenly receptive to beauty throughout the process. Tagore was always a
strong supporter of science and a committed rationalist, stereotypes of
him as an unworldly mystic notwithstanding. His humanism was not
antimodern, and it was profoundly wedded to the spirit of contestation
and argument.[15] Unlike some other Indian intellectuals, and to some
extent unlike Gandhi, Tagore did not repudiate the Enlightenment, but,
instead, sought to create a fusion of the best of Indian and European
traditions.[16] He understood, however, that scientific modernity would
prove hollow and unreliable unless nourished and steered by the humanities. Above all, Tagore relied on the arts as key vehicles of development. Students were always moving—dancing, singing. Elaborate dance-
dramas written, composed, and choreographed by Tagore himself were
centerpieces of the curriculum.[17] As Amita Sen has written, Tagore

somehow knew how to be a good technical dance teacher, imparting discipline and mastery to children of widely varying abilities, while at the same time communicating emotional self-expression and passionate involvement:

> His dance was a dance of emotion. The playful clouds in the sky, the shivering of the wind in the leaves, light glistening on the grass, moonlight flooding the earth, the blossoming and fading of flowers, the murmur of dry leaves—the pulsing of joy in a man's heart, or the pangs of sorrow, are all expressed in this expressive dance's movements and expressions.[18]

The type of passionate humanism on offer at Santiniketan formed a certain sort of citizen, strong and unsubmissive, full of challenges to dead traditions. Like everything else in the school, the dance-dramas mingled critical reasoning with emotion, and were by no means antirational. For example, *Land of Cards* (*Tasher Desh,* 1933), written shortly after *The Religion of Man,* focuses on the intense importance of generating challenges to tradition, and suggests that women will be especially likely to lead such challenges.[19] The link between Socratic inquiry and the arts made the critical spirit alluring.

Comte's project relied on women, but in a way that did not empower them. Women were supposed to teach sympathy to children, but they were kept entirely inside the home, and they were given no creative freedom. They had to dispense love and sympathy under the watchful eye of the philosophers, who would tolerate no individual creativity. Tagore's critical reformulation places individual love and creativity at the center of the conception, but in *The Religion of Man* he says nothing about women—beyond the extremely central observation that the foundation of all love and sympathy is in the child's highly individual loving relationship with its mother. Tagore's empowerment of women through dance and the other arts was a famous feature of his school, but it is not one that he ever wrote about in detail. For these aspects of Tagore's vision, then, we must turn to Amita Sen, who both lived that empowerment, as a student and as a lead dancer in many of Tagore's dance-dramas, and, later, described it in her book *Joy in All Work.*

Joy in All Work cannot well be paraphrased, because it expresses the spirit of Tagore's school in its poetic and personal style. The English translation was carefully supervised by Amita's granddaughter Indrani Sen and captures the poetic nature of the original well, I am told. The first thing that strikes us about this book is that it is a highly individual creative statement, full of emotion and daring, and that it is made by a woman. Such a statement would have been heretical and utterly unacceptable in the Comtean project, but it is exactly as things should be in Tagore's religion of humanity, in which each person finds herself in freedom and personal love.

Let us now consider the book's opening. It begins with women in rapid and passionate motion. We have a description of moonlight on the mango flowers, and then the strains of a song come floating on the spring breeze. "It is impossible for the young wives to stay at home. Out rush all: Kamala Devi, Labanya Devi, Manorama Devi, Surobala Devi, Sukeshi Devi, Kironbala Devi." This list of names is significant: in Comte, women lack individuality, but in the Tagorean project their individuality is key. The young wives quietly tiptoe up to listen to Tagore dancing to the tune of one of his own songs. Then the voice of the author enters: "We listened to these stories from our mothers as if we were listening to fairy tales. We were entranced as we heard about the wonderful acting of Rabindranath Tagore as the blind Baul, playing his *ektara* and showing the way as he sang: 'Let us give all to Him to whom everyone gives all.'" We learn, then, that Amita Sen was raised in a tradition of women's empowerment: the very fairy tales of these children were tales of women's emotional freedom, and they also emphasize the normative significance of the Baul culture: proper wives are encouraged to emulate the Bauls. It is in this framework that Amita Sen now announces her goal: "to write of the joy flowing through the music, dance, drama, programmes and festivals in Santiniketan and also the joy coming from association with Tagore in the hearts of the wives and daughters of the *ashram*."

As we reflect on the relationship of Tagore to Comte, five aspects of Amita Sen's tale of Santiniketan's women stand out. First is her constant emphasis on the cultivation of a wide range of deep emotions, ranging from compassion to deep grief to, of course, a boundless joy in both nature and human beings. The central purpose of the narrative is to show how Tagore cultivated emotions through poetry, music, and dance, and the text contains many very moving examples. One significant fact that other writers had not observed is that Tagore taught by personal demonstration, using his own extremely expressive body and voice to show students areas of possibility—not dictating to them, but simply carving out a space for expression and inspiring them to inhabit it. These emotions were deeply personal, but Amita Sen makes clear that students were never unaware of the larger social and political context, including prominently Gandhi's noncooperation movement and the urgent problems of rural development. Through a cultivation of each person's inner emotional landscape they reached toward this larger world of citizenship in a nation of the future.

Second, the text constantly emphasizes the highly personal and individualized (to that extent un-Comtean) nature of the education Tagore imparted. Even though in many respects students came to feel solidarity with one another, the sense of personal uniqueness was always central, as Tagore wrote poems for individual students and somehow seemed to know them all, as we see from many stories in the text, not least from the lovely one in which Tagore draws a picture of Pratichi house in little Amartya's autograph book and writes that it is "the Green Fairy's Home" (68–69).[20] For women, this sense of individuality was particularly liberating, Sen shows, since women, in traditional society, are frequently deindividualized, seen as somebody's wife or mother, rather than as themselves. "There was no particular posture or fashion of expression," she writes of Tagore's dance teaching. "As we sang we expressed the meaning of the words through our movements" (38). This sense of individuality did not undermine, but actually strengthened, general sympathy, as we see from a moving story of how the girls made a red-bordered sari for a student who was unable to acquire one.

Third, and a large departure from Comte, we see how funny Tagore was, and how lighthearted. Tagore does not convey humor well in his theoretical writings, although he often does in his fiction. Amita Sen thus makes a very important addition to *The Religion of Man* when she shows that Tagore conveyed the laughter of the Bauls, not just their mystical devotion. This is perhaps an aspect that Tagore's Western enthusiasts particularly need to study, since the Tagore that became familiar to the West is a very solemn guru, without the lightness of touch that was such a large part of the whole man.

Fourth is what I would call a spirit of subversive erotic creativity, which is such a key aspect of the Baul tradition. Of course this tradition has been in some ways domesticated as Tagore presented it to young girls, but there is something not entirely domesticated about it after all. Consider Sen's account of the choreography and poetics of *Shapmochan,* which she, as the Queen, danced with Dr. Harry Timbers as the King. Because Timbers did not know Bengali, she tells us, Tagore was especially active in these rehearsals, depicting the "deep pique and love" of the King, and then, right after that, "the dream clad, passion rapt queen" (80). She emphasizes that the "conservative environment" of 1931 made this whole enterprise risky, since "it was a very daring thing for girls from good families to appear on the stage." They even had to change a word in one song. The King was to sing, "Flower-like beauty, come to my breast." But they changed it to: "Come to my home, you who are inside my soul, come out." Amita always used to love telling this story orally too, and when she told it to me she always added something that is not in the book: "We knew exactly what it really meant."

Finally, fifth, the whole text conveys a spirit of fearlessness and freedom—an absence of the constraining shame that typically weighed down women's lives. "The lamp of hope cannot be put out," she concludes. "He has taught us the lesson of fearlessness" (90–91).

Santiniketan was only one school in one region. It became world-famous, inspiring imitators in many countries, and attracting pupils from all over India. (For example, the young Indira Nehru—later Indira Gandhi— seems to have been happier and freer there than, perhaps, at any other time in her life.)[21] But Tagore did not succeed in realizing his ideal on a wide scale, in part because of his unwillingness to delegate and the school's consequent reliance on his creative presence. John Dewey's comparable experiment in the United States had greater success, because Dewey, not being himself a creative artist, was more willing to entrust his general ideas to others. The failure of Tagore's school to have wide influence does not show, then, that such ideas cannot inspire a populous democracy: they only show us that a creator cannot make himself irreplaceable.

V. Implementing the New Religion: Popular Music

Tagore's other contribution has fared far better. His more than two thousand songs drew on Baul and Sufi poetry, widespread musical traditions, and traditions of vocal performance—creating an art form all its own, known in India as Rabindrasangeet (Rabindranath songs), which continues to hold a central place in the cultures of West Bengal and Bangladesh, and in some instances in the nation of India as a whole. Studying the text of the songs has been made easier thanks to Kalpana Bardhan's new set of translations.[22] Bardhan's versions convey a sense of the rhythm of the original, and thus help the reader who will later listen to a recording. Responding to Tagore's music is not easy, because it is always difficult to hear emotions in an alien musical tradition.[23] (What this means for us is that any such project must build upon local traditions and materials: imagine if Martin Luther King Jr. had tried to introduce Rabindrasangeet to the civil rights movement.) Suffice it to say that the songs have been continuously popular, helping to define India's ideals and the culture of emotion surrounding them.

Tagore's songs concern many topics, but some are explicitly political, and are labeled by him as such. One of these is the famous song *"Ekla Cholo Re"* ("Walk Alone"), which was the favorite song of Mahatma Gandhi, and central to his movement. It is a song of resistance, but in a very particular way: not a paean to solidarity, but a song of the questing critical spirit, forging on alone.

> If no one answers your call, then walk on alone.
> Walk alone, walk alone, walk on alone.
>
> If no one says a thing, oh you unlucky soul,
> If faces are turned away, if all go on fearing—
> Then opening up your heart,
> You speak up what's on your mind, you speak up alone.

If they all turn back, oh you unlucky soul,
If, at the time of taking the deep dark path, no one cares—
Then the thorns that are on the way,
Oh you, trampling those with bloodied feet, you tramp on alone.

If a lamp no one shows, oh you unlucky soul,
If in a rainstorm on a dark night they bolt their doors—
Then in the flame of thunder
Lighting your own ribs, go on burning alone.[24]

The music expresses determination: there is a rhythm as of walking on, which continues throughout. It expresses solitude and exposure: the single vocal line, the sense of passionate risk in the voice. But above all, it also expresses joy. It is in fact a very happy, even delighted song, full of gusto and affirmation. People love this song, and their love was highly relevant to the success of Gandhi's resistance movement. As he walked along with his walking stick and his simple loincloth—and his childlike delight in life, so often observed by those who met him—he seemed to embody the spirit of that song, and the fusion of artistic image with living exemplar was (and is) powerfully moving. That's how the spirit of solitary dissent—combined with joy—can galvanize a population.

But perhaps Tagore's crowning achievement, as a forger of popular political culture, was his composition of two national anthems.[25] Chapter 1 has already analyzed *"Amar Sonar Bangla."* Now it is time to look closely at *"Jana Gana Mana,"* the national anthem of India, in which Tagore responds to the challenge of Bankim's *"Bande Mataram,"* proposing a replacement that he believed morally and politically superior, while still being beautiful and even seductive. The Hindu Right does not agree, and its struggle to displace *"Jana Gana Mana"* in favor of *"Bande Mataram"* continues to the present day.

"Jana Gana Mana" is in highly Sanskritized Bengali, a choice on Tagore's part in order to make the song intelligible beyond Bengal, to all who speak one of the languages derived from Sanskrit, which is about as universal as one can get in India—and the speakers of the non-Indo-European languages have gladly adopted it. Originally the song was performed at a meeting of the Indian National Congress in 1911, and was

repeated on the occasion of George V's visit to India shortly after that. Another poet's song honoring the king was performed, and Tagore's was written, he said, as a kind of counterstatement to that one, expressing the idea that the only true leader is the moral ideal, and that India is rightly led toward freedom by that ideal. The part of the song that is sung as the national anthem today goes as follows:

> You are the ruler of the minds of all people,
> Dispenser of India's destiny.
> Thy name rouses the hearts of Punjab, Sind,
> Gujarat and Maratha,
> Of the Dravida and Orissa and Bengal;
> It echoes in the hills of the Vindhyas and Himalayas,
> Mingles in the music of Jamuna and Ganges and is
> Chanted by the waves of the Indian Ocean.
> They pray for your blessings and sing your praise.
> The saving of all people waits in your hand,
> You dispenser of India's destiny.
> Victory, victory, victory, victory to you.

Lest one think that some groups have been omitted, there are actually four more stanzas, of which I cite stanzas two and five (the others are very general, alluding to the ups and downs of life). The second is often also regarded as part of the national anthem, and this is very important, since it includes religious diversity:

> Your call is announced continuously, we heed
> Your gracious call
> The Hindus, Buddhists, Sikhs, Jains, Parsees,
> Muslims, and Christians,
> The East and the West come, to the side of Your throne,
> And weave the garland of love.
> Oh! You who bring in the unity of the people!
> Victory be to You, dispenser of the destiny of India!
>
> . . .

The night is over, and the Sun has risen over
The hills of the eastern horizon.
The birds are singing, and a gentle auspicious
Breeze is pouring the elixir of new life.
By the halo of Your compassion India that was
Asleep is now waking
On your feet we lay our heads,
Victory be to You, the Supreme King,
Victory be to You, dispenser of the destiny of India.

The idea of India awakening to life and freedom is prominent in Nehru's "tryst with destiny" speech, and it is Tagorean, whether he derived it from this source or not.

The song is addressed to an unnamed source, which may be conscience or *dharma* (the moral law), or some other set of moral ideals. Unlike *"Bande Mataram,"* which urges submission to a deity associated with traditional religion, *"Jana Gana Mana"* asks for the victory of this ideal principle—as a result of the passionate love of all the people. In one sense it is obviously a song of resistance and the freedom movement. More generally, though, it is a call for a nation that is moved to its depths both by the beauty of nature and by moral ideals, and that sees the two as somehow fused together. Unlike Bankim's all-Hindu nation, moreover, this one is plural through and through, including all of India's regions and religious groups.[26]

Musically, *"Jana Gana Mana"* is very easy to sing, ranging over just an octave, so people really do sing it with pleasure. It has a swaying rhythm, rather like a dreamy dance, and suggests nothing of the martial. People naturally put arms around one another, or hold hands, or simply sway to the music. It goes naturally with the contemplation of nature, as one can see from the beautiful version by film composer A. R. Rahman (a convert to Sufi Islam, who formerly had the Hindu name Dilip Kumar), released as the official government version on the occasion of India's fiftieth anniversary, and easily found on YouTube. It wonderfully embodies the spirit of the song, showing people (individuals or small groups) from many different backgrounds and walks of life singing in different stirring and beautiful sites in the Indian landscape.[27]

There is something very odd about the way the anthem ends. As *"jaya he,"* "victory to thee," rises to the subdominant, we expect a resolution into the tonic, but we are denied that resolution. When I hear or sing it, I always hear it as unfinished, beckoning to a resolution that is deferred, not yet available. Nor is my experience the mere creation of a Western musical education. My colleague Dipesh Chakrabarty reports to me that when he sang the song in primary school, he and all his classmates kept going on, by returning to the refrain, *"bharata bhagya vidhata,"* and thus reaching what seemed like a more appropriate resolution on the tonic—until the teacher corrected them. I feel that it is not at all implausible to hear this unfinished cadence as the expression of the same idea that Nehru conveyed in his "tryst with destiny" speech, namely, that national pride is most appropriately expressed by emphasizing the unfinished work that lies before the nation: "And so we have to labour and to work, and to work hard, to give reality to our dreams." *"Jana Gana Mana,"* in a bold violation of musical expectations, gestures toward a future of work. Chakrabarty says that this idea makes sense to him, and it makes the invocation of victory more appropriate, in the context of continued suffering, than it otherwise would be.

So Tagore has made not just pluralism, harmony, and mutual respect but also unfinished work popular and even sexy, just as *"Ekla Cholo Re"* made dissent and critical thinking objects of passionate devotion. The Comtean project, we might say, has been remade in the spirit of Cherubino.

VI. Assessing the Comtean Project: Mill and Tagore

Comte's religion of humanity responded to a genuine need, but did so in a way that left much to be desired. Unlike Rousseau, Comte was sensitive to the importance of freedoms of speech and association, and therefore did not propose to enforce his proposals through governmental coercion. Indeed, the role he envisaged for government in the pursuit of important human norms was if anything too restricted, as Mill suggests. Nonetheless, he did envisage an all-embracing type of social control, as his philosophical clergy pronounced norms of moral correctness that were to suffuse each person's daily life in just the way that the norms and moral/spiritual authority of the Roman Catholic Church had done during the Middle Ages. He does not want breathing space for dissent or experimentation, and he does not want to entrust ordinary individuals with the job of working out difficult questions on their own.

For these and other reasons, Mill and Tagore reject Comte's proposal, but they do not reject the general idea behind it. Public culture needs something religion-like, they feel, something passionate and idealistic, if human emotions are to sustain projects aimed at lofty goals. They also agree with Comte (and with Mozart) that the new religion must embody a form of love. Mere respect is not enough to hold citizens together when they must make sacrifices of self-interest. Something deeper in the heart, something more passionate and central in human development, is required. Though they have somewhat different ideas of what this political love should be like, they agree that mere concern and respect are insufficient.

But what can the Comtean project be like if we reject the stifling atmosphere of control and political correctness that animated it? Mill and Tagore have attractive ideas about this, suggesting that a culture of sympathy and imagination is fully compatible with, and indeed can reinforce, a liberal culture of experimentation and dissent. My own proposals will be in their spirit. Nonetheless, as we move forward, there are some questions that we must press.

First, we must ask about the diagnosis of human ills that Mill and Tagore propose. Both suggest that limited sympathy is our primary ethical problem—combined with the herdlike docility that makes people blindly follow traditions in which a limited sympathy is expressed. Mill says little about negative emotions such as fear and anger, and nothing at all about disgust, shame, and group-based hatred. By taking the Bauls as his paradigm, Tagore implies that surmounting disgust with the human body is another major task of the good citizen, closely connected to overcoming hierarchies of gender and caste. (His novel *Gora* further develops this theme, as we'll see in Chapter 7.) But the link between overcoming disgust and broadening sympathy remains largely implicit, given the reticence of Tagore's portrayal of the Bauls. Still, Tagore's psychology opens up important problems that Mill never confronts. In our era, reflecting on a long record of appalling human brutality, we cannot accept Mill's optimism, and we need to search for a deeper understanding.

But of course problems are problems only in relation to a definite view of a political goal. Here both Mill and Tagore are incomplete, and Tagore far more incomplete than Mill. We have a general sense of what they are looking for, but their failure to articulate a vision of a decent society makes their diagnoses seem piecemeal and ad hoc. We need an account of political institutions and what they do for people, and of the limits of political justice. Mill certainly has views about this in other works, and even his critique of Comte makes clear his sense of the larger redistributive responsibilities of government. Still, the emotional part of his project remains insecurely connected to any definite account of government's job. Tagore simply lacks interest in institutions, beyond his evident interest in India's independence from Britain.

Because the two say little about the political sphere and its extent, we are left somewhat unclear about where and how the transformation they envisage will take place. Both talk about education, and favor educational reform as one site of the new "religion," but Tagore is thinking entirely of voluntary private reforms. Mill held that both public and private alternatives should coexist and compete, constrained by a system of public examinations. As for Tagore's songs, he proposed them first as parts of popular culture, not as official public anthems, although two of them ended up that way. Not surprisingly—because the nation was not yet in existence—there is no discussion in his writings about how government and civil society ought to interrelate in promoting a culture of concern. In short, neither Tagore nor Mill has a clear story to tell about how the new "religion" will be disseminated, or why we should think that it will prevail. In part this is because their skepticism about Comtean control and homogeneity leads them to mistrust all public support of definite goals.

For similar reasons, both Mill and Tagore have difficulty articulating the proper balance between solidarity and individual experimentation. Both reject Comtean control; both value free spaces for "madcap" dissent and imagination. But both also think that in certain ways people should learn to be in emotional solidarity. Mill's religion of humanity asks all to identify themselves with the future of all humanity, and all are expected to join in this common emotional endeavor. But how to strike the delicate balance between this shared task and the freedom to experiment and dissent? Mill gives us little information. Tagore offers us more.

In his school he exemplified this delicate balance every day, imparting discipline and some definite ideals while creating spaces for individuality to flourish. His dance idiom combined choreography with experimentation. And his creation of a genre of popular music involves a similar balancing act. For Tagore, the whole point of a song is that people sing it sometimes alone and sometimes in a group, and the group is certainly one powerful vehicle for the shaping of political emotions. Gandhi's use of *"Ekla Cholo Re"* as vehicle of a mass movement was basically in Tagore's spirit, although Tagore certainly prized individual dissent somewhat more than Gandhi. Nonetheless, existing recordings of Tagore and his direct pupils singing his songs show that the songs were vehicles of personal expressive performance; so too they are today, in the voices of interpreters from many backgrounds. Still, these paradigms leave us with a large challenge: How might we keep the good in structure and solidarity without the ludicrous and the stifling, and cultivate dissent without losing shared concern? Any account of the role of the arts in public emotion culture will need to meet this challenge head-on.

To approach this point from a different direction: Mill accuses Comte of lacking a sense of humor, and this insight is profound, as Mozart has already prepared us to see. Comte's idealism is grandiose, and it lacks understanding of the awkward surprising unevenness of real human life. Mill and Tagore have that understanding, but they have a difficult time integrating it with their idealism. Sometimes they too sound like someone who has never laughed—when they talk about the ideal human species of the future, when they urge an attitude that is akin to worship and directed at our own species. Realism about human weakness is difficult to combine with this reverential stance. In his school, as Amita Sen makes clear, Tagore did know how to laugh, and he empowered his students without closing off spaces for idiosyncratic personal expression. Tagore's fictions, too, are rich in humor and the sense of human complexity. The problem of the proper balance between humor and high ideals remains, however, and must be pondered by any society drawing on the arts.

Another unresolved problem is the status of religion in society. Mill improves the Comtean project in many ways, but in one key way he inherits it uncritically: he assumes that at some point traditional religion will wither away, to be replaced by humanism. Although he envisages nothing like Comte's authoritarian *pouvoir spirituel,* he does think that the question about religion's social utility can be resolved decisively against traditional religions and in favor of humanism, and his hopes for humanity are tied to widespread acceptance of this conclusion. Tagore is less clear on this point, but he envisages his humanist religion as at least one powerful social force.

But traditional religions have not disappeared, and by now we have reason to think that under conditions of freedom there will remain a plurality of religious and secular doctrines of life, many of which will continue to attract allegiance. The project of constructing political emotions must either ride roughshod over this reality or learn to accommodate it. Mill's proposal lacks respect for people's consciences, and is to that extent unacceptable in a society based on equal respect. Tagore does better, but he fails to articulate the problem of pluralism clearly, or to offer a definite approach to it, both of which any contemporary political proposal must do.

Finally, since Mill and Tagore break with Comte over the question of freedom, we need to ask what freedom means to them, how it is realized in the personality, and how freedom is connected to, and realized in, political love. Mozart and Da Ponte saw that it was not enough to have good founding documents, or even good institutions. Freedom has to penetrate down to the personality's very core, releasing the constraints of inner anger and fear that lead to hierarchies of domination, creating and then refining a form of love that is both erotic and tender, more like *"Voi che sapete"* than like the "concerto" of guns and cannons from which Cherubino shrinks. Mill certainly understood this, holding that poetry was the key to a healthy personality and that "aesthetic education" should be a linchpin of the new university. But, always reticent about emotional matters, he said little to convey the nature or impact of inner freedom on the mind.

Tagore goes a great deal further, both describing and, at Santiniketan, realizing a freedom that was bodily as well as intellectual, a dance as well as an argument, a set of social practices built upon early childhood love. As we turn to the consideration of political freedom and love in our own day, we would do well to ponder Amita Sen's account of Tagore playing the part of the Wayfarer in his dance-drama *Rituranga:*

Entering the stage, he sang as he walked:

> My fetters will be broken, will be broken, at the time of departure / I
> am free, who can imprison me behind locked doors! / I go in the dark
> as the evening bell rings). [The text also quotes the poem in
> Bangla.]

What a wonderful movement of strong hands breaking fetters! The
free wayfarer advances, the joy of freedom ringing in his steps, and
fearlessness in his clear voice. Even after he had left the stage, the
sound of the evening bell echoed in the spectators' ears. (65–66)

This description was written in 1999 by a citizen of the Republic of
India. India was not a free nation at the time of Amita Sen's education in
Tagore's school, but, as she says, it was a goal toward which much in her
education pointed the way. Tagore gave his pupils a paradigm of free
citizenship that they never forgot. Like the entirety of their education,
this image of freedom is charged with passion, and its paradigm of political love is erotic rather than calm and contemplative. Students realized
this paradigm in their own individual ways, in their own gestures of insubordination and their own distinctive forms of creative joy. And because in Tagore's view a deformed conception of masculinity lay at the
heart of oppression, both internal and external, the key agents in the
creative transformation of society were (whatever their biological sex)
women. In one sense a world separates the Bauls from *Le Nozze di Figaro,* but at a deeper level, Tagore's vision dovetails with Mozart's: "This
day of torment, of craziness, of foolishness—only love can make it end in
happiness and joy."

PART TWO

Goals, Resources, Problems

Introduction to Part II

PART I'S HISTORICAL DISCUSSION showed us why the project of a "civil religion" is important for a liberal society, and also why it should be executed in the spirit of Mill and Tagore, rather than that of Rousseau and Comte. The figure of Mozart's Cherubino gives us an attractive image of the citizen as one who seeks not a dominating, hierarchical type of relationship with others, but, instead, a mutually respectful love that invites and delights in mutually responsive conversation, by turns playful and aspiring. J. S. Mill's discussion of the "religion of humanity" began to give this image political structure, connecting extended compassion to a spirit of experiment and critique. Mill's educational proposals then begin to show how a real society might attempt to form citizens of the "Cherubinic" sort. Rabindranath Tagore's image of the Bauls developed what we might call the "Cherubinic thread" in a similar spirit, but with greater detail, insisting that the citizen of the future should be prepared to throw out all dead traditions and to improvise solutions to problems in a spirit of experimentalism suffused with love and aspiration. Tagore rightly insists on both critical freedom and a spirit of bold innovation—agreeing with Mill's proposal but giving it a much fuller practical development through his practice as an educator, feminist, and composer of popular music. Where he differs from Mill—by respecting existing religions and seeking to include them in a politics of reciprocity, rather than denigrating or seeking to displace them—he makes an attractive contribution to contemporary thought about the public sphere. The political and practical shape of a defensible "civil religion" begins to emerge.

At the same time, we have learned from Mozart and Tagore that any appealing practical proposal must be contextual, informed by an understanding of a nation's history, traditions, and problems. Cherubino and the Bauls are close relatives; each, however, is suited to a place and time, and communicates in virtue of that aptness.

Our historical material helps us think about what we might be prepared to defend and implement today. Promising as this material is, however, we lack some ingredients we need before we can fit these proposals to any existing society. First, we need a road map: an account of where the type of society we have in mind is going. This book deals with societies that are aspiring to justice, not societies already complete. Before we can say anything useful about what will aid and hinder them in their work, we need to have a blueprint of goals toward which they can be imagined as moving. Different emotions take us in different directions, and a sketch of the desired destination is crucial if we are going to sort through the complexities ahead.

We also need a much fuller psychology than we were given by any of our historical sources. As we have seen, our sources focus on limited compassion as the primary emotional impediment to justice. Even this emotion they fail to analyze sufficiently. Thus, one task before us will be to study it in greater depth, asking what its elements are, and why it is typically so narrow and uneven. The historical thinkers did not realize that compassion and altruism are part of our animal heritage; now we know that they are. It seems important to study that heritage in order to understand both the powerful resources on which we can draw and the likely barriers to fair and respectful concern. Animal research, suitably combined with experimental research on human beings, shows us that we are not merely selfish beings, that we are capable of altruism and emotional concern. But it also shows us that much can go wrong with that concern when we think about the goal of political justice.

A further problem with our sources is that they fail to recognize and investigate some darker forces in the human personality that create ongoing impediments to reciprocity and equal concern. So concerned were Comte and Mill to reject theocentric ideas of original sin as the basis of society that they moved too quickly toward what we might call a naïve picture of the personality—one in which we have only good impulses, and our only problem is to extend them and even them out. Life, however, is not like that, and Tagore's Bauls already supply a richer account of what must be overcome in human beings: a problematic relationship to the body, a tendency to feel disgust toward bodily fluids and to project this disgust onto other humans, prominently including women. In Tagore's abstract and chaste formulation, however, issues of disgust and sexuality remain veiled. We need to lift the veil, studying the roots of a bodily disgust and shame that continually threaten to create social hierarchies. Once again, studying the emotions of nonhuman animals will prove essential, giving us a sense of the contrast between our lives and the lives of other altruistic beings, and pinpointing the sources of the uniquely dark capacities of human creatures.

The study of animal/human contrast, then, has a twofold role: it helps us understand the structure, limits, and possibilities of altruism, and it reveals sources of special moral difficulty in human life. This study is then followed, in Chapter 7, by a richer and more detailed human psychology, one that will make sense of the well-known notion of "radical evil" (evil tendencies that precede any particular society) and help us see what resources human psychology offers to surmount it. Donald Winnicott's concepts of "concern" and "play" will help us develop the connection between altruism and the imagination, showing in rich detail how Cherubino and the Bauls correspond to an attractive psychological norm.

By the end of this part, the image of Cherubino will have become more complicated and more real, as we make him a much more ambivalent and "all-too-human" figure capable, initially, of both narcissism and generosity, exclusionary disgust and delighted reciprocity, and show how a plausible account of child development could strengthen some of these tendencies and discourage others. The account of goals in Chapter 5, meanwhile, will have given him a political home: a structure of laws and institutions in a liberal nation aspiring to both liberty and human capability.

CHAPTER FIVE

The Aspiring Society: Equality, Inclusion, Distribution

Do not call him to your house, the dreamer,
who walks alone by your path
in the night.
His words are those of a strange land,
And strange is the melody
played by him on his one-stringed lute.
There is no need for you to spread a seat for him;
He will depart before day-break.
For in the feast of freedom
he is asked to sing
the praise of the newborn light.

—Rabindranath Tagore, *Collected Poems and Plays*[1]

I. Sketching a Goal

Before embarking on a contemporary constructive version of the Mozart/ Mill/Tagore project, we need a sketch of where we are heading. Each political ideal is supported by its own distinctive emotions. Monarchies have long relied on cultivating emotions of childlike dependency, encouraging subjects to depend on the king as on a quasi-divine father. Fascist states (whether German Nazism or the quasi-fascist social organizations of the Hindu Right in India today) engender and rely on solidaristic pride and hero worship, fear of the solitary dissident, and hatred of groups depicted as inferior or subversive. Conservatives who are far from being fascistic also emphasize the political value of solidaristic emotion: Lord Devlin, for example, urged lawmakers to defer to the disgust and indignation of average members of society, even when minorities stood to lose a sphere of cherished liberty. Referring to the struggle against the Axis powers, which had occurred not long before, Devlin argued that such emotions hold society together and make it capable of defeating its enemies.[2]

Even the minimal libertarian state has its own characteristic culture of emotions. Libertarians sometimes suggest that it is an advantage of their ideal that they do not need to rely upon extensive sympathy. They can use human nature just as it is, relying on acquisitiveness, Hobbesian fear, and limited sympathy to propel the machinery of competition. By contrast, liberals, they allege, want to engage in intrusive and uncertain projects of improvement. There is less to this contrast, however, than meets the eye. Even libertarians are opposed to force and fraud. Even they, therefore, need to shape emotions such as anger and fear so as to produce stability and law-abiding behavior—not the behavior that, by their own (Hobbesian) account, we should expect in the "state of nature." And libertarians may have an even larger problem of stability on their hands. To the extent that they do not try to rein in narcissistic emotions such as envy, shame, and disgust, they may render even their own minimal state unstable. Competitive acquisitiveness and the desire to rise above others can upset even that type of state, causing it to degenerate into lawless tribalism. So they will have to ask, at least, whether they don't need a broader program of emotional persuasion, one that addresses these destabilizing forces.

Furthermore, proponents of the libertarian state typically assume, and do not argue, that their claims about "human nature" are true apart from culture. It is by making such an assumption that they claim to be able to get by with a simpler and less intrusive strategy than that required by liberals. And yet history indicates that people's capacity for extended sympathy varies greatly in accordance with the culture in which they live, as do their desires to outdo others in rank and status, or to dominate other racial or ethnic groups. We should surely not assume that the form emotions take in the corporate culture of the United States reveals a universal and timeless truth about how things must be.

The libertarian challenge, however, contains a valuable lesson for our project: we must pay attention to the facts of human psychology, insofar as these are at all understood, and we must not ask of people what they cannot deliver, or can deliver only with great strain. *The Marriage of Figaro* is an important guide because it reminds us to embrace real people as they are, rather than engaging in unrealistic projects that are all too likely to lead, down the road, to a hatred of the actual.

And yet we should not want a political culture that simply pats people on the back, rather than trying to make things in the world better and more just than they currently are. The world as it is is beautiful, but it is also a mess, and much of the suffering it contains can be ameliorated by a wiser use of our time in the world. A creative reach toward something better is a key feature of most societies that strive for decency and justice, and that striving needs a vision of its goal. Striking the right balance between aspiration and acceptance is one of the most difficult and delicate tasks of the political life, as of the personal. But the right balance cannot be one that erases the longing for justice. Any realistic portrait of human beings, as Tagore emphasizes continually, includes the "surplus," the creative vision of a distant goal that, in his view, distinguishes humans from other creatures. "It is an insult to his humanity," he writes, "if man fails to invoke in his mind a definite image of his own ideal self, of his ideal environment, which it is his mission to reproduce externally."[3] If a nation's political culture is domesticated and comfortable, he suggests, then its people have given up being fully human.

Every nation has its pockets of conformity and complacency, but all, too, have a quest, a "feast of freedom" toward which the imagination yearns. So: where is our own imaginary traveler heading, and what songs is he singing on the way? We are considering not the achieved well-ordered society of Rawls's work, but, instead, nations aspiring to justice, with some definite goals and aspirations in view. Some of these goals will be current commitments that have already been given the form of constitutional entitlements or other legal mandates. Some (such as, for example, the elimination of racism) may be more diffuse aspirations in the spirit of constitutional principles.

Any rich account of a nation's goals and core commitments must ultimately be historical and contextual, and Part III will develop that theme.

Nonetheless, we may still say something general about the salient features of a family of political ideals that will be our focus from now on. In his late work, John Rawls emphasized that his own conception of justice was one of a family of liberal political conceptions whose principles of distribution, though similar in their general direction, might differ in some ways. My aim in this chapter is to set out the general features of such a family of political conceptions, members of which will be Rawls's own conception, my liberal "capabilities" approach, and numerous others.[4]

I have argued for a particular version of these norms in other writings; I do not do that here. This chapter supplies a stipulated and hypothetical normative backdrop for what follows. People who have different normative commitments may judge that my analysis of what went right and what went wrong, in the examples studied in Part III, is correspondingly in error. Such people, however, can still agree with the analysis of emotions presented here and with my account of how public strategies form emotions and cause certain goals to be realized or not realized. Thus, a partisan of the British Empire will judge that it did just the right thing in Delhi in 1857, whereas I disagree and say that it did just the wrong thing, but we can agree on the analysis of fear presented, and on the account of how fear was engendered and maintained by urban architecture. Similarly, people who disagree with various aspects of the New Deal will not share my enthusiasm for what Roosevelt accomplished, but they can still be persuaded by my analysis of how his political rhetoric addressed emotions of fear and envy and helped to create progress toward his goals.

II. Core Values of a Just Society

The first thing we can say about the societies we are imagining is that they are not aimed solely at economic growth, and they do not consider that increase in GDP per capita is the only indicator of their quality of life. Instead, they pursue on behalf of their people a wide range of goals, including health, education, political rights and liberties, environmental quality, and many more.[5] We might say that they aim at *human development,* meaning the opportunities of people to live rich and rewarding lives. Sometimes looking at GDP is a useful proxy for this wide range of human opportunities, but it is at best a proxy, and it is not always such a good proxy, particularly when a nation contains large inequalities between rich and poor.

Moreover, they pursue these goals for each person, considering that *each person is an end,* and none a mere means to the goals or ends of others. In other words, they would not think it appropriate to give one group of citizens exceedingly miserable lives in order to create a larger total or average. Nor would they think it appropriate to treat males as citizens, women as a support system for citizens. The distribution of entitlements and benefits matters greatly. As John Rawls puts it, "Each person possesses an inviolability founded on justice that even the well-being of society as a whole cannot override."[6]

But how is each person seen? In some conceptions of national life quality, people figure merely as containers of satisfaction. Our societies care about satisfaction, but they also care about a wide range of other things: opportunities for choice and action, relationships of reciprocity and affection. Because they are well aware that unjust background conditions frequently lead people to adjust their preferences and satisfactions downward—forming what the economic literature calls "adaptive preferences"—they do not think that satisfaction of preferences is a reliable indicator that society is doing its job well.[7]

At the heart of our societies' conception is the idea of *human equality.* All human beings are of equal worth, and that worth is inherent or intrinsic: it does not depend on a relationship to others (such as being the wife of X, or the vassal of Y). This worth is equal: all human beings are worthy of equal respect or regard, just in virtue of their humanity. Although some past conceptions have held that this worth is dependent upon the possession of some specific capacity, such as rational capacity, or a rather sophisticated ability to make moral choices, our nations do not say this. They are aware that humanity comes in many forms, and human beings with profound cognitive impairments are not less human or nonhuman simply because they have little or no calculative capacity and little or no sophisticated moral capacity.[8] Perhaps they lack those capacities, but possess the capacity for affection and delight, or the ability to perceive and respond to beauty—and it is invidious to say that those capacities are less worthy of our humanity than calculative capacities. The only noninvidious thing to say, if we keep our minds fixed on such cases, is that any child of human parents who is capable of some type of agency or striving (who is not, then, either anencephalic or in a permanent vegetative condition) is fully equal in worth and entitlement to every other human being.

We could capture this idea using a familiar and resonant notion, one that plays a role in many international documents and national constitutions: the idea of *equal human dignity*. This is the right sort of idea, because it suggests equal intrinsic worth and being objects of equal respect—but we should beware of using dignity as if it were an intuitively self-evident notion. By now we can see from debates in bioethics that the concept of dignity is not self-evident, and that it is frequently used to bring debate to a close, rather than as an introduction to further inquiry. The notion of human dignity should be understood as a member of a family of conceptions and principles that hang together and are justified as a whole. Dignity is closely linked to the idea of respect, but it will get its full clarity only from the whole system of which it is a part.[9]

The conception of the human being that lies at the heart of the political conception involves both *striving* and *vulnerability*. Human beings are not just passive recipients of fortune's blows. Instead, they are active beings who pursue aims and who seek lives rich in activity. At the same time, however, they are to a significant degree passive, in the sense that fortune's blows mean something to them, impinge seriously on the quality of their lives. In other words, our nations reject from the start the Stoic idea that the only important good things in human life are always perfectly secure, incapable of being augmented or diminished by the interventions of fortune or other people. In order to live well, people need food, care, protection and sustenance of many kinds. They also have deep needs for protected spheres of activity, such as religious freedom and the freedom of speech. It is not trivial, then, but profoundly damaging, to refuse people such support. Thus deprived, people retain human dignity, since that is inalienable, but in the absence of suitable support and care they will not be able to live lives worthy of human dignity.

Agency and support are connected: it is on account of their capacity for activity and striving that human beings are entitled to support for their vulnerability.[10]

A delicate issue arises here. On the one hand, human beings depend on one another for many things they cannot attain on their own, and these relationships of care and support themselves have dignity. Moreover, citizens live in relationships of asymmetrical dependency for large portions of their lives: childhood, old age if they live long enough, and periods of impaired ability due to accident or illness. Some citizens have profound impairments throughout their lives. Our societies regard it as very important to respect the equal dignity of people who have physical and cognitive impairments, and to respect the relationships of care in which all citizens live for at least a significant part of their lives. So removing the shame and stigma often attached to dependency will be a major goal of such societies. On the other hand, this is not to say that independence and agency cease to matter. For people with disabilities as for others, independence and choice of activities are important goals. Striking the right balance in this matter is a delicate process, and one that requires ongoing debate and listening.

I have spoken repeatedly of human beings. Some members of our family of political conceptions do focus exclusively on the human. By contrast, my own conception sees all animals as entitled to support for their agency and striving. Other liberal conceptions incorporate concern for the world of nature in other ways, some even broader than mine (attributing entitlements to all living beings, for example, or even to ecosystems). Although these differences are surely of the utmost importance, and although they rightly shape the repertory of emotions that a nation will encourage and discourage, they will not be my focus in this particular project, although many of my examples will show how a concern for nature may be cultivated.

The societies that I shall consider throughout this project are nations, with a variety of aspirations and goals. To that extent the *moral salience of national sovereignty* (for which I argue elsewhere)[11] is built into the conception from the beginning. Such a commitment has considerable importance for political emotions, since many familiar political emotions take the nation-state as their focus and involve commitments to its defense and flourishing. At the same time, nations have aspirations, and these aspirations include commitments to the transnational realm. Our nations are aware that they are members of an interconnected world, many of whose problems cannot be solved without cooperation. Among their most urgent goals will be world peace, and they will seek fair terms of cooperation among nations in pursuing that aim. Their commitment to other nations will not, however, be exhausted by matters of war and peace. Citizens will understand that the living standard and life opportunities of people in other nations are also a matter of concern—not just for reasons of peace and stability but because people matter. Richer nations have at least some duties to support the development and flourishing of people in poorer nations. Thus sacrifice and sympathy do not stop at national borders. As Mazzini urged, the nation is a fulcrum for the creation of universal human concern.

For all of the members of our family of nations, the idea of *equal political and civil liberties* plays a key role. All citizens enjoy the right to vote, the right to seek political office, freedoms of speech and association, religious freedom, freedom of movement and travel, and the benefits of a free press, on a basis of equality with others. This commitment to equality means that the conditions of liberty must be the same for all: thus a law that appears neutral but which burdens a particular religious group unequally will be suspect. Majoritarianism is limited by a commitment to the fully equal rights of minorities. Although these rights are frequently called "negative" and are sometimes thought to involve merely state inaction, looking at what it takes to realize them in any modern democracy disabuses us of this error.

This same commitment to equality extends to a more general concern for *due process liberty rights* and for the *equal protection of the laws.* Those commitments, familiar in virtually all modern democratic nations, often have particular salience for minorities or traditionally subordinated groups, classified by race, gender, ethnicity, religion, or sexuality. All societies have to grapple with the history or current reality of group subordination, whether in the form of slavery, religious animosity, caste, or the exclusion of women. All, therefore, need to cultivate emotions that conduce to *equal respect and toleration,* while inhibiting those that militate against these norms. All societies, then, have reason to study and manage emotions such as disgust, shame, and fear. The "religion of humanity" goal of extending sympathy is important, but narrowness of sympathy is not the only or even the worst obstacle on the way to a world of equal respect and inclusion. Grappling with group animosity requires a deeper inquiry into the origins of prejudice and hatred.

The *prevention of violence and fraud* is a key goal of all democratic societies, and fundamental to the development of legal systems. Both anger and fear respond to harm or damage, and members of our family can agree with libertarians that violence and fraud are two very salient types of damage, which it is the responsibility of society to control, not only through law, but through appropriate shaping of anger and fear. Our societies will typically pursue this commitment into the home, understanding that domestic violence and sexual abuse are among the greatest impediments to full human equality.

A sharp difference between our nations and their libertarian cousins now appears. Our societies will protect entitlements for all not only in the political and civil realm and not only in the realm of violence and fraud, but also in the areas of life usually called *social and economic:* health, education, a decent level of welfare, shelter and housing. Once again, the nations in our family will vary in the nature and extent of their commitments and in the way they implement them (through constitutional rights, through legislation), but all will seek to reduce the level of material inequality through programs of *significant redistribution,* accomplished primarily through a fair tax system. Because they engage in far more redistribution than do their libertarian cousins, they will need to be far more concerned with the extension of sympathy needed to sustain such programs, and with the eradication of baneful stereotypes of the poor. They will also need to reduce competitive envy and to be on guard against any emotional forces that make it difficult for one group of citizens to see their fate in the fate of others.

The task of containing envy is made more complex by the fact that our societies do not aim at the complete equalization of all material opportunities. They do insist on equalizing political and civil rights— nobody gets more votes than anyone else, or more religious freedom— but on the side of wealth and income and the opportunities it affords, they do allow *some inequalities to remain, in order to give incentives for striving and innovation that raise the level of the whole society.* John Rawls permitted only those inequalities that improve the income and wealth of the least well-off.[12] But he also acknowledged that other members of his family of liberal conceptions of justice will have different distributive principles. My capabilities approach sets an ample threshold of opportunity for all—including full equality in the political and civic arenas—but it also leaves room for further principles dealing with inequality above the threshold, once the society has taken shape. Other societies will adopt other ways of permitting some inequality while greatly reducing it and maintaining a decent level of welfare for those at the bottom. In all these cases, society must engage in a delicate balancing act where emotions are concerned, permitting and even, to some extent, encouraging the competitive emotions, but preventing them from destabilizing the society's commitments to the welfare of all its members.

Among the social and economic commitments of our societies, *education and health* are key, since citizens can hardly pursue other projects unless their capacities are developed by education and supported by an adequate network of health care. Societies pursue these commitments in many different ways.

Education is a goal, but it is also an opportunity. When society makes a commitment to education, it makes a commitment as well to its own future stability, not just in economic matters, but also in pursuit of its political goals. Education will then be one of the main arenas in which the shaping of politically appropriate sympathy will take place, and in which inappropriate forms of hatred, disgust, and shame will be discouraged.

III. A Critical Culture

Our nations are committed to developing political emotions that support their cherished goals. But they also encourage vigorous criticism and debate. A vigilant critical culture is, indeed, a key to the stability of liberal values. Vigorous cultivation of emotion can coexist, albeit sometimes uneasily, with the protection of an open critical space.

Consider just one example, race relations in the United States. The nation by now has addressed the problem of racism not only through laws and institutions, but also through public celebration, rhetoric, symbolism, the arts, and a wide range of persuasive emotional strategies. And yet, criticism also thrives, at several distinct levels. First, even those who openly espouse racist principles and would like to change the legal and constitutional commitments of our society (reintroducing racial segregation, or even slavery) are free to speak their mind and make their case. Unlike many nations, ours protects racist speech (such as that of the neo-Nazi marchers in Skokie, Illinois, or rallies of the Ku Klux Klan), unless it is threatening speech targeted at an individual. Some nations in our family of nations may judge that this very expansive free speech principle is more than they can afford, given their history: thus Germany has made anti-Semitic speech and political organizing illegal, and it may be correct to do so, with that history. But in general there should be a wide latitude for the expression of criticism of the underlying values and goals of the nation, and this is clearly compatible with a strong public commitment to those values.

When people make such criticisms, they are at a political disadvantage, in the sense that they will have to change the U.S. Constitution if they want to achieve their goals; they cannot straightforwardly introduce legislation making African Americans an underclass, or reintroducing segregation. They are also at an emotional disadvantage, in that children are brought up in school to think that racial equality is a very noble political value and that good Americans are nonracist; they have been moved by the words of Martin Luther King Jr., and by speeches from all sides extolling racial progress and racial respect. If some people want to urge their fellow citizens to feel the disgust at the touch of a black person's skin that millions of Americans in the Jim Crow South once felt, they will have a hard time succeeding. But nobody will charge them with a crime for trying.

Another much larger zone for debate concerns the precise meaning and scope of constitutional protections. Most Americans now agree that racial equality is a cherished goal, but they deeply disagree about whether affirmative action programs are a good or even permissible way of reaching toward that goal. Constitutional values are typically adopted at a high level of generality, and that very generality protects spaces for debate. Thus, even though it is possible to show that Martin Luther King Jr. supported affirmative action, and many will, correctly, hear the emotive force of his remarks as strengthening their own support, there are plenty of people who hear King very differently and who are energized toward the goal of removing affirmative action by what they take his example to be. One group is correct historically and the other is not, but that becomes a relatively minor point in the context of ongoing civic argument. It is possible to be a devoted and emotionally energized American, attached to the general goal of racial equality, and yet to oppose affirmative action and to celebrate that opposition on Martin Luther King Jr.'s birthday. The public emotion culture surrounding King did not close off that space for contestation, and it really did not even put such people at a political disadvantage.

Finally, even when people agree both about general goals and about their precise interpretation, they may differ greatly about strategies, and public celebrations of emotion do nothing to close off that space. Thus, two people who intensely support same-sex marriage and who celebrate Harvey Milk's birthday (now an official California holiday) with deep emotion may disagree intensely about the wisdom of using the courts to advance their cause, not on grounds of principle but on grounds of strategy. One person may hold that countermajoritarian judgments by courts on controversial moral issues lead to backlash, and we would do better to leave the issue to elected legislators. The other may point to the political pressures that lobby groups bring to bear on elected officials and urge that courts, immunized from these pressures to some degree, can do a better job in such high-controversy matters. Agreement in emotions did not close the space of debate.

Indeed, so valuable are critical thinking and dissent to the health and stability of our nations that these nations will try to nourish the critical spirit itself through emotional attachment, as did Tagore and Gandhi. When children hear stories of heroes of the past, they will be urged to love and emulate people who are daring and iconoclastic, who saw a great evil and risked their own safety for the sake of justice. In school they may put on a play about the Birmingham bus boycott, or they assume the role of Rosa Parks as she refused to sit in the back of the bus or the role of Mildred Jeter Loving as she and her husband refused to accept Virginia's criminalization of their interracial marriage. As we'll later see, public art enhances the emotions connected to dissent in many ways.

And of course one nation can learn from another. The excellent Richard Attenborough film of Gandhi's life galvanizes discussion in the faraway schools of the United States. One flaw in the film, however, by comparison with the Indian reality, is that it fails to portray the vital atmosphere of dissent and critical thinking *inside* Gandhi's movement: Jawaharlal Nehru argued with Gandhi on virtually every important issue, while supporting the man with deep emotion.

In both nations, then, being a citizen, as young people are brought up to see that role, is closely linked to ideas of personal conscience, dissent, and courageous resistance. And that value, like other values, needs the emotions for its stability and reproduction.

IV. The Challenge of Political Liberalism

Mill and Comte hoped, and to some extent believed, that traditional religion would be replaced by their "religion of humanity." Tagore was less opposed to the existing religions, suggesting, indeed, that they all could join in the spirit of the religion of humanity through cooperation and partial reform. The religions would have to change to a certain degree in order to join in the cooperative venture he envisaged: they would all have to drop any commitment to religious combat or hatred, and they would also need to accept some reforms, for example the abolition of untouchability in the case of Hinduism. But the picture painted by *The Religion of Man,* as well as by many of Tagore's other writings, is one of evolution toward mutual respect and the affirmation of certain shared principles, within a society that would remain religiously diverse. Each religion could continue to cherish its own rituals and its own gods, and even perhaps to believe in its own superiority as a path to insight (refusing Rousseau's principle of theological toleration)—within bounds set by the common rights of all and equal respect for all. In his school, this spirit of pluralism with equal respect prevailed. Students learned about all the major religions and celebrated the main holidays of all of them, rather than being taught that these holidays are bad relics of a divisive religious era. They were not told that religion is a bad social force, although they were certainly forbidden to practice untouchability or to subordinate Muslims or Christians to Hindus. Although Tagore did not live long enough to make political proposals for a civil religion in the new independent nation, the evidence is that he would have favored the

Nehru-Gandhi policy of nonestablishment, equal political and civil liberties, and a political culture that accepts the ongoing fact of religious pluralism while trying to foster toleration (political, not theological) and shared political principles.

Our nations' approach to the problem of pluralism is that of Tagore, not that of Mill and Comte. Seeing that religious pluralism does not diminish under conditions of freedom, and believing that equal respect for citizens requires giving them plenty of room to search for the meaning of life in their own way, these nations will commit themselves not only to ample religious liberty (and to equal conditions of liberty), but also to nonestablishment, holding that establishment of any particular religious or secular comprehensive doctrine as *the* doctrine of the nation is a way of not respecting people equally. Even if such a doctrine is not coercively imposed, it is a statement that creates an in-group and various out-groups, saying that some citizens are true believers, in line with the official state doctrine, and others are not. Mill and Comte favored such hierarchical statements, since they thought that existing religions were major obstacles to human progress. Our nations, by contrast, believe that restraint is justified by the principle of equal respect.

The view that our nations hold is a version of the doctrine that has come to be known as "political liberalism," on account of the influential work of Charles Larmore and John Rawls.[13] Larmore and Rawls argue that equal respect for citizens requires that a nation not build its political principles on any particular comprehensive doctrine of the meaning and basis of life, whether religious or secular. Political principles ought to be such as to be, potentially, objects of an "overlapping consensus" among all reasonable citizens—those, that is, who are respectful of their fellow citizens as equals and ready to abide by fair terms of cooperation. The idea is that the principles should ultimately be able to fit into the comprehensive doctrines of all these citizens, like a part or a "module" that they will endorse while at the same time endorsing the rest of their comprehensive doctrine, religious or secular, whatever it is. The consensus may not exist at present, but it ought to be a plausible possibility for the future, and we should be able to envisage a plausible trajectory from where we currently are to such a consensus.

Such a consensus will be possible, however, only if the political principles have two features. First, they must be narrow in scope, covering central political entitlements and matters of political structure, but not proposing to cover all topics addressed by the comprehensive doctrines. Thus they will steer clear of controversial metaphysical, religious, and even in some cases ethical matters on which the religions are divided, addressing only those ethical topics that involve fundamental matters of political entitlement or citizen standing on which we hope citizens will ultimately be able to agree. Second, they must be shallow as to their basis: they must not be justified by any set of controversial metaphysical, epistemological, or religious claims. The justification offered for them will be "freestanding," meaning that it will not latch onto some comprehensive scheme, whether of knowledge or of value: it will build on just those ethical notions that are central to the political doctrines themselves, such as the idea of equal respect for persons and the correlative idea of human dignity. Political principles have a definite moral content, prominently including the idea of equal respect; the aim is not to construct a purely procedural politics or one with no moral goals and aspirations. The hope is, however, that over time these moral ideals can become accepted by citizens who hold a wide range of different religious and secular views, since citizens will see them as fully respectful of their freedom and equality.

Political liberalism does not require that all citizens who accept the basic ideas of equal respect and fairness should find it equally easy to accept the political principles. Sometimes there may be strains, even grave strains, as of course there may also be internal strains among the different parts of one's comprehensive doctrine. The requirement is only that the political principles show equal respect for all citizens, understood as holders of a variety of religious and secular doctrines, and that it not establish any one doctrine.

Nonestablishment is not just a matter of laws.[14] It also has implications for what public ceremonies can be like, what public schools can teach or require, and what public funding may support. (Landmark cases in U.S. constitutional law concern just this sort of thing.)[15]

Political principles, then, cannot include or be built upon the religion of humanity. That idea, at least in its Comtean and even Millean forms, is objectionable both in its content and in its basis. The content of Comte's religion involves all sorts of controversial metaphysical and religious notions, such as the idea of linear human progress and the idea of humanity as an object of worship. Its rituals interpret common human events, such as birth and death, in a highly specific, antireligious way. As for its basis, it relies on the rejection of theism that Positivism has allegedly proven; it rests, as well, upon other positivist doctrines about the nature of the universe and humanity's role in it. Mill's idea that extensive sympathy would be taught in the family and in schools and, as he explicitly states, reinforced by aesthetic education in the university curriculum is not, in and of itself, vulnerable to this criticism. But if human sympathy were put forward as Mill himself recommends—as a substitute for theistic religion in a new post-religious age—it would be inappropriate. The sort of humanism that does appear to survive scrutiny is Tagore's, understood as demanding allegiance to a common core of notions revolving around the idea of human equality and freedom, ethical ideals that can be built into a nation's political principles while allowing plenty of room for the pursuit of a variety of religious and secular views of life, and while subordinating none to others.

Tagorean humanism does require the major religions to undergo some serious scrutiny, and its rejection of caste may be thought intrusive by some. But race in the United States and caste in India are very similar. The U.S. Constitution—as by now interpreted—endorses racial equality in a very strong form. Laws mandating segregated schools and laws banning interracial marriage have been declared unconstitutional on equality grounds. Similarly, in India, the constitution forbids the practice of untouchability. In both cases, then, basic political principles include a moral ideal of equality that certainly was not accepted at the time by all the major religions. Over time, however, the political principles have exercised a normative pull, and no major religious group in the United States today defends racial hierarchy or even racial segregation (which was always a form of hierarchy but was not always portrayed that way) as a key element in its religious ideal. Similarly in India, although caste discrimination continues to be widely practiced, the constitutional norm has exerted its pull, and even conservative Hindus today would not publicly defend untouchability. This is how an "overlapping consensus" takes shape: certain practices are forbidden in the public sphere, and over time this, along with other arguments and other social forces, leads people to rethink elements of their comprehensive view of life.

How intrusive, then, are the political principles and the ceremonies and artworks they generate? This remains, of course, a matter of much controversy, as many Americans object to the "political correctness" that they find in many of our public observances. Racial segregation is indeed very difficult to practice in any large facility in the United States today, and the construction of public emotions has a lot to do with the strong disapproval racists face. Still, it would be wrong to suggest that no space is left for private choices to pursue ideals that are at odds with the political norm. For one thing, freedoms of speech and association are carefully protected. Overlapping consensus does not require an absence of tension between the comprehensive view and the political view. Most people live with tensions in at least some parts of their belief system, and they are constrained only by the degree of their commitment to consistency as a norm.

But thinking about such ongoing tensions reminds us that Comte and Mill had an advantage. They were not ethically correct—in the sense that their political ideas did not fully respect people's equality and freedom. But when we think about stability, we can see that their ideas have some advantages over the ones that I am defending. If you feel entitled to replace all the doctrines that cause tension and conflict with doctrines that comprehensively support your political ideals, and if you are successful, your political ideals may be more secure than the ideals of a nation that delicately accommodates the claims of many different religious and secular ideas, some of which are in tension with the nation's political principles, although their adherents do accept those principles. It is certainly advantageous to a set of political norms if the entire society and its major religious doctrines are pulling unitedly in the same direction. My view chooses to do without that advantage for the sake of equal respect. It will, then, have to live with a greater degree of tension. Society will not be revolutionized, and people will not be turned into reliable agents of the political ideal. Although we hope that they will support it enthusiastically, and not merely as a modus vivendi, they may be of two minds, and live with divided allegiances. Even in the achieved well-ordered society, Rawls recognizes that such tensions may endure; all the more are they present in our societies, which aspire to, but have not yet achieved, full social justice. The scene of the action shifts from society as a comprehensive whole to the political realm itself, and to its strategies to make its ideals prevail in a world of pluralism.

How does the political sphere enforce its political ideals? Even in our "political liberal" view, which makes a strong distinction between the political realm and the rest of society (what Rawls calls the "background culture"), there is room for a distinction between legal coercion and informal persuasion. Core political values, such as racial equality, can and should be coercively enforced. Furthermore, this fact by itself has a persuasive effect over time, since illegality is stigmatized as well as penalized, and people have strong incentives to bring up their children to conform willingly to legal norms. But public officials can use persuasion too—both encouraging support for legal norms and encouraging more general habits of mind that render those norms stable. When the U.S. Congress made Martin Luther King Jr.'s birthday a major holiday (finally defeating the intense opposition to that plan), and when leaders all over the country take part in its celebration, they are using persuasion to back up existing constitutional norms, but they are also encouraging more general emotional attitudes that lie behind these norms and helping the norms to achieve greater firmness.

In the process, government officials must avoid suggesting that the political norms grow out of one religious or secular view of life rather than another. In principle, the abolition of racial segregation and caste discrimination should be defended by arguments that are independent of any particular religious outlook. The dangers of sectarianism and inadvertent establishment are particularly great when we are thinking about emotions, because emotions respond to memory, and memory is often linked to religious rituals and the habits of mind these form.

Sometimes, however, in a situation of great injustice, there may be no way to mobilize the requisite energy for change without using the resonance of religious imagery. When Gandhi drew on Hindu traditions of asceticism for images of brotherhood and human dignity, he risked suggesting that India is primarily for Hindus. He needed to do this, he believed, in order to win Hindus over to a radically new view of what Hinduism requires, but he understood that, having made this choice, it was incumbent upon him to take every opportunity to include Muslims and Christians in his ritual performances (such as his fast unto death in Bengal, when he accepted his first nourishment from the hands of Maulana Azad, a Muslim). Similarly, Martin Luther King Jr. drew on prophetic imagery from the Judeo-Christian tradition to powerful effect, and it is difficult to imagine him achieving the same emotional effect without that language. He risked sectarianism—but he seemed aware of the danger, taking pains to show that the ideals toward which he spurred people were ideals for all Americans.

Thus public emotions ought to be both narrow and shallow, compared to the comprehensive doctrines that citizens hold. Occasionally, for urgent purposes, they may use the depth and resonance of one those doctrines, but they had better counterbalance this gesture immediately by a commitment to pluralism and equal respect. Narrowness of subject matter means that many areas of human life in which grief, fear, disgust, and other emotions operate will not be topics for political cultivation at all. So we might wonder whether the political culture can, in the end, say and do anything interesting or deep about these emotions. It needs to do so, however, and it had better solve the problem of sectarianism as best it can, for the roots of many pernicious political tendencies are laid down in childhood and in the family, in the images of the body, of self and other, that people form. Racial disgust and fears of physical contamination cannot be addressed by laws alone, and not just by injunctions to avoid disgust in the political realm. Whitman and Tagore see that problems of caste and gender in their societies require us to think and talk publicly about the body, about its eroticism, its limits, its mortality. In the end, the roots of the political ramify widely, and the cultivator of emotions should try to follow them wherever they cause trouble or promise support, while avoiding sectarianism as much as possible.

Sometimes the views that we shall put forward (following Cherubino and the Bauls) will be in some tension with those currently held by the major religions. It will seem that in such cases the danger of sectarianism has not been avoided. But the public culture is a dialogue, and it is dynamic—so over time, as with racial and caste stigma, we hope that these more general tensions may be resolved. Challenging segregation and untouchability once seemed highly sectarian, but today it seems clear that the major religions can survive and prosper without those commitments. To some extent, our issues about disgust and the body have also been transcended: shame about the body is at least on the wane in most modern societies. Ideas of equal human worth or dignity are also in tension with ideas about human beings that some religions hold (e.g., Calvinism), but those ideas do not seem objectionably sectarian or establishmentarian; indeed, it seems possible for even Calvinism to flourish in a nation that affirms human dignity and equal human rights. Most Protestant churches in the United States no longer focus intently on human lowness or worthlessness, but they could do so while affirming human dignity in the public realm, and just learn to live with that tension. With disgust, the same possibility remains: one can hold that disgust is a bad basis for laws that subordinate one group to another, while still allowing disgust to guide many aspects of one's private behavior. Similarly with eroticism and the animal aspects of the body: for political purposes we adopt the view that our embodiment is part of our human dignity. Traditional ideas of transcendence of the merely human can be given a political interpretation (in the spirit of Tagore) that focuses on the aspiration to transcend injustice and achieve justice; they need not retain, at least in the political context, their association with the rejection of the body and disgust toward the body.

As for shallowness, the political culture of emotion should not support itself by drawing on theological or metaphysical traditions. But there is no reason why it cannot draw on empirical psychology, on studies of the relationship between humans and animals in primatology, and on studies of prejudice in history and sociology. Donald Winnicott, whose ideas about imagination and play will be important to the project, was not a metaphysical sort of psychoanalyst; he was a clinician, and very empirically oriented. His ideas converge with those of other empirical researchers.

V. Institutions and People

Public emotions are a source of stability for good political principles, and of motivation to make them effective. So it will naturally focus on making people experience certain emotions in certain contexts and with particular objects (the nation itself, its goals, its specific tasks or problems, its people). But emotions are themselves in need of stabilizing. Even the most positive and helpful emotions, such as expanded sympathy, can be quite volatile, expanding and contracting as the focus of attention expands or contracts. As Adam Smith rightly observed, people can be deeply moved by an earthquake in China, but then quickly diverted from that focus by a pain in their little finger. The attempt to run an ambitious program of social redistribution only on the basis of emotion is doomed to failure.

Understanding this limitation, people who feel keen sympathy for a particular plight will seek not only to energize the emotions of their fellow citizens, but also to create laws and institutions to give stability to their cause. When you feel sympathy for the poor, it is fine to view that as occasion for philanthropy, but it is better to use that energy to create a decent tax system and a set of welfare programs. Emotions in this way operate at two levels. Once laws and institutions are reasonably just, emotions sustain them. But they also create motivations to improve those laws and institutions. When that happens, we might say that the institutions themselves embody the insight of emotions. That is what Mill meant when he said that anger and resentment lie behind the law: laws embody the insights of experiences of personal resentment, distilled by reflection and extended by sympathy to all.[16] So too with tax and welfare policies: they embody sympathy, but in a way that is more stable and less prone to special pleading than is sympathy in real life.

When laws and institutions already embody the insights of good emotions, they facilitate the experience of those same emotions. Thus Tocqueville remarked that American institutions, situating people closer to one another in opportunity and status than European institutions, facilitate sympathy: it becomes easier to see one's own fate in that of another when that other is not at a huge distance.[17] Similarly, a welfare system that is entrenched and habitual makes it easier for people to feel sympathy for people who have suffered an economic calamity, since it establishes the principle that these people are entitled to support (rather than to blame for laziness, for example). Franklin Delano Roosevelt had a much more difficult emotional task prior to the New Deal than a leader would have in a settled and stable social democracy with a safety net. On the other hand, as the subsequent history of New Deal programs shows, good laws and institutions need the ongoing support of real people's emotions—and need to be preserved from the corrosive effect of bad emotions.

The focus of this project will be on the role of emotions in advancing a society that is already pretty good to fuller social justice and then giving stability and motivational force to its political principles. We should never forget, however, that emotional experience often becomes crystallized in institutional form, since only that formal structure, in many cases, solves problems of both evanescence and partiality to which human emotions are all too prone.

CHAPTER SIX

Compassion: Human and Animal

I think I could turn and live with animals, they are so placid and
    self-contain'd,
I stand and look at them long and long.

They do not sweat and whine about their condition,
They do not lie awake in the dark and weep for their sins. . . .
Not one is dissatisfied, not one is demented with the mania of
    owning things,
Not one kneels to another, nor to his kind that lived thousands of
    years ago,
Not one is respectable or unhappy over the whole earth.

So they show their relations to me and I accept them,
They bring me tokens of myself, they evince them plainly in their
    possession.

—Walt Whitman, "Song of Myself"

I. Psychology and Justice

The nations we are imagining aspire to justice. They want to figure out
how emotions can help them in their work, motivating good policies and
rendering them stable. They also want to thwart, or at least to control,
emotions that would derail their efforts. But if a society pursues such
ambitious goals, it will need to learn from research that sheds light on
the resources and the problems that human nature, insofar as we can
know it, makes available. Before we can even begin to consider specific

policy recommendations about specific emotions, we need a general overview—in the light of what we currently know—of the possibilities and dangers inherent in simply being human, a narrative whose particular episodes we can later flesh out with greater complexity.

Because our nations are firmly committed to political liberalism, they agree not to base their policy recommendations on any overarching religious or ethical view about human nature. They can, however, use the results of empirical psychology, the study of animal behavior, and clinical observations of human development. They also see no reason not to turn to imaginative literature for illumination of human life, albeit with critical alertness, since literary works frequently prove sectarian, articulating some partisan religious or secular view of society's goals and purposes.

A good place to begin is with the other animals, for they show us a lot about ourselves.[1]

II. Animal Grief and Altruism

In September 2010, in West Bengal, India, two baby elephants became trapped on a train track as the herd was crossing the railroad line in the middle of a dense forest. As a speeding train approached, five females of the herd turned back to surround the babies, attempting to protect them from harm. All seven died. (The train was traveling at 43 mph, despite a speed limit of 24 mph.) The remaining members of the herd remained at the scene, watching over the dead and dying.[2]

Nonhuman animals care and grieve; they experience compassion and loss. They perform acts of altruism that appear to be motivated by powerful emotions. By now we know a lot about these areas of animal behavior, and we can make solidly grounded conjectures about the emotions that sustain them. By studying the emotions and emotion behavior of complex social animals such as apes and elephants, we learn about our heritage, and hence our current possibilities. As Whitman says, these animals "bring" us "tokens of" ourselves, and we should "accept them."

Human beings often deny this kinship and the possibilities of learning that come with it. We like to think of ourselves as "above the beasts." So often, we define our very humanity by reference to characteristics that humans allegedly ours alone. (Reason? Morality? Emotions associated with morality, such as compassion and love? Altruistic behavior and sacrifice?) When we think of characteristics that are "higher," we usually name characteristics that humans possess in a superior degree and omit those that other species possess in a superior degree: thus, calculative ability, but not spatial perception, or auditory or olfactory acuity. And the history of the study of animal behavior is marred by repeated denials that particular types of nonhuman animals possess abilities that they are later shown clearly to possess (for example, the ability to use tools, or to learn language).

Indeed, for many people in many places and times, the very thought that we humans are actually animals is revolting, as are the bodily secretions and smells that remind us of that kinship. The suggestion that our ancestors were apes is enough to make people feel sick at the thought of contact with those hairy, smelly creatures. Jonathan Swift's Gulliver was extreme in his loathing of the signs of "Yahoo" animality: after his return, Gulliver at first cannot endure even the physical presence of his wife and children, so keenly does he loathe the smell of "that odious animal," and he never reaches a point at which he permits his wife and children to touch his body, or even his food and drink. Still, much of human life is structured by a similar disgust, as we cleanse our bodies of odors, remove body and facial hair, cover our limbs with cloth (Gulliver's primary stratagem to conceal from the Houyhnhnms his kinship with the despised Yahoos), and hide with special caution our genital and excretory parts and activities. It was because his habits were those of a typical Englishman of his time that Gulliver was able to escape being recognized by the Houyhnhnms as a smelly, hairy Yahoo.

Nor is revulsion at animality an old-fashioned emotion that we have now shaken off. When John Updike's hero Rabbit hears that his defective heart valves will be replaced by pig valves, he feels a powerful revulsion. "What else you think you are, champ?" asks the doctor. Rabbit says nothing, but he thinks: "A god-made one-of-a-kind with an immortal soul breathed in. A vehicle of grace. A battlefield of good and evil. An apprentice angel"[3]—giving answers he has learned from a specific type of Christian culture, but answers that are ubiquitous in human history in some form. Of course, one valuable aspect of this culture is that it teaches us the idea of the irreplaceable uniqueness and dignity of each human being, and that part of Rabbit's reflection I want to endorse. It is the other side, the revulsion at the animality of the body, that is deeply problematic. The picture of the human being as "apprentice angel" makes many people shrink from the very idea that we can learn about ourselves from studying apes and elephants. They think that engaging in such a study means denying the soul, religious accounts of the origins of life, and perhaps even the special binding force of morality itself.

Study, however, means no such thing. It just means trying to learn, and it seems unreasonable to suggest that we protect people's sensibilities by cultivating ignorance in the public realm. Moreover, the best theorists who survey the human-animal divide do not stake out sectarian or reductive positions about the soul.[4] A political culture committed to a shared morality of human dignity can still ground its policies in the findings of science in this area if it refrains from premature inferences about what might or might not be shown about issues that divide people along lines of their religion or nonreligion.

Scientists studying primates and elephants, and experimentalists doing complementary work with human babies, can give us three types of understanding that we badly need. First, we need a sense of the common ground that links us to the other animals—which might be seen as our evolutionary heritage, those "tokens of myself" that Whitman welcomes, although we should certainly extend our study to include species (elephants, for example) to which we have no direct evolutionary link, because an understanding of nature's variety is itself illuminating. Studying other animals is not merely studying our own history: it is illuminating in the way that the study of other cultures is illuminating, showing us to ourselves in a clearer light through the investigation of the ways in which another group of intelligent beings has organized the world. Some of the "tokens" that animals bring us give us opportunities, while some constitute limitations. And the study of animal social behavior is itself valuable, since it constitutes an acknowledgment of our own animality, which it is hypocrisy to deny.

Second, by contrasting animal behavior with what psychology tells us about human behavior, we can begin to figure out how far, and in what respects, humans are indeed special, what extra resources we may have for moral behavior that apes do not have. When the "common ground" shows us a limitation, as for example narrow or partial sympathy, we can then ask what special resources we may have to overcome that obstacle.

Third, however, a study of nonhuman animals also reminds us of some deformations and diseases that are endemic to the human condition. Whitman mentions excessive guilt, maniacal greed, and fanaticism. But we could add others. The disgust-ridden way of life depicted by Swift is not very promising as a basis for political community—all the less so when we notice in Gulliver's narrative motifs that recur with monotonous regularity in the history of prejudice and discrimination (the refusal to eat from the same vessel as another, the loathing of a woman's allegedly contaminating bodily secretions).

Consider too the specifically human deformities exhibited by the ending of Theodor Fontane's tragic novel *Effi Briest*. Effi, a high-spirited girl of sixteen, has been married by her parents to a much older man, good but humorless, who takes her to live in a gloomy house on the North Sea. Lonely and afraid, she allows herself to be pressured into a brief affair with a visiting Lothario, but soon breaks it off out of guilt. When her husband takes a position in Berlin and the two have a child, the marriage becomes a happy one—until, some eight years after the event, the husband discovers a note giving unmistakable evidence of the long-ago affair. Although he wants to forgive Effi, he feels that norms of manly honor require him to repudiate her and to fight a duel with her lover, whom he kills. Effi's parents, fearing the social stigma of association with a fallen woman, refuse to take her in until almost the end of her life. When she dies, they are unable to mourn. Only the faithful Newfoundland dog Rollo, knowing nothing of fallen women or social stigma, remains loving until the end, lying, inconsolable, on Effi's grave. Effi's father senses dimly that Rollo is better than they are. He asks his wife whether the dog's instinct is not sounder than their fallible judgment. Parental love is basically good, but their parental love has been blocked by social conventions, which portray Effi as a "bad" woman and a "bad" woman's suffering as deserved. Their hearts are frozen; Rollo's is not.

While depicting the parents' warped emotions, Fontane cultivates in his reader, from the start, a Rollo-like disposition: unjudgmental, skeptical of social norms about female sexuality, and focused on actual suffering. The entire structure of the novel is an exercise in learning to be an animal, learning to love like an animal, unconditionally, but with a human being's power of reasoning and social critique.

Focusing—like Fontane—on compassion, nonhuman and human, we will look for answers to our three questions. What is our common heritage? What extra abilities do we have that may prove helpful? And what does the contrast with other animals show us about pitfalls that must be avoided?

It seems best to begin with an area of apparent commonality and overlap: the experience of compassion.[5] This emotion has been fundamental to our project from the very beginning but was not analyzed with care by Mill and Tagore, whose lead I am following. Because they do not articulate its different elements, they cannot make targeted prescriptions for its appropriate extension, or understand the impediments to extending it.

III. Compassion: The Basic Structure

We must begin with some definitions. By "compassion" I mean a painful emotion directed at the serious suffering of another creature or creatures. A long philosophical tradition agrees, in general terms, about the thoughts that are typically involved when a human being has this emotion.[6] According to my account (to some extent agreeing with this tradition, to some extent criticizing it), compassion has three thoughts as necessary parts.[7] In earlier work I called these thoughts "judgments," but I emphasized at the same time that the word is not a perfect fit, because we need not think of these thoughts as linguistically formulated or formulable. Most animals can see items in their environment as good or bad, and this is all we are saying when we ascribe emotions, as I define them, to animals.[8] I begin by setting out the conditions as they apply to humans; we shall then ask how far they can be extended to the compassion of animals. Throughout, I shall speak of "thoughts" rather than "judgments," in order to mark the fact that most animal emotions and many human emotions involve combination or predication (of an object or situation with the idea of good or bad), without involving linguistically formulable propositions.

First, there is a thought of *seriousness:* in experiencing compassion, the person who feels the emotion thinks that someone else is suffering in some way that is important and nontrivial. This assessment is typically made, and ought to be made, from the point of view of an external spectator or evaluator, the person who experiences the emotion. If we think that sufferers are moaning and groaning over something that is not really bad, we won't have compassion for them. (For example, we don't feel compassion for rich people who suffer when they pay their taxes, if we think that it is exactly right that they should pay their taxes.) If we think, on the other hand, that a person is unaware of a predicament that is really bad (e.g., an accident that removes higher mental functioning),[9] then we will have compassion for the person even if the person doesn't think his or her situation is bad.

Second is the thought of *nonfault:* we typically don't feel compassion if we think the person's predicament chosen or self-inflicted. This thought is not a conceptual condition for all species of compassion, since there are forms present in both the human and the animal cases that do not involve any assessment of responsibility. It is, however, a conceptual element in the most common forms of adult human compassion. In feeling compassion, we express the view that at least a good portion of the predicament was caused in a way for which the person is not to blame. Thus, Aristotle held that compassion for the hero of a tragedy views that hero as *anaitios,* not responsible for his downfall.[10] When we think that a person brought a bad situation on him- or herself, this thought would appear to inhibit formation of the emotion. Thus, as Candace Clark has emphasized in her excellent sociological study of American compassion,[11] many Americans feel no compassion for the poor, who they believe bring poverty upon themselves through laziness and lack of effort.[12] Even when we do feel compassion for people whom we also blame, the compassion and the blame typically address different phases or aspects of the person's situation: thus we may blame a criminal for a criminal act while feeling compassion for him, if we think that the fact that he got to be the sort of person who commits criminal acts is in large part an outgrowth of social forces.

Blame comes in many types, corresponding to different categories of fault: deliberate malice, culpable negligence, and so forth. These will remove compassion to differing degrees. People's responsibility for their predicaments can also be more or less serious, as a causal element in the overall genesis of the event. In many such cases, compassion may still be present, but in a weakened form. To the extent that compassion remains, it would appear that it is directed, at least in part, at the elements of the disaster for which the person was not fully responsible. A trivial error may have huge consequences, including a suffering entirely disproportionate to the fault.

The tradition then includes a third allegedly necessary element of compassion, namely, the thought of *similar possibilities*. The person who has compassion often does think that the suffering person is similar to him- or herself and has possibilities in life that are similar. This thought may do important work, removing barriers to compassion that have been created by artificial social divisions, as Rousseau valuably emphasizes in Book IV of *Emile*. For most humans, the thought of similar vulnerability probably is, as Rousseau argues, an important avenue to compassionate response. But the thought of similarity is not absolutely necessary as a conceptual condition, even in the most common adult human type of compassion: we can in principle feel compassion for others without seeing their predicament as like one that we could experience.[13] Our compassion for the sufferings of animals is a fine example: we are indeed similar to animals in many ways, but we don't need that thought in order to see that what they suffer is bad, and in order to have compassion for them. For the purposes of the present argument, however, we shall see that the thought of similar possibilities has considerable importance in preventing or undoing denial of our own animal nature; its absence is thus a sign of grave danger.

Finally, there is a further thought that is not mentioned in the tradition, which, according to me, must be mentioned: it is what I call the *eudaimonistic thought*. This is a judgment or thought that places the suffering person or persons among the important parts of the life of the person who feels the emotion. It says, "They count for me: they are among my most important goals and projects." As I said in Chapter 1, the major human emotions are always eudaimonistic, meaning focused on the agent's most important goals and projects, and seeing the world from the point of view of those goals, rather than from some impersonal vantage point.[14] Thus we feel fear about damages that we see as significant for our own well-being and our other goals; we feel grief at the loss of someone who is already invested with a certain importance in our scheme of things.

Eudaimonism is not egoism. I am not claiming that emotions always view events and people as mere means to the agent's own satisfaction or happiness; indeed, I strenuously deny this.[15] But the things that occasion a strong emotion in us are things that correspond to what we have invested with importance in our thoughts, implicit or explicit, about what is important in life, our conception of flourishing. The thought of importance need not always antecede the compassionate response; the vivid presentation of another person's plight may jump-start it, moving that person, temporarily, into the center of the things that matter. Thus, when people hear of an earthquake or some other comparable disaster, they often become very focused on the sufferings of the strangers involved, and these strangers really matter to them— for a time. Daniel Batson's important experimental work on compassion demonstrates this repeatedly: instructed to listen with imaginative participation to the story of the plight of a student whom they do not know, the students in the study experience compassion, and this compassion, in turn, is correlated with helping behavior when a helpful action is easily available.[16] (Students instructed to ignore the story and to consider only the technical qualities of the broadcast do not have the same emotional experience.) Focus produces at least temporary salience.

As Adam Smith already observed, however, using the example of an earthquake in China, this focus is unstable, easily deflected back to oneself and one's immediate surroundings, unless more stable structures of concern are built upon it that ensure a continued concern with the people of that distant nation.[17] Thus one task of any political use of compassion will be to create stable structures of concern that extend compassion broadly; but, eudaimonism tells us, this will require creating a bridge between our current concerns and a broader circle of concerns that is still recognizably "us" and "ours."

What of empathy?[18] We may define empathy as the ability to imagine the situation of the other, taking the other's perspective. Thus, it is not merely knowledge of the other's states (which might in principle be obtained without perspectival displacement, for example by inference from past events); nor is it the same as thinking how one would feel oneself in the other person's place, difficult though it sometimes is to make the distinction.[19] Empathy is not mere emotional contagion, for it requires entering into the predicament of *another,* and this, in turn, requires some type of distinction between self and other, and a type of imaginative displacement.[20]

Empathy is not sufficient for compassion, for a sadist may have considerable empathy with the situation of another person, and use it to harm that person.[21] Lawyers may use empathy with a witness to help their clients by confusing or tripping up the witness. An actor may have consummate empathy with his or her character without any true compassion. (Indeed, an actor might play empathetically the part of a person to whom he or she deliberately refuses compassion, believing, for example, that the person brought all his suffering on himself, or that the person was upset about a predicament that is not really worth being upset about.)

Compassion, however, is often an outgrowth of empathy. Batson's experiments show that, other things held constant, the key variable distinguishing those in whom a story of woe elicits compassion from those in whom it does not is the experience of vivid imagining.[22] We can in principle feel compassion for the suffering of creatures whose experience we cannot imagine well, or perhaps even at all. Of course, we need some way of making sense to ourselves of the idea that they are suffering, that their predicament is really bad. But we can be convinced that animals of various sorts are suffering in the factory food industry, for example, without making much of an attempt to imagine what it is like to be a chicken or a pig. So empathy is not necessary for compassion. Often, however, it is extremely helpful. Given the imperfection of the human ability to assess predicaments, we should try as hard as we can to imagine the predicaments of others, and then see what we think about what we've imagined.

We should also grant that empathy involves something morally valuable in and of itself: namely, a recognition of the other as a center of experience. The empathetic torturer is very bad, but perhaps there is something worse still in the utter failure to recognize the other as a center of experience.[23]

IV. Compassion in Humans and Animals

Now we are in a position to think about continuities and discontinuities between human and animal compassion. The first thing to be said is that no nonhuman animal, so far as we know, has a robust conception of fault and nonfault; thus, the compassion of animals will potentially include many suffering people and animals to whom humans refuse compassion on grounds of fault. Animals notice suffering, and they notice it very keenly; they do not, however, form the idea "This person is not a worthy object of compassion, because she brought her suffering upon herself." This difference is at work in *Effi Briest.* But it is present as well in more morally attractive examples: for example, when a person is fired from a job for embezzlement, we will not feel compassion (or not much), although we would were the person fired because of an employer's practice of gender or racial discrimination.

Not all human compassion raises the issue of fault. There is a species of human compassion that is in that sense very similar to Rollo's, focusing on suffering without asking who is to blame.[24] Young children often have that sort of compassion, as Rousseau observes in *Emile,* saying of the boy's emotion: "Whether it is their fault is not now the question. Does he even know what fault is? Never violate the order of his knowledge. . . ."[25] (Later on, Emile does learn about fault, and this is an important ingredient of his social maturity, since compassion must be regulated by the sense of justice.)[26] Rousseau, however, places the sense of fault too late in human development: ideas of fault appear even in young infants. Even after the notion of fault firmly takes root, humans remain capable of the simpler type of compassion. The idea of fault, however, will often block this simpler response, as it does in the case of Effi's parents.

Further research in this area may show that some animals have a rudimentary idea of fault. To the extent that they have an idea of rule following, and of deviation from rule following, as does seem likely for some species, they may well be able to form the idea that some creatures bring their predicaments upon themselves by violating rules.[27] To the extent that they lack the idea that one can choose to pursue some purposes rather than others, however, they would not be likely to go very far in the direction of distinguishing appropriate from inappropriate choices. To the extent that they lack that conception, the idea of bringing misery on oneself would remain in a rudimentary form.

Beyond this, the comparison between humans and animals should focus on the idea of seriousness, the idea of similar possibilities, and what I have called the eudaimonistic thought. Frans de Waal argues that experiments with a wide range of animals show us a hierarchy of types of compassionate emotion. The simplest or most basic type of compassion (or behavior in the area of compassion, we ought to say) is *contagion.* (And, though it is difficult to make this distinction in practice, one really ought to distinguish here between mimetic behavior, or *behavioral contagion,* and a more inner and attitudinal *emotional contagion* that might be produced by the behavioral contagion, although it might also be produced in some other way.)[28] A more sophisticated type involves *perspective taking;* associated with this is *consolation,* behavior that shows concern for what the other creature is suffering, and, where possible, what de Waal calls *targeted helping,* helping behavior that responds to the specific features of the other creature's plight as seen from that creature's viewpoint. Perspective taking comes in degrees. It may be relatively rudimentary, not anchored to a firm grasp of the distinction between self and other. (Most monkeys, for example, are at this level, and we should probably place dogs here, since they exhibit considerable sympathy and yet fail the mirror test.) The second level becomes more sophisticated when the creature in question has a concept of the self and of the distinction between self and other, thus passing the mirror test. Chimps, bonobos, some elephants, and probably dolphins are at this level—along with humans. Thus, although I shall focus on elephants out of sheer interest, what I find there can also be found in studies of chimps and bonobos, our nearest biological relatives. So we are studying our own evolutionary heritage as well as our commonality with other living creatures. And of course this most complex level varies in extent: some creatures are capable of these attitudes only toward other members of their species; some, toward creatures with whom they have lived, even if of different species; and some appear to be capable of these attitudes toward people and animals that are at a distance and that are very unlike themselves.

De Waal uses the image of a series of nested Russian dolls: the inner-most small doll is contagion, and the large outer one is complex compassion, which will still bear traces of the inner. This image, however, is in some respects misleading. It does not include the ways in which the "outer" layers are non-isomorphic to the "inner," adding new materials (such as the judgment of fault); nor does it include the way in which the "outer" layers actually modify the "inner," as when the Briests' judgment of fault blocks their emotional contagion, or, in a happier case, when human judgments of fairness and impartiality block sympathy for a "mean" person or puppet who has taken something from someone else. Finally, it does not include ways in which simpler or more primitive experiences persist and modify the adult human emotion, as when, in Proust's novel, Marcel's adult sympathy for the woman he loves is colored (and interrupted) by the young child's primitive longing for comfort, which persists, unassuaged, in the adult personality.

Bearing these problems in mind, let's now consider three different cases of animal compassion/sympathy, which illustrate different levels of response that may also arise in the human case.

> *Case A.* In June 2006, a research team at McGill University[29] gave a painful injection to some mice, which induced squealing and writhing. (It was a weak solution of acetic acid, so it had no long-term harmful effects.) Also in the cage at the time were other mice who were not injected. The experiment had many variants and complexities, but to cut to the chase, if the non-pained mice were paired with mice with whom they had previously lived, the non-pained mice showed signs of being upset. If the non-pained mice had not previously lived with the pained mice, they did not show the same signs of emotional distress. On this basis, the experimenters conclude that the lives of mice involve social complexity: familiarity with particular other mice prepares the way for a type of emotional contagion that is at least the precursor to empathy.
>
> *Case B.* In Amboseli National Park in Africa, a young female elephant was shot by a poacher. Here is a description by Cynthia Moss of the reaction of other elephants in her group, a reaction typical in all three species of elephants:

> Teresia and Trista became frantic and knelt down and tried to lift
> her up. They worked their tusks under her back and under her head.
> At one point they succeeded in lifting her into a sitting position but
> her body flopped back down. Her family tried everything to rouse
> her, kicking and tusking her, and Tallulah even went off and col-
> lected a trunkful of grass and tried to stuff it into her mouth.

The elephants then sprinkled earth over the corpse, eventually
covering it completely before moving off.[30]

Case C. George Pitcher and Ed Cone were watching TV one
night in their Princeton home: a documentary about a little boy in
England with a congenital heart ailment. After various medical reversals, the boy died. Pitcher, sitting on the floor, found his eyes
filled with tears. Instantly their two dogs, Lupa and Remus, rushed
to him, almost pushing him over, and licked his eyes and cheeks
with plaintive whimpers.[31]

In the first case, we see something that we might call emotional contagion, at least of the behavioral type: that is, distress behavior at the sight
of another's distress behavior. We may very cautiously ascribe to these
mice some subjective feeling of discomfort, and perhaps there is contagion of feeling as well as behavior, but we have no reason to ascribe to the
mice any complex empathetic exercise of imagination, and no reason to
ascribe any sophisticated thoughts, such as the thought of seriousness or
the thought of similar possibilities. (Thus we do not see the responses
that de Waal called "perspective taking," "consolation," and "targeted
helping.")

Because the response seems not to include a cognitive appraisal of the
situation of the other mice as bad, I would not be inclined to call the response a genuine emotion, though it probably involves subjective feelings and not just mimetic behavior. The experiment is certainly interesting, showing a natural response to the sight of the pain of another that is
certainly among the precursors of compassion. (Rousseau made much of
this natural response, observing that the sight of pain is more powerful
in this respect than the sight of happiness: thus our weakness becomes a
source of our connection to others.) The most interesting feature, obviously, is the fact that the mice are moved by the plight of mice they know,

and not by that of mice they don't know. This suggests a surprising degree of cognitive complexity, and something like an ancestor of my eudaimonistic judgment. The mice are not precisely *thinking*, "These are my familiar pals, and their fate matters to me, whereas the fate of strangers doesn't matter"—but they have responses that are at least the basis for forming that very standard human thought. (Moreover, in humans the thought often influences action without being fully formulated, so humans are in that sense not always so far from these mice.) They have a personal point of view on the world—at least in a rudimentary sense—that differentiates between one group of mice and another group.

The second and third cases are rather similar, though with significant variations. In both, we see a recognition of the seriousness of the other creature's plight. The elephants are obviously aware that something major has happened to their friend: they recognize that her collapsed posture is the sign of some serious problem, and their increasingly frantic attempts to lift her up show their gradual awareness that the problem will not be rectified. We can ascribe to them some type of perspective taking, consolation, and targeted helping, although of a futile sort.

Pitcher's dogs know him well; like the elephants, they see that something unusual is going on, something that looks serious. Notice that the thought of seriousness tracks the actual suffering manifested by the other party: there is not the same possibility as in the human case of forming the thought, "This person is moaning and groaning, but the plight is not really serious." Thus, if Pitcher were a rich person for whom the thought of paying a just amount of tax brought tears of suffering to his eyes, Lupa and Remus would behave in just the same way. On the other side, if Pitcher were in a seriously bad way without being aware of it, and thus without manifesting suffering, the dogs would not have compassion for him. The dogs' behavior at least appears to involve a rudimentary perspective taking; it certainly displays consolation and targeted helping, since the dogs were familiar with the fact that their affectionate behavior was associated with improvement in Pitcher's manifest condition.

This case is different from that of the elephants in several ways. First, the dogs' behavior is more individualized and less group-based: they attend to particular humans, and they do not coordinate their behavior in group terms. Second, their behavior may not involve as sophisticated a perspectival capacity as that of the elephants, since dogs fail the mirror test. Third, the behavior takes a cross-species object, reflecting the fact that dogs are a symbiotic species, whose evolutionary history has selected for a high level of attentiveness to the behavior of humans, and particular humans are usually built into their circle of concern. Elephants sometimes bond with humans; thus, when researcher Joyce Poole returned to her elephant group in Kenya after a maternity leave, bringing her little baby with her, the elephants put on the ceremony of trumpeting and defecating with which they standardly greet the birth of a new baby elephant.[32] This behavior, however, suggests that they treated Poole as an honorary member of their group, rather than that they attended to her as an individual outside their group who mattered for their well-being.

Returning to Pitcher and the dogs, there is a subtle difference between Pitcher's compassion for the little boy in the documentary and the compassion of the dogs for Pitcher, for the former is mediated by the thought of non-fault in a way that the latter is not. Pitcher draws attention to the fact that he was raised by a Christian Scientist mother who thought that children (and others) were always to blame for their illnesses, a very severe upbringing. Having rejected these ideas as an adult, Pitcher is able to see the little boy as a victim of circumstances. I think that his intense reaction to the documentary may have been connected to the thought of himself as a boy, cut off from compassion because of the blame that illness always brought with it: in part, he is having compassion for his own childhood self and the lack of care he experienced. The thesis of Pitcher's book is the Fontane-like thesis that dogs are capable of an unconditional type of love—not even raising the issue of fault—that humans have difficulty achieving; in that sense, the often errant judgment of fault, with its ability to disrupt compassion, is very important to his whole analysis.

Pitcher, then, suggests that the judgment of fault is usually a defect, and that animals are better off morally because they lack it. We should not follow him all the way. Dogs' inability to form the judgment of fault at times leads them to remain loyal despite cruel behavior. Women have frequently experienced a similar inability to judge fault, and their failure to judge their abusers can be a very serious failing. In general, for a subordinated group, recognizing reasons for anger and blame can be an important part of asserting one's equal dignity. While not following Pitcher all the way to a fault-free doctrine of unconditional love, however, we can certainly observe that humans often find fault erroneously, hastily, and on the basis of bad social norms—as indeed Pitcher's mother did, blaming his illnesses on his own guilt. To that extent, looking to animals for guidance would seem to be a wise thing to do.

Turning now to the eudaimonistic thought, we see that, as with seriousness, there is some reasonable analogue in our second and third animal cases. The elephants think that the well-being of their fellow female matters, and their behavior betrays their sense of that importance. Similarly, the elephants in my opening railroad example show such a keen awareness of the importance of the calves for their well-being that they are prepared to take what turns out to be a fatal risk. The eudaimonistic circle is narrow, focusing on kin and the immediate group. (At times it appears to extend to other species members, as when elephants recognize the bones of other elephants with a type of apparent ritual behavior.) The dogs, as is usual with dogs, ascribe immense importance to their narrow circle of humans, and react to Pitcher's distress as they would never react to the distress of a stranger, whether canine or human.

Given that it has recently been shown that elephants can form a conception of the self, passing the mirror test,[33] we should probably conclude that the elephants' ability to form something like the eudaimonistic judgment is more sophisticated than that of the two dogs: having the ability to distinguish self from other, they are able to form a conception of the self as having a distinctive set of goals and ends, to a greater degree, at any rate, than is possible for animals who do not form a conception of the self.

There is something like the eudaimonistic thought in our two animal cases, then, but there is no reason to suppose that this thought possesses much flexibility. Elephants care about other elephants, above all members of their group, and also at times other species members. Occasionally this concern is extended, through long experience, to a human who becomes something like a member of the group, as with Poole and her baby daughter. Dogs are much more standardly symbiotic: indeed, far from showing particular concern for dogs as such, they are far more likely to include in the circle of concern whatever creatures they know and live with, including humans, dogs, and occasionally even cats or horses. In neither case, however, is the circle of concern very responsive to argument or education. We cannot expect elephants to learn to care for the survival of other African species; we certainly cannot expect predatory animals to learn compassion for the species they kill; and we cannot expect dogs to attach themselves to a person or dog without prolonged experience. Indeed, as Pitcher makes clear, Lupa and Remus continued to be very suspicious of all other humans, and most animals as well. In the human case there is—at least, we hope there is—a good deal more flexibility than this: people can learn to care about the sufferings they inflict on animals by killing them for food; they can learn to care about the sufferings of people they have never met.

What about similar possibilities? Humans learn, fairly early, that there are some forms of vulnerability that human life contains for all: bodily frailty and disease, pain, wounds, death. Indeed, Rousseau believed that the inevitability of this learning was morality's great advantage in the war against hierarchy and domination: whenever a privileged group tries to think of itself as above the common human lot, this fragile self-deceptive stratagem is quickly exposed by life itself. Life is constantly teaching the lesson of human equality:

> Human beings are not naturally kings, or lords, or courtiers, or rich people. All are born naked and poor; all are subject to the miseries of life; to sorrows, ills, needs, and pains of every kind. Finally, all are condemned to death. This is what truly belongs to the human being. This is what no mortal is exempt from.[34]

So: to what extent do animals in our second and third cases form such ideas, and in what form?

It seems likely that elephants do have some conception of death and of various related bad things, as standard events in elephant life. Their standard and almost ritualized responses to death indicate that they have at least a rudimentary conception of a species form of life and of the events that can disrupt it (or, as in the case of the birth of a child, enrich it). The fact that elephants can form a conception of the self is helpful in forming a conception of the elephant kind: for one can hardly recognize oneself as a member of a kind without recognizing oneself as a unit distinct from others. It seems less clear whether dogs have such ideas, though they certainly can remember experiences of hunger and pain (the traumatized and abused Lupa always trembled at the sight of a stick), and, to that extent, conceive of such bad events as future possibilities for themselves.

V. Looking at Animals: Shared and Nonshared Roots of Morality

From the point of view of our nations, which are striving for justice, the animal heritage of human compassion is promising, but has obvious shortcomings. It is narrow in extent, relatively rigid, typically hostile to strangers, incapable of connecting to the distant through the imagination. Animal compassion, furthermore, contains no sense of the difference between fault and nonfault, and no deliberative evaluation of what is worth getting upset about. Moreover, animals appear not to rank and order ends (or not in a reflective way), and thus are typically unable to inhibit desire satisfaction for the sake of a more valued goal—although the altruism of the elephants in my opening example, like other examples of risk-taking altruism in the apes studied by de Waal, shows that there is a generosity in animal behavior that goes beyond mere satisfaction of desire.

Research on human infants has shown that humans, from a very early age, prior to social learning, are well equipped to go further in these respects. Like many animals, they exhibit emotional contagion, connected to a propensity for mimicry.[35] But quickly they progress to perspective taking and empathy: they are adept "mind readers" from an extremely early age,[36] and they quickly learn to make a distinction between their own pain and the pain of another person: babies cry to recordings of the cries of other babies more than to other noises, *and more than to recordings of their own cries.*[37] So they could already be said to be experiencing the emotion of compassion. By the time they are ten months old, they engage in spontaneous helping and consolatory behavior, and by two years old they also display signs of guilt after they harm someone. (Girls show more of this behavior than boys of a similar age.)[38]

Finally, fascinating findings by Paul Bloom establish that the idea of fault, and emotional adjustments based upon this idea, are firmly established by around the age of twelve months. Bloom's experiments show puppets engaging in helpful and in selfish actions; babies overwhelmingly prefer the former to the latter.[39] They also prefer the helper to a neutral character, and the neutral character to a mean character. But then he shows four more complex scenarios: (a) a "helper" is rewarded by another character; (b) a "helper" is punished by another character; (c) a "meanie" (who has done something harmful to another) is rewarded by another character; (d) a "meanie" is punished by another character. The researchers found that, despite the general preference for "good" actors over "bad," they liked the "bad" (mean) actors when those actors are punishing bad behavior. So the babies not only have contagion plus empathy and compassionate emotion, they also have a sense of fault that promotes and/or inhibits compassion. All of this is part of our human equipment prior to social shaping, and it gives us resources.

A crucial resource, again apparently absent among animals, is the human capacity for impartiality, and our recognition that partiality is an ethical problem. (Bloom calls this "the core of mature morality.") This part of human culture, however, does not appear in the behavior of babies. Babies, like nonhuman animals, are biased toward their own kind. They prefer the faces of the racial type that is most familiar to those of unfamiliar races; they prefer speakers of their language to speakers of a foreign language.[40] Paul Bloom concludes, "The aspect of morality that we truly marvel at—its generality and universality—is the product of culture, not biology."[41]

What types of narrowness does culture particularly need to overcome? Batson shows that there is no intrinsic limitation to empathic concern for people at a great distance, provided that their predicament is described vividly.[42] Nor is prior personal experience of the need in question necessary for concern.[43] But other limitations, very likely rooted in our animal heritage, make compassionate concern imperfectly correlated with what any reasonable morality would require. First of all, concern is wavering and inconstant, often diminishing over time and thus failing to sustain helping efforts required to address chronic problems.[44]

More troubling still, people often act immorally, by their own lights, as a result of empathy-induced compassion. Subjects who are given a vivid story of another person's plight tend overwhelmingly to diverge from a principle of fairness that they themselves have endorsed, in matters involving both trivial rewards and life-or-death choices (organ donations). The person whose story they have imagined is overwhelmingly preferred to candidates more deserving by standards of fairness to which people already assent.[45] Human beings, in effect, have two systems of judgment: a system based in the imagination and perspectival thinking, and a system grounded in principle.[46] (These do not correspond to the well-known psychologists' distinction between "System I" and "System II," a contrast between an undeliberated and quasi-instinctual set of reactions and a system grounded in conscious deliberation. The imagination can involve conscious effort to see clearly, and the application of rules can be reflexive and undeliberated. Although the two are often complementary—imagination showing the human meaning of the cases ranged under the principle—they also diverge and even conflict.)

For this reason we must not regard compassion as an uncriticized foundation for public choice. Emotional foundationalism is as pernicious as neglect of the emotions. Nor, however, should we discard the information compassion contains, or else our principles risk being empty of significance and motivational efficacy. We must arrange for a continual, and watchful, *dialogue* between vivid imagining and impartial principle, seeking the best and most coherent fit, always asking what we're entitled to give to those whose situation we vividly imagine and how far we need, by contrast, to follow impartial principle. And we must also try energetically to construct a *bridge* from the vividly imagined single case to the impartial principle by challenging the imagination, reminding people that a predicament to which they respond in a single vividly described case is actually far broader. A public culture of compassion must be concerned with both the dialogue and the bridge.

Looking at our animal heritage, then, we see some seeds of the moral attitudes that sustain just institutions, but we also see many limitations that we should try to transcend, and we see that we have both the biological and the cultural equipment to address them—in principle at least.

VI. Looking at Animals: Nonshared Pathologies

Thinking about those dogs and elephants, and about the altruistic chimps and bonobos studied by de Waal,[47] we notice that their world does not contain some very bad tendencies that the human world clearly contains. In *Effi Briest,* the dog Rollo looks like a morally superior being, because, unlike Effi's own father and mother, he is not deflected from compassion for Effi's illness and premature death by a warped judgment of fault that rejects a "fallen woman" as unworthy of parental love. What nonhuman animal would have such a bizarre idea? Similarly, the dogs Lupa and Remus showed George Pitcher a kind of unconditionality in love that he had not experienced in his own childhood, dominated as it was by harsh and unfortunate judgments of fault, in particular the religious doctrine that sick children have caused their own physical illness through moral failure. Having the generally valuable capacity to see ourselves as beings who can make choices, pursuing some inclinations and inhibiting others, we also develop the capacity to impute defective choice to others, and we inhibit compassion on that account. This capacity to think about fault and choice is generally valuable, a necessary part of moral life. And yet it can go badly astray.

Sometimes it goes wrong because people want to insulate themselves from demands made by others. Thus, it is very convenient to blame the poor for their poverty and to refuse compassion on that account. If we think this way, we don't have to do anything about the situation of the poor.[48] Sometimes, defective social traditions play the deforming role: the idea that a woman who has sex outside marriage is for all time irredeemably stained, unworthy of friendship or love, was a prominent cultural attitude in nineteenth-century Germany, and it is this attitude that blocks the Briests from responding to their daughter's misery. Although in Pitcher's case the warping judgments are religious in origin, and although our imaginary nations have agreed to respect a wide range of religious and secular comprehensive doctrines that reasonable citizens hold, the doctrine that children's evil is responsible for their physical illnesses is surely an unreasonable doctrine, and one that our nations would be entitled to repudiate in public rhetoric and public education.

Judgments of fault clearly suffer from a variety of distortions, which cannot be traced to a single source.

Thinking about the animal world, we notice some other types of bad behavior that animals do not engage in: genocide, sadistic torture, ethnic cleansing. In the following chapter we'll investigate some of the possible roots of these deformities. Here, however, it is time to mention one prominent distortion in human emotions: what de Waal has called "anthropodenial," the tendency of humans to refuse to acknowledge their animality and their kinship with other animals. Remember Updike's Rabbit: asked whether he isn't, after all, a chimp, he says to himself that he is "A god-made one-of-a-kind with an immortal soul breathed in. A vehicle of grace. A battlefield of good and evil. An apprentice angel." People brought up on such thoughts usually develop correspondingly negative reactions to the signs of their own animality: sweat, urine, feces, sexual fluids. The animal body inspires the aspiring angel with disgust and shame. Swift's Gulliver, having enjoyed the somewhat ethereal society of the Houyhnhnms—clean, non-smelly, and hardly bodily at all—cannot endure the touch of Yahoos like himself.

No nonhuman animal denies that it is an animal, hates being an animal, shrinks from others of its kind because they are animals. None aspires to be an angel, above the body and its smells and fluids. Anthropodenial affects human relationships with the other animals, clearly: Rabbit's view of what a chimp or a pig is is inflected by his conception of himself as an angel. Humans frequently deny compassion to the suffering of animals on account of this irrational splitting of the world of nature. This splitting also inhibits the dispassionate study of the animal roots of human morality and emotion.

But things are worse than this, as we already see in the Swift example, for Gulliver behaves extremely badly, refusing all sympathy and love to his own family out of aversion to their smell and touch. No nonhuman animal has such pathologies, pervasive sources of bad behavior in social life. So the study of animals also shows us clearly what we don't do well, and what a good society will need to repress or reeducate.

Notice that the desire not to die, to extend one's own life span and that of one's loved ones, is not anthropodenial. Animals typically strive to live longer, and the more complex animals grieve at the death of those for whom they care. So the idea that death is bad and that we should struggle against it is ubiquitous, and does not reflect a fundamental refusal of the condition of being animal. The phenomenon that is troubling is not always easy to distinguish from the normal aversion to death, but it consists in a disgusted repudiation of mortality itself, and the body as its seat.

By studying the other animals, we learn a great deal about common roots of compassion and altruism on which we can potentially draw. We also learn that we have both resources and problems that animals do not have, and that we have at least some latitude in determining what tendencies will prevail in our social lives. Deliberating about these tendencies is a major task of our aspiring nations.

CHAPTER SEVEN

"Radical Evil": Helplessness, Narcissism, Contamination

The runaway slave came to my house and stopt outside,
I heard his motions crackling the twigs of the woodpile,
Through the swung half-door of the kitchen I saw him limpsy
    and weak,
And went where he sat on a log and led him in and assured him
And brought water and fill'd a tub for his sweated body and
    bruis'd feet,
And gave him a room that enter'd from my own, and gave him
    some coarse clean clothes,
And remember perfectly well his revolving eyes and his
    awkwardness,
And remember putting plasters on the galls of his neck and
    ankles;
He staid with me a week before he was recuperated and pass'd
    north,
I had him sit next me at table, my fire-lock lean'd in the corner.

          —Walt Whitman, "Song of Myself"

"I must insist on it. It is impossible to take food in your room so long as you keep on that Christian maidservant Lachmi."

"Oh, Gora dear, how can you bring yourself to utter such words!" exclaimed Anandamoyi, greatly distressed. "Have you not all along eaten food from her hand, for it was she who nursed you and brought you up? Only till quite lately, you could not relish your food without the chutney prepared by her. Besides, can I ever forget how she saved your life, when you had smallpox, by her devoted nursing?"

"Then pension her off," said Gora impatiently. "Buy her some land and build a cottage for her; but you must not keep her in the house, mother!"

—Rabindranath Tagore, *Gora*

I. "Radical Evil" in Human Social Life

A just nation needs to try to understand the roots of human bad behavior.[1] It is difficult to know how citizens' dignity and equality should be protected, if we do not know what we are up against. Take antidiscrimination laws. Libertarian thinkers argue that these laws are unnecessary, because discrimination is economically inefficient. All the just state needs to do is to remove artificial barriers to trade, minority hiring, and so forth.[2] Employers, being rational, will quickly see that hiring minority workers is in their interest. Such an account rests on a particular story about human motivation: employers are taken to be rational actors who seek to maximize the satisfaction of their own preferences; moreover, their preferences do not include malicious or sadistic preferences, such as a preference for subordinating or humiliating others. The same is taken to be true of workers and customers: they will happily work in or buy from integrated businesses because they will see that these businesses offer an efficient solution to a social problem. They will not be held back by entrenched hatred, disgust, or, again, the desire to humiliate through segregationist practices. All are understood, moreover, to have a nondeformed view of the potentiality of African Americans, rather than a view deformed by racist stereotypes, whether those impute laziness, low ability, or criminal propensity.

Libertarian politics is naïve, because people are just not like that. Denials of equal opportunity to Jews, African Americans, Asian Americans, and (in India) members of lower castes were not supported by a clear-eyed assessment of economic costs and benefits;[3] indeed, they resulted in a colossal waste of human capital. And as John Stuart Mill observed, the most ubiquitous and enduring exclusion of all, the exclusion of women from employment opportunities and political participation, is a bizarre policy for a utility-maximizing society, and one that could be held in place only by irrational prejudice. Mill, however, lacks a theoretical account of what produces these exclusions. In central theoretical passages, he focuses on the need to extend compassion; in discussing women, he gestures at some darker motives but fails to explore them philosphically. We need to develop some plausible account of the forces that produce these and related ills, since a just society must take steps to combat them.

Different religious and secular views of human life have different accounts of the roots of bad behavior. The doctrine of "original sin" takes various forms, and some religious accept it, while others do not. Secular moralities vary greatly too: some use an idea of natural goodness, ascribing bad behavior to defective social formations, while others use ideas of original narcissism or Oedipal envy that suggest deeper and more universal roots for the tendency to behave badly. It might seem impossible, therefore, for a pluralistic society to choose among the contending views without establishing a particular religion or secular comprehensive doctrine. I shall suggest, however, that by following the lead of empirical work on disgust, compassion, peer pressure, authority, and other human tendencies—as well as clinical work on child development and the capacities for empathy and concern—we can extract the core of a "reasonable political psychology" that people of many different overall views may endorse as a basis for political thought, considering it to be one element in their more comprehensive (and, to that extent, different) understandings of human nature.

Our study of our kinship—and lack of it—with nonhuman animals has given us a start on this problem. We have learned that human beings, like other animals, tend to be narrow in sympathy, inclined to prefer a narrower group to a broader one. But our account has gone beyond that insight, identifying the salient role human reluctance to acknowledge animality and mortality plays in explaining some failures of compassion. We still lack an account, however, of how these problems arise in the personality, how they develop, and how wise interventions might make a difference.

Stigma and exclusion are central among the problems our societies must combat. Unlike our optimistic nineteenth-century predecessors, we cannot help knowing that human beings have deeper problems than mere narrowness of sympathy. The society that for centuries maintained the Hindu caste system taught upper-caste people to feel disgusted and violated by contact with a lower-caste or noncaste person. (Given that she is a household servant, the Christian woman described in Tagore's *Gora* is very likely to be a convert from the lowest castes; thus she is doubly unacceptable.) Gora cannot eat food served by such a person, nor does he want such a person residing in his house. His case is unusual, because, brought up by a mother without caste prejudice, he once accepted and even loved this Christian woman; nor does he seem personally disgusted by her. His assumption of caste attitudes is late and external, as if he is applying a learned rule of conduct to himself. Most traditional Hindus of his caste, by contrast, would have learned a more visceral disgust. Southern bigots in the United States had a similar visceral loathing for African Americans. Jim Crow laws prohibiting miscegenation and segregating lunch counters, swimming pools, and drinking fountains expressed the dominant white population's strongly visceral aversion to any sort of contact with the African American body. Such laws refused humanity to that body in a very basic sense. Whitman's hospitality to the runaway slave—and, especially, his willingness to share food and clothing with him—is a deliberately shocking image of the new democratic and egalitarian society that American might become, could it ever cast off these irrational ideas of defilement. Perhaps the most daring detail in the section is the bandaging of the slave's open sores, an act involving intimate contact with bodily fluids.

Group hatred and loathing are a major part of what our nations agree to oppose. Even in Rawls's well-ordered society, where such discrimination is absent, it cannot be guaranteed that it will not arise, given the reality of human psychology; our societies, however, are aspiring rather than fully well-ordered, so they have to struggle with real problems of exclusion. They therefore need a more nuanced understanding of human motivation than that underlying the optimistic nineteenth-century account. What Mill and Comte omit is real evil: deliberately cruel and ugly behavior toward others that is not simply a matter of inadvertence or neglect, or even fear-tinged suspicion, but which involves some active desire to denigrate or humiliate. This tendency is central to in-group hatred and group discrimination. Comte and Mill ignored it at their peril. Their naïve faith in humanity and in moral progress is impossible to sustain today. Tagore sees more deeply: in the school at Santiniketan shared bodily rituals (music and dance, above all) played a crucial role in addressing group divisions.

This chapter will propose a working understanding of some prominent human tendencies to bad behavior. While the account will agree with Immanuel Kant in finding in all human beings something like "radical evil"—namely, a set of presocial tendencies to bad behavior, tendencies that go beyond those rooted in our shared animal heritage and which lie beneath cultural variation—it will also conclude that culture can do a lot to shape these tendencies. The remedies proposed by the Comteans were bound to be inadequate, given that their conception of human psychology was thin and incomplete. The fuller story we uncover here will show why respect and even sympathy, without love, is insufficient and dangerously unstable.

The role of love in the story unfolded here comes in two stages. In a first stage, a child's helplessness and primitive shame lead to rage and destructive tendencies, which can be surmounted in the direction of concern only by a strong emotion of love toward the object whose destruction is both feared and sought. But even when a child has managed to develop capacities for genuine concern, persisting insecurities make it prone to "projective disgust" and the subordination of others, as people learn to split the world of humans into favored and stigmatized groups—a tendency exacerbated by the narrowness inherent in our animal heritage. Here, at a second stage, love needs to come to the rescue: only a vigorous imaginative engagement with another person's particularity will undo or prevent the ravages of group-based stigma and reveal citizens to one another as whole and unique people. It is crucial not only to have had love in one's childhood, then, but also to be able to renew it on each occasion when one's "inner eyes" are dim.

II. Kant on Evil: The Need for a Fuller Account

Any philosophical account of innate tendencies to evil would do well to begin with Immanuel Kant's famous account of "radical evil." Kant was deeply influenced by the social contract doctrines of both Locke and Rousseau, and, like Rousseau, he understood that a just society has to think about the political emotions and the likely roots of bad behavior. Unlike Rousseau, and like our aspiring nations, he was committed to a genuinely liberal society, with firm protections for freedoms of speech and association.[4] Thus his efforts to supply a psychology of bad behavior fall squarely within the parameters of our project.

Kant holds that the roots of bad behavior lie deep in human beings, deeper than any particular social formation. In effect, they are embedded in the very nature of human life. In *Religion within the Boundaries of Mere Reason,*[5] he articulates his famous doctrine of "radical evil."[6] Evil is radical, according to Kant—that is to say, it goes to the root of our humanity—because human beings, prior to concrete social experience, have a propensity to both good and evil, in the form of tendencies that are deeply rooted in our natures.[7] We are such that we can follow the moral law, treating others as equals and as ends, but there is also something about us that makes it virtually inevitable that under certain circumstances we will disregard it and behave badly.

What are those conditions? Animality itself is not the problem; our animal nature, says Kant, is basically neutral (6.32, 6.57–58). Thus Kant agrees with the diagnosis offered in our last chapter: the fact that we are animals is not the primary source of our moral difficulty. Kant, of course, articulates the distinction between human and animal with less nuance and awareness of continuity than contemporary research would support (and, indeed, with less subtlety than was present already in Aristotle); nor does he acknowledge that at least some of our moral problems (narrowness of sympathy, in-group preference) are rooted in a shared animal heritage. His key contention, however, is plausible: the tempter, the invisible enemy inside, is something peculiarly human, a propensity to competitive self-love, which manifests itself whenever human beings are in a group. The appetites all by themselves are easily satisfied, and animal need is limited (6.93). The human being considers himself poor only "to the extent that he is anxious that other human beings will consider him poor and will despise him for it." But a sufficient condition of such anxiety is the mere presence of others:

> Envy, addiction to power, avarice, and the malignant inclinations associated with these, assail his nature, which on its own is undemanding, *as soon as he is among human beings.* Nor is it necessary to assume that these are sunk into evil and are examples that lead him astray; it suffices that they are there, that they surround him, and that they are human beings, and they will mutually corrupt each other's moral disposition and make one another evil. (6.94)

Kant's account is powerful. Although he surely is too sanguine about the opportunity of many of the world's people to satisfy bodily need, he is also surely right in holding that mere satisfaction is not the biggest cause of bad behavior. Even when people are well fed and housed, and even when they are reasonably secure with respect to other prerequisites of well-being, they still behave badly to one another and violate one another's rights. And even though a presocietal propensity is a difficult thing to demonstrate, Kant is surely right when he suggests that people require no special social teaching in order to behave badly, and indeed regularly do so despite the best social teaching.

Radical evil might be an innate tendency, or it might be a tendency that grows out of general structural features of human life that are encountered prior to a child's experience of any particular culture, or at least in all experiences of all particular cultures. Kant probably imagines an innate tendency, but the spirit of his account is preserved if we emphasize that innate tendencies are activated by general structural features of human life (mortality, scarcity, interdependence of various kinds), and that the tendencies to bad behavior are likely to be outgrowths of this interaction.

Kant's account of radical evil, while attractive in many respects, is incomplete. It is all very well to say that there are propensities in human beings such that the presence of others will elicit competition and aggressive behavior, but Kant says little about their nature. Perhaps he thinks that there is nothing more to be said: radical evil is just the disposition to manifest competitive and morality-defying behavior in the presence of others. We need to say more. Kant does not even identify a sufficiently wide range of types of bad behavior: he includes envy and competition, but omits racial and ethnic hatred, the desire to degrade and humiliate, the love of cruelty for its own sake.

III. The Center of the Universe

What lies behind the anxious competitiveness that Kant calls "radical evil"? Unlike Kant, we should grant that "animality"—a shared animal heritage—is at least part of the problem. Our relatively narrow sense of who matters is certainly learned in the course of life, and it is somewhat responsive to learning, but it has its roots, as well, in a structure of imagination and affection that is a part of our likely evolutionary heritage, what enabled humans to survive as a species. We reject many aspects of that heritage (for example, we do not think it right to abandon elderly people and people with disabilities, as animals typically do), and we should in some respects seek to transcend this one, pursuing the goal of impartiality that humans can attain only through culture and morality. In Part III we'll consider how this might be attempted. But we have also agreed with Kant that animality is not our only, or even our primary, problem: the primary sources of group hatred, stigmatization, and exclusion must be sought in structures peculiar to human life.

All creatures are born weak and needy, and all seek both sustenance and security. (These needs are to some degree independent: experiments have shown that even monkeys, when the source of food is separated artificially from the source of comfort, spend more time getting cuddled than feeding.)[8] Human beings, however, have an odd type of infancy, known nowhere else in the animal kingdom. With other animals, the skills of survival begin to be present right from birth, as standing, moving around, and actively searching for the sources of nourishment and security begin virtually immediately; cognitive maturity (the ability to articulate the perceptual field, grasping the good and bad in it) and bodily maturity develop in tandem. By the time the creature has a robust sense of its practical goals, it also has resources for attaining them.

Human life is not like this. In part because of the large size of the human head, which imposes severe constraints on intrauterine development, humans are born in a state of physical helplessness unknown in any other species. A horse that could not stand up soon after birth would soon die. A human stands no earlier than ten months of age, and walks—with difficulty—only at around a year of age. Articulate speech is also limited by physical capacities (although it begins to appear that sign language can be learned much earlier). Meanwhile, infants have cognitive powers that are more fully appreciated all the time, as psychologists find new ways to test cognition that do not rely on speech or motion. They can distinguish many parts of the perceptual field soon after birth—distinguishing, for example, the smell of their own mother's milk from that of another mother's milk within the first two weeks of life. The capacity to divide self from others and to "read" the minds of others develops rapidly, as Bloom shows, during the first year of life. So human infants are both highly intelligent and helpless, a combination that shapes emotional development, not always for the good.

In the beginning, the infant experiences itself as a diffuse center of experience, impinged upon by various external forces, benign and malign. Psychologist Daniel Stern describes an infant's hunger in language that powerfully conveys, through imagery, what we have been able to learn experimentally (most of it in Stern's own work):

> A storm threatens. The light turns metallic. The march of clouds across the sky breaks apart. Pieces of sky fly off in different directions. The wind picks up force, in silence. There are rushing sounds, but no motion. The wind and its sound have separated. Each chases after its lost partner in fits and starts. The world is disintegrating. Something is about to happen.
>
> Uneasiness grows. It spreads from the center and turns into pain.
>
> It is at the center that the storm breaks out. It is at the very center that it grows stronger and turns into pulsing waves. These waves push the pain out, then pull it back again. . . .
>
> The pulsing waves swell to dominate the whole weatherscape. The world is howling. Everything explodes and is blown out and

then collapses and rushes back toward a knot of agony that cannot last—but does.[9]

As Stern notes, this description captures the power of hunger, an experience that sweeps through the entire nervous system, disrupting whatever was going on before and imposing its own rhythms and sensations. The sensations affect movement, breathing, attention, perception—everything. The experience disorganizes the world, ripping attention away and even fracturing the normal rhythm of breath. Moreover, breathing and crying are not coordinated, and neither of these is coordinated with arm and leg movements. Finally the full cry emerges, with great gulpings of air. The coordination of yelling with deep breathing gives momentary relief, but agony continues to mount.

A short time later, the "hunger storm" abates as the infant begins to nurse:

> At once the world is enveloped. It becomes smaller and slower and more gentle. The envelope pushes away the vast empty spaces. Everything is shifting. A faint promise spurts. The pulsations of explosion and collapse are being tamed. But they are still there, still wild, still ready to break through.
>
> Somewhere between the boundary and the very center of the storm, there is a tug, a pulling together. Two magnets wobble toward each other, then touch, lock tight.
>
> At the point of contact, a new, fast rhythm begins. It rides on top of the slowly pulsing waves of the storm. This new rhythm is short and greedy. Everything strains to strengthen it. With each beat, a current flows to the center. The current warms the chill. It cools the fire. It loosens the knot at the center and saps the fierceness of the pulsations until they subside once and for all.
>
> The new rhythm shifts into an easy, smooth pace. The rest of the world relaxes and trails in its wake.
>
> All is remade. A changed world is waking. The storm has passed. The winds are quiet. The sky is softened. Running lines and flowing volumes appear. They trace a harmony and, like shifting light, make everything come alive.

These descriptions—every detail of which is grounded in research—help remind us of some important points that can easily be missed from the vantage point of adulthood. First is the sheer magnitude of hunger as a disruption of the entire system. Adults looking at infants can easily underestimate the experience, because adults know that it is normal and not a sign of danger, and that the infant will shortly be fed. Nor is adult hunger disruptive in anything like the same way, unless it is prolonged. It is natural that an event this cataclysmic, as the infant develops a sense of the future and of itself as a persisting being, would become the object of intense fear, and its relief the object of joy and gratitude.

Second, we are reminded of how completely solipsistic the infant's world originally is. All experiences radiate from its own internal states, and although the infant is not yet able to demarcate itself from the surrounding environment in a secure way, its awareness is entirely of itself, and of external agencies only insofar as they lock, magnetlike, onto itself and cause an alteration in its own states.

This solipsism is not total: as Stern also describes, infants love light, and in calm moods they stare at whatever most attracts their attention. From the beginning, the world is somehow lovable and interesting, not simply an agent of pain relief. There is a self-directed tendency toward relief—security and freedom from distress—but there is also an outward-pulling tendency to investigate, a kind of incipient wonder, which prepares the way for love.

As the infant becomes more fully aware of itself as a demarcated center of experience (learning, for example, the difference between its own toes and another object at a similar distance), it also becomes aware that its hunger and distress are relieved by agencies external to itself—the breast, and the arms that shelter and comfort. For quite some time these agencies are not seen as parts of whole people; they are pieces of the world that do things for the infant. So, the solipsism of infancy colors its first relations to objects: other people figure in the infant's perceptions and emotions as pieces of the world that help (by feeding and holding) or hinder (by not being there immediately, or for long enough). In this way the infant develops an idea that the world is all about its own needs and ought to meet those needs, and is bad if it does not. *Everything should be waiting on me,* is the general shape of this thought—the source of Freud's

wonderful image, "His Majesty the Baby." Babies are indeed like royalty, seeing the world as revolving around them and their needs. They
are also like royalty in their helplessness, their demand for constant service if their needs are to be met. (For this reason, Rousseau concluded
that instruction in practical self-sufficiency was a key requirement of
democratic citizenship.) But of course their helplessness is far more complete, and so they are in the ridiculous position of expecting to be the
center of the world, but having no way of enforcing or even promoting
their wishes, other than crying. From this situation develops a host of
intense emotions: fear of abandonment and hunger; joy at the restoration of the world; anger when the needed food and comfort do not arrive when wished; and, gradually, shame at the dissonance between
expectation and reality. *I am the monarch, and yet here I am alone,
hungry, and wet.*

From this early situation of narcissism grows a tendency to think of
other people as mere slaves, not full people with needs and interests of
their own. How might this narcissism ever be surmounted in the direction of stable concern for others? That is the problem that all good
societies need to try to solve, and we might say that the combination
of narcissism with helplessness—a helplessness that is resented and
repudiated—is where "radical evil" gets its start, in the form of a tendency to subordinate other people to one's own needs. We now can situ-
ate the "anthropodenial" of Chapter 6 in a richer developmental context:
what is really resented and denied is not humanity *tout court,* it is the
helplessness that we feel, on account of bodies that are vulnerable and
often powerless.

The frustration of need creates an opportunity, as well as pain: the
opportunity to come to grips with the reality of an external independent
person. As Donald Winnicott puts it, "[I]ncomplete adaptation to
need makes objects real, that is to say hated as well as loved."[10] But the
infant's narcissism powerfully resists this reality, since perfect adaptation to need is omnipotence, and omnipotence is easier to deal with than
interdependence.

It's obvious that narcissism of this type goes on exercising a pernicious
influence in most human lives, as people focus greedily on their own security and satisfaction, neglecting the claims of others, or even seeking to

convert them into a slave class who can be relied on to promote security. If we imagine an angel growing up—never having been wet and hungry, never having been helplessly dependent upon others—we see that such a being would have few reasons to be greedy or self-promoting.

Sometimes people overcome narcissism in a narrow circle of close personal relations, for whom genuine concern is learned, but sometimes they don't even do that. Think of the central character in Proust's novel. Although an adult of remarkable sensitivity and strong emotion, he remains utterly self-focused, thinking of others as servants of his inclinations, whom he must control or suffer terrible torment. He has not progressed beyond the rigid and terrified little boy who used to long for his mother to sleep in his room all night—knowing in advance that the joy of her arrival would already be sullied by the pain of her expected departure. Moreover, articulate rationalizer of his own pathology that he is, he repeatedly informs us that all apparent love and friendship are nothing more than this desire for possession and control. (He does think that the activity of the writer of fiction involves genuinely loving attention to the world—only, however, because the writer is not dealing with real people and the uncertainties they impose.)

In essence, this is anthropodenial: the refusal to accept one's limited animal condition, a stance toward the world that no nonhuman animal has. To expect to be complete (or continually completed) is to expect to be above the human lot. Infants cannot imagine a human sort of interdependency, since they are not aware that human life is a life of need and reciprocity and that, through reciprocity, needs will be regularly met. Their helplessness produces an intense anxiety that is not mitigated by trust in the world or its people. The only solution is perfection, and the only way of achieving perfection is making other people one's slaves.

How could a human being cease to be like this? Part of the story must indeed, as Rousseau urged, involve increasing practical mastery: like other animals, human beings can become far less helpless than they are at first, and the confidence that one can meet one's own needs to some degree removes the need to enslave others. Still, the terror of early helplessness leaves a mark, and it is not surprising that many human beings do succumb to the alluring fantasy of completeness, never fully accepting the reality of others. Something has to happen in the emotional realm to dispel or transform that fantasy. And life has already supplied the material for a transformation. Consider that love of light, and, more generally, that generous outward-seeing movement of the mind, finding the world fascinating and curious, that is both intelligent and emotional: the world is seen as lovable. Somehow, this attitude can and often does combine with the emotions of relief and gratitude to make the comforting/ feeding parent or parents objects of wonder and love. It is this outward erotic movement toward the world and its alluring objects—which we can already call wonder, and which we can call love in at least a nascent sense[11]—that proves crucial in propelling infants beyond the frozen state of narcissism that Proust depicts.

IV. The Growth of Concern out of the Spirit of Love

At some point, probably late in the first year of life, infants become aware of the adults in their world as whole people. The joy of connection is by now complex: children don't merely get security and nourishment from their parents, but also play with them and develop, gradually, the ability to read their minds. The games they play with parents are delightful in their own right, increasing the child's sense of the world as an enjoyable place. The dialogue that develops between parent and baby exhibits great (and increasing) subtlety and responsiveness, and it develops the capacity for both face reading and "mind reading," or sympathetic perspective taking, on the part of the infant.[12] Wonder at the amazingness of the other drives and channels curiosity, and curiosity leads to increasingly sophisticated efforts at mind reading. At the same time, however, children are becoming aware that their anger and frustration are directed toward the same whole person who is also the object of delight and enjoyment. This recognition of their own aggression provokes intense anxiety, and this is another point in development when the personality might simply shut down, cease to move outward—out of fear of the damage that one's own aggression can do.[13]

Suppose, however, as is often the case, the parent or parents remain constant and loving, showing that they have not been destroyed by the infant's hate. This constancy allays anxiety, since the infant is becoming aware that its needs will be met on a regular basis. It also gives the infant a sense of continued joy: the security of being held and the fun of playing go on, despite outbursts of destructiveness. And it also offers a new possibility: that the infant can actually give something to the mother, pleasing her and showing affection. The distinguished psychoanalyst and clinician Donald Winnicott—whose empathy for the situation of infants was remarkable—describes this "benign cycle" in a classic essay, "The Capacity for Concern."[14] The "facilitating environment" required in order for concern to develop is not very special, and is often present. The parent or parents must be available and must "survive the instinct-driven episodes"; the function of the "mother" (Winnicott always stresses that this is a functional concept and could be filled by a parent of either gender) is "to continue to be herself, to be empathetic towards her infant, to be there to receive the spontaneous gesture, and to be pleased" (76). Under such circumstances—which prominently include the parent being lovable as well as just being there—the infant develops confidence that it can make good contributions to the lovable parent despite its aggression, and its anxiety is gradually transmuted into a morally rich sense of guilt at its aggressive impulses. Its relationship to the parent becomes a moral one.

Couldn't morality and rules of fairness do this work all on their own? Can't we imagine infants coming to the realization that the parent has rights and that these rights should be respected, even without love? Well, we can try to imagine a family like this, in which rules are lifeless and loveless. However, such a family would lack trust, spontaneity, and the creative sense of reciprocity that children develop in Winnicott's "benign cycle." It's not clear that a morality of that sort could ever be stable, since it would be shot through with suspicion and mistrust, and it would be rigid rather than flexible. Moreover, infancy really is painful: first, the pain of lack and frustration, and, later, the pain of recognizing one's own aggressive urges against those who love and care for one. Because of this pain, there is an ongoing risk of shutdown, of a retreat into a narcissism that understands others only as tools. It's possible for a narcissist to understand and apply rules, but those rules would remain lifeless and highly unstable.

As at the earlier stage of anxiety, then, love has to come to the rescue. Only love propels the infant into creative reciprocity and the sort of empathetic perspective taking that makes action an expression of genuine concern rather than rigid formulae. The opportunity for concern is created in the first place by the parent's lovable (sustaining, nonterrified, empathetic) behavior.

What do these psychologists mean, and what do I mean, by love? The relationship they describe includes a delighted recognition of the other as valuable, special, and fascinating; a drive to understand the point of view of the other; fun and reciprocal play; exchange, and what Winnicott calls "subtle interplay"; gratitude for affectionate treatment, and guilt at one's own aggressive wishes or actions; and, finally and centrally, trust and a suspension of anxious demands for control. (There could hardly be fun and "subtle interplay" without that.) It is only through trust in an uncertain world and the people in it that one ever finds the way out from a smothering narcissism, if one does. But trust cannot be generated out of rules of fairness alone; it really has little to do with such rules. What makes it possible is the lovable behavior of the parent— combined with the wonder, love, and creativity of the child, which has its ultimate roots in the child's wonder at the light, its erotic outward-moving curiosity.

This, in essence, is the idea behind Tagore's religion of humanity, behind Mozart's "yes," and behind the argument of this book: that, as Mozart and Da Ponte put it, "this day of torment, of craziness, of foolishness—only love can make it end in happiness and joy."

One place to see the difference between a morality generated out of rules and a morality generated from love is in *The White Ribbon,* Michael Haneke's terrifying film of Germany between the two world wars. Apart from the schoolteacher, who provides the film with a moral compass, all of the young people in it have grown up in authoritarian and loveless families.[15] They pay lip service to rules of fairness, but they don't understand their meaning, and each one appears to carry around an immense burden of undischarged aggression and hate—the very drives that might have found a creative outlet in a relationship of loving reciprocity. In one family, children are forced to wear white ribbons as reminders of the innocence against which they have all in various ways transgressed; the ribbon becomes a brand of eternal and undischargeable guilt. While the schoolteacher loves his fiancée, Eva, and fills his days with creative plans to visit her and delight her, the children of the town turn their pain into acts of sadism. So the absence of love leads to two distinct problems: children have no constructive way of managing their own aggression, and they never become capable of endowing the rules with inner life. Although the film is a nightmare, it is a nightmare about a reality, as Theodor Adorno's study of the German family bears out.[16]

Heineke's fantasy does not exactly *prove* that love is necessary if respect is to lead to stable concern, but it reminds us that morality cannot survive in a world where anxiety is unrelieved by trust and love; that genuine concern for others rests on a capacity for empathetic understanding and the sense that the other's perspective matters; and, finally, that genuine concern requires confidence in one's own ability to give, an attitude that is deeply imperiled by both shame at helplessness and the awareness of one's own aggressive wishes. If even respect is to be sustained stably, there has to be a moment of generosity, in which one is willing to be at the mercy of another who is mysterious, and approachable only in a spirit of play and wonder. That generosity, that "yes," is made possible only by the spirit of love; or, more accurately, it is that spirit.

All this concerns intimate early relationships (although the same dynamic recurs at different developmental stages, perhaps especially in the insecurity of adolescence). Why does a political project need to think about these personal matters? My suggestion will be that the political culture needs to tap these sources of early trust and generosity, the erotic outward movement of the mind and heart toward the lovable, if decent institutions are to be stably sustained against the ongoing pressure exerted by egoism, greed, and anxious aggression.

V. Play and Projection

By the age of one, infants are adept mind readers. They have developed a sense of the distinction between self and other and capacities to see the world empathetically from the perspective of the other. "Contagion" of affect exists more or less from birth: babies cry in response to the sound of other babies crying, a familiar phenomenon repeatedly confirmed. But, as psychologist Ross Thompson writes, "An important transition in empathic responsiveness occurs when the child becomes aware that others have internal, subjective states that are distinct from her own and that merit attention in social interaction"—a transition that now is agreed to occur quite early in development.[17] The transition is subtle: even the earlier evidence of contagion shows that babies react more strongly to the crying of other babies of similar age than they do to the crying of older children or adults: so, like the mice in the McGill University experiment, they already carve up the world into proximate and more distant groups, and perhaps they are at least beginning to be able to view the world from the viewpoint of the proximate.[18] But now they begin to grasp that another person is a separate world of experience, and that their behavior has consequences for what happens in that world. That realization is greatly assisted by the reciprocal interactions in which parents and infants engage. For some time they have been engaging in game playing, exchanging smiles, gestures, and sounds, and they are used to seeing that other face react to what they do. Now the world of play takes on a greater complexity and becomes a vehicle for the further development of both empathy and reciprocity.

Psychologist Donald Winnicott's important work on play is not experimental psychology in its most traditional sense: Winnicott was a psychoanalyst and pediatrician. He was, however, a person of remarkable insight and wide experience, and his empathetic understanding of the world of small children was unparalleled, so one does not need to accept any particular, or indeed any, psychoanalytic theory in order to use his contributions in connection with the experimental literature. Winnicott, like the experimentalists, focuses on children's growing sense of the full reality of others and their evolving capacity for genuine concern. He connects this in an insightful way to a discussion of play.

Play, for Winnicott, in its most general sense, is an imaginative activity in which one occupies a "potential space," a realm of unreality that is peopled with stories that enact hypothetical possibilities. In this realm children do exercise a greater measure of control than in the world of reality, since they write the script. Nor are the consequences of what takes place in this realm the grave consequences that reality offers: loneliness, hunger, destructive aggression. For those two reasons, play offers a pleasant way to explore the world of human possibilities. In effect,

Winnicott is extending to play generally what Aristotle said of tragedy: that we confront, in a way that is pleasurable and not personally painful, "things such as might happen" in human life, thus learning about the general nature of human life. He emphasizes that an important part of what is learned is the reactions of other people: play centrally involves role playing, and is thus a development of empathy.

An early and crucial form of play involves a "transitional object," a concept that is one of Winnicott's most famous and influential contributions. Extremely young infants can be comforted only by an actual person who holds them. But slightly older infants learn to comfort themselves, selecting a stuffed animal or a blanket and endowing that with magical security-conferring properties. (Winnicott believed that *Peanuts* cartoonist Charles Schultz had gotten the idea of Linus's security blanket from his work; whether or not this is true, it is the same idea.) By clinging to this object, infants become able to comfort themselves, and thus wean themselves, gradually, from the need to view other people as instruments and servants. They also learn to experiment with emotions connected to loss and recovery, as they drop the cherished object and find it again with delighted giggles. As the capacity for empathy matures, infants invent narratives with the stuffed animal as a character, inventing feelings for that animal, in response to a variety of situations; sometimes, for example, the invented fear or anger of the stuffed animal becomes a vehicle for a child's exploration of its own fear or anger. Infants still control transitional objects to some extent, but the very investment in a piece of external reality involves surrender: "Some abrogation of omnipotence is a feature from the start."[19]

Gradually, the world of play becomes rich and sustaining, enabling a child, in Winnicott's simple but resonant phrase, "to play alone in the presence of its mother," to inhabit a world in which others may go their own way and there is no need to subordinate them constantly to the child's own anxious projects.

But play is not always solitary. Just as it helps to enrich the world of solitude, building inner resources, play also enriches the interpersonal world, as parents and children, and children together, enact a variety of roles and possibilities, learning about one another and about further possibilities in the process.

Winnicott's larger purpose is to suggest that all human relationships involve the characteristics of early play: the capacity to be alone in the presence of the other (not constantly demanding slavish attention); trust in the other and the willingness to relax the demand for complete control in the presence of the other; the capacity to respond to subtle cues with an appropriate reaction; the ability to imagine what the other intends and feels. Indeed, in the analysis posthumously published under the title *Holding and Interpretation,* he suggests that all love is a form of "subtle interplay"—which his patient, a frozen young man, was experiencing for the first time in the analytic relationship. Love means many things, "but it has to include this experience of subtle interplay, and we could say that you are experiencing love and loving in this situation."

"Subtle interplay" is closely connected to the willingness to give up omnipotence. Winnicott's patient, whom he calls "B," was raised by an anxious mother who believed that her husband demanded that she become a perfect parent. (Winnicott points out that this means that she really did not love her husband: she saw him as a demanding authority figure, for whom any real human being was not good enough.) The stress of this fantasized demand made her demand perfection in her child, which meant, in turn, that she was unwilling to accept any of the signs that he was a real baby: crying, anger, hunger, and so forth. Nor could she play with him, because relaxation and trust were undermined by anxiety and the desire for control. Not surprisingly, her child became himself incapable of play or spontaneity; he could not interact successfully with individual people, and all his behavior displayed rigidity and impersonality.[20]

B represents an extreme, a failure of the developmental process that occurs relatively rarely, since most parents take delight in their children's reality. Winnicott liked to emphasize this fact, in part in order to reassure real parents that perfection is not required and thereby calm their anxieties. Nonetheless, he also emphasized that human life inherently involves anxiety and difficulty: "the inherent difficulty in regard to human contact with external reality." The desire for control and the unwillingness to trust are endemic to a world that contains surprises of many kinds, and in which the discovery of one's own infirmity and, ultimately, mortality gives new meaning, as life goes on, to the sense of non-control. For this reason, human development is an ongoing process, and it needs the resources of play and imagination at every stage in order to reinforce trust, reciprocity, and respect for the separate world of others.

How do people play in later life? Well, as Winnicott says to B, love is one answer. Most successful human relationships, whether familial or friendly or erotic, have this element of "subtle interplay." But these relationships are also sources of stress, and so it is valuable, Winnicott argues, to have a "potential space" in which roles and options can be tried out without real-life stress: the world of the arts and culture. Because "the task of reality-acceptance is never completed, [and] no human being is free from the strain of relating inner and outer reality, . . . relief from this strain is provided by an intermediate area of experience which is not challenged. . . . This intermediate area, rich in enjoyment, is in direct continuity with the play area of the small child who is 'lost' in play."[21] Indeed, if we pose the question "Where are we? Where do we live?" the answer is that we spend much of our lives in a "potential space" of imaginative possibilities. This "potential space" is neither private internal experience nor pure external reality: it is an intermediary between the two, "a product of the *experiences of the individual person* (baby, child, adolescent, adult) in the environment that obtains,"[22] Winnicott underlines the continuity between infantile experiences of play and adult participation in culture:

> It will be observed that I am looking at the highly sophisticated adult's enjoyment of living or of beauty or of abstract human contrivance, and at the same time at the creative gesture of a baby who reaches out for the mother's mouth and feels her teeth, and at the same time looks into her eyes, seeing her creatively. For me, playing leads on naturally to cultural experience and indeed forms its foundation.[23]

In adult life, then, the infant's experience of trust, reciprocity, and creativity finds a wide range of outlets, in culture and the arts, that deepen and renew the experience of transcending narcissism.

I began by arguing that love, and a type of play that expresses and deepens love, are necessary if an individual child is to exit from the impasse created by narcissism and fear toward genuine concern for another separate being. To have concern for another is already an achievement. As life goes on, however, that achievement is hardly stable, as awareness of weakness and mortality prompt a recrudescence of narcissism. Because narcissism is ongoing, the resources that make its defeat possible must also be ongoing, in the form of increasingly sophisticated forms of love, reciprocity, and play, to some extent in personal relationships, but in large part in the "potential space" of culture and the arts. Respect that is not infused with the spirit of play and wonder is likely to be itself unstable. To understand this point in greater detail, we must now turn to a major expression of "radical evil" in political cultures: disgust, and the stigmatization of groups.

VI. Projective Disgust and Segmentation: Gora and the Runaway Slave

People form hierarchies. For Kant, "radical evil" centrally concerned competitive ranking and the obstacle it poses to the recognition of equal human dignity. A tendency to form hierarchies is clearly a part of our evolutionary heritage, but narcissism, the desire for omnipotence, and "anthropodenial" make hierarchy take a particular shape that threatens the life of any moderately just society.

A key device of subordination is disgust: people in power impute animal properties that typically inspire disgust (sliminess, stickiness, bad smell, connection with decay or with bodily fluids and excrement) to other groups of people, whether African Americans, women, lower castes, Jews, or gay men—and they then use that alleged disgustingness as a reason to refuse contact. This syndrome must be grasped and combated by a just society. "Projective disgust" grows out of the same anxieties that inspire infantile narcissism. Like it (and as a part of it), it can be surmounted only by the spirit of love.

By the time children are two or three, they have in most cases become capable of love and trust toward a small number of individuals. Nonetheless, anxieties associated with bodily vulnerability exert their sway throughout life. These anxieties now crystallize in the newly developed emotion of disgust. Disgust, as a large body of experimental research shows, is, at least in the first instance, a negative response toward substances with marked bodily characteristics: ooziness, bad smell, stickiness, sliminess, decay. Even in these simple cases, in which the objects of disgust really have the properties imputed to them, disgust is not the same as mere sensory distaste, because it is highly influenced by the person's conception of the object. Thus the very same smell elicits different disgust reactions depending on whether the person is told it is feces or cheese.[24] The idea of feces is evidently a part of what renders the object disgusting. This happens ubiquitously. Nor is disgust the same as the fear of danger: substances that are not dangerous may be highly disgusting (people refuse to ingest even a detoxified, sterilized cockroach).[25] Meanwhile, many highly dangerous objects (for example, poisonous mushrooms) are not found disgusting. Thus, even though disgust probably evolved as a rough and ready heuristic warning us away from dangerous substances, its content and function are subtly different.

Disgust, the research concludes, concerns an idea of contamination: it expresses an anxiety that the self will be contaminated by taking in something that is defiling. "You are what you eat," as the saying goes. And the "primary objects" of disgust are all "animal reminders": our own bodily excretions (sweat, urine, feces, semen, snot, blood), which remind us of our commonality with nonhuman animals, and corpses, which remind us of our mortality and fragility.[26] Disgust is in this way closely linked to the earlier dynamic of narcissism, omnipotence, and anthropodenial, because the aspects of animality that elicit disgust reactions are those that are reminders of helplessness, not things such as strength and speed that suggest good potentialities shared with other animals.

Disgust for primary objects is already a form of anthropodenial: a repudiation, that is, of the fact that we are mortal animals with bodies that emit odors and substances and will ultimately decay. It is not as such, however, terribly harmful, and it even has some positive value in steering us away from genuine danger, even though it does not perfectly track the dangerous. Given the late arrival of disgust in the developmental process, however—it is not in evidence before the time of toilet training—societies have more than the usual opportunity to mold its content and to extend it to other objects. For in no society is disgust limited to "primary objects."[27]

Rather soon after learning primary-object disgust, children begin to carve up the world in accordance with the social phenomenon of "projective disgust."[28] Projective disgust is disgust for a group of other humans who are segmented from the dominant group and classified as lower because of being (allegedly) more animal. Members of this group are thought to have the properties of disgust's primary objects: they are found dirty, smelly, slimy. They are associated with sexual fluids, excrement, and decay. They are represented as quasi-animals, as occupying a border zone between the truly human (associated with transcendence of the body and its substances) and the utterly nonhuman. Being able to point to a group of people who allegedly are revolting Yahoos makes it easier for the dominant group to consider itself above the merely animal.

Projective disgust, then, is a form of anthropodenial, and very likely motivated by deeper anxieties about mortality and helplessness that lead to anthropodenial more generally. The groups onto which disgust properties are projected do not really have those properties—any more than those doing the projecting. The common fantasy that African Americans smelled worse than whites, and the more general anxiety that their bodies would contaminate food, drinking fountains, and swimming pools, is just one example of disgust's irrationality. As Paul Rozin, disgust's leading experimental researcher, concludes, disgust is extended from one object to another by totally irrational processes, forms of "magical thinking."[29] What all these forms have in common is a willed segmentation of the social world, combined with lies about the self. The dominant group says: *This group must be kept at a distance because of its animality, but we, of course, have nothing in common with them.* Thus males imputed animality to women because of their alleged sexual eagerness and their connection with pregnancy and birth, all the while implicitly denying their own connections to these phenomena. Straight society often represented the sexuality of gay men as foul, connected to excrement and germs, while "forgetting" the ubiquity of "sodomy," anal and oral sex, in the sex lives of opposite-sex couples. Similar irrationalities are found in all instances of projective disgust. The subordinate group is stigmatized, then, in order to serve the inner need of the dominant group for a surrogate for its own animality.

Projective disgust is social, in the sense that the particular group or groups that get singled out as the vehicles of animality vary from culture to culture in accordance with particular facts of history and social order. It appears, however, not to be merely social, in the sense that all known societies exhibit some form of it. Male disgust for women's bodies is one species of projective disgust that is unusually widespread and tenacious. Similarly, disgust often targets sexual minorities, and one way of marginalizing a minority is to impute to it a deviant sexuality: both Jews and African Americans, for example, have been represented as hypersexual and predatory, and national self-definition frequently involves the creation of an underclass that is thought to have these characteristics.[30] But that the group should be Jews, in the case of Germany, or African Americans, in the case of the United States, is an artifact of particular history. Walt Whitman suggests that society might exist without disgust if we all established a healthier relationship to our own bodies and the bodies of others. This idea, however attractive, remains speculative, since no such society has ever existed. The very fact that all societies engage in such irrational types of segmentation and stigmatization suggests very strongly that projective disgust is not a mere error, but is linked to the deeper anxieties that we have discussed. Recent research, indeed, has suggested that people who experience an unusually high degree of disgust aversion toward primary objects are more likely than others to engage in the stigmatization of others by projective disgust—something that suggests that even primary-object disgust is harmless only up to a point.[31]

Projective disgust creates a radically segmented world: the world of the self and people like the self, who are all apprentice angels (as Updike's Rabbit imagined himself),[32] without bad odors, without messy fluids, perhaps even immortal; and the world of animals who masquerade as quasi-human, but who betray their animal nature in their (fantasized) bad smell, dirtiness, and connection to loathed bodily substances. Swift's fable of the Houyhnhnms and the Yahoos brilliantly shows this segmentation for the lie it is: Gulliver's body is a Yahoo body, and yet he learns to loathe the very smell and touch of Yahoos, relegating them to a distant place of inferiority. The disgust he feels is physically real, just as southern whites were physically repulsed when they found themselves at a northern dining table eating with African Americans.[33] And yet, its source is an irrational cultural fantasy.

This type of segmentation lies close to what psychologist Robert Jay Lifton, in his book *The Nazi Doctors,* calls "doubling." Lifton describes the way in which these doctors, working in Auschwitz, could live with love and trust in the bosom of their families and yet at the same time perform horrible experiments on Jews. "Doubling" involves the irrational creation of two worlds to which different rules of conduct apply, although the underlying reality (the human body) is actually the same; the agent too is "doubled," operating by one set of rules in one world, by another in the other. Lifton describes doubling, however, as a reaction to an extreme situation, as the only alternative, in that situation, to a radical breakdown of the self.[34] Projective disgust, by contrast, is not a reaction to unusual stress or authoritarian political control; indeed, nothing is more daily, even in thriving democracies. Nor is projective disgust as radical as doubling in its operations, creating two distinct selves operating in two separate environments. Disgust operates at the heart of daily life. It requires but one environment and one self; the world is segmented simply by the creation, right inside the daily world, of an underclass whose members bear, in fantasy, the properties that are feared and repudiated in the self. So it is more ubiquitous and more quotidian than doubling, and we have all the more reason to view it with alarm, as a threat not only in a society taken over by evil, but in every society, even the most decent.

Disgust blocks equal political respect. How might its baneful influence be overcome? We can now turn to the two examples with which this chapter began: Tagore's *Gora,* and Whitman's description of an encounter with a runaway slave. Both concern nation building; both argue that projective disgust and splitting must be overcome in order to attain a morally satisfactory type of national unity.

Gora is a large, pale young man in a high-caste Hindu family in Bengal. (His name means "paleface.") In late adolescence, he becomes convinced that India's future requires a return to traditional Hindu caste practices, including untouchability. A high-caste Hindu must never eat food prepared or served by a member of the lower castes or a person without caste, such as a Christian or Muslim. Caste norms express an aversion to the idea of bodily contamination by animality. Because the lower castes are associated with occupations such as cleaning latrines and disposing of corpses, a fantasy develops that members of those castes are themselves contaminated by animal wastes and pass on that contamination to whatever they touch. (Gandhi pointed out that the idea of lower-caste filth is false: during the cholera epidemic, the lower castes, defecating in fields far from their dwellings, were cleaner and less at risk than upper castes, who defecated into chamber pots that were then poured into the gutters outside their windows.)

For Gora, the world is now divided into two groups: people with whom he can share food and drink, and lower beings with whom he cannot. This bifurcation takes precedence over normal human relations: he now refuses to take food from Lachmiya, a Christian servant who nursed him and treated him with love. (Christians were very often converts from the lowest castes, so Lachmiya is stigmatized in two different ways.) His tolerant mother is aghast at his conduct; she tries to get him to focus on properties that seem relevant to the social treatment of others, but the fantasy of contamination dominates, blocking out everything else.

The reader of the novel knows, from the start, that Gora's life is absurd and self-contradictory. Not only is he, as in all practices of untouchability, repudiating a part of the identity of all human beings (excretion, decay), he is also, in a very direct and particular sense, repudiating his own particular identity. For Gora is pale because he is not Hindu at all, but Irish. His mother adopted him when he became orphaned, as an infant, at the time of the Sepoy Mutiny. According to the Hindu rules he follows, he is not and can never be a Hindu. His mother tries to set him on the right track, saying, "But do you know that it was when I first took you in my arms that I said goodbye to convention? When you hold a little child to your breast then you feel certain that no one is born into this world with caste."[35] Gora, however, is convinced not only that his own life needs the caste hierarchy, but also that the future India of his dreams can emerge only if these ancestral customs are maintained. He imagines his life's work as that of "realizing India," and he conceives of India's stability as a hierarchical order.[36]

The discovery of his real origin devastates Gora. In the wake of the crisis, however, he finds a new sense of freedom. No longer oppressed by the weight of maintaining a thousand dead conventions, he can think about the situations and needs of real people, and he can see, for the first time, what the caste hierarchy means for human welfare. His nascent capacity for empathy is unleashed, and he can now live freely in the potential space of the future welfare of India's hundreds of millions of diverse people. He returns home and, embracing his mother, says: "[Y]ou have no caste, you make no distinctions, and have no hatred—you are only the image of our welfare! It is you who are India!" And then, after pausing for a moment, he says, "Mother! . . . will you call Lachmiya and ask her to bring me a glass of water?"[37]

Gora's split world has been made whole through a recognition of the equal worth of all Indians. But that recognition did not come about through abstract ideas of respect alone: it had its birth, essentially, in love and childhood play. By arranging his fable in such a way that the key revelation comes from a rediscovery of a child's love of his mother, Tagore reinforces the idea that the political needs to draw on the archaic sources of trust and joy that animate childhood love.

Whitman, too, inhabits a radically segmented world: that of the United States during the Civil War. He repeatedly draws attention to the connection between that split and the manifold ways in which people, through projective disgust, segment themselves from allegedly lower aspects of their own bodily humanity by projecting those aspects onto others: African Americans, women, homosexuals. His insistent suggestion is that Americans can transcend the separations that vex their national life only if they can forge a new relationship to their own bodies, seeing them as beautiful rather than disgusting. On the way to that central idea, he confronts one of the central sources of stigma in the (dis)United States: the body of the black man.

In this brief fable, the poet takes a runaway slave into his house, keeps him there, feeds and clothes him, and tends his injuries, all the while prepared to fight with potential captors (the gun in the corner); ultimately he helps him go further north. The slave begins as an animal: a noise in the woodpile. But as soon as the poet sees him, he treats him with both compassion and respect, giving him medical treatment, food, reassurance, and, finally, a place of equality at the table. The transition to full equal respect comes about, crucially, through bodily contact, confronting sources of alleged defilement and contamination that remained potent through the modern civil rights movement and still exert influence today: shared living quarters (the slave's room has a door into Whitman's), shared bathing facilities, shared clothing, and intimate contact with bruises and open sores.

How has disgust been transcended? The poem's insistent claim is that disgust is surmounted only through the play of the imagination— only, in effect, through and in poetry, through a poetic spirit that endows shapes with inner life and dignity, that "sees eternity in men and women."[38]

Like Tagore's fable, Whitman's enacts what it depicts. It goes to work on the minds of its readers, humanizing and dignifying the viewpoint of the split-off, the despised. Tagore's novel leads the reader to inhabit the viewpoints of its varied characters, showing us during the act of reading the meaning of the idea that India is all of its people. Whitman, similarly, inhabits a multiplicity of perspectives as he constructs an America where equality truly reigns among diverse citizens, "without retrograde."[39] Shortly before the section about the slave, Whitman alludes emphatically to the continuity between children's imaginative play ("A child said, 'What is the grass?' fetching it to me with full hands") and the adult's attempts to understand life's mysteries; the poet's answers concern serious matters of life, death, and war, and yet they are themselves playful, childlike, and they encourage this playful disposition in the reader.[40]

The poet begins by putting himself on a basis of parity with the child, admitting incompleteness and cognitive vulnerability: "How could I answer the child? I do not know what it is any more than he." His subsequent interpretations are put forward as guesses. First he compares the grass to "the flag of my disposition out of hopeful green stuff woven." Next it might be "the handkerchief of the Lord . . . bearing the owner's name someway in the corners, that we may see and remark, and say *Whose?*" Or it might be itself "a child, the produc'd babe of the vegetation." Or it might be a "uniform hieroglyphic" whose meaning is equality:

> . . . Sprouting alike in broad zones and narrow zones,
> Growing among black folks as among white,

Kanuck, Tuckahoe, Congressman, Cuff, I give them the same,
I receive them the same.

And now it seems to me the beautiful uncut hair of graves.

The idea of equality leads, thus, to the idea of equal vulnerability and mortality. The poet then imagines that the grass is springing up from the corpses of young men dead in the war, or from "old people," or from prematurely dead children—reminding the reader that death comes by surprise, and none of us is immune. So the playful game is also a playful acknowledgment of an extreme type of vulnerability. By placing this section so shortly before the account of the slave—and, following it, the account of the woman bathing in secret fantasy with the young men—he connects political equality and reciprocity to a playful renunciation of omnipotence, which is staged by and in the poetry.

Both Whitman and Tagore suggest what Winnicott explicitly argues: that a cultivation of the imagination, through artistic play, is necessary if adults are to maintain and broaden their concern for the other people in their surroundings, overcoming the tendency of all societies toward stigmatization and "doubling."

I have responded to Kant's vague account of "radical evil" by developing a more detailed account of forces in the personality that impede mutual respect and reciprocity, in both personal and political life. These forces are indeed "radical" in the sense of being rooted in the very structure of human development—our bodily helplessness and our cognitive sophistication—rather than being the creation of this or that particular culture. So far, I have made three claims. First, in early child development the spirit of love (including trust and "subtle interplay") is a necessary key to the development of genuine concern and respect for others, out of the imprisoning egoism of early life. Second, the dynamics in human life that made love necessary (helplessness, fear and anger at helplessness) are not removed by time and growth, but persist—and thus love is an ongoing necessity for the personality in adult interactions, if these are not to lapse back into narcissism. This is as true in the political life as it is in familial and friendly relations. Third, there are ways in which narcissism rears its head in the political realm—reflecting the operations of projective disgust—that pose special problems for a society that aspires to equal human dignity; these problems themselves must be addressed not only by rules promoting equal concern, but also by the spirit of play and imaginative sympathy, including the vulnerability and the willingness to forgo omnipotence that this "poetic" spirit renders possible. In short: we always need the poetic spirit, but we need it all the more urgently where we are most inclined to splitting and repugnance.

VII. Authority and Peer Pressure: Props for Badness

Our working account of "radical evil" is not complete. We now need to add two tendencies that also appear deeply rooted in human nature, and which pose a serious threat to the stability of democratic institutions: the tendency to yield to peer pressure, even at the cost of truth, and the tendency to obey authority, even at the cost of moral concern. Both of these tendencies are very likely rooted in our evolutionary heritage: in primate life, both hierarchy and group solidarity are useful.[41] Both continue to be useful in human societies up to a point: obedience to legitimate authority is usually good, and, in the absence of personal expertise, deference to peer judgments is essential. Both, however, threaten democratic public culture.

In a series of rigorously designed experiments conducted over a long period of time,[42] psychologist Solomon Asch demonstrated the high degree of deference average subjects exhibit toward peer pressure.[43] The experiments involve a group of participants, one of whom is the experimental subject, and the others (the number of others varied in size, but it was found that the effect required at least three others, and there were usually more) are working for Asch, unbeknownst to the subject. The subject is told that the experiment is a test of perception. Some simple perceptual questions are posed: typically, matching a line on one card to the line of closest length out of three lines on a second card. Typically, the subject begins by giving correct answers, but the stooges repeatedly give incorrect answers. (Once in a while they give correct answers, in order to reduce the likelihood that the subject would suspect what is really going on.) The subject becomes more and more uncomfortable, and after a while he or she usually responds to group pressure by yielding and going along with the majority. In ordinary circumstances, a subject will err less than 1 percent of the time. Given group pressure, subjects yield about 36.8 percent of the time. (About one-quarter of the subjects remained completely independent through all trials and never agreed with the majority. Some went with the majority nearly all the time. Many yielded only after repeated iterations of group pressure.) It's important to notice that the percentage of capitulation is not actually very high, though higher than one might wish in a situation where truth is obvious. (Summaries of Asch's work sometimes suggest that most people yield to group pressure.)

The reasons people gave for yielding to the group interested Asch. Some quickly concluded that they were wrong and the others were right. Others yielded in order not to "spoil your results." Many suspected the majority were victims of an optical illusion, but went along anyway. "More disquieting were the reactions of subjects who construed their difference from the majority as a sign of some general deficiency in themselves, which at all costs they must hide. On this basis they desperately tried to merge with the majority, not realizing the longer-range consequences to themselves."[44] Meanwhile, the subjects who did not yield showed a "capacity to recover from doubt and to reestablish their equilibrium." Other dissenters thought the majority might be correct, but still thought it their obligation "to call the play as they saw it."

Asch sometimes gave the experimenter a partner, a stooge who was instructed to give truthful answers. The effect of just one truth teller was extraordinary: "The presence of a supporting partner depleted the majority of much of its power." Subjects answered incorrectly only onefourth as often as they did without the partner. Even the weakest people did not yield as readily. Other variations in the experiment established that it was less the truthfulness of the partner than his act of dissent that freed the subjects: when the partner answered even more erroneously than the majority, this "produced a remarkable freeing of the subjects; their errors dropped to only 9 per cent," and the errors were all moderate. Moreover, the effects of a dissenting partner lasted even after the partner had departed.

These experiments have great interest for us. Although the group pressure effect appears independent of the dynamics of narcissism and projective disgust, we can predict baneful interactions between the two, as, under the influence of group pressure, people concur in erroneous judgments about the physical properties of Jews, gays, or African Americans. Group pressure is dangerous in all circumstances, since it is an impediment to truth telling. It is all the more pernicious when brought to bear in situations already characterized by stigmatization and hierarchy.

Asch's results do not justify an extremely pessimistic conclusion, because the size of the effect he observed was limited. Still, the effect is large enough to be troubling. Particularly interesting is the effect of just one dissenter on the behavior of others. As Asch himself concluded, all decent societies have strong reasons to nourish and reward dissent and critical thinking, both for its intrinsic importance and for its effects on others.

More troubling still are the famous studies of obedience to authority conducted by Stanley Milgram at Yale University.[45] Milgram told participants in advance that they would be participating in a study of memory and learning. Participants were not students, but were recruited by a newspaper advertisement from the surrounding New Haven community; he sought a wide range of ages and backgrounds. Subjects were offered payment ($4 per hour, not bad in the 1960s) and carfare. Not enough volunteers answered the ad, so Milgram also solicited participants by direct mail invitation, sampling names from the New Haven phone book, a tactic that had a response rate of 12 percent. (We should note that people often volunteer for something when the money makes a difference to them and is more significant to them than the lost time. This factor may have been underestimated in analyzing why the participants obeyed the scientist: they wanted to remain in the study and get paid. The payment also constructed a class hierarchy between Yale scientists and subjects, reinforcing their sense of the scientist's prestige and authority.) The study was conducted in an "elegant" laboratory that was part of Yale University, a factor that Milgram thought significant in creating a sense of prestige and legitimacy.[46]

When the subjects arrived, pairs were formed. One member of each pair was designated "teacher"; the other member (who was actually an actor working for the experimenter) was designated the "learner." Both were told that the study would focus on the effects of punishment on learning. The learner was taken into a room, "seated in a chair, his arms strapped to prevent excessive movement, and an electrode attached to his wrist. He is told that he is to learn a list of word pairs; whenever he makes an error, he will receive electric shocks of increasing intensity."[47] The teacher sees all this and then is taken into the main experimental room "and seated before an impressive shock generator. Its main feature is a horizontal line of thirty switches, ranging from 15 volts to 450 volts, in 15-volt increments. There are also verbal designations which range from SLIGHT SHOCK to DANGER—SEVERE SHOCK." Now the teacher is told to administer a learning test to the learner. When the learner gives the correct answer, he is to move on; when he makes a mistake, the teacher is to give him an electric shock—beginning at the lowest level, but increasing the level each time a mistake is made. No shocks are actually received by the learner, but he feigns increasing discomfort, and ultimately pain. "At 75 volts, the 'learner' grunts. . . . At 285 volts his response can only be described as an agonized scream."[48] If the teacher showed reluctance to go on, the experimenter used a sequence of "prods," in ascending sequence:

Prod 1. Please continue, *or,* Please go on.
Prod 2: The experiment requires that you continue.
Prod 3: It is absolutely essential that you continue.
Prod 4: You have no other choice, you *must* go on.[49]

If the subject asked whether the learner was liable to suffer permanent damage, the experimenter said, "Although the shocks may be painful, there is no permanent tissue damage, so please go on." In the basic version of the experiment, in which subject and learner could see each other through a "silvered glass" but not touch, slightly over 60 percent of subjects continued all the way to the maximum voltage level. When the two were in the same room, the rate dropped to 40 percent. When the subject was required to touch the learner and force his or her hand onto the shock plate, the rate dropped to 30 percent. Subjects did, however, experience varying levels of stress. Some attempted to help the victim by mouthing the correct answer. In a separate set of studies, Milgram found that people's predictions about what the experiment would show were way off: most people predicted that subjects would not follow the experimenter all the way, and this gap persisted over the years, despite the growing fame of the experiments.

Milgram himself was always unequivocal about what he thought his experiments showed: that "ordinary people, simply doing their jobs, and without any particular hostility on their part, can become agents in a terrible destructive process."[50] He compared his findings to Hannah Arendt's study of Eichmann, and agreed with her that evil is not found in a "sadistic fringe," but in normal people under circumstances in which they surrender personal accountability and simply go along with someone else's directives—a personality state that he called the "agentic state," somewhat confusingly, since what he means by that term is a state in which people surrender personal agency and become simply the vehicles for another's plan—often becoming absorbed by technical minutiae rather than taking responsibility for the larger course of action. Milgram recognized that the tendencies he observed had value, not only in evolutionary prehistory but also in contemporary society.[51] His concern was with the extent to which these problems threaten the operations of a just society, and his conclusion was pessimistic, although he emphasized that face-to-face situations, in which individuality is accentuated on both sides, mitigate bad behavior.

One reason the conclusions were so pessimistic is that Milgram simply assumes that the "background conditions" for obedience are similar in all subjects. He did no study of the upbringing and character of individual subjects, and was therefore unable to correlate dissent (or even stress) with any background features. Moreover, he appears to think that such differences do not matter. Although he never studied the family or child development, he tells his readers that all subjects have grown up in the midst of a hierarchical structure in the family, and that no family can teach moral values without at the same time teaching obedience to authority. Children can never separate the two, he alleges, and the demand for obedience is "the only consistent element across a variety of specific commands."[52] At school, similarly, moral substance and obedience to authority are again conflated—he alleges, again, without having studied schools of different types. In short, "The first twenty years of the young

person's life are spent functioning as a subordinate element in an authority system."[53] These sweeping statements utterly ignore large differences
in family and educational styles that have been much studied, beginning
at least with Theodor Adorno's *The Authoritarian Personality,* which
imputes much of the obedient behavior of Germans to the specific style
of family upbringing common in German homes at that time.[54] Schools,
of course, vary at least as much as families do. Without knowing the extent to which the propensity to dissent was linked to prior experiences
of various sorts, we have no way of knowing whether the tendencies
Milgram uncovers persist despite socialization in critical thinking and
dissent. Certainly Asch's studies suggest that the presence of dissent has
a powerful influence on behavior.

Over the years, the experiments were repeated in many different
places, and the basic findings were confirmed, with some further discov-
eries added. Many studies considered the question of gender, and their
bottom line is that gender is not a significant factor in predicting the degree of a subject's obedience. Other studies establish that obedience was
a response both to the general idea of legitimate authority and to the idea
of scientific expertise. (This finding limits the extent to which we can
generalize his findings to social life at large.) When we consider that the
subjects were selected as volunteers (a category in which economic need
and low income may well have played a part), and then transported to
the "elegant" lab at Yale, given some voltage numbers they may not have
understood, and given, too, the reassurances of a lab-coated scientist,
this factor looms large. Third, although Milgram reported a large gap
between expected and actual obedience, subsequent studies find a much
smaller gap.[55]

Milgram's studies are important, and we can learn from them. Hierarchy and tendencies to obedience are indeed a deep part of our human
inheritance, rooted, no doubt, in evolutionary prehistory; these tendencies can in many ways collaborate with the other psychological tendencies we have studied. Historian Christopher Browning, studying a police battalion that murdered large numbers of Jews during the Third
Reich, used both Milgram and Asch to good effect in explaining the
conformity of these young men—showing, indeed, that those who could
not bring themselves to shoot Jews reported feeling shame.[56] Military

organizations of all sorts are highly skilled at using both obedience and peer pressure to create solidarity and a sense of shame about deviant conduct—which often overrides personal morality. They need to do this; but there are inherent dangers in this inculcation.

Nothing in Milgram's work, however, shows that a robust training in independent thought, personal accountability, and critical dialogue cannot control and even surmount these tendencies. Despite his grim predictions that any nation in the world could fill dozens of Nazi death camps, in fact not all nations have done so. And none have done so under robust conditions of democratic freedom. A vigorous critical culture counts for a great deal.[57] Asch's work shows, in fact, that in a culture of dissent people become willing to stand up against the "pack." Milgram's research tells us nothing about how different styles of upbringing or education might influence political culture, but Asch's gives us good reasons to predict that schools teaching reasoned dissent and critical thinking would create bulwarks to terrible acts. And even Milgram shows ways in which the dangerous effects of obedience may be mitigated: through proximity, letting people see one another as individuals.[58] Batson's work suggests that this tendency can be developed by listening to narratives of individual predicaments. Other studies too have confirmed that people behave worse if the people over whom they have power are presented to them as dehumanized nonindividual units—given a number, for example, rather than a name—and better when they are encouraged to see the other as an individual with a name and a specific life story. People also behave worse when they can evade personal scrutiny and accountability, and better when they are encouraged to feel personally responsible and be seen as individuals, not as part of a faceless mass.[59]

In addition to encouraging ongoing tendencies to independence and critical thinking through education and the public culture, our societies can structure situations in such a way as to maximize personal accountability and the perception of others as full individual human beings. The mainstreaming of children with a variety of disabilities in public school classrooms, as individuals with names, tastes, and stories, rather than as "a mongoloid idiot" or "a cripple," is just one example of a social revolution that can be brought about in large part through situational design, and then supported by the use of the narrative arts.

The tendencies uncovered by Asch and Milgram are facets of "radical evil," constraints on human behavior that no doubt evolved because they had some utility, and which continue to have utility in some situations, but they also involve great dangers. They interact in manifold ways with what we have identified as the central "narrative" of "radical evil," the effort to cope with helplessness and finitude. (For example, peer group bonding reduces the shame of helplessness, as does submission of the will to an allegedly omnipotent authority, through whom a person may seek to regain lost omnipotence.) These tendencies are just tendencies, however deeply rooted. They can be modified by upbringing and education, and they can also be shaped by situations. Nations can foster cultures of dissent, encourage personal accountability, and discourage bureaucratic anonymity. Perhaps most important, they can build cultures of empathy, encouraging the ability to see the world through the eyes of others and to recognize their individuality.

PART THREE

Public Emotions

Introduction to Part III

IT IS TIME TO PUT this analysis to work in the context of real societies—imperfect, yet aspiring toward justice and human capability. What some might expect at this point is a general philosophical theory of the construction of political emotions. The preceding analysis, however, has given us reason to suppose that no highly general theory will prove helpful—beyond the theories of personality and the general political norms we have presented so far. This is true for two reasons. First, what we have been after all along is an experimental approach to social problems, in the spirit of Mill and Tagore, with lots of space for improvisation, critical independence, and quirky individuality. Any highly general account of how government should proceed risks closing off the spirit of experiment and play. Comte and Rousseau could offer such a general theory—but that was because their theory was wrong!

Second, we have already had reasons to think that any good proposal for the cultivation of public emotion must be not only experimental but also highly contextual. Cherubino embodies a human norm that can be realized in India, but Tagore was right to speak of the Bauls of Bengal, rather than a Mozart character. What moves people is a function of their sense of their nation's history, traditions, and current problems, and leaders attempting to generate emotional support for valuable projects must engage with people as they are, their particular historically and socially shaped loves and cares—even if ultimately to lead them to a place altogether new. So if we want to see what could be done well, we will need to look at what has been done, with a keen eye to a nation's concrete situation. Good public emotions do embody general principles, but they clothe them in the garb of concrete narrative history.

For these two reasons, we should not be looking for a top-down general theory, and if we did propose one, we would have failed to understand our own project.

On the other hand, we can do more than simply offer a series of heterogeneous examples of what has gone well. Public emotions must deal with a wide range of different themes and problems, and it is possible to offer a semitheorized account of how each of these areas of life might be well addressed—before illustrating that account with concrete historical examples (drawn, as before, from the United States and India) where we can discuss in greater detail the choices that were made and the work they did. This part aims to strike a delicate balance between too thick a theory and no theory, something that is not easy to do, but which must be attempted.

One of the most obvious questions before our aspiring societies is how to shape the emotions that citizens feel toward their nation. What is patriotism? It's easy to see the damage it can do, but can it also be a crucial force for good? We turn first to this question, about which there is a great deal to be said in general, and a theoretical argument to be made, before turning to examples of the good work that it can do, when suitably constructed. Abraham Lincoln, Martin Luther King Jr., Mohandas Gandhi, and Jawaharlal Nehru will help us understand this work more fully.

All societies must also manage two very disturbing emotions: grief and disgust. The former needs to be channeled in ways that promote reciprocity and extended, rather than narrow, compassion; the latter needs to be contained, lest it become an impediment to general concern. All societies, then, need something like the spirit of tragedy and the spirit of comedy—the former shaping compassion and the sense of loss, the latter indicating ways to rise above bodily disgust in a spirit of delighted reciprocity. The ancient Greek tragic and comic festivals embody much insight about how this can be done. Starting from that case—highly theorized in antiquity, and widely influential historically—will give us a general quasi-theoretical account of where we are going, which we can then pursue in connection with historical projects in a wide range of media. This case also completes our argument complementing that of John Rawls, since it shows a variety of ways in which public art and rhetoric may forge a bridge between particular emotions and general compassion, while retaining the focus and energy of love.

At this point our account of the "Cherubinic" citizen is virtually complete, since we have now shown how this citizen's emotions include attachments to general principles and institutions, but mediated and infused by a loving spirit of "musical" reciprocity.

But there are other emotions that, neglected, threaten to derail admirable projects based on extended compassion: fear, envy, and shame. Each of these three needs theoretical analysis before we can understand how they might be managed. The third chapter of this part undertakes that task before, once again, turning (in each case) to the analysis of concrete cases.

Another way of putting the aim of this part is in terms of the following argument:

1. Aspiring societies have strong reasons to seek stability and efficacy for their good political principles.
2. If love and compassion can be appropriately extended in the spirit of Cherubino (and impeding emotions contained and discouraged), this will greatly strengthen the stability of decent aspiring societies.
3. Love and compassion can indeed be appropriately extended, and impeding emotions contained and discouraged, by strategies A, B, and C.
4. Decent aspiring societies have strong reasons to pursue strategies A, B, and C.

This part will provide some additional reasons for accepting premise 2, by showing in general a type of work emotions of a given sort can do, in three areas of great importance. That is the contribution of its semitheorized portions. But the primary focus of this part is on premise 3: our historical examples should convince skeptics that public emotions can indeed be vital parts of an aspiration to justice, and can actually work, without removing and indeed while enhancing liberal freedom.

Where are public emotions generated? We think immediately of the rhetoric of political leaders, and that, certainly, is one very important "site" of emotion cultivation. But leaders lead in many ways. They lead with their bodies, their clothing, their gestures. And government, more broadly conceived, generates public emotion through many strategies: through public artworks, monuments, and parks, through the construction of festivals and celebrations, through songs, symbols, official films and photographs, through the structure of public education, through other types of public discussions, through the public use of humor and comedy, even by shaping the public role of sports.[1] Our examples in this part will not investigate every medium in connection with every emotion, of course, but they will be representative, and suggestive of where present-day politics might look for further material.

CHAPTER EIGHT

Teaching Patriotism:
Love and Critical Freedom

Hail the flag of America on land or on sea,
Hail the Revolutionary war which made us free.
The British proceeded into the hills of Danbury,
But soon their army was as small as a cranberry.
Remember the brave soldiers who toiled and fought;
Bravery is a lesson to be taught.

—Martha Louise Craven[1]

I. The Janus-Faced Nature of Patriotism

In 1892, a World's Fair, called the Columbian Exposition,[2] was scheduled to take place in Chicago.[3] Clearly it was turning out to be a celebration of unfettered greed and egoism. Industry and innovation had become its central foci, as America planned to welcome the world with
displays of technological prowess and material enrichment. Gross inequalities of opportunity in the nation and in the city were to be masked
by the glowing exterior of the pure white Beaux Arts–style buildings
(right next door to the University of Chicago) that came to be called "the
White City."[4] The architectural choices of the exhibition's designers,
Daniel Burnham and Chester French, expressed the idea that America
rivaled Europe in grandeur and nobility. Everything funny, chaotic, and
noisy was relegated to the Midway, a grassy strip now in the middle of
the university campus, but then outside the official buildings of the exhi-

bition. The first Ferris wheel, though officially part of the exhibition, was on the Midway—along with Buffalo Bill's Wild West Show, noisy children, racial and ethnic differences, bright colors, and poor people. Instead of real human bodies, disturbing in their heterogeneity and their frailty, the official exhibit put forward the "Statue of the Republic," a sixty-five-foot-tall gilded statue of a woman holding a scepter and orb, a smaller replica of which, only twenty-four feet high, created in 1918 to commemorate the exposition, now stands at Hayes Drive and Cornell Avenue. The *Chicago Tribune* wrote, "It impresses by its grand presence, its serene and noble face, and its perfect harmony with its magnificent surroundings, by its wonderful fitness."[5]

Advocates for the poor, increasingly upset by the plan, got together to think how the celebration might incorporate ideas of equal opportunity and sacrifice. A group of Christian socialists finally went to President Benjamin Harrison with an idea: at the exposition the president would introduce a new public ritual of patriotism, a Pledge of Allegiance to the flag that would place the accent squarely on the nation's core moral values, include all Americans as equals, and rededicate the nation to something more than individual entrepreneurialism. The words that were concocted to express this sentiment were: "I pledge allegiance to the flag of the United States of America, and to the republic for which it stands: one nation, indivisible, with liberty and justice for all."[6] At the same time, *The Youth's Companion,* a popular children's magazine, began an aggressive campaign to promote the use of the pledge, along with the flag salute, in the nation's schools.

As so often happens with patriotic sentiment, however, the pledge soon proved a formula of both inclusion and exclusion. Francis Bellamy, the pledge's author, was himself both a socialist and a xenophobe who feared that our national values were being undermined by the flood of new immigrants from southern Europe. By the nineteen forties, required by law as a daily recitation in schools in many states, the pledge became a litmus test for the "good American," and those who flunked the test faced both exclusion and violence. Jehovah's Witnesses, who refused to recite the pledge for religious reasons, seeing it as a form of idolatry, soon found their children expelled from school for noncompliance. Then, in a wonderful Catch-22, the parents were fined or jailed for "contributing to the delinquency of a minor" because their children were not in school! The idea grew in the public mind that Jehovah's Witnesses were a danger: a "fifth column" subverting America's values in the lead-up to the war against Germany and Japan. Accused of German sympathies (despite the fact that Jehovah's Witnesses were being persecuted under the Third Reich for similar reasons and had to wear a purple triangle in the concentration camps), Witnesses faced widespread public violence, including many assaults and some lynchings—particularly after the U.S. Supreme Court upheld the compulsory flag salute as a legitimate expression of devotion to national security.[7]

Any account of public emotion must grapple with the complexities of patriotism. Patriotism is Janus-faced. It faces outward, calling the self, at times, to duties toward others, to the need to sacrifice for a common good. And yet, just as clearly, it also faces inward, inviting those who consider themselves "good" or "true" Americans to distinguish themselves from outsiders and subversives, and then excluding those outsiders. Just as dangerous, it serves to define the nation against its foreign rivals and foes, whipping up warlike sentiments against them. (It was for precisely this reason that Jean-Jacques Rousseau thought that a good nation needed a patriotic "civil religion" in place of the dogmas of Christianity, which he found too meek and pacifistic.)[8]

The story of the pledge shows us that quite a few different things can go wrong when a nation sets out to inspire strong emotions with itself as the object, all of which are pertinent to the project of teaching patriotism in the schools. The Burnham plan for the exposition shows the danger of misplaced and exclusionary values: we see a nation defining itself in terms of elite achievements and aspirations that exclude common people and their urgent needs. The aftermath of the pledge shows us the danger of burdening minority conscience with enforced homogeneity. Finally, both the Burnham plan and the ritual of the pledge show us the danger that patriotism will short-circuit the critical faculties and undercut social rationality.

With such problems in mind, many reasonable people look skeptically on appeals to patriotic sentiment. They favor deemphasizing it in education. Instead, they argue, we should focus on developing citizens who can think for themselves and deliberate about the nation's future on the basis of rational principles. In favoring critical reason, they are surely not wrong. In ignoring or discarding patriotic emotion, however, such people may have lost sight of an insight firmly grasped by our group of historical thinkers: that patriotic emotion can be a necessary prop for valuable projects involving sacrifice for others. Mazzini argued that national sentiment was a valuable, even necessary "fulcrum" on which one could ultimately leverage generous sentiments extending to all humanity. Comte, Mill, and Tagore, while strongly internationalist, all gave the idea of the nation an honored place in their account of extended sympathy.

Mazzini was correct that national sentiment can play a valuable and even essential role in creating a decent society, in which, indeed, liberty and justice are available to all. The nation can grab people's hearts and imaginations because of its eudaimonistic connections (we might say): it is "us" and "ours," and thus it enables, as Mazzini says, a transition from narrower sympathies to more extensive sympathies. In loving the nation, people can, if all goes well, embrace general political principles—but in a motivationally efficacious way. The public love we need, then, includes love of the nation, and a love that conceives of the nation not just as a set of abstract principles, but as a particular entity, with a specific history, specific physical features, and specific aspirations that inspire devotion. But it can be constructed in many different ways, with different consequences for valuable political goals and the ultimate embrace of general principles. A group of vexing problems stands before us, a type of Scylla and Charybdis that are all too likely to waylay even the wary voyager.

Scylla, the monster that lured voyagers on one side of the narrow strait, had many heads, each equipped with sharp teeth—and so I shall imagine her here. One "head" of Scylla is the danger of misplaced and exclusionary values. A second "head" is the danger of burdening minority conscience by the imposition of ritual performances. A third "head" is an excessive emphasis on solidarity and homogeneity that threatens to eclipse the critical spirit. On the other side of the strait, however, awaits Charybdis, a whirlpool that threatens to entrap and destroy any ship that steers too far away from Scylla. Charybdis, in this argument, is the danger of "watery" motivation, the problem that Aristotle thought would beset any society that tried to run its business without particularized love.

After discussing and illustrating these dangers, I shall give examples from both U.S. and Indian history of leaders who were able to construct a form of patriotism that steered successfully through the narrow strait: George Washington, Abraham Lincoln, Martin Luther King Jr., Mohandas Gandhi, and Jawaharlal Nehru. Their achievements will help us see how a valuable form of patriotism might be taught in schools, and how it might give an aspiring nation strength in its struggle for justice.

II. Why Patriotism?

Patriotism is a strong emotion taking the nation as its object. It is a form of love, and thus distinct from simple approval, or commitment, or embrace of principles. This love involves the feeling that the nation is *one's own*, and its rituals usually make reference to that idea. Consider: "My Country, 'Tis of Thee," where the embrace of the nation as "mine" is explicit; the first line of *"La Marseillaise," "Allons enfants de la patrie,"* where the first-person plural exhorts all Frenchmen to see the nation as their parent; or India's *"Jana Gana Mana,"* in which the "we" identifies itself as comprising people drawn from all of India's geographical regions and her major religious traditions.

This love may be modeled on quite a few different sorts of personal love. As with the love of a sports team, so here: different people think differently about the nation's relationship to them. For some, the nation is a beloved parent, and that idea is prominent in many symbolic appeals to patriotism. At other times, the nation is seen as more like a beloved child, whose growth and development one desires to promote. At still other times, the nation is seen in a more romantic light, as a beloved beckoning to the lover. Different patriotic rituals and songs conjure up subtly different forms of love, and sometimes the same song appeals to more than one. (*"La Marseillaise"* begins by imagining France as a parent, but the beautiful concluding stanza is far more erotic, as *liberté chérie* is addressed in tones of awe. *"Jana Gana Mana"* appeals to a parental idea in its depiction of the moral principles of the nation as sustaining and guiding it, but the music is quite erotic.) Even within one and the same ritual or part of a ritual, different people may experience different types of love, in keeping with individual needs and predilections.

In all its forms, however, patriotic love is particularistic. It is modeled on family or personal love of some type, and, in keeping with that origin or analogy, it focuses on specifics: this or that beautiful geographical feature, this or that historical event. The thicker it is in these respects, the more likely it is to inspire. Thus Americans love "America the Beautiful" and Woody Guthrie's "This Land Is Your Land" (albeit often ignoring the latter's political meaning) more than they love the boringly abstract "My Country 'Tis of Thee." The specificity and musical eroticism of *"Jana Gana Mana"* and Bangladesh's *"Amar Shonar Bangla"* inspire love, while a thin plodding abstraction, such as *"La Concorde,"* Gabon's national anthem, is likely to have more trouble sustaining attention.[9]

Our focus here is on the nation, but we should not forget that other forms of patriotic love—addressed to the state, the city, the region—can coexist with love of the nation and reinforce it. Sometimes there will be tensions, as when a city or state pursues goals that the nation as a whole has not embraced. (This often happens, for example, when great cities espouse pluralistic values that rural areas of the nation may not endorse.) Some cases of more-local love will concern us in the following chapter.

Why do we need an emotion like this? The very particularity and eroticism of patriotic love make it ripe for capture, it would seem, by darker forces in our personalities.

Mazzini's answer[10] was that our lives are immersed in greed and self-interest, so we need a strong emotion directed at the general welfare to inspire us to support the common good in ways that involve sacrifice. But to have enough motivational strength, this emotion cannot have a purely abstract object, such as "humanity," but must have more concreteness. The idea of the nation, he thought, was that sort of idea: sufficiently local, sufficiently ours, sufficiently concrete, or at least susceptible of being made concrete, to motivate us strongly, and yet large enough to involve our hearts in an object beyond greed and egoism.

Our account of compassion shows that Mazzini is correct. Compassion strongly motivates altruism, but it is also rooted in concrete narratives and images. If altruistic national emotion is to have motivational power, it needs to hitch itself to the concrete: named individuals (founders, heroes), physical particulars (features of landscape, vivid images and metaphors), and, above all, narratives of struggle, involving suffering and hope. Such an emotion gives strength to moral motives, but it can also pose a threat to impartial principles. This tension can be addressed in two different ways: by extending compassion, and by a dialogue between emotion and principle. We can extend compassion by attaching it to images and institutions that stand for the well-being of all people—preferably including people outside the nation itself. That is what a good form of patriotism does. It provides a bridge from people's daily emotions to a broader and more even-handed set of concerns. But, even then, we continue to need a dialogue between good moral principles and the type of particularistic emotion that is rooted in concrete images. And this means that patriotic emotion continually needs critical examination.

Patriotic emotion seeks devotion and allegiance through a colorful story of the nation's past, which points, typically, to a future that still lies in doubt. Indeed, the idea of a nation is, in its very nature, a narrative construct.[11] To say what a given nation is is to select from all the unordered material of the past and present a story line that emphasizes some things and omits others, all in the service of pointing to what the future may hold—if people dedicate themselves sufficiently. French philosopher Ernst Renan influentially and convincingly argued that a nation is not simply a physical location; it is an idea, a "spiritual principle."[12] This spiritual principle involves, on the one hand, a story of the past, usually a story of adversity and suffering, and then a commitment to the future, a willingness to live together and face adversities for the sake of common goals. The two sides are linked, because the story of the past has to tell people what is worth fighting for in the future. Renan remarks that the past has to have in it something great or glorious, but it also needs to have loss and suffering: "Where national memories are concerned, griefs are of more value than triumphs, for they impose duties, and require a common effort."[13] Meditating on the glories and sufferings of the past, people think, *Yes, for those great ideals I too would be willing to suffer.* Or, in Renan's words, "One loves in proportion to the sacrifices to which one has consented, and in proportion to the ills that one has suffered."[14] Following Batson, we may add that a good story of a nation's past will involve not only abstract ideals, but also particular individuals; not only a conceptual space, but also physical places.

The need for emotions of loving concern becomes even more apparent, and their contours more clearly demarcated, when we consider the threat posed to morality by disgust. Disgust jeopardizes national projects involving altruistic sacrifice for a common good, for it divides the nation into hierarchically ordered groups that must not meet. What "common good" could cross those lines? Given that separations motivated by disgust are so common in real societies, all societies need to find ways to surmount this problem. It seems unlikely that abstract principles on their own can do this job. Given that the other has already been vividly depicted in one way, as subhuman, the antidote to that way of imagining must itself come via the imagination, in the form of experiences of seeing the other as fully human. If the other has been dehumanized in the imagination, only the imagination can accomplish the requisite shift. For example, having formed the view that African American men are loathsome hypersexual animals and sources of unspecified contagion and decay, people will see them differently only if the nation offers its citizens narratives that portray African American lives differently, as fully human and close to those people's own lives and purposes. Any call to altruism that fails to deploy the imagination and emotions in this way leaves in place powerful forces of division that are very likely to subvert any common labor.

Disgust might be counteracted in the private sphere, without recourse to national ideals. But one way to overcome it is surely to link the narrative of the full humanity of the denigrated group to a story of national struggle and national commitment in Renan's sense. We shall see later that one of Martin Luther King Jr.'s great achievements was to promote this emotional transformation in his audience. If educators can portray the denigrated group as part of a "we" that suffered together in the past and is working together for a future of justice, this makes it far more difficult to continue to see the other as a contaminating and excluded outsider. In patriotic emotion, citizens embrace one another as a family, sharing common purposes; thus stigma is overcome (for a time at least) by imagination and love.

III. Scylla: Exclusionary Values, Coerced Conscience, Uncritical Homogeneity

Scylla represents a variety of dangers of strong patriotic passion gone awry. We must confront them if we are to argue that a form of patriotic love can avoid them. Because these dangers are heterogeneous, the many-headed monster Scylla is an apt metaphor.

The first and most obvious danger is that of *misplaced values.* If we are going to whip up strong passions, we want to make sure we don't generate enthusiasm for the wrong thing. And it is easy to see that patriotic love has served a range of unwise causes: foolish and/or unjust wars, racial or ethnic hatred, religious exclusion, distorted norms of masculinity that contribute to the subordination of women, xenophobia and hatred of other nations. It is on such cases that people usually focus when they express horror at the very idea of patriotic love.

It is a little difficult to know what, precisely, this objection is supposed to be. Does the objector think that there is any inherent tendency in patriotism that leads to the support of bad rather than good ends? If so, this analysis needs to be presented. One could, for example, imagine an argument that it is always unwise to whip up disgust in public life, given the specific tendencies of that emotion to lead to the stigmatization and subordination of vulnerable groups. Indeed, Part II made such an argument. However, we are talking here about love, not disgust, and it is much more difficult to see what argument could be given for the claim that love is always likely to be unwise, or connected to bad policy choices.

Perhaps the objection, instead, is to the idea of the *nation* as object of love. Some believe that the very idea of the nation is a primitive one, to be superseded ultimately by the universal love of all humanity (and, presumably, the creation of a world state). But that argument itself needs to be stated and examined. I myself have argued that even in a world dedicated to the pursuit of global justice, the nation has a valuable role to play, as the largest unit we know so far that is sufficiently accountable to people and expressive of their voices.[15] And even though we cannot deny that attachment to one nation has often been linked with the denigration of other nations, there appears to be no necessity to this: we can, and often do, imagine nations as cooperating toward common goals. Similarly, love of one's own family has often been linked to the wish to denigrate or subordinate other people's families, but this need not be: we may think that all families deserve a decent level of support, and family love can be securely tethered to that norm.

Most often the misplaced-values objection is probably to be parsed as follows: *Emotions are always dangerous: look what trouble they have caused in this case and in that. We can do without them as we pursue our good values. So we'd better do that.* There are, however, several problems with this very common way of thinking. First, the objector typically lists the bad goals that emotions have supported (Nazism, religious persecutions, unjust and unwise wars) and not the good (the abolition of slavery, the civil rights movement, the cause of greater economic justice, just and wise wars, the enfranchisement of women). Does the objector believe, for example, that Hitler could have been defeated without strong passions connected to the idea of the survival of one's own nation, whether it be Britain or the United States? That Winston Churchill's appeal for "blood, sweat, and tears," and other emotional appeals of that same sort, were irrelevant to stiffening Britain's resolve in that difficult time? Second, as this example already suggests, the objector just assumes that good goals propel themselves into existence and sustain themselves without any strong emotional motivation. History, I believe, proves that picture wrong. When people don't care enough about something to endure hardship for it, things usually go badly. Edward VIII was not an adequate leader, because he did not display (or, probably, possess) strong emotions about Britain's sovereignty, and he did not encourage others to have those emotions. Third, the objector seems to forget that the bad goals and bad emotions don't disappear as we calmly pursue the good, so the question of what happens to the emotionless good in competition with the emotion-laden bad is not posed. (Once again: imagine combating the canny propaganda machine of Hitler's Germany, so full of emotive devices, without any sources of love or emotional motivation.)

The best response to give to this group of objections is that we must be extremely vigilant about the values we encourage people to love and pursue, and we must encourage continued vigilance by the cultivation of a critical public culture, the teaching of history in a critical mode, and the teaching of critical thinking and ethical reasoning in the schools. As we'll see, this can be done.

One way to avoid this danger is to make sure that the narrative of the nation's history and current identity is not exclusionary, not emphasizing the contribution of a single ethnic, racial, or religious group to the denigration or even omission of others. A national narrative may, and frequently is, based on a set of political ideals that can embrace all citizens, including new immigrants. Conceiving of the nation in such a way (as both the United States and India have done, but most of the nations of Europe have not) helps avoid the danger of ethnocentrism, a crucial aspect of the danger of misplaced values.

A somewhat trickier issue will be connecting the narrative of national inclusion to an adequate world narrative, so that nationalism is buttressed not by warlike and aggressive aims, but rather by projects that in principle can extend to include the good of other nations. Once again, though tricky, this task can be and often has been accomplished.

One more version of this objection remains. The objector now says that if, as suggested, the emotions are particularistic, then we cannot utterly depend on them to generate even-handed policies that treat people as equals—even when the object of strong love is the entire nation. This seems to me to be the best objection of the misplaced-values type, because it identifies a genuine tendency in the emotions (well demonstrated in Batson's research). And history shows many cases in which the appeal to the nation is uneven and even exclusionary, defining certain groups and people as not really part of the nation. We should grant that this is a real problem, and we shall shortly see how patriots from Lincoln to Gandhi address it. But we should acknowledge, too, that a crucial role in any decent society is played by institutions that take matters out of people's hands in some key respects. Compassion, however altruistic, can't run a fair tax system. So, we turn many things over to institutions and laws. Nonetheless: these institutions and laws will not sustain themselves in the absence of love directed at one's fellow citizens and the nation as a whole. The erosion of the New Deal in the United States results from an imaginative and emotional shift, and this shift prompts major changes in institutions and laws. Thus it isn't sufficient to create good institutions and then run away and hide. We have to get our hands dirty by entering the feared emotional terrain.

The second head of Scylla has deep historical roots, and yet it is relatively easy to confront. Indeed, it has already been effectively confronted. At one time in our history, the urgent importance of patriotism was understood to justify coercion of the young: many states required the

Pledge of Allegiance and the flag salute, as we have seen, and they sus-
pended or expelled children who refused to join in. In at least one case,
that of Russell Tremain, the parents lost custody of their child as a result, and little Russell was placed in a children's home, where he was
compelled to recite the pledge.[16]

More than one religious group objected to the pledge as a form of
"idolatry," but the Jehovah's Witnesses were the most publicly influential such group, because they were willing to engage in litigation, whereas
some other groups (including the sect to which the Tremains belonged)
saw litigation as incompatible with their pacifism.[17] Lillian and William
Gobitas[18] offered convincing and articulate[19] testimony that the pledge
was, to them, a violation of religious requirements.[20] Nonetheless, the
local school board had no sympathy for their arguments, contending
that their objections were not genuinely religious. Eventually their complaint reached the U.S. Supreme Court, where they lost.

Minersville v. Gobitis[21] is one of the most infamous cases in the history of the U.S. Supreme Court. A number of factors explain the result.
Joseph Rutherford, leader of the Witnesses, argued the case himself and
did a very bad job. More important still, Felix Frankfurter's strong views
about patriotism carried the day. Frankfurter stressed throughout—
both in his majority opinion here and in his later dissent in *West Virginia State Board of Education v. Barnette*[22]—his personal sympathy
with the situation of the Gobitas children. "One who belongs to the most
vilified and persecuted minority in history is not likely to be insensible
to the freedoms guaranteed by our Constitution," he wrote, at the time
the lone Jew on the Court.[23] Nonetheless, his strong views about the
limits of judicial power, combined with his fervent patriotism,[24] led him
to conclude that the regulation requiring the pledge was not unconstitutional. His patriotic fervor outlived the controversy over his two opinions: in 1944, as speaker for the District of Columbia's I Am an American
Day celebration, he compared love of country to romantic love, saying
that it was too intimate an emotion to be publicly expressed except in
poetry. He then read a rather sentimental ode to the flag by Franklin K.
Lane, which included the lines "I am not the flag, not at all. I am but its
shadow."[25] Frankfurter, then, shows the dangers of coercion that do at
times inhere in a sincere and fervent patriotism. It is understandable, if

not commendable, that the world situation in 1939 led him to take this enthusiasm too far.

In *Minersville,* Frankfurter grants that the First Amendment entails that restriction on conduct expressive of religious conviction can be justified only by "specific powers of government deemed by the legislature essential to secure and maintain that orderly, tranquil, and free society without which religious toleration itself is unattainable."[26] He then argues that national unity and cohesion supply the state with "an interest inferior to none in the hierarchy of values."[27] The school board's view that requiring the pledge is crucial to promote that central interest is plausible, since the flag is "the symbol of our national unity, transcending all internal differences, however large."[28] He does not, however, address the real question in the case: Is it plausible to hold that national unity and cohesion require enforcing the pledge rule against a small number of children with sincere religious objections? He focuses on the general issue of national unity in a time of danger, rather than the conscientious acts of two respectful teenagers who certainly would not be imitated by their scoffing peers. So Justice Harlan F. Stone pointed out in his stinging dissent: "I cannot say that the inconveniences which may attend some sensible adjustment of school discipline in order that the religious convictions of these children may be spared, presents a problem so momentous or pressing as to outweigh the freedom from compulsory violation of religious faith which has been thought worthy of constitutional protection."[29]

Frankfurter was wrong and Stone was right, as the nation soon agreed. The decision was immediately greeted with a storm of criticism. At the same time, escalating violence against Jehovah's Witnesses was to some extent blamed on the Court, as if the decision had given sanction to the popular idea that Jehovah's Witnesses were disloyal.[30] Several justices[31] gave indications that they might have changed their mind, and later a shift in membership on the Court[32] suggested that the other side might now prevail. The Court shortly accepted another case raising the same issues. In *West Virginia State Board of Education v. Barnette,*[33] the Court found in favor of the Witness plaintiffs. Justice Robert H. Jackson's majority opinion has become one of the defining landmarks of U.S. political life. Treating the case as a compelled-speech case rather than one falling under the religion clauses, he offers a resonant defense of the idea of freedom of dissent:

> If there is any fixed star in our constitutional constellation, it is that no official, high or petty, can prescribe what shall be orthodox in politics, nationalism, religion, or other matters of opinion or force citizens to confess by word or act their faith therein. If there are any circumstances which permit an exception, they do not now occur to us.[34]

He adds that compulsory unity is not even effective: "Those who begin coercive elimination of dissent soon find themselves exterminating dissenters. Compulsory unification of opinion achieves only the unanimity of the graveyard."[35]

Barnette gives the right reply to our second objection. Patriotism and respectful dissent are not incompatible. Indeed, our particular tradition emphasizes the freedom of dissent, and we should take pride in that defense of liberty. Given values of a particular sort, emphasizing individual liberty and the rights of conscience, the second objection can be straightforwardly answered: our values preclude such burdens on conscience, unless a national security interest is far stronger and more immediate than it was in this case. In general, children may not be burdened against their conscience by required patriotic rituals in the schools.

Today the idea of noncoercion is well understood, and even its subtler aspects have had sympathetic attention. In *Lee v. Weisman*,[36] for example, the Court understood the subtle coercion that might be present if a student were required to stand during a middle-school graduation prayer, especially when the only alternative was not to attend her own graduation. Justice Anthony Kennedy's opinion focused on the dangers of coercive pressure to conscience and enforced orthodoxy in the schools.[37]

The *coercion* objection is no longer a serious issue. Young people who find their conscience burdened in the schools are sure to be excused from the ritual. Nonetheless, there are many other ways in which minority beliefs are burdened in the schools, particularly through peer pressure. Lillian Gobitas recalls how, when the school bus drove by their home, children jeered and threw things at them.[38] So it is not just legal imposition of conformity that we have to worry about in schools, but also the tyranny of peers, a tendency we have seen to be among a decent society's major problems. Therefore, teachers and other school officials need to be vigilant in their defense of minorities—religious and political, and also racial and sexual. The problem of bullying, however, is hardly unique to the issue of patriotism, and it supplies no reason not to teach patriotism that is not also a reason not to educate children in groups at all.

The question of peer pressure brings us to our third objection on the side of Scylla: Won't a culture in which patriotic emotion is a major theme be likely to be all too solidaristic, all too homogeneous, lacking free spaces for individual expression and for dissent? As with the second issue, we should begin by saying that this is not a problem peculiar to patriotism. As we have seen, human beings are all too prone to defer to peer pressure and obey authority, as Asch and Milgram showed. This problem has beset democracy ever since democracies began to exist. But certainly, strong patriotic emotion might be one area in which people seek to silence critical voices. How might this danger be headed off?

Justice Jackson gives us the best path to follow: we must insist that the truly patriotic attitude is one that repudiates orthodoxy and coercive pressure and celebrates liberties of speech and conscience. His stirring rhetoric is one example of a patriotic statement that can move people powerfully, even while making them think and endorsing the value of dissent. In general, we need to cultivate the critical faculties early and continuously, and to show admiration for them, insisting that critical freedom, not herdlike obedience, is the mark of the true patriot. This can be done in many ways, and some of them involve strong emotions. Children are herd creatures, but they are also, at other times, dissenters, and the joy of freedom and critical dissent can be encouraged from the beginning of a child's life. In my own case, the serialization in a popular children's magazine of the captivating story of Sybil Ludington, who rode farther than Paul Revere in the cause of freedom, tapped into a young child's love of the idea of breaking with tradition and pursuing freedom, linking that idea to the founding ideals of the nation. The idea of America, for me, was thus characterized from the beginning by a strong flavor of dissent and experimentation, even defiance, for the sake of justice—a note firmly struck in many narratives of the Revolution, then and now, and in many other beloved parts of the American literary and filmic canon, from *Twelve Angry Men* to *To Kill a Mockingbird.* In India, the same has been true, as Gandhi turned many symbols of defiance into national symbols, not least Tagore's song *"Ekla Cholo Re."*

Patriotism of the right sort can, it seems, avoid the three dangers represented by Scylla. But still, one might ask, why play with fire?

IV. Charybdis: "Watery Motivation"

Given these dangers, one might wonder whether it is not better to dispense with patriotic love altogether, in favor of sentiments more principle-dependent, cooler, and therefore, it might seem, more reliable. Jürgen Habermas takes this course, and one might read John Rawls as taking it, although I believe that in the end his proposal is fully compatible with mine. Habermas's "Charybdis" proposal fails to offer a blueprint for the cultivation of strong sustaining emotions because it is insufficiently alert to the problem of "watery motivation."

The phrase "watery motivation" comes from Aristotle's criticism of Plato's ideal city. Plato tried to remove partiality by removing family ties and asking all citizens to care equally for all other citizens. Aristotle says that the difficulty with this strategy is that "there are two things above all that make people love and care for something, the thought that it is all theirs, and the thought that it is the only one they have. Neither of these will be present in that city" (*Politics*, 1262b22–23). Because citizens will not think of any child that it is all theirs, entirely their own responsibility, the city will, he says, resemble a household in which there are too many servants, so nobody takes responsibility for any task. Because citizens will not think of any child or children that they are the only ones they have, the intensity of care that characterizes real families will simply not appear, and they will have, he says, a "watery" kind of care all round (1262b15). In short, to make people love something requires making them see it as "their own," and preferably also as "the only one they have." This point, of course, is the point we have made all along: the major emotions are "eudaimonistic," tied to the person's conception of flourishing and the circle of concern that is involved in any such conception. To make people care, you have to make them see the object of potential care as in some way "theirs" and "them."

Let us now examine two highly principle-based accounts of patriotic emotion, those of John Rawls and Jürgen Habermas. Both accounts are promising, and yet both prompt us to raise Aristotle's question, since one might wonder whether the sentiments they cultivate will prove distant and anemic.

John Rawls's account of political emotions is not mechanistic: like mine, it relies on imagination and a story of an object. He also recognizes the obstacle to general concern posed by the narrowness of altruistic emotion.[39] His solution takes the form of a detailed account of the way in which family love may be extended, over time, to become a broader type of associational love, and how this love, in turn, can be extended to the political principles that shape the nation. The basic psychological principle is that of reciprocity: we have a tendency to love and care for those who manifestly love and care for us. The existence of this psychological law Rawls takes to be "a deep psychological fact."[40] First, this happens in the family: children recognize their parents' love and care for them, and they come to love their parents in return. Second, given that a surrounding system of social associations is "just and publicly known by all to be just," people develop "ties of friendly feeling and trust toward others in the association as they with evident intention comply with their duties and obligations, and live up to the ideals of their station."[41] Finally, given that people have passed through the first two stages, and given that they see that the basic institutions governing their society are just, they develop a sense of justice and sentiments supportive of those institutions.

Rawls's account is rich and, especially in the context of its time, bold in the way in which it confronts psychological issues that philosophers usually did not address. And yet it prompts three questions. First, don't we urgently need an account of how people love and strive in nonideal conditions? Of course, this is not Rawls's project, but even the just society always risks becoming unjust, and thus the sentiments that sustain even that society will have to have at least some features of the nonideal case, such as hope for a just future, a critique of an unjust present and past, and a visionary love of the distant. In the real world, and in the context of my own project, which focuses on aspiration rather than achieved justice, two crucial roles for the right type of patriotism will be to prompt the rectification of historical injustice and to sustain a struggle for greater economic justice that will always be difficult for human beings to support, given the strength of self-interest. So, even if Rawls does not need such a nonideal account, I do.

Second is a related question: Isn't Rawls's account too thin in its picture of how people are? Rawls was attempting to sketch a political psychology without taking any stand on controversial questions about what human beings are like, and this works only up to a point. Thus, we simply do not see some of the problems that any good political psychology will have to address—for example, the problem of disgust and stigma—and these problems are likely to be looming in even the well-ordered society, which has just institutions prohibiting exclusion, since even that society assuredly contains real and not perfected people. Filling in this picture more fully is entirely compatible with Rawls's project; for a variety of reasons he felt it was best to avoid a lot of potentially controversial detail, but this detail seems in some areas of vital importance.

Third—and this is really where the whirlpool of Charybdis draws the voyager in—Rawls's proposal, as developed, is highly abstract. Rawls recognizes this, trying to assure us that his proposal involves not simply abstract principles but "active sentiments of love and friendship."[42] It's obvious, for example, that he imagines children loving real, particular parents, not abstract norms of Parenthood. Rawls is not Plato, and he is not really vulnerable to Aristotle's objection. And yet he says nothing about how the particularity of these loves will actually lead on to a grasp of general principles. People really don't fall in love with abstract ideas as such, without a lot of other apparatus in the form of metaphor, symbol, rhythm, melody, concrete geographical features, and so forth. Shrewd leaders understand this very well. Had Martin Luther King Jr. written in the manner of Rawls, world history would have been very different. Vividness and particularity are crucial determinants of emotional response, and thence of altruistic action. Rawls appears to grant as much in his critical remarks about the excessive abstractness of Utilitarianism. But by omitting the quirky ways in which real people are moved, Rawls omits both resources and potential dangers. His project is only to show the general shape of what is possible, and thus far it succeeds. However, the ideas need a great deal of supplementation if we are to have confidence that they can move real people—even in the well-ordered society,

I would say, but certainly in the aspiring and as yet imperfect societies we are considering.

Rawls's account has gaps but can be fruitfully developed. A moralized account of supportive sentiment that really does seem vulnerable to Aristotle's objection was offered by Jürgen Habermas, in his defense of a "constitutional patriotism."[43] Once again, it is to his great credit that Habermas sees the need for some type of emotional support for good political principles and proposes to address the question. Nonetheless, unlike Rawls, he does not even get to the point of offering a picture of what emotions are like and how they work, and his vision is so moralized and so abstract that one can't have any confidence that it would work in real life. His reticence is no doubt comprehensible.[44] Germany's past makes people particularly squeamish about any appeal to strong emotion in the political realm, and it is consequently particularly difficult to address the topic of patriotic emotion there. What Germany's history shows, however, is that people defending liberal values must not cede the terrain of emotion cultivation to fascists, or else they will certainly have to cede much more in the long run.[45] (One might reflect on Habermas's proposal, intended for the European Union, in connection with recent problems in that entity. One way of thinking about the argument of this book is to think about what the European Union has so far lacked.)

A likely source of Habermas's excessive abstractness is his strong commitment to impartiality. Since Habermas tells us little about how this commitment plays out in emotional terms, it will prove useful to see it how led an admirable thinker and political leader into the whirlpool of Charybdis: Marcus Aurelius, the Stoic philosopher and Roman emperor, whose *Meditations,* one of the most widely read works in the Western philosophical canon, was written while on campaign in Parthia, thus while he was actively leading his people in a military effort.[46] Marcus tells us that the first lesson he learned from his tutor was "not to be a fan of the Greens or Blues at the races, or the light-armed or heavy-armed gladiators at the Circus" (I.5). His imagination had to unlearn its intense partiality and localism. It is significant that the negative image for the moral imagination is that of sports fandom, for in all ages, perhaps, that has been such a natural way for human beings to imagine yet other types of loyalty, to family, city, and nation.

The question is whether this negative lesson leaves the personality enough resources to motivate intense concern with people anywhere. For Marcus, unlearning partiality requires an elaborate and systematic program of uprooting concern for all people and things in this world. He tells us of the meditative exercises that he regularly performs in order to get himself to the point at which the things that divide people from one another do not matter to him.

But getting to the point where we can give such concern even-handedly to all human beings requires, as Marcus makes abundantly clear, the systematic extirpation of intense cares and attachments directed at the local: one's family, one's city, the objects of one's love and desire. Thus Marcus needs to learn not only not to be a sports fan, but also not to be a lover. Consider the following extraordinary passage:

> How important it is to represent to oneself, when it comes to fancy dishes and other such foods, "This is the corpse of a fish, this other thing the corpse of a bird or a pig." Similarly, "This Falernian wine is just some grape juice," and "This purple vestment is some sheep's hair moistened in the blood of some shellfish." When it comes to sexual intercourse, we must say, "This is the rubbing together of membranes, accompanied by the spasmodic ejaculation of a sticky liquid." How important are these representations, which reach the thing itself and penetrate right through it, so that one can see what it is in reality. (VI.13)[47]

Unlearning partiality means learning to think of sex as just the rubbing of membranes: it requires, that is, learning not to find special value or delight in a particular. Not being a fan of the Blues means, too, not being a fan of this body or that body, this soul or that soul, this city or that city. This is the Platonic project that Aristotle criticizes, fully and conscientiously executed.

But getting rid of his erotic investment in bodies, sports teams, family, nation—all this leads Marcus into a strange world, a world that is gentle and unaggressive, but also lonely and hollow. To unlearn the habits of the sports fan we must unlearn our erotic investment in the world, our attachments to our own team, our own love, our own children, our own life.[48]

And this means something like a death within life. For only in a condition close to death, in effect, is moral rectitude possible. Marcus tries repeatedly to think of life as if it is a kind of death already, a procession of meaningless occurrences:

> The vain solemnity of a procession; dramas played out on the stage; troops of sheep or goats; fights with spears; a little bone thrown to dogs; a chunk of bread thrown into a fish-pond; the exhausting labor and heavy burdens under which ants must bear up; crazed mice running for shelter; puppets pulled by strings . . . (VII.3)[49]

The best consolation for that bleak conclusion comes also from the thought of death:

> Think all the time about how human beings of all sorts, and from all walks of life and all peoples, are dead. . . . We must arrive at the same condition where so many clever orators have ended up, so many grave philosophers, Heraclitus, Pythagoras, Socrates; so many heroes of the old days, so many recent generals and tyrants. And besides these, Eudoxus, Hipparchus, Archimedes, other highly intelligent minds, thinkers of large thoughts, hard workers, versatile in ability, daring people, even mockers of the perishable and transitory character of human life, like Menippus. Think about all of these that they are long since in the ground. . . . And what of those whose very names are forgotten? So: one thing is worth a lot, to live out one's life with truth and justice, and with kindliness toward liars and wrongdoers. (VI.47)

Because we shall die, we must recognize that everything particular about us will eventually be wiped out. Family, city, sex, children, all will pass into oblivion. So really, giving up those attachments is not such a big deal. What remains, and the only thing that remains, is truth and justice, the moral order of the world. In the face of the looming inevitability of our end, we should not mind being dead already. Only the true city should claim our allegiance.

Marcus is alarming because he has gone deep into the foundations of impartialist "patriotism," a patriotic love based purely on abstract principle. What he has seen is that impartiality, fully and consistently cultivated, requires the extirpation of the eroticism that makes human life the life we know. The life we know is unfair, uneven, full of war, full of me-first nationalism and divided loyalty. But he sees that we can't so easily remove these attachments while retaining humanity.[50]

Patriotic love can be lofty, and it can in some sense cultivate an impartial altruism, by asking people to love the nation as a whole, and thus all of its people. But it had better do so by getting people to love something that is all their own, and, preferably, the only one they have.[51] Rawls's account can, and should, be developed in that direction.

V. History: Washington, Lincoln, King, Gandhi, Nehru

Let us now turn to history.[52] There are many constructions of patriotism that negotiate the narrow strait between Scylla and Charybdis, promoting particular love while not silencing the critical faculties. Let us look at two very different cases: the attempt to found a nation of equals and, later, to end the injustice of slavery and racial discrimination in the United States, and the attempt to forge a new Indian nation that would be dedicated to combating poverty and inequality. In each case I shall focus on political rhetoric, the personal conduct and attire of leaders, and the choice of national songs and symbols—not because all the other sites are not important, but because these particular sites are especially central in bringing patriotism into the education of children (as well as the continuing education of adults).

As we consider these sites, we must remember Renan: a nation is not an entity whose essence is simply given, but a "spiritual principle" that is constructed out of many possible ingredients. These speakers are, then, not so much alluding to a preexisting national identity as they are constructing it out of the materials made available by history and memory; some realities are made salient, others downplayed or omitted. Our task will be to see how these people perform that task in a way that enables them to avoid both Scylla and Charybdis, inspiring strong love of a particular without coercive homogeneity or misplaced values.

Washington's Clothes: A Nation of Equals

After the Revolution, the American patriots had a demanding task: to establish a new nation based on republican ideals. Although many citizens had experienced equality and nondomination in the context of local and state government, there was as yet no framework for a nation of citizen equals. Although the Revolution had given the newly free Americans experience of what it was to stand together against tyranny, they still had to find ways of imagining a common life without a king. This was difficult, because history was replete with examples of monarchical emotions, involving devotion to and obedience to a good father, and not so full of symbols and metaphors of republican emotions—although the Roman Republic constantly provided the patriots with resonant symbols, names, and rhetoric.

Particularly contested was the institution of the presidency, which some saw as incompatible with Republican self-government. Laws and institutions (the separation of powers, judicial oversight) were important in crafting a presidency strong enough to hold the nation together, without being a kingship or a potential dictatorship; so too were symbols and the conduct of the office's first occupant. Although George Washington has often been thought more a military than political leader, he proved remarkably thoughtful in the way he approached this challenge.

Many stories of the American Revolution that were already becoming proverbial at the end of the Revolution—and which are still taught to children today—fire the imagination with the thought of citizen equals fighting tyranny. The famous bloody feet of the soldiers (and their officers) at Valley Forge are a sign of the courage and determination of the patriots in the cause of freedom. The drunken Hessians taken by surprise at Trenton are symbols of monarchical corruption, outflanked, as such corruption always must be (the story goes), by patriot shrewdness and resourcefulness. In the famous painting "Washington Crossing the Delaware" by Emanuel Gottlieb Leutze, Washington is there in the front of the boat, but the painting and the usual accompanying narrative still tell a patriot story, a liberty story, not a story in which the common people remain passively dependent on the care of a fatherly ruler.

Washington was charismatic (tall, dashing, a fine horseman), and also famous and beloved as a military hero. But he was also already a patriot hero, first among citizen equals, and thus well positioned to undertake the delicate negotiation between an excess of monarchical paternalism and an excess of unemotional routine. It is now clear, thanks to Ron Chernow's pathbreaking (and Pulitzer Prize–winning) biography, that Washington thought about these issues with unusual subtlety.[53] Anti-Federalists such as influential historian and playwright Mercy Otis Warren probably would not have been happy with any choices made by Washington in his role as president, since they opposed the office as quasi-monarchical. Warren loved the Roman Republic and the figure of Brutus,[54] and she would have preferred not to have a strong executive. In this situation, with many doubts about whether the presidency was compatible with republican virtue and liberty, we can appreciate the shrewdness of Washington's choices.

Already as commander he made a point of emphasizing the vulnerable humanity he shared with his soldiers: a famous story describes him suddenly putting on reading glasses during a speech and commenting, "I have grown gray in your service and now find myself growing blind."[55] He astonished foreign visitors by the simplicity of his dress: "[A]n old blue coat faced with buff, waistcoat and britches . . . seemingly of the same age and without any lace upon them composed his dress."[56] When he was subsequently elected as the nation's first president, he acknowledged the difficulty of crafting this new office and the importance of his judgment for the nation's future: "I should consider myself as entering upon an unexplored field, enveloped on every side with clouds and darkness."[57]

One of the greatest dangers, as anti-Federalists saw it, was that the presidency would become hereditary. Already upset at Washington's membership in the Society of the Cincinnati, a patriotic club in which membership initially was hereditary, they were somewhat assuaged by the fact that Washington himself strongly opposed hereditary membership and soon got others to end it. Best of all, however, was something that Washington did not choose, but which he did emphasize in a way that made it part of what he symbolized: he and Martha were childless. Washington was well aware that this otherwise unhappy situation made him uniquely suited to be the first president, and this fact may have influenced his decision to allow his name to go forward.[58]

When the time came to craft the first presidential inauguration, his taste for a combination of dignity and simplicity was strongly in evidence. He made a major decision when he refused to wear a military uniform at the inauguration—or ever after that (although he did wear a sword on formal ceremonial occasions). Instead, he decked himself out with patriotic symbols. To encourage American industry, he chose "a double-breasted brown suit made from broadcloth woven at the Woolen Manufactory of Hartford, Connecticut. The suit had gilt buttons with an eagle insignia on them."[59] We see, then, military smartness, combined with humility in color and cut and a preference for the domestic. Washington remarked that Americans ought to imitate their president and favor domestic industries. During the entire period surrounding the inauguration, although he was always imposing because of his good looks and six-foot stature, and although he continued to favor white horses whose coats had been treated with a shiny paste, he also took care to walk around the streets of New York like an ordinary citizen, greeting people affably. As one antimonarchical correspondent observed, "It has given me much pleasure to hear every part of your conduct spoke of with high approbation, and particularly your dispensing with ceremony occasionally and walking the streets, while Adams is never seen but in his carriage and six."[60]

Washington has long been thought of as a heroic leader rather than a thinker. It is clear by now, however, that he exercised judgment superbly, both in isolated gestures (the glasses) and in overall patterns of symbolic conduct (his walks, his style of dress)—knowing that his heroic attributes were helpful in the nation's first leader, sending a message of strength and command, but also that they had to be balanced and to some degree undercut by gestures of a more egalitarian sort if fears of a monarchical presidency were to be proven groundless. The symbols Washington favored (the eagle, native woolens, the eyeglasses) united people and cemented devotion, and they led the mind toward, rather than away from, the central ideals of the nation.

It is entirely appropriate, and a sign that he communicated his ideas about public symbolism effectively, that the Washington Monument is not the portrait of an individual, far less a shrine inviting the worship of an individual. It is, instead, an abstract symbol, an obelisk—alluding to Washington's Masonic connections. At the same time, it is not a monolith, like classical obelisks, but is composed of separate blocks. At its dedication this design was said to symbolize the unity of the states, and, with its graceful ascent, the high goals of the nation.[61]

Significantly, a related debate rages today about a monument for another military hero/president, Dwight D. Eisenhower.[62] The planned monument, just south of the National Mall, designed by architect Frank Gehry,[63] features as its centerpiece a roofless classical temple; the colonnade supports a metal screen that carries images (metallic tapestries) of the Kansas landscape, and it will include a representation of Eisenhower as a boy amid the cornfields of Kansas, as well as two very large bas-reliefs of the mature Eisenhower, one as general and one as president. Two of Eisenhower's grandchildren have objected to the design as too humble and not heroic enough.

Public monuments are frequently controversial at first—including the Vietnam Veterans Memorial, the Lincoln Memorial, and the now iconic Picasso sculpture in Daley Plaza in Chicago,[64] whose abstractness drew jeers at first, but whose humor and zest are now beloved. In the case of the proposed Eisenhower Memorial, the particular objection of the grandchildren seems seriously misplaced. What a military hero who becomes president needs above all to beware of is deification; Eisenhower's own tendency to refer to himself as a "Kansas farm boy" was, like Washington's brown suit, a way of deflecting idolatry, and it should be honored in honoring him.

Lincoln's Gettysburg Address and Second Inaugural: A National Narrative Pointing toward Justice

The Gettysburg Address (November 19, 1863) is one of the defining documents of education in the United States. Children memorize it, and learn from it the ideals to which they ought to dedicate themselves. Its brevity, thought a disgrace at the time, has proven a great asset in forging sentiments in generation after generation. Studying it, we can see how a narrative of the nation—including its past history, its founding ideals, and its possible future—plays a central role in Lincoln's attempt to make people willing to continue to shoulder the emotional and physical burdens of an extremely painful and doubtful war, in which victory was undoubtedly crucial for the nation's future and that of her ideals. Here it is in its entirety:

> Four score and seven years ago our fathers brought forth on this continent, a new nation, conceived in Liberty, and dedicated to the proposition that all men are created equal.
>
> Now we are engaged in a great civil war, testing whether that nation, or any nation so conceived and so dedicated, can long endure. We are met on a great battle-field of that war. We have come to dedicate a portion of that field, as the final resting place for those who here gave their lives that that nation might live. It is altogether fitting and proper that we should do this.
>
> But, in a larger sense, we cannot dedicate—we cannot consecrate—we cannot hallow—this ground. The brave men, living and dead, who struggled here, have consecrated it, far above our power to add or detract. The world will little note, nor long remember what we say here, but it can never forget what they did here. It is for us the living, rather, to be dedicated here to the unfinished work which they who fought here have thus far so nobly advanced. It is rather for us to be here dedicated to the great task remaining before us—that from these honored dead we take increased devotion to the cause for which they here gave the last full measure of devotion—that we here highly resolve that these dead shall not have died in vain—that this nation, under God, shall have a new birth of freedom—and that government of the people, by the people, for the people, shall not perish from the earth.[65]

Lincoln is sometimes mistakenly thought of as a naïve and unselfconscious orator, contrasting his simple style with Edward Everett's rhetorical sophistication. Nothing could be further from the truth. Lincoln's notes, drafts, and letters all testify to a deep interest in rhetoric, including classical Greek norms.[66] Throughout his career, he strove increasingly for brevity, classical simplicity, and compression, for the telling use of parallels and antitheses and for fertile patterns of imagery. In the address, in addition, he emulates the structure of the classical Greek *epi-taphios,* or funeral oration (exemplified, for example, by Pericles's funeral oration in Thucydides), including its generality (no proper names occur), its praise of the dead, its movement to praise of the ideals for which they died, and its injunction to the living to take up their work.[67] Through these formal devices, and through the ingenious deployment of patterns of imagery of birth and death, Lincoln undertakes a project of breathtaking boldness: nothing less than a refounding of America as a nation dedicated to human equality.[68] By attaching these abstract ideals to a concrete occasion of mourning, he creates a bridge between narrow concerns for an "us" and the embrace of these abstract principles.

Lincoln begins with memory, with the mention of a number of years. But the reference also has biblical resonance, echoing a passage in Psalm 90 in which fourscore years is given as the outer limit of the human life span: hearers are thus reminded of the brevity of human life and, as well, of the vulnerability of a human nation at a time of enormous uncertainty in the middle of war.[69] Alluding to the Declaration of Independence, Lincoln reminds his audience that the nation, so imperiled at present, had a beginning. It was "a new nation," with a distinctive set of ideals focusing on liberty and equality. By omitting the Constitution, with its protection for slavery, and returning to the ideal of equality in the Declaration (set in a new light through the implicit reference to the end of slavery), Lincoln in effect refounds the nation: it is a nation dedicated to that simple and yet difficult ideal.[70] Lincoln now observes that the present war tests whether any nation of this sort "can long endure." He thus positions the Civil War as a war over the deepest and most cherished ideals, and over their fate in the entire world, not just in America (suggesting a Mazzini-style link between love of the nation and concern for the whole world).

Lincoln's account of the ideals of the founding is clearly interpretive in Renan's and Hobsbawm's sense. He rereads the Declaration, and he corrects, implicitly, a key aspect of the Constitution. Through his emphasis on a critical narrative of national aspirations and failings, he avoids the Scylla head of misplaced values and also the Scylla head of excessive solidarity and docility. Because the speech itself made nothing happen, its tone is inevitably optative, and its rhetoric creates a sense of emotional intensity around the ideals it praises.[71]

Praising the sacrifice of those who died (in a battle that was one of the war's bloodiest), he then says that the living cannot hallow the ground: only the bravery of the fallen can do so. Living people are thus led toward an attitude of reverential emulation of the sacrifice of the dead. Next, Lincoln famously asks that dedication of the living: we are all to be dedicated to the task of preserving the American democracy, and to giving it "a new birth of freedom." He ends on the note of urgency he has sounded throughout: the struggle is really a struggle over whether such a democracy itself can exist.

Lincoln's speech contains appeals to a constitutional patriotism that would have pleased defenders of abstract principle such as Rawls and Habermas. But it does much more. In its vivid invocation of the founding, its heartfelt mourning for the fallen soldiers, its appeal to renewed commitment, it puts historical and contemporary flesh on these moral bones. If it had lacked these eudaimonistic elements, the speech would not have succeeded in getting people to embrace the principles. The very rhythm and resonance of his language reaches beneath principle to touch springs of emotional attachment.

Lincoln developed this idea of the nation further in his Second Inaugural Address, delivered on March 4, 1865. Since it is a much lengthier speech than the Gettysburg Address, I quote only a few key passages:

> . . . On the occasion corresponding to this four years ago all thoughts were anxiously directed to an impending civil war. All dreaded it, all sought to avert it. While the inaugural address was being delivered from this place, devoted altogether to saving the Union without war, urgent agents were in the city seeking to destroy it without war—seeking to dissolve the Union and divide effects by negotiation. Both parties deprecated war, but one of them would make war rather than let the nation survive, and the other would accept war rather than let it perish, and the war came.
>
> One eighth of the whole population were colored slaves, not distributed generally over the Union, but localized in the southern part of it. These slaves constituted a peculiar and powerful interest. All knew that this interest was somehow the cause of the war. . . . Both read the same Bible and pray to the same God, and each invokes His

aid against the other. It may seem strange that any men should dare to ask a just God's assistance in wringing their bread from the sweat of other men's faces, but let us judge not, that we be not judged. . . . With malice toward none, with charity for all, with firmness in the right as God gives us to see the right, let us strive on to finish the work we are in, to bind up the nation's wounds, to care for him who shall have borne the battle and for his widow and his orphan, to do all which may achieve and cherish a just and lasting peace among ourselves and with all nations.

A key feature of the Gettysburg Address was its emphasis on the nation's singleness: it is a single "people," not a collection of states.[72] The Second Inaugural Address continues this task of reimagination, constructing the nation with care and subtlety, using sonorous parallelisms. It includes both North and South as full elements in the nation, but positions the Union as the side that wanted and desperately tried to avoid division. The survival of the unitary nation—"nation" is used interchangeably with "Union"—is the starting point: the South would *make* war rather than see it survive, and the North was willing to *accept* war rather than see it perish. Thus the two sides are asymmetrical in their relationship to the nation: the secessionist struggle of the South is portrayed as a war of aggression against the body of the nation, and the Union's response is portrayed as a just response. The speech inspires a love of the nation's wholeness and a determination to protect it from that aggression.

The situation of the slaves now enters the picture, and the fact that the South was motivated by greed is emphasized, as Lincoln constructs a patriotism that rises above narrow self-interest. On the one hand, then, we have people motivated by self-interest, who "wring their bread from the sweat of other men's faces"—resonant quasi-biblical language—and even ask God to help them do it. On the other hand, we find those who would include the slaves as human beings and as citizens who count, totaling one-eighth of the population. The nation is now allied with respect, equality, inclusion, and a transcendence of narrow self-interest, the secessionist movement with egoism and false religion. Lincoln is alive to the role played by disgust and stigma in racism: disgust is sternly countered by insisting on the full and equal humanity of the slaves, who are "other men" with "faces" like one's own. (Note that it would have been easier to say "bodies," but Lincoln places his emphasis on the site of humanity.)

Finally, however, the speech appeals, famously, to mercy and forgiveness, since the nation is wounded and its wounds must be "bound up." By personifying the nation as a wounded soldier, he evokes compassion for all. Mercy is not acquittal—it does not compromise "firmness in the right"—but it gives us a way of going on together into an uncertain future.

The urgent need for reconciliation may have led Lincoln to stress a nonjudgmental attitude of forgiveness prematurely. A critic might argue that mercy for the convicted is compatible with condemnation, whereas forgiveness is not appropriate—unless there is, first, apology and change of heart—and Lincoln's "judge not" blurs the distinction between these two attitudes.[73] On the other hand, one might reply that the speech is actually shrewd and also generous, rising above partisanship and seeking reconciliation, trying to create a united "us" once again, while continuing to blame the South.[74] These aspects of the speech still give rise to controversy. Nonetheless, there can be little doubt that its sentiment of healing was urgently needed at the time, and contributed to at least the first stage of a reconciliation that is still in process.

Once again, the rhetoric of the speech is part of its meaning. Its sentiments are not simply abstract sentiments directed at constitutional principles. Its use of image and narrative, its rhythmic cadences of language, and its pithy and memorable phrases make the moral principles come alive. It has been observed that at times the speech verges on the musical, its cadences approaching those of a hymn.[75] Like the Gettysburg Address, it is easily memorized by children, forging their deepest images and, later, memories of what their nation is. Said in schools by black and white children together, it reminds them of the history of pain and struggle, but also of the evidence that respect, love, and sheer endurance can overcome pain. Once again, it constructs a patriotism that is interpretive, holding up general ideals and using them to criticize historical wrongs.

The speech ends, like the Gettysburg Address, on a strongly universalistic note: "to do all which may achieve and cherish a just and lasting peace among ourselves and with all nations." Lincoln once again constructs a type of national love that is not bellicose toward other nations, but seeks a future of universal peace and justice. This comes easily, because when national love focuses on ideals of inclusion and human dignity, such a love can easily lead on to a struggle for these things everywhere. Respect and inclusion are indeed the terms of a just and lasting peace.

Martin Luther King, Jr.: From Anger to Hope, Promise to Justice

The Emancipation Proclamation was signed in 1863. One hundred years later, its promise had not been fulfilled. Martin Luther King Jr.'s great "I Have a Dream" speech, delivered in Washington, D.C., on August 28, 1963, is another formative document of American education, and all young Americans have heard it thousands of times, recited in the moving cadences of King's extraordinary voice on the national holiday that honors him. Nobody could doubt that it is a masterpiece of rhetoric, and that its achievements go well beyond the abstract sentiments that it conveys. Its soaring images of freedom and revelation, its musical cadences, all give the general ideas of freedom, dignity, inclusion, and nonviolence wings, so to speak, making real people embrace them as ideals because of the way in which it cannily gets them to think of these notions as about them and their own.

Let us now examine the way in which King appeals to the history and traditions of the nation, constructing sentiments connected to an idea of America that is, once again, critical and interpretive, bringing forward valuable general ideals from the past and using them to find fault with an unjust reality:

> Five score years ago, a great American, in whose symbolic shadow
> we stand today, signed the Emancipation Proclamation. This mo-
> mentous decree came as a great beacon light of hope to millions of

Negro slaves who had been seared in the flames of withering injustice. . . .

But one hundred years later, the Negro still is not free. One hundred years later, the life of the Negro is still sadly crippled by the manacles of segregation and the chains of discrimination. . . . And so we've come here today to dramatize a shameful condition.

In a sense we've come to our nation's capital to cash a check. When the architects of our republic wrote the magnificent words of the Constitution and the Declaration of Independence, they were signing a promissory note to which every American was to fall heir. This note was a promise that all men, yes, black men as well as white men, would be guaranteed the "inalienable Rights" of "Life, Liberty and the pursuit of Happiness." It is obvious today that America has defaulted on this promissory note, insofar as her citizens of color are concerned. Instead of honoring this sacred obligation, America has given the Negro people a bad check, a check which has come back marked "insufficient funds."

But we refuse to believe that the bank of justice is bankrupt. We refuse to believe that there are insufficient funds in the great vaults of opportunity of this nation. . . .

But there is something that I must say to my people, who stand on the warm threshold which leads into the palace of justice: In the process of gaining our rightful place, we must not be guilty of wrongful deeds. Let us not seek to satisfy our thirst for freedom by drinking from the cup of bitterness and hatred. We must forever conduct our struggle on the high plane of dignity and discipline. We must not allow our creative protest to degenerate into physical violence. Again and again, we must rise to the majestic heights of meeting physical force with soul force.

[After the prophetic "I have a dream" sections]:

And this will be the day—this will be the day when all of God's children will be able to sing with new meaning:

> My country 'tis of thee, sweet land of liberty, of thee I sing.
> Land where my fathers died, land of the Pilgrim's pride,
> From every mountainside, let freedom ring! . . .

And if America is to be a great nation, this must become true.

And so let freedom ring from the prodigious hilltops of New Hampshire.

Let freedom ring from the mighty mountains of New York.

Let freedom ring from the heightening Alleghenies of Pennsylvania.

Let freedom ring from the snow-capped Rockies of Colorado.

Let freedom ring from the curvaceous slopes of California.

But not only that:

Let freedom ring from Stone Mountain of Georgia.

Let freedom ring from Lookout Mountain of Tennessee.

Let freedom ring from every hill and molehill of Mississippi.

From every mountainside, let freedom ring.

And when this happens, when we allow freedom to ring, when we let it ring from every village and every hamlet, from every state and every city, we will be able to speed up that day when all of God's children, black men and white men, Jews and Gentiles, Protestants and Catholics, will be able to join hands and sing in the words of the old Negro spiritual:

> Free at last! Free at last!
> Thank God Almighty, we are free at last!

The speech begins with an allusion to the Gettysburg Address, positioning itself as its next chapter. Just as Lincoln looked back to the founding as a moment of commitment to ideals that he (reinterpreting them) saw as gravely threatened, so King looks back to Lincoln's freeing of the slaves as a moment of commitment whose promise is still unrealized. He uses a very mundane and very American image for that failure: the nation has given the Negro people a bad check that has come back marked "insufficient funds." This insistent appeal to fiscal rectitude is also a way of alluding to America, since Americans so love to think of themselves as characterized by that virtue. It is a way of including the white members of his audience, by alluding to a value that they can be expected to share. They too are part of America; thus King creates a united "us" while also encouraging different members of his audience to respond in subtly different ways.

Throughout the speech, King sounds a note of urgency: the "swelter-ing summer of the Negro's legitimate discontent" means that there will be no peace in America until justice is done. And by this allusion to the evil schemes of Richard III, he inspires what he describes: a legiti-mate, justified anger at the wrongs done by American racism. But he also cultivates in his followers a patriotism that is restrained and criti-cal of violence: they must, in Gandhian fashion, attain moral superiority by forgoing violent deeds. Like Gandhi, who was a major inspiration, he makes nonviolence seem high, "majestic," and violence look sordid. At the same time, like Lincoln, King appeals to trust between the races, re-minding his followers that many white people are present and have joined the struggle for justice: "We cannot walk alone." By cultivating hope and trust, along with legitimate anger and insistent criticism, he defuses the urge to violence.

The visionary "I have a dream" section of the speech, so well known, is central to the speech's construction of an image of a future America in which all may join together on terms of equality. But then, immediately following upon this vision of a new America, King returns to national memory and national tradition by quoting in full the famous song "America," or "My Country 'Tis of Thee." Very significantly, he now says, "And if America is to be a great nation, this must become true." In other words, the song, which people usually sing complacently, as the account of a reality, is itself prophecy, and its words of freedom must be *made* true by committed action for justice. Even that complacent song, then, is turned into an exercise of the critical faculties.

The next section of the speech can well be described in the language of jazz, as a series of riffs on the song, as freedom is asked to ring from a series of regions of America. What is going on here? Several very inter-esting things. First, the image of America is being made concrete and physical by being linked to well-known features of geography. Second, geography itself is being moralized: the mountains of New York are now not just mountains, they are sites of freedom. Third, the body of the na-tion is being personified in a sensuous, indeed sexy way: the "heighten-ing Alleghenies," the "curvaceous slopes." (Thus the invitations to dis-gust so ubiquitous in malign patriotism are replaced by an embrace of the sensuous reminiscent of Walt Whitman.) But also: the end of the

Civil War is finally at hand, as freedom is asked to ring from a series of sites in the South. In a manner reminiscent of Lincoln's Second Inaugural Address, King expresses malice toward none and charity toward all. The note of sly humor as he gets in his dig at Mississippi ("let freedom ring from every hill and every molehill of Mississippi") is a reminder that bad behavior has not been forgotten; King thus avoids Lincoln's ambiguity about blame for bad deeds. Justified resentment has, however, been transcended in a surge of joy whose object is the nation of the future.

Like Lincoln's speeches, King's ends on a global note: the victory of integration in America will "speed up that day when *all* of God's children" will enjoy freedom. Thus critical patriotism melds naturally into a striving for global justice and an inclusive human love.

Lincoln and King express, and inspire in others, a profound love of America and a pride in her highest ideals. They do so, however, while constructing a narrative of America that is aspirational, foregrounding the best values to which America may be thought to be committed, and also deeply and explicitly critical, showing that America has failed to live up to her ideals. Both sound a note of critical yet hopeful rededication. The speeches seem made for critical pedagogy, for they lead naturally into classroom discussion: Where did America go wrong? What might be good ways of realizing the dream inherent in national ideals? How, even today, are we falling gravely short of the promise in our founding documents?

VI. India: Two Anthems, Two Flags

The case of India concerns the founding of a nation. There are no canonical documents or traditions, no memories—at least no shared and canonical memories—of long-past struggles that can command the agreement and the sentiments of all. Indeed, to this day a struggle continues over the proper image of the nation and its history, as partisans of the Hindu right endeavor to characterize that history as one of indigenous Hindu peace and alien domination, first by Muslims and then by (British) Christians.[76] Gandhi and Nehru, setting out to forge the image of a pluralistic India, united by commitment to a truly shared history of struggle for self-rule and by a shared commitment to the nation's people, had an uphill battle, since colonial oppression bred in many a strong desire to perform deeds of manly aggression, countering perceived humiliation with tough-guy domination. Their struggle involved, then, not just a set of ideals that were controverted by other more exclusionary ideals, but a conception of true manliness and strong patriotism that was controverted by a more warlike form of patriotism.

This contest of ideals is neatly exemplified by the debate, which is ongoing, over which of two songs should be the national anthem of India. *"Jana Gana Mana"* is rejected by the Hindu Right as too inclusive and not warlike enough; they prefer Bankim's *"Bande Mataram,"* which urges warlike aggression, uncritical devotion, and a Hindu conception of India's identity. *"Jana Gana Mana,"* as I argued in Chapter 4, cultivates a patriotism that is sensuous and passionate, but at the same time moral, highly inclusive, and friendly to the critical spirit.[77]

There is a parallel debate about the Indian flag. The official national flag, designed by Gandhi and Nehru and adopted at a meeting of the Constituent Assembly in July 1947, shortly before independence, is based on an earlier flag of the Indian National Congress. It has at its center the wheel of law, a symbol associated with the Buddhist emperor Ashoka, a favorite historical figure of Nehru's because he fostered religious toleration and a spirit of brotherhood. It is, then, a symbol of religious inclusiveness, nonviolence, and the supremacy of law over faction and sect. If a flag can suggest the critical spirit, this one does so. The colors of the flag are also significant. The saffron color represents courage; white represents truth and purity (crucial to Gandhi's reformulation of Hinduism); the green signifies peace and prosperity. The linkage of the three colors suggests that courage and sacrifice are to be pursued in a way compatible with Gandhian truth (i.e., inclusion of all citizens as equals), and with the goal of peace and prosperity for all. Equally significant is the law regarding the material composition of the flag: it is to be made of *khadi*, or cloth made from hand-spun thread. It is thus an outgrowth of Gandhi's critique of caste and class, since hand-spinning, in his movement, symbolized the renunciation of elitism and privilege and an embrace of the daily life of the poor. (When Nehru's daughter, Indira, got married in a *khadi* sari, this was a huge symbol of material equality.)

The right to manufacture the flag resides with the Khadi Development and Village Industries Commission. These laws shed a further light on the wheel at the flag's center: as well as law and right, the wheel alludes to Gandhi's *charka* or spinning wheel, and to its potent symbolism of equal human dignity.

The flag preferred by the Hindu Right is the saffron banner of the eighteenth-century Maharashtrian hero Shivaji, who conducted a briefly successful rebellion against Muslim rule. The flag is pure saffron with no other color or image—thus the courage part of the national flag without its truth, peace, law, and equality. It is an aggressive and exclusionary symbol, a symbol that says that Hindus will strike back against centuries of humiliation and seize power for themselves, subordinating others. And it is closely associated with the oath of loyalty taken every day by members of the Rashtriya Swayamsevak Sangh (RSS) as they raise that saffron banner: "I take the oath that I will always protect the purity of Hindu religion, and the purity of Hindu culture, for the supreme progress of the Hindu nation. I have become a component of the RSS. I will do the work of the RSS with utmost sincerity and unselfishness and with all my body, soul, and resources. And I will keep this vow for as long as I live. Victory to Mother India."[78] The patriotism engendered by the saffron flag deliberately silences the critical faculties. "We worship the saffron flag as our guru," young group leaders tell filmmaker Lalit Vachani. Addressing the flag, they say, "We bow before you, we are prepared to serve your cause."

Flags are usually taken for granted, and yet they have a powerful, if often unarticulated, emotional resonance. Members of the Hindu Right explicitly and passionately associate the saffron banner with a nation of unequals, with the idea of a "pure" Hindu culture free from the taint of "alien" religions and cultures, and with the abnegation of the critical spirit in a spirit of submission and peer solidarity. The actual Indian flag, while much more subdued in its emotive characteristics, is nonetheless a powerful symbol of a completely different kind. When citizens take pride in it (particularly when singing the national anthem at the same time), they are taking part in being members of an inclusive religiously plural nation, its strength drawn from many cultural, regional, and ethnic sources, all knit together by political principles and the rule of law.

Gandhi's Body: An Image of Justice

There was no more canny creator of critical patriotism than Mohandas Gandhi. Gandhi had views about patriotic emotion very close to those of Mazzini's: he thought that love of the nation, mediated by symbols such as flags and anthems, was an essential part of the path to a truly effective internationalism.[79] And yet he also urged critical thought, and chose symbols that proclaimed its centrality, such as *"Ekla Cholo Re."* As Rajmohan Gandhi emphasizes in his biography of his grandfather, Gandhi sang this song often himself, in a low but tuneful voice. "Tagore was the author of the song but Gandhi . . . had become the song."[80]

Gandhi wrote copiously, but his success in forging an activist and yet critical patriotism for the new nation, a vast majority of whose inhabitants could not read and write, owes little to his writings. What Gandhi brilliantly did was to make his own body a living symbol of a conception of the nation that was at one and the same time traditional and revisionary, stirring and highly critical. In keeping with his idea that the essential site of national struggle is inside each person, a struggle to conquer greed and anxious desires for domination of others in favor of compassionate concern, he portrayed himself as someone whose entire life focused on that struggle against greedy desire. His lean and yet vigorous physical persona, developed by walking hundreds of miles, showed a body that was devoted to justice for all, not to personal gratification, and certainly not to aggression. And knowledge of his abstemious personal practices (a vegetarian diet without dairy products, a vow of celibacy) colored people's response to the body they beheld. His repeated fasts for political ends dramatically used bodily renunciation in the pursuit of truth.

Gandhi did not fashion himself in a vacuum: he relied heavily on traditional Hindu images of the ascetic sannyasi, which were powerfully evocative, yet risked bolstering an exclusionary Hindu-first conception of national identity. He therefore had to be very careful lest his image of the nation seem Hindu in any exclusionary way. Consequently, throughout his life he took care to put Muslims in central positions in his freedom movement and to turn to them at what we might call key ritual moments. Thus, his famous fast unto death in 1947 was broken when he turned to Maulana Azad, a Muslim cleric and Congress party leader, and asked him for some orange juice and some bread. In doing so, he broke totally with traditional Hindu ideas of purity, which were exclusionary along lines of both caste and religion. Wielding the enormous power of traditional asceticism, he at the same time diverted it to an utterly new cause. As Rajmohan Gandhi summarizes, "All in all, curiosity and warmth were the Muslims' strongest instincts towards Gandhi, and they noticed his regard for their sensitivities."[81]

More problematic, in my view, was Gandhi's attempt to use his body as a symbol of gender equality. He created a persona that was found androgynous by many who met him; the words "childlike" and "maternal" frequently occur in discussions of the impression he made. And of course he often represented the vow of *brahmacharya,* or celibacy, as pro-women, a device to free women from men's sexual demands. He included women prominently in his circle. For Gandhi, the fight against aggression could be won only by a violent repudiation of the body and its erotic longings. In a marvelous imaginary dialogue with the dead leader in *Gandhi's Truth,* psychologist Erik Erikson says to him, "You should stop terrorizing yourself, and approach your own body with nonviolence."[82] Only when we can accept our own bodies and their sexuality without the violence of moralistic denial, he argues, will we really be able to surmount the tendencies to violent domination of others that lurk in every society.

Tagore, by contrast, sought to empower women as full agents, including erotic agents. He accepted the profound eroticism of the mother-child relationship and of many deep adult relationships. He conceived of personal love, including its erotic aspects, as the basis for a worldwide religion of humanity. Women, who had been taught renunciation and abnegation of desire for centuries, were freed by Tagore to pursue their own passionate course. For Amita Sen's wedding, he wrote a poem that, after her death, still hangs in the family house in Santiniketan, describing her as "a dancing torrent . . . immersing your playful steps / in the deep, taking on the universe, unafraid."[83] And that was his wish for all women. Like Erikson, Tagore held that it was not eroticism but its denial that was a primary source of destructive aggression. The Bauls practice gender equality and nonaggression through, not in spite of, an acceptance of the body.

Nonetheless, this one fault noted, Gandhi used his own body as the protagonist in the most ingenious drama of nation building ever staged. A central act in this drama was the march of protest against the British tax on the manufacture and sale of salt in 1930. The Salt March, in which tens of thousands marched 240 miles over twenty-three days from Gandhi's Sabarmati ashram to the sea at Dandi, was no casual mass protest. Every aspect was meticulously choreographed.[84] Gandhi's prepared statement for the journalists who gathered said simply, "I want world sympathy in this battle of Right against Might." First was the drama of the issue itself: as Gandhi put it, "Next to air and water, salt is perhaps the greatest necessity of life."[85] It was something that united rich and poor. Next were the costuming and staging of the actors: All the marchers wore *khadi* (homespun) and all the men wore a simple white cap. In the lead were chosen representatives of fifteen Indian provinces and of India's three major religions (Hindu, Muslim, Christian), as well as members of the "untouchable" castes. At the same time, and most central, were the director's rules for his actors. Gandhi insisted with dictatorial firmness on a list of mandates: no violence, no insults to British officials, no swearing or cursing—but also no saluting the Union Jack. Finally, at the center of the stage, we find the lead actor. In the words of Jawaharlal Nehru, whose deep emotion comes across clearly in this account:

> Today the pilgrim marches onward on his long trek. Staff in hand, he goes along the dusty roads of Gujarat, clear-eyed and firm of step, with his faithful band trudging along behind him. Many a journey he has undertaken in the past, many a weary road traversed. But longer than any that have gone before is this last journey of his, and many are the obstacles in his way. But the fire of a great resolve is in him, and surpassing love of his miserable countrymen. And love of truth that scorches and love of freedom that inspires.[86]

We find here two layers of public poetry: first, Gandhi's self-presentation, then Nehru's poetic chronicle, whose archaic and abstract style creates a virtual sense of lofty remoteness, ready for use in teaching generations of young Indians about the history of their nation. What do they learn?

That their nation was founded out of a righteous struggle against brute power; that it was born of solidarity with all who require the necessities of life; that it included all religions, classes, and castes. That its twin ideals are truth and freedom. Gandhi's body thus constructed a bridge from people's sense of their own life narratives to abstract principles.

When, at the culminating moment of this drama, Gandhi bathes in the sea and makes salt illegally, letting the water evaporate in his hand, a nation has been born.

Both supremely moral and supremely strategic, Gandhi knew that when the eyes of the world were on India, dignified nonviolent behavior both seemed and was strong and self-governing. Repeatedly—as in the famous protest at the Dharasana Salt Works—he knew how to theatricalize the moral superiority of the India cause, arranging episodes of civil resistance that would surely lead to countless Indians getting beaten up by British soldiers; the latter's violence looked increasingly desperate and small, while Indians resisted with dignity and nonviolence.[87] In the process, he made both his followers and countless others see manliness in a new way: the body that stood with dignity, taking blows, looked strong and proud. The body that kept dishing out the blows looked utterly at sea, hopelessly weak, not able to touch what it was trying to control. These acts of resistance were often accompanied by the Tagore song, a reminder that true national love requires constant critical vigilance and the willingness to defy convention.

Was Gandhian patriotism critical enough? One might have doubts, and Tagore surely did, expressing concern at Gandhi's unwillingness to change his mind in response to argument.[88] Gandhi, however, was not Sandip of *Ghare Baire*. He was gentle, respectful, and receptive. Particularly in his correspondence and his lifelong friendship with Jawaharlal Nehru, we see intense critical exchanges that create an attractive image of respectful dialogue for the new democracy. This too was constantly on public display.

Gandhian patriotism asked a lot of people. It asked the rich to live in solidarity with the poor and to make huge sacrifices of personal comfort. It asked all men to adopt a new type of nonviolent manliness that itself entailed a great deal of sacrifice, since revenge is pleasant. Only the use of symbols, Gandhi repeatedly said, could succeed in making people willing to take on these difficult tasks. Fortunately, he was a brilliant forger of symbols, symbols that moved because they were old and yet included because they were utterly new.

Nehru's "Tryst with Destiny" Speech: Work and Striving

Gandhi was a revolutionary. He was not a politician, and he could not have led a nation on a daily basis, dealing with legislatures, courts, and foreign leaders. Nor could he have administered economic policy: his ideas on that score were naïve and romantic. Thus the creation of India was in fact a complex partnership. At the founding of the new nation, the task of articulating its goals fell to Jawaharlal Nehru, the masterful politician who led India from 1947 to 1964. The speech that he delivered on the eve of independence is another landmark of critical patriotism.

It would have been easy to celebrate that auspicious occasion by delighted bashing of Britain, or simply by celebration of the victory that had just been achieved. Nehru takes a very different course. The speech is yet another example of the public construction of a story of the nation (and thus of an "us") that is at once inspiring and critical, dedicated to human inclusiveness and equality and to the meeting of essential human needs for all people near and far. Imagining Indian citizens not as aggressive warriors, but as mothers laboring to bring forth a new and just nation, Nehru borrows Gandhi's androgyny and draws a sentiment map that links proper patriotism to extended compassion and a commitment to economic justice. Indeed, he constructs an idea of the nation that is, centrally, an idea of work for a distant goal.

> Long years ago we made a tryst with destiny, and now the time comes when we shall redeem our pledge, not wholly or in full measure, but very substantially. At the stroke of the midnight hour, when the world sleeps, India will awake to life and freedom. . . . It is fitting that at this solemn moment, we take the pledge of dedication to the service of India and her people and to the still larger cause of humanity. . . .
>
> . . . Before the birth of freedom, we have endured all the pains of labour and our hearts are heavy with the memory of this sorrow.

Some of those pains continue even now. Nevertheless, the past is over and it is the future that beckons us now.

That future is not one of ease or resting but of incessant striving so that we may fulfill the pledges we have so often taken and the one we shall take today. The service of India means, the service of the millions who suffer. It means the ending of poverty and ignorance and disease and inequality of opportunity. The ambition of the greatest man of our generation has been to wipe every tear from every eye. That may be beyond us, but as long as there are tears and suffering, so long our work will not be over.

And so we have to labour and to work, and to work hard, to give reality to our dreams. Those dreams are for India, but they are also for the world, for all the nations and peoples are too closely knit together today for any one of them to imagine that it can live apart. Peace is said to be indivisible, so is freedom, so is prosperity now, and also is disaster in this one world that can no longer be split into isolated fragments. . . .

When one listens to a recording of this great speech, one thing that is immediately surprising is the absence of cheering. There are enthusiastic cheers at "awake to life and freedom"—but then, for the rest of the speech, the audience is silent, and Nehru's voice is, as ever, grave and solemn. This is remarkable at the celebration of the birth of a new nation. (Even the Gettysburg Address, an occasion of mourning, was interrupted frequently by applause.)[89] The basic decision Nehru took in crafting his speech was to portray independence as a challenge, not an achievement. And the dominant note is therefore not celebration but earnest contemplation of the work ahead.

Independence, as Nehru constructs the story of the new nation, is also no occasion for warlike self-assertion. For the idea of an exclusionary and warlike India, an image cherished by many of his countrymen, Nehru substitutes the idea of an India at work, characterized by incessant labor and striving toward the goal of eradicating human suffering—not only in India, but everywhere. He alludes to Gandhi's compassionate desire to wipe every tear from every eye, and makes this goal the job of the India of the future. Instead of the heroism of epic battles, we have a new Gandhian conception of heroism: effort and sacrifice in solidarity with the poorest. The speech is certainly emotional, but the emotions it constructs do not include resentment (of the Raj), hatred (of European imperialists), or even fear (of being dominated again). The dominant notes are compassion and determination, as all Indians are asked to look out from within their own egos to the sufferings of those who have the greatest misery, and to unite in determination to eradicate poverty. The speech contains hope as well as challenge, but it is a hope carefully limited by an awareness of the magnitude of the task. Hope is realistic only if people work very hard and with intense commitment.

Nehru's narrative of the nation looks backward as well as forward. He alludes with sadness to the violence of Partition, comparing the combined trauma of Partition and the independence struggle to the labor pains in which the new nation was born, and remarking that some of those pains continue. And yet, like Lincoln, he insists that the past of internal struggle is over. The nation exists, and it is the future that beckons—a future that unites all Indians regardless of religion, caste, or class. By referring to India as a whole and refusing to distinguish religious groups, Nehru makes plain his repudiation of the sectarian patriotism of the Hindu right. And crucially, at both the beginning and the end of the speech, he defines India as part of a movement for the eradication of poverty that embraces the entire world.

Nehru has the literary and rhetorical style[90] of the cultivated upper-caste and upper-class person he was. He is capable of showing intense emotion in his voice and in his words—not least in his eloquent speech after Gandhi's death, where one can hear tears in his voice. But he still speaks like a British-educated and privileged person, and he speaks in English. These qualities, valuable in establishing India on the world stage, needed the complementary skills of Gandhi, who was born in humbler (lower middle-class *bania* or trader) circumstances, who typically wrote in Gujarati rather than English, and who had a chameleon's ability to refashion himself as one of the lowest and poorest. But, despite his elite background, Nehru was himself a passionate champion of equality, and his insistence on economy and simplicity marked all his choices as India's first leader—or, as he put it in a famous speech, the "first servant of the Indian people." Like George Washington, Nehru also showed this commitment to equality in his lifestyle, creating an "us" that included leaders and citizens in a single circle of concern. His home, Teen Murti (preserved as a national museum), shows the taste for simplicity that he displayed throughout his life in his clothing, inspired by Gandhi's *khadi* movement. Nehru would have preferred the even greater simplicity of a small private house; security concerns led his colleagues to urge him to move to the larger building. Even so, to the visitor Teen Murti is a model of simplicity, with no ornateness and a very crisp design, amid spacious but simple gardens. Nehru insisted on paying all the expenses of his own family and personal guests, although the government paid for official hospitality. He even declined the entertainment allowance provided to all cabinet ministers.[91] In a cost-cutting measure, he removed the air-conditioning.[92] And he opened the grounds to the public. As historian Judith Brown concludes, "His whole lifestyle was in a sense iconic of the new nation and also of the new relationship between government and people, in contrast to the contrived display of the imperial regime and British concern for social separation and security as a small group of foreigners."[93]

These examples show us that patriotism can be inspiring, making the nation an object of love and cultivating extended compassion, while also activating rather than silencing the critical faculties. Such achievements are always unstable, since love needs to be cultivated anew in each generation, and kept alive throughout people's lives. Let us now ask how schools can contribute to this mission.

VII. Patriotism in the Schools: Content and Pedagogy

The topic of teaching patriotism in the schools is part of the far larger topic of how schools form citizens, a topic that would require us to talk about the importance of the humanities and arts for a decent public culture.[94] Our larger question about the formation of a citizen who is both loving and critical requires an entire account of how critical thinking is taught at various ages, how Socratic pedagogy complements that content, and how the imaginative ability to inhabit the points of view of people different from the self can be refined and cultivated at different ages. All this I have discussed elsewhere,[95] and so I shall confine myself here to a very narrow understanding of my topic, speaking only about the formation of emotions explicitly directed toward the nation and its story. Rather than a synthetic account, I shall present a list of maxims that ought to guide instruction in patriotism. These maxims are but a supplement to the historical examples given above, which provide a good idea of how a critical yet loving patriotism works; those examples would be prominent in any education for patriotism in the schools of those two nations.

1. *Begin with love.* Children will not be good dissenters in or critics of a nation unless they first care about the nation and its history. My own education did this very well, hooking me in by the dramatic tale of Sybil Ludington in the Revolution, a character who resonated with my love of adventure and my ambition to be something daring, a girl who did what girls usually don't do. By the time I was seven, I already loved the American founding and saw myself in it—but, and this is important, in a way that laid the groundwork for a lot of criticism later on, since I saw the story of America as a story of dissent, of the rejection of false values and the search for freedom. Something as abstract as political liberty acquired motivational force through its embodiment in the persona of a little girl whom I wanted to be, riding horses and pursuing a remarkable adventure. She was a defiant girl, not a submissive traditionalist, and so I linked love of country to that spirit of autonomy. We might say that the abstract values of liberty and individualism were eroticized—connected to things such as my father's love and admiration, and the feeling of riding a horse. This was an excellent starting point for further investigations. So start with love, but it is important that from the beginning love should be linked to good values that can become, later on, a basis for criticizing bad values—and, preferably, linked to the critical spirit itself.

2. *Introduce critical thinking early, and keep teaching it.* There is a lot of research on the teaching of critical reasoning, and it shows that young children can learn skills of reasoning with joy, indeed love, if they are

presented cleverly and in an age-appropriate way. So the dangers begin to be headed off here. At first critical thinking can be taught with any content, but at some point it is good to move it onto the stage of the patriotic narrative itself, getting children to think about the reasons the patriots fought, about the difficult struggle of the Civil War, and so forth. It is natural to mingle these two parts of the curriculum: thus, when visiting the Lincoln Memorial, and when deeply moved by Lincoln's grief and humility, one might study the Gettysburg Address and ask questions about its argument, and about the reasoning of the two sides before, during, and after the war.

It's obvious that critical thinking is not just a subject matter but an entire approach to pedagogy. If education is based on rote learning and regurgitation, all too common in government schools in India, and sadly on the rise in the United States on account of national testing, there is little hope of teaching patriotism critically, because the critical faculties are being stifled by the entire system.

3. Use positional imagination in a way that includes difference. Since one of the big dangers in the misplaced-values department is underinclusiveness, and another is stigmatization and disgust, it is important to teach patriotism in a way that keeps students actively imagining the situation of various minorities—slaves and ex-slaves, new immigrants, religious dissenters (such as Lillian Gobitas, a very nice story for elementary school)—and even acting those roles in classroom theatricals. When children feel the pain of stigma and exclusion in their own bodies, this gives them an understanding they can acquire nowhere else. When the imagination is drawn to something, one naturally wants to act it out; however, children often shrink from the difficult roles, and it's important that they all get a turn to be the outcast, the stigmatized, Rosa Parks in the back of the bus.

In India, children learn critical patriotism in part through their own manual labor, a very Gandhian form of learning. For example, they engage in craft labor that was formerly a source of caste division and stigma. Thus, a privileged Brahmin girl told me with no trace of self-consciousness of her project in leatherworking, and when I asked whether there was any reluctance to engage in it, she seemed quite surprised. Perhaps this is because her school is in close proximity to Santiniketan, but she assured me that this is a staple of public education everywhere.

Teachers should connect the struggles over inclusion in their nation's history to the ongoing efforts in the classroom to confront issues of stigma and bullying, since every classroom has such issues. Are there children in the class who are experiencing a little bit of what Rosa Parks suffered? What a *dalit* used to suffer (or, perhaps, still does)? If the treatment of Rosa Parks was un-American, in the light of our evolving concept of America, and if the treatment of a *dalit* child was un-Indian in the light of that nation's founding values, what about the treatment we mete out to others (gays and lesbians, people with disabilities)?

As children come to love an America, or an India, that really stands for inclusiveness (reading such poems as Emma Lazarus's "The New Colossus," which contains the line "Give me your tired, your poor," or singing *"Jana Gana Mana"* and *"Ekla Cholo Re"*), they had better also ask disturbing questions about what their nation is doing about poverty today, and whether certain things about America in the present might not be un-American in the light of some of the accounts of patriotism the class has been learning. There will naturally be much debate about this, and it should continue. Not all the positions taken will be congenial to all students and parents. (My father threatened to withdraw me from school when I came home defending FDR and the New Deal. He said that I had been brainwashed by my teachers.)

Once again, the advice to include positional imagining in a particular way presupposes that teachers are already cultivating the positional imagination in the first place, using theater, narrative, and other arts to develop the capacity to see the world from someone else's point of view. This cannot be taken for granted.

4. Show the reasons for past wars without demonizing. Since the beginning of the modern nation, one of the serious reservations about patriotic sentiment has been that it leads people to demonize other nations and their people and to charge out unwisely to make war against them. Herder, we recall, urged a "purified patriotism" that would teach a horror of war and of a "false statecraft" that would lead to war.

Here we arrive at one of the most delicate areas of our topic. On the one hand, one of the purposes of patriotic sentiment is to fortify people to endure the hardships of war when they must. So we don't want people to think that war is always wrong. Here we must reject the guidance of Gandhi, who suggested that if the Axis powers invaded India, Indians should not fight back; he proposed reasoning with the Nazis in a non-violent manner. Nehru, who understood the horrors of fascism well, took profound exception to Gandhi's pacifism concerning the Second World War, and he was correct. On the other hand, we do not want children to learn to rush into wars as if they were occasions for glory rather than bitter struggle. So, learning about the horrors and pains of war is altogether appropriate, despite the fact that it is not always popular with parents.

It is appropriate, as well, to learn about the pain that one inflicts upon others. Thus objections to a critical exhibit about Hiroshima and Nagasaki at the Smithsonian Institution in 1994 were misplaced. (Unfortunately, the concessions made by the museum led to alterations in the exhibit[96] and to uncontroverted statements that misrepresented the historical record.)[97] Teachers and students should debate vigorously in the classroom the case for and against the use of nuclear weapons, but we must begin by acknowledging the terrible toll they took. It is all too easy to stigmatize foreign nationals as subhuman, and to justify war against them in that way. Any wise policy in the area of war and peace begins from the acknowledgment that the people on the other side are fully human. On the Indian side, there's an unfortunate lack of public monuments and rituals connected to the horrors of Partition, which might have addressed festering resentments that extended into the future, fueling interreligious violence. Recent tragedies, such as the anti-Sikh riots in Delhi in 1984 and the 2002 Gujarat massacre of more than 2,000 Muslim civilians, also deserve public commemoration in an extremely critical spirit, although this is most unlikely to happen, given that many of the malefactors in these two cases have not even been brought to justice.

Finally, as the example of Nehru/Gandhi shows, it is important to emphasize that all the world's nations share some goals, such as the eradication of poverty, toward which we can and must strive together.

An emphasis on these cooperative goals contributes a great deal to the construction of a story of national purposes and ideals that is not wrongly bellicose and adversarial.

5. Teach a love of historical truth, and of the nation as it really is. One of the problems of patriotism, which can often abet misplaced values, the stigmatization of minorities, and uncritical homogeneity, is historical distortion. So one of the most important aspects of teaching patriotism in the schools is teaching how to evaluate historical evidence, how to construct, criticize, and then defend a historical narrative. Students need to learn that the past is not self-evident, that it must be painstakingly put together from materials that are not self-interpreting. And yet, they must also learn that not all narratives are equal, that some are terrible distortions and evasions, that ideology is not the same thing as patient historical reconstruction.

Unfortunately, political groups today sometimes try to capitalize on postmodern attacks on historical truth to commend their own slipshod and error-ridden tales. India's Hindu Right has become especially adept at this practice, both in India and in controversies in the United States over the teaching of Hindu history.[98] So, we should make students alert to the fact that any historical narrative is created by humans situated somewhere, often with interested motives. But we must also prevent them from concluding that anything goes, it's just your narrative against mine, and there's no such thing as what really happened. As historian Tanika Sarkar said of the attempt by the Hindu Right to deny the rapes and killings of Muslims in Gujarat in 2002:

> There can be no political implication, no resource for struggle, if we deny the truth claims of these histories of sadism, if we . . . denigrate the search for true facts as mere positivism, a spurious scientism. For the life and death of our political agenda depend on holding on to the truth claim, . . . to that absolute opposition to their proclamation that they will make and unmake facts and histories according to the dictates of conviction. . . . We need, as a bulwark against this, not simply our story pitted against theirs, but the story of what had indubitably happened.[99]

This point is especially urgent. Patriots often dislike reality, preferring a glorified version of the past and present. They fear that presenting the nation as it is will undercut love. But really, what they are saying is that the human heart can't stand reality, that lovers can't stand the real bodies of those they love, that parents can't embrace children who do not live up to an idealized picture of achievement. Though sometimes true in sad cases, this is a terrible starting point for the education of a nation's children. Indeed, if particular children do show difficulty loving other people once the signs of their bodily reality are manifest, schools should worry about those children and intervene. The mind hooked on perfection is destined to despair.

VIII. Institutional Support Structures

Schools do not exist in a social and political vacuum. Attempts to teach a patriotism that steers clear of both Scylla and Charybdis will be much more likely to succeed in societies that surround the schools with a set of institutional safeguards. Given the unreliability of majority sentiment, we would be well advised not to trust entirely to the goodwill of local school boards, or even state legislatures, to keep good traditions of patriotism going. Law and institutional structure are essential props to the good in patriotism, and we can mention three factors that will contribute to our getting the good out of patriotic education without the bad.

1. *Constitutional rights, and an independent judiciary.* Constitutional rights are bulwarks for minorities against the panic and excess of majorities. Because minorities (such as the Gobitas children) are always at risk from patriotism, which can often whip up majority sentiment against them, patriotism needs to be advanced in conjunction with a firm and comprehensive tradition of constitutional rights protecting all citizens, and an independent judiciary, detached from public bias and panic, as these rights' interpreter.

2. *Protections for the rights of immigrants.* Patriotism always risks veering into xenophobia, and xenophobia often takes new immigrant groups as its targets. In addition to protections for minorities who already enjoy

citizens' rights, a decent patriotism needs to be taught in conjunction with firm protections for the rights of legal immigrants who are not (or not yet) citizens, and rational and consistent policies and laws concerning illegal immigrants.

3. Freedoms of speech and press. Perhaps the most important factor of all is the one emphasized by Kant, in all of his works about the prospect of a peaceful international community: strong legal protection of the freedom of speech and dissent, and of the freedom of the press; more generally, protection of the voices of intellectuals who play leading roles in shaping a critical public culture. To the extent that a nation succeeds in building such a culture, to that extent it has in every town and region built-in safeguards against the excesses of patriotism run amok. *Barnette* shows us the importance of the press and its critical freedom to the relatively happy ending to the *Minersville* story of patriotism run amok.

Love of one's own nation is not a good thing in itself. Very often it is a very bad thing. National stories can be constructed badly, and even a basically good narrative can be badly taught. Such instruction can do great damage. Nonetheless, a nation that pursues goals that require sacrifice of self-interest needs to be able to appeal to love of the nation, in ways that draw on symbol and rhetoric, emotional memory and history—as Washington, Lincoln, King, Gandhi, and Nehru all successfully did. If people interested in relief of poverty, justice for minorities, political and religious liberty, democracy, and global justice eschew symbol and rhetoric, fearing all appeals to emotion and imagination as inherently dangerous and irrational, people with less appetizing aims will monopolize these forces, to the detriment of democracy, and of people.

CHAPTER NINE

Tragic and Comic Festivals: Shaping Compassion, Transcending Disgust

Brave men rejoice in the output of their own energy, they create their own festivals. These cowards who have not the power to rejoice in themselves have to rely on what others have left. Afraid lest the world should lack festivals in the future, they save up the scraps left over by their predecessors for later use. They are content with glorifying their forefathers because they know not how to create for themselves.

—A Baul singer, quoted in Tagore, *The Religion of Man*[1]

I. The Theatre of the Body

On his way to Troy to fight with the Greeks in the Trojan War, Philoctetes walked by mistake into a sacred shrine on the island of Lemnos. His foot, bitten by the serpent who guards the shrine, began to ooze with a smelly ulcerous sore, and his cries of pain disrupted the army's religious observances. So the commanders abandoned him on the island, with no companions and no resources but his bow and arrows. Unlike others who wrote tragedies on this theme, Sophocles imagines Lemnos as an uninhabited island, in this way giving enormous emphasis to Philoctetes' isolation from human company and human speech. He is seen and heard only by the animals who must also become his food.

Ten years later, learning that they cannot win the war without his magical bow, the Greeks return, determined to trick him into returning to Troy. The leaders of the expedition show no interest in Philoctetes as a person, speaking of him only as a tool of their ends. The chorus of common soldiers has a different response. Even before they see the man, they imagine what it might be like to be him, and they enter a protest against the callousness of the commanders:

> For my part, I have compassion for him.
> Think how
> with no human company or care,
> no sight of a friendly face,
> wretched, always alone,
> he wastes away with that savage disease,
> with no way of meeting his daily needs.
> How, how in the world, does the poor man survive?[22]

They picture his hunger, his physical pain, his isolation, his outcry of distress, the echo that is its only reply.

As the men of the chorus vividly imagine the life of a man whom no human eye has seen for ten years, a man whose very humanity has been rendered invisible by ostracism and stigma, they stand in for, and allude to, the mental life of the spectators. All are invited to imagine a type of needy homeless life to which prosperous people rarely direct their attention—a life, they are repeatedly told, that might become the lot even of the fortunate. Tragic spectatorship cultivates emotional awareness of shared human possibilities, rooted in bodily vulnerability.

On a different day, the same audience watches, laughing, a confrontation between two different styles of manliness. Lamachus, the aggressive manly man, the heroic general, comes back from battle torn and suffering, crying out in pain. Rural farmer Dikaiopolis, who has opposed the war, contentedly celebrates the pleasures of eating, drinking, and imminent sex. His erection (vividly represented by his costume) is a sign not of macho aggression, but of its successful refusal. And by representing Lamachus as distressed by his fate, the play reminds us of what we should have known already: war hurts. The tough-soldier personality can be inculcated very deeply in men, but it does not really survive the confrontation with one's own blood and guts, not to mention the absence of life's pleasures. Lamachus is a real historical figure, but his name is also symbolic, alluding to battle, *machê*. Dikaiopolis is a fiction, and his name means "the just city."

Lamachus at this point wishes he were Dikaiopolis. He is not—but at least he has become the tragic hero, crying out like a veritable Philoctetes in the spasms of his pain, acknowledging that he has a vulnerable body. Lamachus: "Hold my legs, hold them, *papai* [the same rather unusual interjection of pain that Philoctetes uses], hold them tightly, comrades." Dikaiopolis: "And as for me, hold my prick, hold the middle, hold it tightly, you dear girls." Lamachus: "My head is reeling, I feel like a rock hit my head, and I am about to pass into darkness *[skotodiniô]*." Dikaiopolis: "As for me, I feel like going to bed. I have a hard-on, and I want to fuck in the darkness *[skotobiniô]*."[3] As each tragic utterance is comically answered, the very excess and shamefulness of the comic hero look like a kind of healing: normal life, and the pleasures that all human beings love, rather than the cruel depredations of war, such as bed for pleasure, rather than bed for wounds. Lamachus went to war recklessly, and he is punished—because, as it turns out, the comic body is also the soldier's body, only he doesn't realize it until he returns home in pain.

The ending of Aristophanes's *Acharnians* (425 BCE) was enacted before a group of citizens who were heavily invested in the Peloponnesian war effort. The comedy was part of an official and highly sacred civic festival, and their city has long been at war. But the drama reminds them of the ultimate goal of peace. No sane member of the audience would truly choose the lot of Lamachus for its own sake, as a way of being brave. All will recognize their own longing for the good things in life symbolized by Dikaiopolis. This identification is a way of going over, for a time, to what one might not implausibly call the "soft" side of things, to the side that loves pleasure, is scared of dying, and has much skepticism about "manly" aggression.[4] Laughing at the juxtaposition of Dikaiopolis's triumph to Lamachus's torment, even the most militaristic members of the audience recognize a part of their own souls. (We recall Cherubino's horror of "manly" battle, his preference for music and love.)

The ancient Athenian democracy assigned a central place, in the education of citizens, to tragic and comic dramas. During the festivals at which these dramas were performed, all other business stopped. During the City Dionysia, a major civic festival, three tragedians competed with three tragedies each, plus a satyr play. Citizens watched all of these (alongside women and some foreign visitors), and later determined which playwright would get the prize. And they also acted: the trainers of the chorus were wealthy citizens, and all its members were male citizens, usually young.[5] Lead actors were also usually respected citizens. At the Lenaia, a smaller festival during winter, tragedies were again performed, but comedies joined them: usually five, in competition with one another. They too were part of a civic occasion to which considerable importance was attached.

Dramas, both tragic and comic, were assessed for their message as well as their style, and the accent was on civic reflection and instruction.[6] Even the arrangement of the theater contributed to this emphasis: instead of being seated in the dark, in seeming isolation from one another, gazing ahead at an illuminated spectacle—as in many modern performances—spectators, seated in the sunlight, saw across the staged action the faces of their fellow citizens.

The performances were occasions for deep emotion; tales abound of intense emotional reactions on the part of the audience, including pregnant women whom the tragic action precipitated into labor. These emotions, however, were not considered antithetical to the idea of a democracy based upon deliberation and argument: indeed, just the opposite. They were considered important inputs for political discussion.

Often the input was highly critical—as when Euripides's *Trojan Women* invites its audience to question the rightness of the recent decision to kill all the men of the rebellious colony of Melos and to enslave (and rape) the women and children. All too often, people deliberate about the fate of others without having any clear imaginative sense of their human reality. A drama such as this promotes an experience that might penetrate that obtuseness, informing future choices. Argument cannot function well without the imagination. Rational deduction alone will not tell us whether women are full-fledged human beings, or whether rape really hurts. It's easy to construct a logically valid argument for the conclusion that it is right to enslave the women of Melos. Arguments are only as good as their starting points, and tragedies such as these promote an emotional insight that connects people to the reality not only of what their own side is suffering but also of what they are doing to others.

All societies need to manage public grief in ways that do not defeat aspiration, and to extend compassion from the local to the general in appropriate ways. All need, too, to create an attitude to the bodies of others that helps citizens overcome a bodily disgust that can easily turn aggressive. Large modern nations cannot precisely replicate the dramatic festivals of ancient Athens, but they can try to understand their political role and find their own analogues—using political rhetoric, publicly sponsored visual art, the design of public parks and monuments, public book discussions, and the choice and content of public holidays and celebrations. First, however, they need to understand more deeply what the tragic and comic festivals accomplished. This example is intrinsically, theoretically interesting, and it also happens to be historically influential, given the centrality of the ancient Greek classics in the United States, and, really, all over the world.[7] As we'll see, tragic festivals focus on the development of compassion, but do not neglect disgust; comedy of the Aristophanic type primarily confronts disgust, but also cultivates a spirit of fellowship.

II. Tragic Spectatorship and Appropriate Compassion

The central emotion aroused by tragic spectatorship is compassion, an emotion that responds to the misfortunes of others. Chapter 6 defined it, following both Aristotle and Rousseau, as having three elements: a thought that the suffering is serious; a thought that the person is not the primary cause of his or her own suffering; and (in many cases if not all) the thought that the suffering involved things "such as might happen" in a human life, and is thus a possibility for the spectators as well as the suffering characters. Finally, we need to add a "eudaimonistic thought": the thought that the suffering person is part of one's own circle of concern.

The "thought of similar possibilities" is not strictly necessary for compassion, I argued, since we can feel compassion for creatures whose possibilities are very different from our own. But the idea of similar possibilities is extremely useful in preventing a common type of moral obtuseness, in which people see the other as a remote and distant being whose possibilities and vulnerabilities are utterly unlike those of the spectator.

Such distancing is a constant possibility in societies divided by class, race, gender, and other identities, particularly when disgust and stigma are involved. As we've seen, disgust operates by representing the other as a base animal, utterly unlike the (allegedly) pure and transcendent self. Disgust often, in effect, denies the reality of the (dominant group's) body, projecting bodily vulnerability onto the subordinate group (they have Yahoo bodies, we do not), and then using that projection as an excuse for further subordination. A failure to have the thought of similar possibilities leads to a failure in the eudaimonistic thought: the other is expelled from the circle of concern by the thought of unlikeness, or base animality.

Tragic spectatorship, emphasizing common human vulnerabilities, undoes the lies involved in the segmentations produced by disgust and what we have called anthropodenial,[8] making it possible to extend concern beyond the dominant group.[9] It is always perilous to offer sweeping generalizations about "tragedy" and "the tragic," and there are tragedies that contain moral obtuseness. Nonetheless, reflecting further about the *Philoctetes* (the focal point of a long theoretical tradition reflecting about tragedy, bodily pain, and common humanity) will help us discern structures of reversal and mourning inherent in the genre itself, which tend in their very shape toward the undoing of these ethical errors. Appreciating these general structures will enable us to think well about how we might produce a similar effect in different environments.

The *Philoctetes* is surely a play that leads its spectator to acknowledge the horror of bodily pain and the social isolation that often accompanies it. By bringing its spectators close to extreme bodily suffering, though with enough distance not to repel people (the attack of pain is depicted formally, by a metrical outcry rather than a shriek), it promotes an experience that is in the best sense democratic, one that acknowledges the equal frailty of all human beings and their fully equal need for the goods of life that Philoctetes so conspicuously lacks: food, shelter, relief of pain, conversation, nondeceptive friendship, political voice.

In the *Rhetoric,* Aristotle offers a highly influential list of the common occasions for tragic compassion. The list is surprisingly timeless: a list of occasions for compassion volunteered by contemporary Americans is very similar.[10] And it reads like a plot outline of Sophocles's play. The list contains two categories: painful and destructive things, and bad things for which luck is responsible. (The rationale for the division is unclear.) In the first group are deaths, bodily damages, bodily afflictions, old age, illnesses, and lack of food. In the second group are friendlessness; having few friends; being separated from one's friends and relations; ugliness; weakness; deformity; getting something bad from a source from which you were expecting something good; having that happen many times; the coming of good after the worst has happened; and that no good should befall someone at all, or that one should not be able to enjoy it when it does. Philoctetes has every item on this list excepting old age—including the more unusual ones (getting something bad from a source from which you were expecting something good, having the good come when it is too late to enjoy it). It is as if Aristotle, who clearly knew the play (since he refers to it in the *Nicomachean Ethics*), used it as a template for his own discussion. In any case, from this list we can see the extent to which the play provides us with a map of compassion and its occasions, as well as the underlying thoughts (seriousness, blamelessness, similarity) that enter into the structure of the emotion. The play shows the magnitude of these events, making it difficult to deny that they matter deeply. We are given incentives to fight against these bad things: to alleviate pain, to extend the life span, et cetera. But this struggle is not anthropodenial: it does not express a refusal of the basic conditions of mortal life.

The play shows us, as well, the extent to which deprivation affects the mental life itself, poisoning speech and thought. Philoctetes has to think all the time of how he is going to get his food; the effort to survive is so difficult and so continual that it threatens to swallow up other thought. "Pitiable alike in his pain and his hunger, he has anxieties with no let-up" (185–187). Second, this effort is not a peaceful one: it introduces emotions of agitation and confusion into the inner world. Philoctetes is "bewildered at each need as it arises" (174–175). His suffering is "spirit-devouring." He is as helpless as a child without his nurse. Pain infan-tilizes. Pain and solitude together also make thinking crude. Philoctetes has not used language for years, and he knows that he is "grown savage" (226). And when pain comes in full force, as the remarkable central scene depicts, it comes perilously close to removing human thought and speech altogether. Philoctetes's metrical cry "*apappapai papa papa papa papai*" (746) shows us the razor's edge that separates human be-ings from other animals, for his cry retains meter and thus a semblance of human ordering, but it has lost syntax and morphology, the hallmarks of human language.[11] Pain can give us lives unworthy of our human dignity.

Thus the play corrects potential defects in the judgment of serious-ness: these things matter deeply, and they matter for us all. It also persis-tently corrects errors in the judgment of fault, for repeatedly Philoctetes asserts that he is not at fault—a mere accident was the source of his woes. And in that way the play underlines the idea of similar possibilities, since if this can happen to this well-intentioned and blameless man, it could happen to any of us.

Philoctetes is physically disgusting. His isolation is a result of stigma. Disgust is an undercurrent throughout the play, as Neoptolemus ex-claims in revulsion on discovering pus-filled rags next to Philoctetes's dwelling, and as Philoctetes himself expects to be shunned. The play therefore does something further: it brings spectators close to the life of an outcast, who has been found not fully human, and it convinces spectators—like the chorus and ultimately Neoptolemus—of his full and equal humanity. Tragedies deal with matters that are difficult to con-front, but they do so in a way that is made palatable to a squeamish audi-ence, by the seductions of poetry, rhythm, and melody. In real life fear for oneself might lead to paralyzing self-focus, and physical disgust might lead to distancing and exclusion. By addressing such a scenario, but without the sensory qualities that elicit disgust and without the real-life involvement that could arouse fear, tragedy undermines exclusion.

Many errors in compassion stem from a narrowness in the way we construct our circle of concern, a part of our innate animal heritage that is made worse by uniquely human responses of disgust and anthropodenial. Nonetheless, we also saw (as Batson's experiments showed) that an extension of the circle of concern can be jump-started by a vivid narrative. Tragedies perform the Batson task with enormous skill, deploying resources of poetry, music, and dance to make the characters' plight vivid and moving. A person who has been ejected from the characters' circle of concern is restored to it by the power of art.

Tragic spectatorship, in short, with its insistent focus on bodily vulnerability, is a powerful device toward overcoming segmentation in social life.[12] Even if right now the privileged have opportunities and possibilities that are very different from those of the less privileged, tragedy (taking privileged people, usually, as protagonists) reminds them that terrible plights are the common lot of all, even the most privileged. These valuable tendencies are particularly salient in a work such as the *Philoctetes*, but they are in many respects inherent in the genre, whose very plot structure emphasizes common human vulnerability.

Because of its emphasis on common human plights, tragedy also has an outward or universalizing movement that tends to correct the narrowing focus that Batson's research shows to be all too prevalent in compassion. We said that because of this narrowness emotional experience needs to be in dialogue at all times with good moral principles, but we also said that it was a good thing if the emotional experience itself could contain a bridge toward the universal. Tragedy provides such a bridge. We still need the conversation with principle, but it helps us get there from our narrower and more particular immersions.[13] In effect, it can lead us to emotions that are principle-dependent in Rawls's sense—but retaining the energy and symbolic precision of art.

Finally, tragedy generates a valuable dialogue about fault and social change. Why was Philoctetes suffering? Because of the callousness of those who left him unattended. Why are the Trojan women suffering? Because rape and slavery are the common lot of conquered peoples. Although some philosophers have held that tragedy promotes resignation or a sense of inevitable necessity, ancient Athenian tragedy far more often produced a critical ferment in which people ask themselves how much of the suffering they see is indeed the result of things that cannot be changed, and how much the result of bad human conduct.[14] Tragedy does convey the limits of human ambition, but not in a way that leads to paralysis of the will, and not in a way that silences difficult questions about blame, responsibility, and the possibility of change.

III. Tragic Dilemmas and Fundamental Entitlements

All societies, however decent and aspiring, face difficult choices. Because the societies we are considering protect a plurality of entitlements for all citizens, considering each person as intrinsically valuable and deserving of concern, they will sometimes encounter cases in which those plural values come into conflict.[15] Tragic spectatorship has already helped citizens learn to identify key opportunities that ought to be protected for all, since their absence poses an especially grave obstacle to a life worthy of human dignity. But it makes another important contribution: tragedies also promote understanding of these conflicts, and of the limits of some common approaches to them. Although the idea of value conflict is prominent in ancient Greek tragedy, it is equally at home in India—seated, indeed, at the very heart of the great epic *Mahabharata*. So let us turn to a key case from that work.

Arjuna stands at the head of his troops. A huge battle is about to begin. On his side are the Pandavas, the royal family headed by Arjuna's eldest brother, legitimate heir to the throne. On the other side are the Kauravas, Arjuna's cousins, who have usurped power. More or less everyone has joined one side or the other, and Arjuna sees that many on the enemy side are blameless people for whom he has affection. In the ensuing battle he will have to kill as many of them as possible. How can it be right to embark on a course that involves trying to bring death to so many relations and friends? How, on the other hand, could it possibly be right to abandon one's own side and one's family duty?

Arjuna saw his closest kinsmen, related to him as father or grandfather, uncle or brother, son or grandson, preceptor as well as companion and friend, on both sides. Overcome by this sight, he said in sorrow and compassion, "O Krishna, when I see my own people ready to fight and eager for battle, my limbs shudder, my mouth is dry, my body shivers, and my hair stands on end. Furthermore, I see evil portents, and I can see no good in killing my own kinsmen. It is not right and proper that we should kill our own kith and kin, the Kauravas. How can we be happy if we slay our own people? . . . O Krishna, how can I strike with my arrows people like the grandsire Bhisma and the preceptor Drona, who are worthy of my respect?" . . . Having said these words, Arjuna threw away his bow and arrows, and sat down sorrowfully on the seat of his car.[16]

Arjuna poses himself not one but two questions. The first question, which I shall call the obvious question, is the question of what he ought to do. That question may be difficult to answer. It may also be difficult to identify the best method for arriving at the answer. In this case, Arjuna and his advisor Krishna differ sharply about method, Krishna recommending a single-minded pursuit of duty without thought for the unpleasant consequences, Arjuna proposing a careful consideration of all the foreseeable consequences.[17] What is not difficult, however, is to see that it is a question that has to be answered, since some action must be taken, and even inaction is, in such a situation, a kind of action. In that sense, the question is obvious; it is forced by the situation. Arjuna cannot be both a loyal dutiful leader of his family and at the same time a preserver of lives of friends and relations on the other side. He has to choose.

The other question is not so obvious, nor is it forced by the situation. It might easily have eluded Arjuna. I shall call this the "tragic question." This is, whether any of the alternatives available to Arjuna in the situation is morally acceptable. Arjuna feels that this question must be faced, and that when it is faced, its answer is no. Krishna, by contrast, either simply fails to see the force of the question altogether, or recommends a policy of deliberately not facing it, in order the better to get on with one's duty.

The tragic question is not simply a way of expressing the fact that it is difficult to answer the obvious question. Difficulty of choice is quite independent of the presence of moral wrong on both sides of a choice. In fact, in this case as in many tragic dilemmas, it is rather clear what Arjuna should do: much though he is tempted to throw away his arrows, that would accomplish nothing, resulting simply in the deaths of many more on his own side, and possibly the loss of their just cause, while countless lives will still be lost on the other side. So he should fight. The tragic question registers not the difficulty of solving the obvious question, but a distinct difficulty: the fact that all the possible answers to the obvious question, including the best one, are bad, involving serious moral wrongdoing. In that sense, there is no "right answer."[18]

What is the point of asking the tragic question? When we think about Arjuna's dilemma, it might seem that Krishna has a point: the real question is the obvious question, and the tragic question is just a useless distraction. "O Arjuna," he says, "why have you become so depressed in this critical hour? Such dejection is unknown to noble men; it does not lead to the heavenly heights, and on earth it can only cause disgrace." Quite right, one may think: when one has seen where one's duty lies, one ought to get on with it, without tragic moaning and groaning. We don't want military leaders who self-indulgently wring their hands about the blood they are about to shed, or throw away their arrows to sit sorrowfully on the seats of their cars. It does no good for them to think this way, and it may do harm, weakening their resolve and that of their troops.

On the other hand, one can argue that Arjuna is a better model of deliberation than Krishna: even in a case like this, where the tragedy does not look like one that could have been avoided by better political planning, there is a point to the tragic question. It keeps the mind of the chooser firmly on the fact that his action is an immoral action, which it is always wrong to choose. The recognition that one has "dirty hands" is not just self-indulgence: it has significance for future actions. It informs the chooser that he may owe reparations to the vanquished, and an effort to rebuild their lives after the disaster that will have been inflicted on them. When the recognition is public, it constitutes an acknowledgment of moral culpability, something that frequently has significance in domestic and international politics.[19] Most significantly, it reminds the chooser that he, and we, must not do such things henceforth, except in the very special tragic circumstance he faces here. Slaughtering one's kin is one of the terrible things that it is always tragic to pursue. In that way, facing the tragic question reinforces moral commitments that should be reinforced, particularly in wartime.

Arjuna is the person who has a tragic choice to make, and he is also the one who both poses and answers the tragic question. This, of course, is not always the case. Anyone who is aware of the case may pose the question. Thus tragic dilemmas are not just occasions for one involved person's pondering: they are occasions for public deliberation, as citizens, tragic spectators, seek to get the best account of a situation that may have large public consequences.

There is a further way in which the tragic question brings illumination. Seeing a tragic clash of major values, we naturally ask how things came to such a pass, and whether better planning might have avoided the tragedy. Consider Sophocles's *Antigone*.[20] Creon tells the entire city that anyone who offers burial to the traitor Polynices is a traitor to the city, and will be put to death. Antigone cannot accept the edict, because it asks her to violate a fundamental religious obligation to seek burial for her kin. As Hegel correctly argued, each protagonist is narrow, thinking only of one sphere of value and neglecting the claim of the other. Creon thinks only of the health of the city, neglecting the "unwritten laws" of family obligation. Antigone thinks only of the family, failing to recognize the crisis of the city. We may add that for this very reason each has an impoverished conception not only of value in general but also of his or her own cherished sphere of value. As Haemon points out, Creon fails to recognize that citizens are also members of families, and that therefore a protector of the city who neglects these values is hardly protecting the city at all. Antigone fails to note that families also live in cities, which must survive if the survival of the family is to be ensured. A person who thought well about Antigone's choice would see that it is genuinely a tragedy: although there may be a better choice, there is no "right answer," because both alternatives contain serious wrongdoing. Burying a traitor is a serious wrong to the city, but for Antigone not to bury him involves a serious religious violation. Because neither sees the tragedy inherent in the situation, because neither so much as poses the tragic question, both are in these two distinct ways impoverished political actors.

This makes a huge difference for the political future. The drama depicts a very extreme situation, which is unlikely to occur often. In this extreme situation, where the city has been invaded by a member of its own ruling household, there may be no avoiding a tragic clash of duties. But a protagonist who faced the tragic question squarely would be prompted to have a group of highly useful thoughts about governance in general. In particular, noting that both the well-being of the city and the "unwritten laws" of religious obligation are of central ethical importance, he or she would be led to want a city that makes room for people to pursue their familial religious obligations without running afoul of civic ordinances. In other words, he or she would want a city such as Pericles claims to find in democratic Athens, when he boasts that public policy shows respect for unwritten law. Just as Americans and Indians believe that they can create a public order that builds in spaces for the free exercise of religion, in which individuals are not always tragically torn between civic ordinance and religious command, so ancient Athens had an analogous antitragic thought—as a direct result, quite possibly, of watching tragedies such as Sophocles's *Antigone*.

It was here, indeed, that Hegel located, plausibly, the political significance of tragedy. Tragedy, he said, reminds us of the deep importance of the spheres of life that are in conflict within the drama, and of the dire results when they are opposed and we have to choose between them. It therefore motivates us to imagine what a world would be like that did not confront people with such choices, a world of "concordant action" between the two spheres of value. In that sense, the end of the drama is written offstage, by citizens who enact these insights in their own constructive political reflection. "The true course of dramatic development consists in the annulment of *contradictions* viewed as such, in the reconciliation of the forces of human action, which alternately strive to negate each other in their conflict."[21]

If the political sphere decides, wisely, to recognize plural spheres of value, it thereby builds in the permanent possibility of tragic clashes among them. Nonetheless, Hegel gives us the best strategy to follow, especially in political life. For we really do not know whether a harmonious fostering of two apparently opposed values can be achieved—until we try to bring that about. Many people in many places have thought that a harmonious accommodation between religion and the state is just impossible. Athens tried to prove them wrong. Modern liberal states— grappling with the even thornier problem of reconciling the compelling interests of the state with a wide plurality of religious and secular views of the good life—all in their own ways try to prove them wrong. To a great extent, decent modern constitutional democracies do enable citizens to avoid *Antigone*-like tragedies, when they say, for example, that government may not impose a "substantial burden" on an individual's free exercise of religion without a "compelling state interest."[22] Political principles do their best to keep tragedy at bay—because citizens understand the force of the tragic question.

Often we do not know what arrangements we are capable of making, until we have faced the tragic question with Hegel's idea in view. Until recently, most nations had not faced up to the tragic choices they were posing every day to women who wanted both to honor their family obligations and to seek paid employment. Many public policies can ease that tension: flexible work time, paid family leave, incentives to men for sharing domestic labor. But because it had never dawned on most men of that generation to think that a person ought to be able to be both a good primary caretaking parent and a good colleague, they had never bothered to think what very simple changes in arrangements might remove the problem. People just thought, and sometimes said, that the incompatibilities were just the way life is. Things simply cannot be otherwise. Whenever our imaginary citizens are inclined to say this about any clash of values, they should pause, remembering the emotions engendered by tragic spectatorship, and ask Hegel's question: Is there a rearrangement of our practices that can remove the tragedy? Tragedy is rarely just tragedy. Most often, behind the gloom is stupidity, or selfishness, or laziness, or malice.

In short, tragic dilemmas have two related roles in the political life. First, they direct emotional and imaginative attention to fundamental entitlements and to the damage done when these are not present. Pursued thoughtfully, they shape compassion and address some of its likely errors. Second, through the emotionally difficult experience of tragic dilemmas, citizens learn that some costs, some losses, have a distinctive nature: they are bad in a distinctive way. No citizen should have to bear them. People are then spurred to use their imaginations, thinking how they might construct a world in which such conflicts do not confront citizens, or confront them as rarely as possible. Such a cast of mind is itself progress.

IV. Comedy and the Good Things of Life

The world of the ancient comic festivals seems as different from the world of the tragic festivals as are the costumes of their respective heroes. Grave in tall boots and sober mask, the tragic hero is the embodiment of human dignity. Rotund and shapeless in a padded costume, his perpetual erection signifying a shameful lack of self-control, his public eating a violation of good manners,[23] the comic hero—often farting and even shitting in a way that ought to embarrass a person of even minimal dignity—stands for the messy, smelly, uncomfortable body, and the delights it can bring. Still, the two heroes are not so far apart after all. Socrates, his sights fixed on becoming "godlike," transcending our merely human situation, was right to suggest, at the end of the *Symposium,* that the tragic and comic poets have a single nature.[24] Tragedy, we said, emphasizes bodily frailty, encouraging a compassion that overcomes tendencies to arrogant denial of mere humanity. Aristophanic comedy, with its insistent frank and delighted references to bodily functions, asks all spectators to revel in their bodily nature.[25] So it's really two sides of the same coin. Excretion, sex, and sweat are shown as signs of great vulnerability—many of the jokes in Aristophanes turn on the way an ambitious plan is derailed by the need to take a shit, or by the embarrassment of having farted at the wrong time, or by an unwelcome erection. But the vulnerability is embraced as common to all, as just a part of being alive, connected to life's joy. And the comedies celebrate that fragile joy—while repudiating the all-too-common pretense that one is invulnerable. Not just Aristophanes, but the ethos of the comic festival itself, argues on the side of peace, since it is in peace that one can enjoy eating, drinking, and sex (and even farting and shitting). Military aggressiveness puts all that at risk—often without good reason.

Like tragic festivals, then, comic festivals deal with painful matters: with the limits of the body, its subjection to indignities, its closeness to death. But the spirit of comedy, and the very structure of Old Comedy as a genre, turns these gloomy matters into sources of delight. The triumph of the comic hero is one that democracy has good reason to promote, if it is wise. As Dikaiopolis says, "Comedy too knows what justice is"— choosing a name for comedy, *trugôidia,* or "song of the wine lees," that makes its kinship to tragedy evident. Comedies, like tragedies, are politically imperfect, and may contain elements that a just society should not approve. My point is not about every statement in every comedy; it is about the comic genre itself, the sense of life that is built into the ways in which this dramatic form related to its audience.

As you will have noticed long since, comedy deals with materials that are sometimes found disgusting. But they do not court disgust, they banish it. Prudish spectators sometimes do react with disgust, but that is because their upbringing has not prepared them to join in comedy's celebration of the body.[26] (It's the reaction that greeted Joyce's *Ulysses*[27] and the comedy of Lenny Bruce.) However, the ancient Greek audience viewed comedies not only as proper, but—as Dikaiopolis says—as closely linked to civic deliberation. What could they have had in mind?

As *Acharnians* opens, Dikaiopolis, a rural farmer, has come to the democratic assembly early to argue on behalf of peace. In his opening speech, he tells us quite a lot about himself. What does he love? Democratic politics, tragic poetry, peace, the countryside. When he arrives early at the assembly, he spends his time in a variety of activities: "I sigh, I yawn, I stretch, I fart, I wonder, I write, I pluck out hairs, I construct arguments." Undignified physical activities such as farting and hair-plucking are oddly joined to activities characteristic of the good democratic citizen: wondering, writing, constructing arguments. Throughout the play, with its absurd scheme to end the Peloponnesian War through an economic boycott, the suggestion is that a politics rooted in bodily functions is likely to make good arguments, arguments duly attentive to the importance of peace and welfare. The aggressive and irresponsible war making of Lamachus and his fellows neglects the ordinary person, who suffers greatly in war. Even if the play's audience ultimately supports the war effort, they need to think like Dikaiopolis, reckoning the costs of war in a reasonable manner. The goal of war—even if just—is always peace and the good things of life.

An even more vivid example of the insistent connection between comedy and the success of democracy is Aristophanes's most famous play, *Lysistrata* (411 BCE).[28] In the wartime Athens of the play (a later and grimmer stage of the war than that relevant to *Acharnians*),[29] men have forgotten about the good things of life. What they love is waving shields and swords around, or prying up things with crowbars. Lysistrata complains that men don't like to hear alternative viewpoints, or to listen to arguments. When women ask a question about the war, they are told to shut up or given a smack (510–516). Ask another question, expressing skepticism about the war plans, and they are told, "Go do your spinning or you'll get a sound beating. War is men's business" (519–520). Threats of force take the place of good counterarguments.

Notice that the men's world contains neither tragic compassion nor humor. It lacks a sense of the tragic, because it lacks a sense of its own weakness and vulnerability. It lacks a sense of humor for related reasons: men are unable to see anything ridiculous or even slightly odd about themselves. They want to be heroes without flaw, and they can't recognize the body as a site of funny events, illustrative of human frailty.

The women of the play are far from heroic: they love drinking and sex. But they also love arguments, and Aristophanes connects their good sense with their focus on the body. They know what is at stake in war: the home deprived of its men (101 ff.); deaths in battle (524), especially deaths of the children they have labored so to bear and bring up (588–589); women growing old in solitude, unable to marry again, wasting the short space during which a woman can find a husband (591–597). Peace, by contrast, is imagined, as always in Aristophanes, as a time of sensory delight: food, drink, sex, religious and poetic celebration.

In the exchange with the Athenian official that forms the centerpiece of her argument, Lysistrata proposes that the woman's art of weaving is a good model for the type of good sense that is badly needed in this conflict: first washing and combing, as women remove dirt and parasites from the wool, then weaving, as all the separate strands the city contains—migrant workers, foreign friends, metics—are carded together into a basket of goodwill, and woven together into a new outfit for the city (574–586). Weaving is an image of constructive political talk, aimed at the common good: each strand has to be taken into account, and all have to be brought together into a coherent whole.

Erections are the device through which the female world wins its triumph. By denying men the control they have come to expect over women's bodies, the women put them in a ridiculous and humiliated position.[30] To walk around with an erection is a confession of a shameful lack of control, over both self and other. Losing their macho authority, the men become capable, ultimately, of sense. As Lysistrata remarks, it is easy to get men to make peace—if you catch them while they are erect, rather than when they are competing aggressively with one another (1112–1113). The goddess Truce, not surprisingly, has the form of a beautiful woman, and she joins the men together by grabbing hold of any part that happens to be sticking out. The penis, first an emblem of male humiliation and submission, now becomes the emblem of reconciliation, hope, and peace. "Even though I'm a woman," Lysistrata remarks at this point, as Spartans join Athenians, "I have some good sense, and I don't do badly for judgment" (1124–1125).

The end of the play connects bodily play to democratic triumph with sudden solemnity. Hands on one another's organs, Athenian and Spartan men join the women and dance, calling on the Graces, Apollo the healer, Dionysus, and the other gods. In an invocation suggestive of old-time traditions, the Athenians summon Hêsuchia (Stability), a goddess associated with civic tranquility and freedom of action.[31] And, in the final defeat of male shield waving, the Spartans first praise Dionysus and the maenads, and then, dancing, sing in praise of an unnamed goddess who would seem to be the patron of their former enemies, and of the Athenian democracy—Athena.[32] The strands have been interwoven so effectively that national differences break down in the festive dance with which the comedy ends.

Aristophanes suggests, then, that civic stability and peace (even peace with our rivals) is promoted by a spirit of play that focuses on bodily delight. The comic festivals found ingenious ways to celebrate and engender that spirit—inviting us to ask, as did the tragic festivals, how we might perform the same function in a large modern society.

V. Tragic Spectatorship in Modern Democracies

Modern societies do not have tragic or comic festivals where all citizens gather and all business ceases. How, then, can they promote tragic and comic spectatorship?

Like everything else, tragic spectatorship begins in early childhood, in the family. Children hear stories that involve risk, pain, and loss. Often the central character, whether animal or human, loses a loved one: Bambi and Babar both lose their mothers to hunters' bullets; the king of the elephants dies from eating a poisonous plant. Meanwhile, in real life children often encounter loss first by experiencing the death of a beloved animal. This loss typically prepares them for a later confrontation with human losses.

As children grow older, they are ready to grapple with more realistic accounts of families and their plights. In the popular Hayao Miyazaki film *My Neighbor Totoro,* which appeals to children as young as three or four, the adventures of the two sisters are framed by the serious illness of their mother, who is hospitalized throughout the movie, and by the frequent absences of their father, who visits her, full of anxiety. In the series of autobiographical books about American frontier life by Laura Ingalls Wilder (one of my own favorites as a child), the Ingalls family confronts hunger, extremes of heat and cold, disease, and danger from animals and from hostile humans. Laura's sister Mary becomes blind as the result of illness; their father almost dies in a blizzard. The climax of the series is the near-death of an entire town in North Dakota, recounted in *The Long Winter,* when unprecedented amounts of snow cut it off from food supplies. These are but a few examples of the popular works for children that can both bring them into contact with human vulnerability and prompt valuable discussions in families and elementary schools. One thing a decent society can do is to make sure that works of this type and quality are part of the public school curriculum and that authors, visual artists, and filmmakers who do good work for children get a due amount of public attention and concern.

But there are other strategies. All societies, unfortunately, have to confront disasters of various kinds, and the way in which the public sphere represents those disasters makes a difference. Let's consider three cases from the United States in which the sort of tragic spectatorship we've described was successfully and insightfully promoted: the mourning for the Civil War promoted by Lincoln's speeches, the Lincoln Memorial, and the poetry of Walt Whitman; Franklin Delano Roosevelt's use of photography during the New Deal; and Maya Lin's Vietnam Veterans Memorial. Then we'll consider a different type of case, in which public discussion of fictional works can spur public debate about the silent tragedies that unjust societies inflict every day upon the capacities and the very spirit of disadvantaged people and groups.

Tragedies get their emotional effects through the distinction of their poetry, music, and visual spectacle. They inspire not only compassion, we might say, but also *wonder*, an intense and delighted absorption in the object of contemplation.[33] The fact that Sophocles is a great artist is hardly irrelevant to the power of his work to move us; so the modern society that wants to emulate the Greeks needs real artists and real artistry, and it needs to permit the artists to create in surprising ways, not seeing them, in Comtean fashion, as obedient servants of an academy of philosophers.

Lincoln and Whitman: Mourning and Rededication

The U.S. Civil War was a tragedy of great magnitude. It was clear to all that the nation would have difficulty recovering from it. Perhaps it has not yet fully recovered. The tragedy called for grief, mourning, and compassion; it also called for responses of justified anger and resentment, which could prevent healing if not channeled in the direction of mercy and healing. One of Lincoln's most important contributions as president was to chart a path from mourning to reconciliation. We have discussed two of his speeches as constructions of a new patriotism. Let us revisit them, to study the images of mourning they contain.

The Gettysburg Address speaks to the magnitude of the national tragedy, and connects the sacrifice of the fallen soldiers to the nation's deepest ideals. It begins by an allusion to the nation's beginning. It was "a new nation," with a distinctive set of ideals focusing on liberty and equality. The nation itself, then, is presented as fragile: it began not terribly long ago, and it is not clear whether it "can long endure." He thus positions the Civil War as a war over the deepest and most cherished ideals, and over their fate in the entire world, not just in America. The decent society is itself a vulnerable body.

Lincoln does not try to mitigate the tragedy that has befallen the soldiers. Praising the sacrifice of those who died (in a battle that was one of the war's bloodiest), he then says that the living cannot hallow the ground: only the bravery of the fallen can do so. In other words, nothing redeems death or consoles us for death, but death cannot eclipse human virtue or dignity. And then Lincoln famously asks that dedication of those who hear his speech: we are all to be dedicated to the task of preserving the American democracy, and to giving it "a new birth of freedom." He ends on the note of urgency he has sounded throughout: the struggle is really a struggle over whether democracy itself can exist.

Lincoln's speech both dignifies the tragedy of the fallen and uses that tragedy as a metaphor for the vulnerability of the decent nation, which will survive only if those who hear his speech emulate their willingness to risk and sacrifice. It thus draws the audience close to the sacrifice of the fallen, urging them, even while mourning, to invest their own future in the struggle for democracy and freedom. Heard in its own time, it motivated its hearers to work on for victory and reconciliation. Heard today, it both tells us about the painful sacrifice involved in creating this nation as a truly democratic and inclusive nation and reminds us that such sacrifices must be made, because democracy is too precious to be lost on account of egoism, laziness, or fear.

In the Second Inaugural Address, Lincoln turns to the issue of fault. In a most delicate manner, he manages to portray the war as a tragedy without concealing the fact that one side was asymmetrically at fault. He dwells on the grave moral error of "wringing their bread from the sweat of other men's faces." And yet, the note of tragic suffering overwhelms blame and resentment: he urges charity, and constructive work to "bind up the nation's wounds." The scope and magnitude of the tragedy transcends the measure of fault, leading Americans to a shared grief. Tragedy leads to thought and action toward "a just and lasting peace among ourselves and with all nations."

The Lincoln Memorial on the Mall, dedicated in 1922, is an apt visual analogue of these great speeches. Indeed, the Ionic temple contains the text of both speeches, along with a large seated sculpture of the dead president. It also contains the names of all the states (all fifty at present) and the dates on which they entered the Union. It is thus a monument to the success of the Union cause, but in a very solemn and understated way. The sculpture of Lincoln, by Daniel Chester French, is very unusual in a monument honoring a great leader, because it is an image of tragedy. It shows Lincoln bowed down with suffering, exhausted. (Indeed it was much criticized at the time for this unheroic depiction of the great leader. Earlier plans were in the heroic mode: one would have surrounded Lincoln with huge equestrian statues.) It is a solemn reminder that the war ought to be seen not as hateful aggression, but above all as tragedy, a burden we must all shoulder and somehow cope with, and, ultimately, put behind us. Above Lincoln is a simple inscription: "In this temple as in the hearts of the people for whom he saved the Union the memory of Abraham Lincoln is enshrined forever."

A leader's words, a leader's sculpted image—these charted a path for the future. Public poetry also played a formative role in shaping the nation's response to the tragedy, and its future. Walt Whitman, who worked on the battlefield as an attendant, was the war's great poet, and Lincoln's great memorializer. In his lyric "When Lilacs Last in the Dooryard Bloom'd," he takes up Lincoln's task: constructing a new national love that is just and firm in the right, and yet capable of forgiveness and reconciliation. At every point in the poem, we are on the right track if we ask: How does this phrase, this image, bear on the task of creating a new and transfigured America—an America that truly practices equality and inclusion, that is free from the poisonous hatred of the outsider? And also, how does this poetic strategy bear on the more immediate task of binding together an America riven by the waste and horror of a war fought for the most basic and elementary starting point of justice, a war that has destroyed generations of citizens for the sake of establishing what should never have been in question?

> I saw battle-corpses, myriads of them
> And the white skeletons of young men, I saw them,
> I saw the debris and debris of all the slain soldiers of the war . . .
> The living remain'd and suffer'd, the mother suffer'd,

And the wife and the child and the musing comrade suffer'd,
And the armies that remain'd suffer'd. ("Lilacs" 177–184)

The poem, we are told, is a series of "pictures" to "hang on the chamber walls" of Lincoln's tomb, "to adorn the burial-house of him I love." With aching tenderness and an erotic response to visual beauty, Whitman brings Lincoln—brings his reader—pictures of America, an America that contains no line between slave and free states, between North and South, an America at peace, and so beautiful:

Pictures of growing spring and farms and homes,
With the Fourth-month eve at sundown, and the gray smoke lucid
    and bright,
With floods of the yellow gold of the gorgeous, indolent, sinking
    sun, burning, expanding the air,
With the fresh sweet herbage under foot, and the pale green leaves
    of the trees prolific,
In the distance the flowing glaze, the breast of the river, with a
    wind-dapple here and there,
With ranging hills on the banks, with many a line against the sky,
    and shadows,
And the city at hand with dwellings so dense, and stacks of
    chimneys,
And all the scenes of life and the workshops, and the workmen
    homeward returning.

Lo, body and soul—this land,
My own Manhattan with spires, and the sparkling and hurrying
    tides, and the ships,
The varied and ample land, the South and the North in the light,
    Ohio's shores and flashing Missouri,
And ever the far-spreading prairies cover'd with grass and corn.

Lo, the most excellent sun so calm and haughty,
The violet and purple morn with just-felt breezes,
The gentle soft-born measureless light,
The miracle spreading bathing all, the fulfill'd noon,

The coming eve delicious, the welcome night and the stars,
Over my cities shining all, enveloping man and land. (81–98)

Surviving a great tragedy requires love. Respect for human dignity is
important, but if people are being asked to heal one another's wounds
after a great disaster, they need some stronger reason. They need to be
moved to a love of one another and of their common enterprise. Returning to the Whitman stanza we discussed in Chapter 1, and seeing it now
in its poetic and historical context, as a response to a huge national tragedy, we can more fully appreciate Whitman's reasons for insisting, as he
continually did, that poetry is a necessary part of the public endeavor.
Political rhetoric can itself verge on poetry, swaying people by surging
rhythms and evocative images of their common task. Lincoln and King
have that emotive capacity. And yet Whitman's poetry adds something
crucial: the concrete sensuous grasp of America, its beauty, the beauty of
its people—with the shiver down the spine that only great poetic imagery can inspire. The poet-speaker takes his stand in the middle of America: "Now while I sat in the day and look'd forth,/ . . . in the large un-
conscious scenery of my land with its lakes and forests,/In the heavenly
aerial beauty (after the perturb'd winds and the storms)" (108–111). He
becomes, thus, a kind of national light or eye, seeing peace out of war,
and seeing the beauty of the land that makes peace worth fighting for.

Like Lincoln's speeches and like the Lincoln Memorial, Whitman's
poetry contains the great weight of national tragedy, as the reader follows Lincoln's coffin as it passes through the towns and countryside of
America. But it contains, as well, something more, a vivid embodiment
of why the exhausting struggle was worth it—for an America that is an
object of passionate devotion. Even the poem's mythic and symbolic
elements—the lilacs, flowers of mourning, the "powerful western fallen
star," its brightness eclipsed by the shades of night, and the bird war-
bling a threnody alone in the swamp—are sensuously evocative of America's beauty. The thrush is also the poet, who asks, "Oh how shall I
warble myself for the dead one there I loved?/And how shall I deck my
song for the large sweet soul that has gone?" (71–72). All are symbols of
Lincoln's death—and yet all are somehow part of what he died for, the
"loud human song" that continues beyond his death (103).

To respond to a national tragedy and to move beyond it, a nation needs what both Lincoln and Whitman supply: a powerful reminder of national ideals, and a more evocative and quasi-erotic sense of national love.

Roosevelt and Public Photography:
Building Support for the New Deal

During the Depression, President Franklin Delano Roosevelt faced a large rhetorical challenge: how to mobilize public support for the policies of the New Deal, in an America that had never before supported such social welfare measures. The task was complex, for Americans traditionally had not wanted to extend economic relief to people except in the case of a natural disaster. Nor had they been inclined to have compassion for people whose problem was poverty, for they thought of these people as slothful and irresponsible. Moreover, the programs of the New Deal required sacrifice: all Americans would shoulder the tax burden of these programs.

As legal sociologist Michele Landis Dauber has argued,[34] Roosevelt, understanding these attitudes, deliberately set out to convince Americans that an economic disaster has all the features of a natural disaster that are most relevant where the emotion of compassion is concerned. Using an analysis of compassion similar to ours, Dauber shows that winning compassion for the victims of economic disaster required convincing the American public that the calamity they suffered was serious, that they were not to blame for it (any more than one would be to blame for being the victim of an earthquake or a flood), and that it was the sort of thing that any human being might suffer.[35] In short, Roosevelt used an implicit understanding of compassion and motivation that tracks the classic Aristotelian and Greek-tragic models—not so surprising, since this same understanding is deeply rooted in American traditions.[36]

Dauber analyzes many pieces of public rhetoric and many works of art connected to the New Deal, including John Steinbeck's great novel *The Grapes of Wrath*.[37] Here I focus only on her analysis of the photographs commissioned by various New Deal agencies, in particular the Resettlement Administration. Hiring a staff of talented photographers, including Dorothea Lange, Walker Evans, Ben Shahn, Russell Lee, and Arthur Rothstein, the administration gave them specific instructions about how and what to photograph; it also chose, later, which photographs to print and which to "kill."[38] Those selected were shipped to newspapers and magazines around the country, included in reports given to the Congress, and displayed at conventions of social workers, so that the images rapidly came to stand for the Depression itself.

How did these images construct compassion for a skeptical American public? The seriousness of the plight of the poor was the easiest thing to depict. Images showing lines of people applying for various types of relief—unemployment checks, bread, soup—made vivid the lack of basic necessities in lives hit hard by the Depression. The magnitude of the reversal caused by the Depression was also evident in the clothing of some of the applicants, which showed their previous occupations. Other images showed the dwellings of the rural poor and the even worse conditions in which migrant laborers were forced to live.

More difficult to construct were the other elements of compassion. Lack of blame and the idea of similar possibilities actually go together closely, for a spectator will think, "I myself might suffer that," only if it is clear that the cause of misery is not badness or laziness on the part of the suffering person. Roosevelt's agents thought about this problem very hard. First, they forbade photographers to show images of strikes (a favorite subject of Dorothea Lange before this), since that would scare viewers and make them think of the poor as troublemakers who brought their misery on themselves. Instead, people quietly queuing up for bread were preferred. In such photographs, Dauber argues, the "blameless character of the needy" was shown in their orderliness and patience.[39]

Second, the images selected were shorn of biography, in order to prevent thoughts about individual moral character and possible blame from cluttering the mind of the spectator. The only cause of misery that we are permitted to focus on is the Depression itself. In the queue of photographs that were selected (as contrasted with those that were "killed"), "[t]he viewer is prevented from identifying the men as individuals by the hats, shadows, and hazy focus that obscure details of physiognomy. These are people made equal in their loss." Other photographs of intimate suffering have a surface clarity and appeal, but at the same time discourage any interest in the biography of the individual represented. "Thus we have," Dauber concludes, "in some of the most enduring visual images of the Depression, vivid pictures of babies being nursed by migrant women who are otherwise wholly anonymous, without clues as to family status, location, or historical circumstances."[40]

In that sense, the New Deal photographs do better than Steinbeck's closely associated novel, *The Grapes of Wrath*. For Steinbeck identifies his migrants carefully as of northern European origin, and he gives enough of their story to show that they have been in the United States for several generations. Indeed, at times he invites readers to notice these facts as giving the Joads a special claim to sympathy as "real Americans." This is an instance in which tragic representativeness stops so far short of human universality that it risks fostering invidious stigma, valuable though the portrait of economic suffering in the novel is in other respects.[41]

Roosevelt's appeal to emotion through a carefully crafted use of the arts seems to have been an important feature in the success of his New Deal programs. The fact that nobody is thinking much about these matters today goes at least some way to explaining the slide back to the view that the poor cause their own misery, and, in turn, to the decline of the American welfare state.

The Vietnam Veterans Memorial: Mourning and Questioning

Our first two cases involve tragedy, but they are politically simple. The aim in each case is to generate support for values that are alleged to be central to the nation's self-understanding. Even though each case involves difficulty and struggle, citizens are not invited to debate or to question the basic values involved: they are asked, instead, to dedicate themselves to their energetic promotion. In the case of Lincoln, mourning for the fallen soldiers is supposed to lead not to a questioning of the cause for which they fought, but, instead, to a wholehearted rededication to the cause of democracy. The address emphasizes the fact that the values it promotes are the values of the founding—reinterpreted, of course, so as to include the former slaves as equals. That is a radical shift, but it is framed as the only honest understanding of how those values really ought to be realized.

Roosevelt's New Deal programs too were radical—in a sense; but FDR too positions them as continuous with founding ideals of equal respect and equal dignity. The photographs administration officials selected emphasized that idea. The political realm was certainly busy questioning Roosevelt's programs, but his use of the arts is one-sided; it promotes emotional support for redistribution, not a balanced debate about whether redistribution is just. In the end, the programs of the New Deal proved overwhelmingly popular, and most of them remain so today, despite the great change in public feeling since the Ronald Reagan era. Even now, when a critical conversation does take place about specifics, such as the future of Social Security, that conversation takes place against the backdrop of a commitment to equal dignity that Roosevelt's choices affirmed and strengthened.

But our imaginary nations insist on a vigorous critical culture. If some values at some times are so urgently important and so fundamental that it seems right for a leader to ask for commitment rather than a calm critical conversation—the Gettysburg battlefield was not the place to hold a calm debate abut whether slavery is just—still, critical conversation should always wait in the wings, and the ambivalent emotions connected to such a difficult conversation are also of enormous political value. Public art would be suspect if, among its many functions, it could not also operate in ways that support this Socratic and deliberative way of operating. The Vietnam Veterans Memorial is one such Socratic work.[42]

Monuments are reminders of enduring aspirations; memorials are reminders of painful loss. As Arthur Danto puts it, "We erect monuments so that we shall always remember, and build memorials so that we shall never forget." The Vietnam Veterans Memorial is situated between the Washington Monument and the Lincoln Memorial. Its dark walls, hinged at a 125-degree angle, point, like wings, one toward each of these reference points.

The Washington Monument is abstract, impersonal, aspirational. An obelisk—its Egyptian pedigree alluding to Washington's Masonic connections, and thus to imagery of light vanquishing darkness—is regular, the same from all sides. Nonetheless, unlike classical obelisks, it is not a monolith, but is composed of separate blocks. So it also symbolizes the unity of the states, and, with its graceful ascent, the high goals of that

Union and its Enlightenment pedigree. Deliberately, and against counterproposals, it is utterly abstract and impersonal, eschewing a heroic portrayal of the great leader, or even any words denoting his achievements.[43] The Lincoln Memorial, by contrast, shows Lincoln bowed down with care and suffering. It reminds us of the pain and tragic loss of the war, and of the ongoing struggle to produce human equality and respectful political consensus. The Vietnam Veterans Memorial points, then, both toward the nation's highest commitments and toward its most profound loss.

The competition to design the memorial was explicit in its constraints: the memorial must (1) be reflective and contemplative in character, (2) be harmonious with its site and surroundings, (3) provide for the inscription of the names of all those—nearly 58,000—who lost their lives or remain missing, (4) make no political statement about the war, and (5) occupy up to two acres of land. Thus many subsequent objections to the design were really objections to the criteria for the competition. The unanimous choice of the panel of eight experts, out of 1,421 entries, was a design by Maya Lin, an Asian American woman from Athens, Ohio, at the time a twenty-one-year-old student at Yale University. Initially the design was very controversial: some veterans groups saw the black walls as walls "of shame," a "degrading ditch," a "wailing wall for liberals."[44] Many were indignant at the absence of any typical representation of soldiers and their nobility. As a result, a banal bronze statue of four solders by Frederick Hart was later added, opposite the memorial. In only a short time, however, the memorial became immensely popular. The simple dignity of the design, its straightforward and unpretentious mourning for all the individuals lost in the war, drew people in, and it is to this day one of the nation's most-visited works of public art, and the only one on the Mall that is a living memorial, where people interact with and alter the work to express their mourning for specific loved ones. All this is in accordance with Lin's plan: she said that she intended the memorial "to bring out in people the realization of loss and a cathartic healing process."[45] She drew particular attention to the contemplative and personal character of the memorial. In her official statement submitted to the competition, she wrote, "Brought to a sharp awareness of such a loss, it is up to each individual to resolve or come to terms with this loss. For death is in the end a personal and private matter and the area contained within this memorial is a quiet place, meant for personal reflection and private reckoning." Lin was awarded the National Medal of the Arts in 2009.

The memorial is not visible from a distance. You cannot interact with it without being in its space. Nor can you use it casually, like a piece of park furniture. People play Frisbee on the Mall, and children run around. The memorial, by contrast, is a solemn, almost ritual space. You enter it walking downhill; it opens like a gash in the earth.[46] As you walk, you seem to be in the valley of the shadow of death—and yet the space is not tomblike, not enclosed. You can still see the sky overhead, the Washington Monument and the Lincoln Memorial in the distance.

The memorial consists of two slabs of polished black stone, hinged at the center, like a book—the book of the dead.[47] The names, in chronological order, both begin and end at the center. There is no impersonal symbol, no flag, no message, only the names of individuals. The contrast to the Washington Monument is stark: there we find no individuals, only high ideals, while here only the individual is real. As you study the names, you see your own face behind them. It was part of Lin's plan that the stone is highly reflective. So what you see is the names of the dead, and at the same time yourself, hovering indistinctly behind the names. The work in that way poses questions about your own relationship to the war. Were you there? Did you lose a loved one? What do you think of all this loss? Was it worth what the war accomplished? The monument is not only contemplative, but interrogative.[48] One might call it Socratic, but the process of questioning operates through the emotions of grief and loss.[49] As Arthur Danto says, "Be prepared to weep. Tears are the universal experience even if you don't know any of the dead."[50] While you observe the names, you also see people putting flowers next to a name, or a family photo, or a medal—or making a rubbing of a particular name. (Directories of names are provided close to the monument, as are ladders to reach those that are too high, and materials to make the rubbings.) The memorial, while about individuals, is in that sense universal: it includes all visitors in the experience of grief, bringing them together no matter what they think of the war. That is why the memorial, initially so controversial, quickly became popular: it does indeed, as Lin suggests, promote healing of the divisions caused by the Vietnam War, by bringing people together in a contemplative space. The idea that it represents shame was quickly dispelled by visitors' shared perception that it dignifies the individual fallen soldiers and their sacrifice, making their fate a matter of national concern.[51]

The memorial is deliberative in very much the way in which Athenian tragedy is deliberative. By summoning powerful emotions and, at the same time, posing questions about the events connected to these emotions, it gets people to examine their own lives, past and present, in a way that people don't usually do amid the distractions of everyday life. Not like a church or a temple, where congregants mourn in sectarian isolation from people with different beliefs, the space of the memorial, more like the tragic theaters of ancient Athens, brings all citizens together under the open sky, isolating visitors for a time from other sights and activities—much in the manner of a church or a temple, but with the open air and the view of the Mall's other sculptures reinforcing the message of shared national tragedy amid high aspirations.

Difficult Conversations about Everyday Tragedies: *Native Son*, "Giribala"

The Vietnam War is over, though its legacy continues. Our public conversation about the war is retrospective and analogical: we search for what went wrong, and how to think about possible wars in the future. By now we are also searching for an account of our involvement in Iraq and Afghanistan, and a visit to the Vietnam Veterans Memorial now arouses difficult questions about those conflicts. There are some tragedies, however, that never seem to come to an end, that persist in the fabric of a nation's daily life, often little noticed because they involve anonymous poor people living lives of silent deprivation. They raise very difficult issues, often involving fundamental political questions, such as: What is the appropriate stance toward affirmative action? What forms of government interference with the family is acceptable to promote fair equality of opportunity for women and girls? What is a decent welfare program?

Such questions should be debated in many settings and in many ways. Some of these debates will rightly involve little emotion and will focus on gathering the best data and understanding the problems as well as possible. Even here, though, political art that engages emotions has a role to play. If people talk without tapping into their emotions, they often don't really understand the depth of the problem, or communicate their full thinking to others.

It is not surprising, then, that public book conversations have emerged as one device for fostering a deliberative public dialogue that involves emotive material and people's reactions to it. The idea that democracy is aided by the public arrangement of book clubs and book groups has a long history. In one sense, it goes back to ancient Athens, where the tragedies were discussed and rated by the audience—but then eventually published and, in that form, debated yet again. Aristophanes's *Frogs* depicts a character carrying such texts around, and though the context is comic, the audience has to find this habit familiar to make sense of it. Modern democracies, to their shame, rarely had the high literacy rate of ancient Athens until relatively recently, but Weimar Germany did publicly organize book groups for workers as a way of nourishing civic discussion.[52]

In the United States, the book group has been primarily a city or town affair. The city of Chicago, for example, has pioneered a very successful program called One Book One Chicago that celebrated its tenth anniversary in 2011. Initiated by Mayor Richard M. Daley and run by the Chicago Public Library, the program encourages Chicagoans to read a book together—two books are selected each year—and to participate in local discussions of that book around the city. Lectures about the book and, where possible, a personal appearance by the author are also prominent and free of cost. Books chosen have included *To Kill a Mockingbird* by Harper Lee, *Night* by Elie Wiesel, *A Raisin in the Sun* by Lorraine Hansberry, *One Day in the Life of Ivan Denisovich* by Aleksandr Solzhenitsyn, *Go Tell It on the Mountain* by James Baldwin, *The Crucible* by Arthur Miller, *The House on Mango Street* by Sandra Cisneros, *The Plan of Chicago: Daniel Burnham and the Remaking of the American City* by Carl Smith, and *A Mercy* by Toni Morrison. It's evident that selections keep returning to difficult issues faced by the city, including questions of race, ethnicity, and city planning.

What books clubs can do that city parks and monuments cannot is to promote each person's active involvement in a vigorous critical culture.

The works chosen here are not like works of political philosophy: they promote readers' emotional involvement in the events, and encourage a dialogue that grows out of and attends to these emotional experiences. One of the benefits reading offers is a kind of intimacy with the lives of people in different groups or classes, something that would be hard to attain through social science data alone, given existing separations. Through imaginative identification, readers can take the measure of the human cost of existing policies and distributions.

As the Chicago experience shows, an indefinite number of books can promote a good civic discussion (and also promote the love of reading, an announced aim of the program). To illustrate the way such an open-ended discussion can tap powerful emotions and generate productive thought about ongoing problems, I choose two works that I have actually taught, one from the United States and one from India.

Native Son, by Richard Wright (1940), is not on the Chicago list, and yet it should be, since it deals with an ugly era in the history of Chicago, raising issues that are difficult to talk about but that need to be raised. Only in 1993 was it published in unexpurgated form: a scene depicting two black teenage boys masturbating in a movie theater to the image of a glamorous white actress was deemed too sensational for the Book-of-the-Month Club, its original publisher. It is a difficult novel because, deliberately, it repels empathy. Its protagonist is hostile, angry, scary—in such a way, Wright said, as to repel a facile sympathy, a sympathy that assumes that the mind of a person who has suffered terrible deprivation and racism is easily accessible to the white reader. Like Philoctetes, Bigger Thomas has been damaged by his life, which, like Philoctetes's, is a life of both deprivation and stigma.

As the novel opens, readers enter a squalid one-room tenement, where Bigger Thomas lives with his mother, sister, and brother. "Light flooded the room and revealed a black boy standing in a narrow space between two iron beds." Bigger is in prison already. Like the rat he shortly kills, he is trapped in a condition of helplessness. Readers see what it is to try to maintain self-respect and order when you have no privacy to change your clothes, when your pathetic "conspiracy against shame"—the effort to maintain dignity when four people must dress and undress with no privacy—can be interrupted at any time by a rat running across the floor.

They note the way in which the rat, cornered, strikes viciously back, and they sense from then on what Bigger's relation to the world around him will be. At every point his hopes and fears, his sexual longings, and his sense of self are conditioned, and confined, by the squalor in which he lives.

Not only squalor, but hatred and disgust. Bigger is aware of himself through images drawn from the white world's denigration of him; he defines himself as worthless because they have defined him thus. And yet, he knows that he is not worthless, so he hates their denigration. And he also hates their compassion, based as it is on a facile assumption that we are all brothers under the skin. As he drives University of Chicago student Mary Dalton and her boyfriend Jan to the black restaurant she wants to visit, they drive down Indiana, past the tenements where he lives.

> "You know, Bigger, I've long wanted to go into these houses," she said, pointing to the tall, dark apartment buildings looming to either side of them, "and just *see* how your people live. You know what I mean? I've been to England, France and Mexico, but I don't know how people live ten blocks from me. We know so *little* about each other. I just want to *see.* I want to *know* these people. Never in my life have I been inside of a Negro home. Yet they *must* live like we live. They're *human.* . . . There are twelve million of them. . . . They live in our country. . . . In the same city with us . . . ," her voice trailed off wistfully.
>
> There was silence. The car sped through the Black Belt, past tall buildings holding black life. Bigger knew that they were thinking of his life and the life of his people. Suddenly he wanted to seize some heavy object in his hand and grip it with all the strength of his body and in some strange way rise up and stand in naked space above the speeding car and with one final blow blot it out—with himself and them in it.[53]

Readers cannot follow the novel without trying to see the world to some extent through Bigger's eyes. As they do so, however, they see that Mary's conception of what it is to know and to understand is far too simple. Circumstances form the psyche. He does not "live like we live," and therefore he is not simply a generic human, with a mind like any other. Racism has made him different. Beneath the facile kind of sympathy expressed by Mary, however, lies the possibility of a deeper sympathy, one that says: "This is a human being, with the equipment to lead a productive life. See how not only his choices but also his emotional and intellectual capacities have been deformed by racial hatred and its institutional expression." The unlikeness that repels easy identification becomes the object of concern. Readers then feel a further range of emotions—a deeper sympathy for Bigger's predicament, a principled anger at the racism of American society, perhaps a little hope that things might change.

"He knew as he stood there that he could never tell why he had killed. It was not that he did not really want to tell, but the telling of it would have involved an explanation of his entire life," the novel continues. Bigger commits two crimes. One, the accidental killing of Mary Dalton, is at worst negligent homicide. The murder of his lover Bessie, however, is a deliberate premeditated murder. (One of the ironies of the novel is that readers usually react exactly as does the white society in the novel: they forget entirely about Bessie, and think of him as a heinous monster for his killing of Mary. Film versions of the novel always focus on the Mary plot and ignore Bessie.) The novel is the "explanation" that Bigger never gets to give in court—because the criminal justice system, like the white world around him, cannot see him as an individual. Indeed, the novel's careful "explanation" of Bigger's individual life involves a type of thought that seems to be unavailable in the world depicted in the novel.

The denial of individuality is symmetrical: on both sides of the color line, racial anger has eclipsed personal identity. To Bigger, white people are a "mountain of hate." The thought that individual people are on the other side of the line is so terrifying that he cannot bear it. The novel is well known for the speeches of Bigger's lawyer, who, borrowing from Frantz Fanon, sees violence as an inevitable response to Bigger's oppression, and indeed a valuable self-assertion. But it is not on this note that the novel ends. The lawyer is shown to be just as blind to Bigger's individuality as other white characters. The novel ends, instead, with the possibility of individual friendship. During his long imprisonment, Bigger— struck by the courage and decency of Jan, the young Communist who has every reason to hate him (he was Mary's fiancé), but who alone seems to treat him as a person in his own right—begins to think the way readers of the novel have been encouraged to think from the start. He begins to think, that is, about the human aims and abilities that exist on both sides of the color line, though so differently shaped by social institutions. At last, Bigger becomes fleetingly able to see individuality on the other side:

> He wondered if it were possible that after all everybody in the world felt alike? Did those who hated him have in them the same thing [the lawyer] Max had seen in him, the thing that had made Max ask him those questions? For the first time in his life he had gained a pinnacle of feeling upon which he could stand and see vague relations that he had never dreamed of. If that white looming mountain of hate were not a mountain at all, but people, people like himself, and like Jan—then he was faced with a high hope the like of which he had never thought could be, and a despair the full depths of which he knew he could not stand to feel. . . . He stood up in the middle of the cell floor and tried to see himself in relation to other men, a thing he had always feared to try to do, so deeply stained was his own mind with the hate of others for him.

The novel's conclusion seems to go beyond the class-based politics of Marxism, suggesting that even that political stance, which sees people as categories, is an artifact of oppression. If the line were really erased, there might be—friendship. Bigger's last words are, "Tell Jan hello . . ." and then "Good-bye!"

What would the book clubs of Chicago talk about, reading this novel during the Obama administration? High on the list would surely be the question of whether our society has progressed, and if so, how far. Does the election of Obama as president, and, closer to home, the (2011) choice of (Jewish) Rahm Emanuel as mayor by the predominantly African American and Latino as well as the "white" wards, mean that we are moving into an era of post-racial politics? What reasons are there against this conclusion? What is happening in the inner city, and how many young lives are still being at best uncultivated, at worst stained with "the

hate of others"? Does the criminal justice system care enough about minorities and the poor? What reforms should be contemplated? Does a
poor black female victim still go neglected? What role do slumlords like
Mr. Dalton play in perpetuating racial stigma? And how is race related
to class? Some readers will surely say that racism is secondary and class
is the really important issue.

We would also have to talk about that "university-school out there on
the Midway." The University of Chicago has surely improved its relations with the surrounding community since Wright's time, as Chapter
10 will show, and it is a much more multiracial place than it used to be.
But has it done enough? Does it really care about the community enough?
Internally, does it show enough concern for ending the long legacy of
racial exclusion? What policies would that imply?

What do we think of affirmative action, for example? What goals does
it accomplish, and at what risk? And what trade-offs are we willing to
make for it? Such issues are not a matter of remote history. They are debated with anguish, sometimes with anger and the risk of estrangement.

Some book discussions would focus on the depiction of emotions and
their social shaping, and at this point discussion could roam far and
wide, thinking about disgust, shame, stigma, the emotions of women,
gays and lesbians, and other disadvantaged groups. And at some point
we'd have to tackle the hardest issue of all: what it is to understand another human being. This could lead to a discussion of the relationship
between a politics based on group identities and a politics based on the
dignity and separateness of the individual.

It would not be amiss to go further, investigating the larger relationship between the aesthetic and the political, thinking of what makes a
topical work survive its time, what quality of psychological depth or human insight.

India does not currently have a high enough literacy rate to have a public
book club program of Chicago's type: such a program would promote
class division, rather than inclusion. Films would be a better choice for
local discussion groups. And many groups already generate public discussion through music and dance, as did Tagore and as do the Bauls of

Bengal today. For narrower middle-class audiences, however, recent Indian literature offers many valuable texts for public discussion. The work of authors such as Mahasweta Devi, Arundhati Roy, Rohinton Mistry, and many other writers in both English and the vernacular languages would promote discussion of issues of caste, class, and gender, in much the way that I imagine Wright's novel functioning in Chicago—generating a similar broadening of sympathy and an emotionally rich grasp of some of the nation's core political principles. A very short story such as Mahasweta Devi's "Giribala,"[54] which describes the daily tragedies faced by a very poor woman, could function much as other tragic narratives in many places and times (it is quite close to Euripides's *Trojan Women*, for example) to produce a public discussion of women's agency and vulnerability, and, crucially, of which tragedies are really part of the human "lot," and which are caused by defective social arrangements that can be changed.[55]

Of course, people could debate all these issues without a highly emotive work of art. And any complete discussion would need to be fortified with lots of data, since a story might paint a distorted picture of life in rural India, although this one does not. But the story, unlike the data, powerfully brings its reader close to the life of a poor woman, helping readers to understand the power and energy of female agency in circumstances of enormous adversity, and making her part of their "eudaimonistic" circle of concern in a way that a more detached description could not, thus helping them to grasp key principles of the Indian democracy in a form that makes these principles part of their own deliberations about flourishing. The compassion such a work inspires is in principle highly pertinent to helping behavior. For its readers, as for Batson's undergraduates, useful helping action is ready to hand, and one likely conclusion of such a discussion would be an agenda for action.

VI. Comic Celebration

Aristophanes seems more remote from us than Sophocles, because good humor is typically intimate and contextual. It might therefore seem odd to imagine a modern analogue to the function of the comic festivals. But their spirit, like the tragic spirit, animates many works of public art.

Millennium Park, Chicago: Bodily Joy and Inclusion

The poetry of great cities is a particularly powerful source of public emotion in the United States. New York and Chicago, in particular, have generated civic art that expresses a love of differences and celebrates the great energy that comes from them when they are respected and not feared. Here we must return to Whitman, whose public poetry of inclusiveness for all America, during and in the wake of the horror of the Civil War, was modeled on his love of New York and his sense of what New York stood for. "Walt Whitman, a cosmos, of Manhattan the son," he announces himself in "Song of Myself" (24) and immediately he juxtaposes the idea of New York the key values of his ideal America: "Whoever degrades another degrades me./And whatever is done or said returns at last to me . . . By God! I will accept nothing which all cannot have their counterpart of on the same terms" ("Song" 24). New York is a metaphor for the turbulent diversity that is Whitman's America, for the daring and energy of that diversity, and for the daring refusal of disgust and stigma—all the forbidden people and things that dare to speak their names there. As the poem continues, Whitman repeatedly addresses the roots of shame and disgust, connecting them to intolerance. He suggests that if we learn to love and celebrate what is noisy, messy, tumultuous—including, prominently, our own messy sexuality—then we will be less likely to hate and oppress others:

> Through me many long dumb voices,
> Voices of the interminable generations of prisoners and slaves,
> . . . And of the rights of them the others are down upon,
> Of the deform'd, trivial, flat, foolish, despised, . . .
> Through me forbidden voices,
> Voices of sexes and lusts, voices veil'd and I remove the veil. . . .
>   ("Song" 24)

It is not surprising, then, that New York figures centrally in the climactic lines of Whitman's elegy to Abraham Lincoln, as the only place the poet calls his "own": "Lo, body and soul—this land,/My own Manhattan with spires, and the sparkling and hurrying tides, and the

ships . . ."[56] Clearly New York is not just a particular city; it is also a figure of American diversity, inclusion, and aspiration.

This poetry of diversity is not free from difficulty. The dark side of
life is dark. But there is a kind of love undergirding the whole enterprise,
and the suggestion is that this love, which is at bottom a love of the human body, can carry us forward. When we don't like our fellow citizens,
or approve of what they do, we can still love them as parts of the great
city that we celebrate and are. The poetry of inclusion beckons to us, offering pleasure as we investigate corners of life we may view with suspicion. These include, as Whitman knew so well, aspects of bodily life
that we often cordon off as forbidden territory, telling ourselves that
what makes us uncomfortable is outside and "other."

But New York does not have a monopoly on urban poetry in the
United States. We can now turn to Chicago's Millennium Park, which
creates a public space that is its own poem of diversity. Chicago has a
history of bodily self-assertion. By contrast to (Chicago's picture of) the
rarified East, where people might almost forget that they have bodies,
Chicago is proud of its smells and its sweat:

> Hog Butcher for the World,
> Tool Maker, Stacker of Wheat,
> Player with Railroads and the Nation's Freight Handler;
> Stormy, husky, brawling,
> City of the Big Shoulders:
> They tell me you are wicked and I believe them, for I have seen
>   your painted women under the gas lamps luring the farm boys.
> And they tell me you are crooked and I answer: Yes, it is true I have
>   seen the gunman kill and go free to kill again.
> And they tell me you are brutal and my reply is: On the faces of
>   women and children I have seen the marks of wanton hunger.
> And having answered so I turn once more to those who sneer at
>   this my city, and I give them back the sneer and say to them:
> Come and show me another city with lifted head singing so proud
>   to be alive and coarse and strong and cunning.
> Flinging magnetic curses amid the toil of piling job on job, here is a
>   tall bold slugger set vivid against the little soft cities;

Bareheaded,

Shoveling,

Wrecking,

Planning,

Building, breaking, rebuilding,

Under the smoke, dust all over his mouth, laughing with white teeth,

Under the terrible burden of destiny laughing as a young man laughs,

Laughing even as an ignorant fighter laughs who has never lost a
battle,

Bragging and laughing that under his wrist is the pulse, and under
his ribs the heart of the people, Laughing!

Laughing the stormy, husky, brawling laughter of Youth, half-naked,
sweating, proud to be Hog Butcher, Tool Maker, Stacker of Wheat,
Player with Railroads and Freight Handler to the Nation.[57]

Carl Sandburg writes in a Whitmanesque style, and his Chicago is a counterpart of Whitman's New York: a place that deliberately courts the disapproval, and even the disgust, of prudes and would-be angels. It joyfully flaunts its physicality. It is sooty, sweaty, smelly, but it is also full of life and delight. As H. L. Mencken famously wrote, "I give you Chicago. It is not London and Harvard. It is not Paris and buttermilk. It is American in every chitling and sparerib. It is alive from snout to tail."

Not all Chicagoans were happy with this image. In the late nineteenth century, public buildings and parks emphasized, instead, the pseudo-European theme of pristine purity—anthropodenial in stone, we might say. Grant Park, built in imitation of the formal gardens of Europe, has as its centerpiece Buckingham Fountain (1927), white and pure, and humanly inaccessible. It is no wonder that people don't go to Grant Park, because it does not invite them in, and once they are there, there is nothing for them to do. When Chicago welcomed the world during the Columbian Exposition of 1892, it chose to portray itself as pure white. As we saw in Chapter 8, the temporary buildings of the exposition, known as the "White City," constructed a fairy-tale world that masked the diverse world outside it.[58] It lacked a body, and it certainly lacked humor. Such amusements as Buffalo Bill's Wild West Show and ethnic exhibits of many types had to set up shop outside the festival, on the Midway, which now runs through the middle of the University of Chicago.

The White City proclaimed that Chicago was as regal as the great monarchical capitals of Europe. Like them, it counted on not really being human, mortal, sweaty. And lower-class people were not welcome there— any more than they were at the (surrounding) University of Chicago.

Fortunately, Chicago's conception of parks and public art has changed. We shall return to the Midway in Chapter 10. But a central attraction of this revised Sandburgian conception of the city is downtown, next to, and subverting, Grant Park: Millennium Park, opened in 2004 under the auspices of Mayor Richard M. Daley.[59] As you approach the park from Michigan Avenue, you encounter, first, the Crown Fountain, designed by Spanish artist Jaume Plensa. On two huge screens, fifty feet high and about twenty-five yards apart, one sees projected photographic images of the faces of Chicagoans of all ages and races and types. At any given time two faces are displayed, changing expression in slow motion, with wonderfully comic effect. Every five minutes or so, just before two new faces replace the old, the faces spit jets of water, as if from out of their mouths—onto the waiting bodies of delighted children, who frolic in the shallow pool below and between the screens. These children are often joined, at first shyly and gingerly, by parents and even grandparents. Getting wet makes people look silly and lose their dignity. People love it, and the shared loss of formality democratizes the space. It also says no to the stigma that used to separate the races in separate swimming pools and drinking fountains, and also to the stigma attached to women's bodies, seen as liquid and sticky. With the comic ejaculatory bursts of liquid, it says no to laws against miscegenation, and to puritanism more generally. Whitman described a young woman, condemned by the shame of puritanism to hide her body, who imagines going out and joining the young men as they swim. As he said of them, so with the huge faces on the screens: "They do not think whom they souse with their spray."

If you watch all this from a certain angle, you will also see the sprouting plumes of the Frank Gehry band shell curling upward, a silver helmet lying on its side, a relic of war that has decided to abandon aggression and turn into a bird. A beautiful curved shape, it recalls the beauty of martial glory, but it also takes it apart and turns it soft and graceful. Listening to free concerts there, you are in a reverberating shrine of peace.

Walking uphill, you arrive at Cloud Gate, the enormous stainless-steel sculpture by Anish Kapoor, a huge inverted kidney bean. The shape itself is of arresting beauty. Reflected in its surface you see images of sublime beauty: the skyscrapers of Michigan Avenue, the clouds and the sky. The buildings are awe-inspiring straight, but they look even more delicious curved. People of all sorts lie on the ground underneath the sculpture to get a view. But then they also study their own distorted reflections, finding different comic distortions from different vantage points, and they laugh. "The Bean" (its familiar Chicago name) continues the comic festival of the Crown Fountain. Kapoor's sculpture is a cousin of Maya Lin's Vietnam Veterans Memorial in its emphasis on self-awareness: both reflect the spectator's face and body, both are in some sense about the spectator—each in its own different mode and spirit. Lin's black panels reflect, amid the names of the dead, a face looking at those names, a face full of sadness and unanswered questions. Kapoor's bright stainless steel reflects the entire body of both self and others with comic distortions—but juxtaposes them to images of beauty and wonder, producing a sense of celebration and outrageousness.

Meanwhile, on Gehry's improbably curving bridge over the highway—a bridge that seems to go nowhere in particular—people meander, pause, talk to strangers. The interactive public space celebrates diversity together with the contemplation of beauty, and both together with the pleasures of the body, as young and old paddle contentedly or stare at the reflected clouds.

What attitudes and emotions are constructed by this magical place? Well, certainly a love of diversity in one's fellow citizens, and a sense that diversity is a source of pleasure, not of anxiety. Then too, a delight in getting wet—for one of the features of the park least anticipated by its designers has been the extent to which not just children, but people of all ages, want to stand in front of those spewing fountains, enjoying an odd kind of sensuous, if not exactly sexual, intercourse with Chicagoans of many races and genders and ages. Also, not insignificantly, an Aristophanic sense of the ridiculous in oneself and others, a sense that when the body looks odd and funny, or when fluids suddenly shoot out from some part of it, that is good rather than bad. Also, again not insignificantly, a kind of calmness, a willingness to lie around, to walk slowly, to pause and greet people. (In this way the park reconstructs the Aristophanic connection between bodily delight and peace.)

Lagaan: The Sport of National Identity

One of the most loved and admired Bollywood movies of all time, *Lagaan* ("Land Taxes") has a huge international following; it has garnered many honors, was nominated by India for an Academy Award, and is a top DVD seller years after its original box office triumph in 2001. Produced by Aamir Khan, who also stars, it was written and directed by Ashutosh Gowariker. Although it has private origins, it has been widely recognized as an image of national identity, and indeed as a celebration of a particular vision of that identity at a difficult time. Its official nomination as Best Foreign Film, like the choice of A. R. Rahman to make the official version of *"Jana Gana Mana"* for India's fiftieth anniversary in 1997, makes it an official public statement about national values—whether that statement (made during the ascendancy of the Bharatiya Janata Party, in a coalition government) is to be viewed as sincere or as adept public relations.

Lagaan has a subtitle: *Once upon a Time in India.* This subtitle is odd, for surely any historical movie out of Bollywood could be called something that happened once upon a time in India. It is odder still, in that, strictly speaking, "India" the nation did not exist at the time of this story, set in the late nineteenth century. So, even though it is mistaken to claim that no such entity as "India" was recognized prior to the formation of the modern state, the title does pose a question: What, when, and who is India, and who is "in" it? It also suggests that the story it will tell, though in a sense remote and far away, is in another sense "in India," located in the midst of the nation and its current dilemmas. The reference to myth is also significant, suggesting that the movie aspires to the creation of a tale of origins, perhaps a tale of national identity. And by alluding to the familiar activity of telling a child a story, *Once upon a Time* alludes, as well, to the narrative imagination, suggesting that storytelling itself has a role to play in the national project.

Lagaan is a story of successful nonviolent resistance against the British masters—years before Gandhi. Set in the late Victorian era, it concerns peasants from a poor village who are oppressed by high taxes imposed by the British, represented by the cruel and arrogant Captain Russell, commanding officer of the local cantonment. One comic aspect of the film is this character, who is threatening but ultimately buffoonish, and whose pink skin is made to look like an overcooked piece of some rather unappetizing lunch meat, while the various shades of dark skin exhibited by the villagers look pleasing. Bhuvan (Aamir Khan), the leader of the villagers, asks for a remission of taxes on account of the prolonged drought. Russell is utterly unreceptive. On his visit to the officers, Bhuvan witnesses a cricket match and makes fun of the game. Russell, offended at the resistance of the villagers, seeks revenge, offering Bhuvan a wager. If, at a time only a few months hence, the villagers can beat his men at cricket, he will remit the tax for three years; if they lose, they will have to pay triple tax. Bhuvan accepts the wager, much to the villagers' astonishment.

But they don't know anything about cricket. Fortunately, they get help from Russell's sister, who has fallen in love with Bhuvan. She sneaks out and organizes practice sessions. Before they can start to practice, however, a team must be formed. And it is here that the nation building begins. The natural team members are local Hindus, but Bhuvan quickly insists on recruiting Deva, a Sikh who knows the game from his military past as a sepoy in the British army, and Ismail, a Muslim, who shows fine skill as a batsman. Each of these inclusions meets with some initial resistance, but this is nothing compared to the horror with which the villagers and team members react to his introduction of Kachra, an "untouchable" or *dalit*, who has remarkable natural talent as a leg spin bowler. Bhuvan berates the villagers, and the team finally accepts Kachra. Meanwhile, women's empowerment is dramatized not only through the theme of the female coach, but, more pertinently, by the assertive role in the whole business played by Gauri, Bhuvan's girlfriend, to whom he remains loyal. All these "minorities" remain utterly loyal and make a huge contribution to the success of the team. It is in fact a good-caste Hindu who almost ruins everything by colluding with the British and trying to throw the match, out of romantic jealousy, since he loves Gauri. So the film reminds the spectator that treachery is not particularly associated with these "others" (as the propaganda of the Hindu Right constantly suggests, saying that those whose holy land is elsewhere cannot be loyal), but can exist right in the heart of the majority.

The entire second half of this four-hour film concerns the match itself, and I shall not summarize it, except to say that it presupposes a strong interest in the national sport, and shows the sport itself as an act of national self-definition. In the end, the villagers win—thanks in particular to the stellar performance of their spin bowler, but thanks as well to the ability of the group to unmask the deception of the betrayer and bring him over to their side. They win—and then the rains come down, ending the drought. So the village is doubly saved: no taxes, and the promise of a rich harvest to come. As the film ends, everyone is dancing around in the rain.

The basic message of *Lagaan* is that only by including and respecting everyone can India be strong and solve her political and economic problems. Indeed, only in this way can she transcend her history of subjection. The Hindu Right at the time kept sending the message that overcoming the legacy of humiliation required the aggressive assertion of a Hindu-first identity and the marginalization of other groups. *Lagaan* subverts this propaganda. In *Lagaan,* it is the British who are racist and who discriminate on grounds of religion. True Indian values are pluralist. The villagers defeat the British not only by winning the match, but by holding their conduct to a higher standard (a constant theme in Gandhi's independence movement). Western values are those of aggression and domination; Indian values are mutual respect, teamwork, toleration, and the love of diversity.

The choice of cricket is significant because it is a sport associated with good manners—and the manners of the Indians, like their play, surpass those of their rulers. Cricket, however, is significant for another reason: the world of Indian cricket is indeed very inclusive, with easy mingling of the religions and public love of players from diverse backgrounds. The film alludes to the values of Indian cricket as good for all India. And of course the other Indian world that is famously inclusive, the one place in which religious identity means little and interreligious marriages don't raise an eyebrow, is the world of Bollywood, to which the film refers all the time by being itself, mixing people together in the way that Bollywood just does. Here we have a romantic Hindu couple, Bhuvan and Gauri—and, lo and behold, they are incarnated by Aamir Khan, a Muslim who is married to a Hindu in real life,[60] and Gracy Singh, a Sikh. Somehow, in the midst of the terrible religious tensions of the time, nobody was even suggesting that a Muslim symbol of both heroism and sexiness—marrying a Hindu woman in fiction, and a Sikh woman in the reality behind the fiction—was anything but utterly wonderful and normal. And it's even better, for Khan is well known to be a descendant of Maulana Azad, the devout Muslim who played a leading role in Gandhi's movement, and from whose hands Gandhi first accepted food when he broke his fast unto death. The film thus alludes to the overcoming of bodily stigma and disgust as a goal of a truly Gandhian India.

Nor, with the bitterness of the Delhi anti-Sikh riots of 1984 still vividly alive and with the prosecutions wending their way through the courts, does anyone think that someone named Singh ought not to play a romantic leading-lady role. The fictional characters sing and dance as if made for each other, and everyone loves them. The film suggests boldly that someone with the name Singh could do anything—three years before Manmohan Singh's ascent to the leadership of the nation as its first minority prime minister. If only all India were as inclusive as cricket and Bollywood and as rooted in bodily grace and joy, goes the message, the country could flourish as never before.

And the miscegenation in the casting goes further: the Muslim character Ismail is played by Rajendranath Zutschi, a Hindu who in real life is married to Aamir Khan's (Muslim) sister. The Sikh sepoy Deva is played by Pradeep Rawat, an upper-caste (rajput) Hindu, and another Sikh character, Ram Singh, is played by Javed Khan, a Muslim. Nor are the lower castes absent: the character Bhura, the (non-lower-caste) poultry farmer, is played by Raghuvir Yadav, a "backward caste." The untouchable Kachra is an exception, but of a most interesting sort, for he is played by Aditya Lakhia, who is actually a *dalit,* from the Musahar (rat-catcher) caste of Bihar, a scheduled caste. However, his first name, Aditya, is not a name often found in lower castes, suggesting that his family already had some education and upward mobility[61]—so, the poor and uneducated *dalit* is played by that most promising hybrid of all, a middle-class *dalit*.

Every spectator, in 2001, knew that India was not like the world of *Lagaan*. In the aftermath of the destruction of the Babri Masjid at Ayodhya in 1992 and the subsequent rise to power of the Bharatiya Janata Party, discrimination and hostility against Muslims was ongoing, and the ruling party was tacitly encouraging the view of Muslims (and Christians) as outsiders that led to the horrible events of Gujarat in 2002. Nor had justice for the Delhi anti-Sikh riots of 1984 ever been secured, or the guilty government officials brought to justice. As for the scheduled castes, despite various affirmative action programs, discrimination against them was, and still is, a daily reality. So *Lagaan* has a tragic undercurrent, just as do Aristophanes's *Acharnians* and *Lysistrata,* produced in a time of real war and real pain. Even a decade later, the unity it imagines does not exist—or exists only in pockets of Indian society. The fantasy, however, and the real hope, is that India could become like cricket, like Bollywood—a realm united through play. In 2004, at least a part of it came true. It would be absurd to call Manmohan Singh, who at least appears to be one of the most humorless Indian leaders in history, a source of unity through play, but maybe that joke is itself a type of healing. Despite its unreality, the film is still hopeful, indeed festive—it celebrates those pockets of pluralism, and hence the capacity of India to be her best self, rather than her worst, respecting each citizen as an equal and using the human capital of all to enhance the living standard of all. For it is in the end a film about welfare. Its title alludes to economic survival, and it ends with a welcome rain that relieves the drought.

Lagaan's conclusion, in which all castes and religions frolic in the rain, is reminiscent of Aristophanic endings: bodily joy triumphing over animosity and separation. And it is an Indian analogue of the comedy of the Crown Fountain, as the water of miscegenation flows over all, and disgust has been banished.

Bill Mauldin's Cartoons: The Body at War

The body at war is still a human body, longing for the good things of life, burdened by pain and fatigue. So war, as Aristophanes saw, is a central occasion for comedy. As *The Acharnians* reminds us, military leaders have a way of forgetting about the bodies of common soldiers. But this is particularly true in modern warfare, when the officers themselves, unlike Lamachus, may not be in the field. Pro-war propaganda by elites, from ancient Athens to the present day, keeps churning out clean, noble images of combat soldiers, "gallant lads" who win "glory."[62] But life is not like that, and common soldiers want acknowledgment of the bodily reality of their lives—as part of the respect owed them for their sacrifice, and as part of a public acknowledgment that the goal of war must always be peace and the enjoyment of life.

The controversial American cartoonist Bill Mauldin, during World War II, created his own comic festival in the person of his legendary characters Willie and Joe—so successfully that he became an official part of the war effort, endorsed by Dwight Eisenhower himself.[63] The man whom General George S. Patton Jr. denounced as a subversive was in May 2010 honored with a U.S. postage stamp. It depicts his classic characters Willie and Joe, and shows Mauldin himself in uniform beside them, pen and sketch pad in hand.

Mauldin (1921–2003) entered the U.S. Army in 1940 through the Arizona National Guard, and was assigned to the 45th Infantry Division. Having already studied at the Chicago Academy of Fine Arts, he volunteered to work for the unit's newspaper. Here he invented Willie and Joe. Landing with the division in the invasion of Sicily in July 1943, he continued his cartooning, and began working for the official soldiers' newspaper, *Stars and Stripes*—to which he was officially transferred in February 1944. Shortly after this, he was given his own jeep, so that he could roam the front in search of material. His cartoons were seen by soldiers throughout Europe, and also in the United States.[64]

Top brass did not like his irreverence or his satirical depiction of military discipline (such as a cartoon making fun of Patton's order that soldiers must be clean-shaven at all times, even during combat). Patton tried to get him removed from the front, calling him on the carpet for "spreading dissent." He also threatened to ban the newspaper if it did not stop carrying "Mauldin's scurrilous attempts to undermine military discipline." But Eisenhower came to his defense, because he saw that Mauldin gave common soldiers a champion and an outlet for their frustrations, helping them survive the emotional and physical hardship of war. He arranged a meeting between Patton and Mauldin. Mauldin told *Time* magazine, "I came out with my hide on. We parted friends, but I don't think we changed each other's mind." Patton, incensed at this public comment, said that if Mauldin ever came to see him again, he would throw him in jail. Much later, Mauldin commented, "I always admired Patton. Oh sure, the stupid bastard was crazy. He was insane. He thought he was living in the Dark Ages. Soldiers were peasants to him. I didn't like that attitude, but I certainly respected his theories and the techniques he used to get his men out of their foxholes."[65] Mauldin's popularity increased when he was wounded in the shoulder while visiting a machine gun crew near Monte Cassino. In 1945, Mauldin won the Army's Legion of Merit, and, shortly after that, the Pulitzer Prize "for distinguished service as a cartoonist." He is buried in Arlington National Cemetery.

Willie and Joe are the Aristophanic heroes of World War II.[66] Like Dikaiopolis, they draw attention to daily bodily functions and bodily vulnerability. Crumpled and saggy, with cigarettes hanging out of the corner of their mouths, they even resemble the baggy padded costume of the ancient comic hero. Like this hero too, they focus on the good things of life, not on abstractions such as glory. Exhausted and schlumpy, flat-footed, bent over, Willie goes to the army doctor—himself a sad sack, beaten down by cares. The doctor holds out an aspirin bottle in one hand, a box containing a medal in the other. "Just give me the aspirin," Willie says. "I already got a Purple Heart."[67] It's important that Willie is a patriot, no coward or deserter: he already has a Purple Heart. But he is tired and sore, and the cartoon pokes fun at the idea that medals can relieve the feet or the aching back. What doctor would offer you a useless thing like that?

Other cartoons poke fun at the brass for its indifference to the common soldier's experience. One, for example, shows Willie and Joe in a Jeep, exhausted, unshaven, dirty, pulling up outside a fancy club that says "Staff Officers Only" and "Ties Must Be Worn." Mauldin said, "I drew pictures for and about the soldiers because I knew what their life was like and understood their gripes."[68] Officers, in the cartoons, usually don't understand: in one, an officer is standing tall, clean, and proud while Willie and Joe crouch down in the mud behind some bushes. "Sir, do ya hafta draw fire while yer inspirin' us?" the caption reads.[69] Somehow we know that the officer will move on in his nearby vehicle (we just know it's there, off the page), leaving the soldiers to live with the risk his display has created.

Again and again, the cartoons harp on bodily need and discomfort—rain, mud, and cold being the most persistent themes of the Italian series, along with blisters, lack of sleep, and aches and pains—but they also focus on the attempt to live with minimal decency and dignity, a serious aim, even when their attempts are somehow comic. As other soldiers carry out garbage, Joe, in a hole that might be a garbage pit or might be a foxhole, puts up a sign: "This is a residence."[70] On a field strewn with the detritus of combat, Willy and Joe notice a single flower on a barren tree. "Spring is here," reads the caption.[71] It's a jibe at the sentimentalizing of wartime conditions, but at the same time it is real, a little glimmer of pleasure in the middle of pain and fatigue. They even have a capacity for metaphor in the middle of ugliness. As they stand up to their necks in mud, the rain beating down on their helmets, Willie says, "Now that ya mention it, it does sound like th' patter of rain on a tin roof."[72] And they do organize their pleasures, even in the midst of chaos and disorder. When the sun comes out after the rain, Willie says to Joe, "Th' socks ain't dry yet, but we kin take in the cigarettes"—and indeed cigarettes have been lovingly hung out to dry on the line in a neat, orderly row.[73] About sexual deprivation the cartoons are more circumspect, but it's clearly there, as when Willie, turning to a particularly slovenly and disheveled Joe, says, "Why the hell couldn't you have been born a beautiful woman?"[74] Joe drives up to a building promisingly labeled "Mlle. Du Blanc Université des Femmes," only to find that there are no femmes to be found—it has been commandeered by a bunch of his colleagues, leaving only the elderly proprietress to inquire of him, "Are you seeking a company of infantry, mon capitaine?"[75]

At times the comedy verges on tragedy. As the two soldiers huddle together in a swamp, Willie says, "Joe, yestiddy ya saved my life an' I swore I'd pay ya back. Here's my last pair of dry socks."[76]

Patton was wrong and Eisenhower was right. Mauldin was no subversive. He did not look down at Willie and Joe; he clearly respects their courage and their endurance. He himself, it is important to note, is one of them, assuming the same risks and vulnerabilities. But by reminding the brass and the public of the fact that wars are fought by human bodies, he gave a voice to the common soldier, prompting better deliberation about their needs and sacrifices.

Interestingly, Mauldin once had the idea that Willie and Joe would die at the end of the war. But he was talked out of it: it is, after all, a comic festival, and comedy celebrates life. Instead, going home, they make fun of the idea that war is glory. Seated somehow next to a top general on a flight home (a fantasy, of course), Joe says, aping the snootiness of the top brass, "My companion and I find these transatlantic flights very tedious."[77] Later, interviewed by a journalist, with a sign reading "Public Relations" over his head, Joe just sits there schlumpy, exhausted, and numb, and an officer speaks for him: "He thinks the food over there was swell. He's glad to be home, but he misses the excitement of battle. You may quote him."[78] Willie, meanwhile, standing at a podium, addresses a group of returning soldiers, in an official room that bears the sign "Fill Out Forms Properly." He is evidently reading from a demobilization questionnaire. "Next question: Do you wish to remain in the army? It says here I gotta ask." Not one smile around the room—except on Willie's amused face.[79]

They never do die. Indeed, a cartoon in Mauldin's manner, signed Hank Stair, entitled "R.I.P. Bill," shows them, still in World War II uniform, mourning at Mauldin's grave in 2003.[80]

Difficult Conversations?

Book clubs, we saw, can provide a valuable extension of the tragic festival, because they promote a type of emotional experience and exchange that is cooler and more deliberative than the experience of watching a movie or visiting a memorial. Critical conversation and emotional participation join hands in a valuable way. Is there a comic analogue? Well, of course a book club can read books that are funny—but it's striking that the Chicago list does not include first-rate comic works, and we can imagine why. A comic novel such as *Portnoy's Complaint* is "hot," full of charged ethnic material that is potentially offensive to many people and groups. Moreover, comedy, unlike revenge, is not "best served cold." Half the fun of a comic novel is likely to get lost if you start analyzing it in a book group, and it is notoriously difficult to talk about why something is funny, far more difficult than to talk about why something is sad. Furthermore, jokes, unlike tragic predicaments, require a context of intimacy, shared background assumptions.[81] So it is never easy to transfer humor from one era to another, from one nation to another, even from one subculture to another. In several centuries, *Portnoy's Complaint* will likely be as hard to understand as Aristophanes is today, and right now it probably would make a bad book group topic in Chicago's Mexican American and African American neighborhoods. Even if such books could be made to work in a book club context, they would require skilled moderators, and the city program thrives on spontaneity.

Still, live comedy can perform some of the functions of the book group, provoking a difficult conversation about the toughest issues a society faces. The comedy of Lenny Bruce is a notorious example.[82] Consider the famous routine in which he shocked people by using the *N*-word and all sorts of other unacceptable ethnic slurs—until it became clear that the labels included everyone in the room. This was a demonstration—initially terrifying, ultimately healing—of an idea whose roots we studied in Chapter 7: that stigma is not the property of some underclass, different from you and me, but a property of the human body, and of everyone who will admit to having one. The recognition of stigma's omnipresence helps overcome the baneful effects of stigma in everyday life.

How might a society arrange to reap the benefits of this abrasive, alarming, ultimately unifying experience?

Lenny Bruce could not have achieved his effects had he been on retainer from Mayor Daley (whether Richard J. or Richard M.). It seems important that this sort of provocative comedy is informal, unofficial, at the margins. So that's an asymmetry between comic and tragic festivals, and a reason the official comic festivals, like our three examples, are always going to involve comedy of a gentler sort, lacking the critical edge that makes some comedy capable of digging deep into particularly vexing social problems. So what could a decent society do to support the more radical type of comedy, aware that to domesticate it would kill it?

Well, for a start it could refuse to persecute it. Lenny Bruce's sad life now stands as a monument to public obtuseness. Hounded by the law in a way that now seems utterly grotesque, he did so much less than he might have done. So, firm protection for the speech of edgy artists is one of the obvious ways in which society can cultivate comedy.

Obviously, though, more might be done. Grants given to edgy artists through some decent system of peer review used to be a familiar part of our political landscape, until the National Endowment for the Arts became a political target (and it's now threatened with total extinction). Nothing would be worse than Congress selecting the comic artists who would get grants. But Congress can, as it used to, appropriate money and protect the freedom of the peer review system—in the way that now, in a state university, faculty hiring is done by peers and the speech of unpopular faculty is standardly protected from infringement.

National prizes can also confer semiofficial status. Maya Lin won the National Medal of the Arts, so why not Bruce? Bill Cosby has actually won the Presidential Medal of Freedom, as well as Kennedy Center honors—but his comedy, while admirable, is of a much gentler and more cautious type. Aamir Khan and A. R. Rahman have both won the Padma Shri, the Indian prize for meritorious contributions to the democracy (as have many cricket players and actors). So why not work that is more experimental and emotionally challenging? It's not going to happen now in the United States, with all federal money for the arts about to be cut, but that's a huge error.

With this mention of federal money, we arrive at a delicate issue: How are these public art projects to be funded, and how will this avoid the obvious dangers of banality and the exclusion of really challenging artists? Since I have selected high-quality projects, we can ask how they emerged. Some were initially private (*Lagaan,* Bill Mauldin' cartoons, in a sense Walt Whitman's poetry) but were then put into an official role because of their quality. Some were statements by a single leader. In others cases, a shrewd political leader arranged things so as to promote high artistic quality: Roosevelt did not submit every art project to Congress, though the Works Progress Administration paid for them. Mayor Daley did not ask for a majority vote of the City Council on plans for Millennium Park, and indeed funded it mostly through private donations. Gehry was approached directly by the city and also through the private donors, without any competition—although the Chicago public and its architecture critics always like to weigh in, and celebrated his involvement. (The public and the media in Chicago are currently debating another major project, for the renovation of Navy Pier, though in an advisory capacity.) The Vietnam Veterans Memorial was a public competition, and this is actually relatively rare.[83] There is no rule about the best way for public culture to be commissioned and funded, but these examples suggest that direct legislative approval of funding for specific projects is, and should be, the exception. And the long track record of high-quality public art produced in other ways shows us that those other ways are not inherently undemocratic.

All nations face tragedies that call upon the spirit of extended compassion. All nations struggle with a disgust that stigmatizes and excludes. Pondering the work of tragic and comic festivals, we see a wide range of diverse experiments that make them real in modern times, as modern societies find ways to forge a coherent unity out of enormous plurality— weaving, as Lysistrata says, the separate threads into a tapestry of general welfare.

At this point, the image of Cherubino as citizen has reached its full development. We began by adding to his interest in reciprocity a genuinely political commitment to freedom and critique in the spirit of J. S. Mill (Chapter 3), and a determination to overcome bodily disgust in the spirit of the Bauls (Chapter 4). We next advanced a psychological theory that located these parts of his personality in a plausible account of human development that indicated how concern and compassion might be extended and disgust overcome, and how play and imagination function as key elements in that project (Chapters 6 and 7). Also in Part II, we made explicit a political structure and a set of distinctively political aspirations, giving him a home, so to speak (Chapter 5).

We then turned to the difficult question of how the just political principles to which his nation aspired could be embodied in emotions that are motivationally powerful. We showed how love of that political home could be constructed as a form of extended compassion in which, as a citizen, Cherubino loves what is his own, having powerful eudaimonistic emotions, while at the same time grasping general principles of justice, and grasping them in those very emotional experiences. (Thus Rawls's demand for principle-dependent emotions is fulfilled, but in a eudaimonistic and therefore personally powerful way—and, in addition, a way involving the sort of love that we have found to be required if narcissism is ever to be transcended.) We argued that love of the nation, appropriately constructed, is fully compatible with quirky individuality and a commitment to liberty. And now, in this chapter, we have shown in a more general way, not focused simply on love of the nation itself, how a love-infused compassion can become, extended, a vehicle of political principles, while not ceasing to bind citizens to what they love; how laughter, while remaining lighthearted and earthy—indeed, precisely because it is these things—can surmount disgust and promote the common good.

CHAPTER TEN

Compassion's Enemies:
Fear, Envy, Shame

I will plant companionship thick as trees along all the rivers of
America, and along the shores of the great lakes, and all over
the prairies,
I will make inseparable cities with their arms about each other's
necks,
By the love of comrades . . .

—Walt Whitman, "For You O Democracy"

I was glad to observe that the privileges of the garden were enjoyed
about equally by all classes.

—Frederick Law Olmsted, 1851 (of Birkenhead Park, Liverpool)

I. Compassion under Siege

Creating civic compassion requires us to understand what threatens it.
Our entire project starts from an unfortunate reality: people are inclined to be narrow and greedy in their sympathies, reluctant to support projects aimed at a common good if these require sacrifice. They
are also prone to ugly practices involving the projection of disgust
properties onto subordinate groups, who then function in majority ideologies as quasi-animals. At this point in our inquiry, we have some
understanding of how compassion may be strengthened and generalized and projective disgust minimized through civic projects of many
kinds.

Compassion, however, has other enemies. These other hostile forces are not utterly unrelated to the narcissism that makes compassion narrow, or to the fear of the bodily that generates projective disgust. They are, however, different—both from disgust and from one another—in their specific emotional content and therefore in the strategies required to keep them from doing public damage. Fear, envy, and shame are three such enemies. Each has a good aspect or at least a good relative, but all have pernicious tendencies that can erode support for good political causes. All, then, need to be understood as well as possible, so that we can imagine strategies to minimize the specific damages they do. Our project thus becomes more complicated: we need not only the working understanding of compassion, love, and disgust that informed our study of patriotism and our proposal for new tragic and comic festivals. We also need political projects aimed at containing the damages these three emotions commonly do, even in basically stable democracies. Because they all (or, in the case of envy, a close relative) have some good roles to play, a nuanced understanding of each of them and their different species is essential: we don't want to lose civic benefits while preventing civic damages.

In all three cases, one of the best preventions against damage is the strengthening of extended compassion itself. We might therefore easily make the mistake of thinking that specific strategies aimed at containing these three potentially pernicious emotions are not necessary and that all we need to do is to build sufficient fellow feeling, like the thick forest of companionship of which Whitman speaks. This is not exactly false, but it misses something important. The three bad emotions interact in highly specific ways with different elements of compassion, jeopardizing it from different directions. While it's true that a general strengthening provides a general defense, no well-run army would defend itself without trying first to understand as well as possible from what direction the enemy is marching and how it is planning to attack. With such an understanding, leaders can prepare a much more efficient defense, strengthening specific vulnerable areas, rather than spreading resources around haphazardly.

Of course, law is crucial. Laws and institutions protect us against the damage of bad civic passions, and law often precedes and guides the creation of decent sentiments. We certainly don't want to wait until most people love each other before we protect the civil rights of the vulnerable.

Hannah Arendt wrongly opined that we should wait for racial harmony in society before passing nondiscrimination laws.[1] But the force of law was essential in starting, however painfully and slowly, a process of emotional change that is still taking place. The armed federal guards who protected the young men and women who integrated the universities of the South preceded emotional change in the southern states. But they were a beacon of hope and a protection for the oppressed, and in this way they contributed to a gradual change of sentiments. All this seems obvious enough.

Our project, however, is not a study of the emotional consequence of good laws. It is the more subtle and diffuse one of ascertaining how public strategies can help good laws by influencing the emotional climate of the public culture. It relies on the thought that good laws rarely come into being or remain stable over time without emotional support. Thus, at the same time as we figure out how to protect the rights of minorities by law (expecting that this itself will influence public emotions toward them), we should also think about shaping the emotional climate so that it supports and sustains good laws and institutions. Thus Martin Luther King Jr.'s highly successful efforts to engender hope and a new picture of the history and essence of the nation proved an essential complement to the strategies of President Lyndon Johnson and others that culminated in the Civil Rights Act of 1964. The national holiday celebrating King's legacy is one strategy to nourish and further develop good laws in this area—although, like many such strategies, it is vulnerable to fatigue and overexposure, and thus will need to be continually renewed. (This danger is endemic to most strategies we use to nourish emotions. It is connected to the role of wonder in kindling love of this type. For this reason, as Tagore and Whitman understood, we need to involve changing generations of creative artists who have the capacity to fashion new and arresting images. But we should also grant that a really great work of art, like a great friendship, can be continually revisited and new possibilities can be discovered in it, or the same thing seen freshly, because in a new context.)

II. Compassion against Itself

Before we begin studying the three hostile emotions, we need to be vividly aware that compassion is at times its own worst enemy. Batson's studies have shown that compassion, engendered prototypically by an individual narrative of distress, can often destabilize good principles through just this particularism.[2] Thus (in his study) once a compassionate understanding of the plight of people who need organ transplants has led us to adopt good policies in this area, hearing a vivid story of one would-be recipient's plight can lead people to discard good policy and procedure, advancing that person unfairly to the top of the list. The one blocks the many.

The Batson phenomenon is so familiar that it is hardly necessary to illustrate it. Parents may support a set of inclusive goals for a school system—and then become utterly deflected by the particular struggles of their own children. Citizens may support policies that are fair to all—until reversals close to home elicit powerful sympathy for one's own family or group, eclipsing the good of the whole. But this is not only a problem when selfish interests are in play: it can affect any situation in which an individual case is salient and thus available to the mind.[3] When new laws are passed protecting the rights of minorities, we typically hear a lot of individual testimony, which moves legislators to support the measures. Still, the very individualism of the reference point can at times become an impediment to policies that are truly evenhanded.

In our discussion of tragic festivals we addressed this issue in two ways. First, we insisted that it is good for a tragic predicament to be presented in a somewhat generalized and abstract form, so that people's minds are led naturally to the choice of general and fair policies, not to the relief of specific individuals. (Roosevelt understood this issue extremely well, overseeing the selection of photographs that seemed representative of economic woes, rather than idiosyncratically particular.)[4] Such generalized experiences of compassion create a bridge toward good principles, and in themselves they are emotions that have principles as part of their content—for example, King's emotions of hope and longing for a just America, and Lincoln's evocation of a compassion for dead soldiers that also embodies a love of the principles for which they died. Generalization has its risks, for it can enshrine hostile stereotypes, but when it is focused on shared human aims and vulnerabilities it can avoid this difficulty, and actually undermine hostile stereotypes. Second, we said that compassion should never be an uncriticized foundation for policy: it should always be in dialogue with principles and general moral norms. Moreover, a vigorous critical culture should keep it from degenerating into a sectarian and uneven sympathy.

These safeguards are important, and they go some way toward alleviating the worry. Nonetheless, Batson's experimental results remind us that even when good principles are established, vivid compassion for particulars remains a threat to their fair operation, so we must be aware of this danger and prepared to head it off, without losing the emotional force and the insight of that emotion.

The Batson problem becomes more acute when we recall that we are after no mere tepid or detached sympathy, but, instead, something more closely akin to and periodically illuminated by love. We argued that overcoming disgust and generating trust requires love during the developmental process, and that the mature sympathy of an adult too needs to be enlivened by and retain access to that passionate and quasi-erotic emotion, if trust is not to become a lifeless simulacrum. Tagore's religion of humanity, putting the Bauls of Bengal at the center of the program for citizenship, harmonized with the conclusions of our developmental inquiry, in which a type of loving play, what Winnicott calls "subtle interplay," is given a central role. Accordingly, the type of patriotism that seemed truly capable of surmounting narrowness and egoism had that element of love—whether in King's powerfully poetic rhetoric or in Gandhi's use of Tagore's songs—addressed to the history, geography, people, and institutions of the nation. Because this love is not an abstract Rawlsian or Habermasian principle-based love, it is particularly vulnerable to narrowness and deflection, so we need to think hard about how this problem can be prevented from infecting our project at its very core. This problem is only partly a problem of selfishness: it is also a question of how particulars catch the eye, drawing attention away from the whole.

One obvious answer is the rule of law. But how can we engender emotions that support fair laws and policies, including policies that promote decent international relations and the hope of peace? Let us think again of our two correctives. First, the type of compassionate love we engender, while vivid and particular in one sense, addressed to concrete features of the nation's history and geography and culture, should nonetheless be inclusive and somewhat abstract, as Rawls suggests, in order to include all members of the nation. There is no contradiction here. The New Deal photographs (like Sophocles' character Philoctetes, enacted by a real and particular body) were vividly, searingly individual, showing the impact of economic disaster on unforgettable particular bodies—and yet at the same time they were representative rather than simply idiosyncratic. *Lagaan* (like Aristophanes' *Lysistrata*) created a set of characters whom the spectator could love as individuals but at the same time see as representative of classes of Indians. Gandhi's body was inspiring because it was his, and he was an utterly unique individual; yet it constantly represented general political values. Martin Luther King Jr.'s soaring poetry, rather like Walt Whitman's, could create passionate involvement while at the same time encouraging listeners to think of the whole history of the United States, past, present, and future.[5]

Indeed, if we accept Tagore's argument, and my reformulation of it in Part II, it is precisely because poetry of the sort that touches the heart is involved that the mind is enabled to be led, as if by that long curvaceous bridge in Millennium Park, to contemplate a large and inclusive collectivity. Creating the right sort of emotion, poised between the particular and the general, is a challenge, but hardly an impossibility.

But because the balance is so crucial and so difficult to achieve, even well-chosen symbols need to be part of a dialogue that also includes arguments addressing issues of fairness and inclusion—especially in our nonideal societies, where these goals are not yet fully achieved. Emotion, once again, is not foundational, but part of a conversation. This, indeed, is Batson's own remedy for the problem he finds. Don't reject the insight embodied in emotional response, he concludes, since without it a large part of our ethical connection to others is lost. But pay attention to principles too, and constrain emotions accordingly.

Notice, then, what we do and do not mean by saying that love matters for justice. We surely do not mean that love is an uncriticized foundation for political principles. Nor do we mean that it can achieve anything good on its own, without arguments and general norms. We also do not even claim that all citizens have to be moved by political love, and we certainly don't mean (we'd better not mean) that it must be a constant experience. (Love is never well imagined as a constant experience; it is a relationship involving kaleidoscopically many feelings, actions, and reactions—including intense focus on the other person, but also including the solitary cultivation of one's own personal interests, and even sleep.) The idea is, instead, that the public culture cannot be tepid and passionless, if good principles and institutions are to survive: it must have enough episodes of inclusive love, enough poetry and music, enough access to a spirit of affection and play, that people's attitudes to one another and the nation they inhabit are not mere dead routine. Whitman and Tagore describe an ingredient that leavens the whole.

So what can a wise public culture do to head off the threat to common pursuits posed by specific types of fear, envy, and shame, while retaining the good roles played by other species of those same emotions?

III. Fear: A Narrowing Emotion

Fear is very useful, indeed necessary. It steers us away from danger. Without its promptings we would all be dead. Even in the political and legal realm, fear can be reasonable, giving good guidance. The Anglo-American criminal law, with its doctrine of "reasonable fear" in the area of self-defense, suggests that the fear of death and gross bodily injury is a legitimate motivation for self-defensive conduct. But, of course, the targets of this "reasonable fear" correspond to a central part of what the criminal law already regulates; thinking of what we reasonably fear is a good guide to lawmaking. And, as has been plausibly argued by constitutional theorist András Sajó, former judge of the European Constitutional Court, fear plays a valuable role in constitutional law too: thinking of the dangers that they reasonably fear at the hands of authority, societies frame their account of basic rights that cannot be violated.[6]

In order to be the ally of law, however, fear needs to be combined with general concern. By thinking about what we fear for ourselves, we see the sort of thing that ought to be warded off from all. But it takes sympathy to extend that concern to others, and fear is not always combined with sympathy. Indeed, it can often distract us from general sympathy. To see why, let us consider what we know about it.[7]

Fear is an unusually primitive emotion. It is found in all mammals, many of whom lack the cognitive prerequisites of sympathy (which requires positional thinking), guilt and anger (which require ideas of cause and blame), and grief (which requires an appraisal of the value of the lost individual). We now know that animals as "simple" as rats and mice are capable of appraising objects as good or bad for the self. All fear requires is some rudimentary orientation toward survival and well-being. Joseph LeDoux's important work has shown that the transmission of fright signals involves a number of distinct parts of the brain, but that a crucial role is played by the amygdala, a part of the brain that is common to all vertebrates[8] and is not connected to higher cognition. LeDoux explains that he has not shown that fear is seated in the amygdala. He is studying fright behavior, not the emotion of fear, either in rats or in humans. He believes that fear itself is a subjective state of awareness, whose connection to fright behavior would need further study. Even where fright behavior is concerned, it is a function of the entire network, he argues, not of the amygdala alone.[9] Still, LeDoux does show that human fear involves deeply implanted evolutionary tendencies: the shape of the snake, for example, elicits fright behavior even in people who have no experience of snakes. Moreover, habituated fright conditions the organism and is very difficult to unlearn.

Fear, then, is a form of heightened awareness, but one with a very narrow frame, initially at least: one's own body, and perhaps, by extension, one's life, and people and things connected to it. It is triggered by mechanisms that are rooted in genuine evolutionary usefulness, but which are also very recalcitrant to learning and moral thinking. Fear can be reasonable, based on well-grounded views of good and ill, and it can also be broadened to include the entire community, as in the case of constitution making described by Sajó, but there are tendencies inherent to the emotion that resist these good developments.

Our fear reactions can be misguided in many different ways. Natural fears (including the fear of a snaky shape and the fear of sudden noises or startling appearances) can be useful, but they can also be exploited. People may learn by association to fear groups whom culture associates with stealth or hiding, or with being wily and sinuous—all stereotypes used to demonize minority groups. But of course natural reactions carry human beings only a small way: we have to learn from our society what is helpful and harmful, in ways that go well beyond evolutionary biology, and we then attach our fear mechanism to that conception. Ultimately we have to form a conception of our own well-being and what threatens it that addresses the dangers of our complex world.

Here lie many potential problems. In every society, rhetoric and politics work on ideas of what is dangerous, making danger salient where it really exists, but also constructing the perception of danger where it does not. Aristotle's *Rhetoric,* which anatomizes the process through which political rhetoric creates a sense of danger or removes it, shows us clearly a number of points where error can enter in. We may have misidentified the threat, or misestimated its size. Or we might be right about the threat but wrong about who has caused it. Or we might have a conception of our well-being that is off-kilter, which makes us fear something that is not bad at all (for example, the inclusion of new ethnic groups in our nation).[10]

Even in the most reliable cases, where fear is "reasonable" concerning a narrow circle of concern, fear is all too often excessively narrow. Because of tendencies to intense self-focusing that derive from its biological origins, fear often hijacks thought powerfully, making it difficult to think about anything else but oneself and one's immediate circle, so long as intense anxiety lasts. In consequence, a public culture that wants to encourage extended compassion needs to think as well about limiting and properly directing fear, for once it gets going, the good of others is all too likely to fade into the background.

Fear is everywhere, for both good and bad. Societies can shape it in many venues and modes. Here, two contrasting examples will suffice: the use of political rhetoric by Franklin Delano Roosevelt to temper and manage a potentially dangerous level of public fear, and the use of urban architecture in both Delhi and Chicago to create fear where there was previously sympathy—or, reversing that process, to create a basis for sympathy by managing fear.

Tempering Fear with Optimism and Effort: Roosevelt's First Inaugural Address (1933)

Sometimes present events are genuinely alarming. It would be rational to fold up one's tent and move elsewhere, give up, or just run away— above all to protect oneself and one's family from the damage that seems imminent. War is such an event, and yet leaders need to rally people to face an aggressor with courage and fellowship. Fear is centrifugal; it dissipates a people's potentially united energy. What leaders say can make a great deal of difference, bringing people together around a common project.

An obvious case, which we may study as a paradigm of the wise political management of fear, is Winston Churchill's famous speech of May 13, 1940, his first speech to the House of Commons as prime minister. At that time there was a real danger that the British people would collapse in fear and exhaustion. Churchill's goal, brilliantly executed, was to characterize accurately the immense effort that would be required and to dispel defeatist fear in favor of a spirit of hope and solidarity. Here is the crucial part of the speech:

> I would say to the House, as I said to those who have joined this government: "I have nothing to offer but blood, toil, tears, and sweat." We have before us an ordeal of the most grievous kind. We have before us many, many long months of struggle and of suffering. You ask, what is our policy? I can say: It is to wage war, by sea, land and air, with all our might and with all the strength that God can give us; to wage war against a monstrous tyranny, never surpassed in the dark, lamentable catalogue of human crime. That is our policy. You ask, what is our aim? I can answer in one word: It is victory, victory at all costs, victory in spite of all terror, victory, however long and hard the road may be; for without victory, there is no survival. Let that be realized; no survival for the British Empire, no survival for all that the British Empire has stood for, no survival for the urge and impulse of the ages, that mankind will move forward towards its goal. But I take up my task with buoyancy and hope. I feel sure that our cause will not be suffered to fail among men. At this time I feel entitled to claim the aid of all, and I say, "Come then, let us go forward together with our united strength."

From the point of view of sheer technical rhetoric, this speech, with its resonant biblical phrases, its incantatory repetitions, and its artful repetitions and crescendos, is as carefully crafted as anything in Cicero, who undoubtedly inspired it (despite the fact that Churchill was a weak classical scholar!). Emotionally, it traces a map of a most interesting sort. Churchill begins, in effect, in the middle of people's fear—and instead of turning away from it, he confronts it: *Yes, it is that bad. It is a terrible ordeal.* But at that very moment the task begins to take on heroic and in that sense appealing and somewhat glamorous proportions, as Churchill summons a range of images—the labors of Hercules against monsters, a classic schoolboy's tale of battle and danger, images of past British victories over tyranny (Lord Nelson is not far away). Then Churchill returns to the alternative. It is not friendly partying with German elites (as Edward VIII and Mrs. Simpson probably thought). It is extinction of everything fine about Britain—and here Churchill sounds a note he loves to sound, the note of Britain's empire as the necessary condition of world civilization and progress. He makes the audience feel the fear fully by representing its object as nothing less than the extinction of the human race, via the extinction of the values of the British Empire. Empire is made to look so necessary and so beautiful that sacrifice is amply justified—and now Churchill turns to "hope" and even "buoyancy." He becomes, in effect, the undaunted schoolboy hero fighting the forces of darkness, a figure beloved of the British public, from Tom Brown at Rugby to Harry Potter. Then he forms a community around him: the emotional arc of the speech has entitled him to refer to "our united strength."

Now let us turn to Roosevelt's earlier speech. War in the literal sense was not yet at hand, but Roosevelt's treatment of the economic crisis closely parallels Churchill's treatment of military emergency. Like Churchill, Roosevelt traces an arc from fear to hope and solidarity—but in a characteristically American mode, self-reliance and Christian morality taking the place of empire.[11]

Roosevelt begins, like Churchill, with a profession of honesty: Americans rely on him to "address them with a candor and a decision which the present situation of our Nation impels." Throughout the speech, Roosevelt insistently characterizes the present state of the nation as one of war, saying we must treat "the task as we would treat the emergency of a war." His policies are "lines of attack." The American people are "a trained and loyal army"; he assumes the leadership of "this great army of

our people dedicated to a disciplined attack upon our common problems." He only asks for broad executive power "to wage a war against the
emergency." And yet, early on, he sounds his other major note: the problem is not so grave that it cannot be solved by American ingenuity and
self-reliance. It is less grave than the "perils which our forefathers conquered because they believed and were not afraid." Indeed, his very first
characterization of the economic crisis contains a combination of grim
accounting with the cheerful reminder that it is not a problem that goes
to the core of America's identity:

> In such a spirit on my part and on yours we face our common diffi-
> culties. They concern, thank God, only material things. Values have
> shrunken to fantastic levels; taxes have risen; our ability to pay has
> fallen; government of all kinds is faced by serious curtailment of in-
> come; the means of exchange are frozen in the currents of trade; the
> withered leaves of industrial enterprise lie on every side; farmers
> find no markets for their produce; the savings of many years in thou-
> sands of families are gone. More important, a host of unemployed
> citizens face the grim problem of existence, and an equally great
> number toil with little return. Only a foolish optimist can deny the
> dark realities of the moment.

Like Churchill, Roosevelt enumerates with dark honesty the problems of his time, showing that fear is warranted and rational. But at the
same time he points the way beyond these problems by saying that they
"concern, thank God, only material things." For although the primary
argument of the speech concerns confidence and united work, a major
subtheme concerns blame. Roosevelt responds to the (unspoken) anxious question whether America's economic system itself, indeed its
whole democratic way of life, is to blame for the present crisis. Socialism
was waiting around the corner, and the speech later concludes, "We do
not distrust the future of essential democracy. The people of the United
States have not failed." Here near the beginning, Roosevelt insists that
there is no "failure of substance," no defect in Americans and their time-
honored traditions, including (in a general way) their economic traditions. Inclusive compassion should not be impeded by the thought that

there is a flaw in America itself. He thus positions his proposed reforms as not radical changes but minor corrections in course that enable America to remain true to herself.

It is in this context that we should hear the most famous part of the speech, near its opening: "[L]et me assert my firm belief that the only thing we have to fear is fear itself—nameless, unreasoning, unjustified terror which paralyzes needed efforts to convert retreat into advance." Just as Churchill faced the danger that Britons would give up on the war effort, so Roosevelt faces the danger that Americans will abandon America. What would that mean? It means giving up on the common effort to solve the economic problems within the general context of the (to-be-reformed) American economic system. It would mean giving up, or seeking a radical transformation. It would mean scattering and retreat, rather than united effort.

Churchill had a villain, and his image of the buoyant schoolboy crusading against the monster relied on a vivid sense of the real evil on the other side. Roosevelt's villains, by contrast, are not evil, but they are profoundly mistaken, "cast in the pattern of an outworn tradition." They are, in fact, somewhat ridiculous. They are "incompetent" rulers of the financial world who have simply "abdicated," left their posts when the going got tough. And what is left now that they have abdicated? A kingdom that is both archaically biblical and totally American.

> The money changers have fled from their high seats in the temple of our civilization. We may now restore that temple to the ancient truths. The measure of the restoration lies in the extent to which we apply social values more noble than mere monetary profit. Happiness lies not in the mere possession of money; it lies in the joy of achievement, in the thrill of creative effort. The joy and moral stimulation of work no longer must be forgotten in the mad chase of evanescent profits. These dark days will be worth all they cost us if they teach us that our true destiny is not to be ministered unto but to minister to ourselves and to our fellow man.

The "ancient truth" of the Protestant ethic of work and the Christian mandate of brotherly love gives Roosevelt his shrewd analogue for

Churchill's questing hero. The money changers are wrong because they do not do a day's useful work, but instead engage in a "mad chase" after "evanescent profits." They are also wrong because they don't love their neighbors, but are in it only for selfish ends. Real work is American and moral, and work on behalf of others is more American and more moral than work for oneself. Fear and defeatism are now positioned as both unchristian and un-American.

When he turns to his ideas for economic recovery, at the end of the speech, Roosevelt follows this same line, characterizing the recovery efforts as drawing on the "American spirit of the pioneer" and the "policy of the good neighbor—the neighbor who resolutely respects himself and, because he does so, respects the rights of others—the neighbor who respects his obligation and respects the sanctity of his agreements in and with a world of neighbors." By this point in the speech, the financial enemy is seen as a useless character, both flighty and selfish, while the true American, joining the common effort, is a pioneer and a good neighbor, and helping others is seen as the responsible way to live.

Roosevelt has another opponent, whom he arranges not to confront. Addressing mainstream America, he encourages his audience not to have fear concerning the essential soundness of America's institutions. But by his insistent, albeit negative, references to blame he betrays the presence of a left-wing opposition (including Huey Long, who was already becoming a threat) that does in fact blame American institutions for the nation's ills. What he cleverly does is to downgrade this opponent from a conscientious critic of the nation to a coward: because there's no place for real blame, the negative response can only be fear. This is rhetorical sleight-of-hand, and it is certainly not a reasoned confrontation with the arguments of his socialist opponents. We may criticize him for treating them disparagingly in this way—or, on the other hand, if we share his goals, we may feel him justified in telling his main audience, the uncertain mainstream, that there is no legitimate principled opposition out there, but only fear.

By comparing Roosevelt's speech with Churchill's, both masterpieces of emotional motivation, we can see that a good rhetorician knows his audience thoroughly, knows what images will resonate and what appeals will arouse strong emotion. The British public wants victory at all costs and wants the glorious spirit of empire to survive. The American is a moralist: he wants to be responsible and courageous, to show his own self-reliance and to do his duty for others. Roosevelt purports to describe America and Americans, but of course the reality was volatile. His intervention constructed emotions critical to creating the kind of united effort that the New Deal involved, with regard to which it was indeed true that a major impediment was fear itself. We do not need to think that Roosevelt was unerring with regard to fear (the later internment of Japanese Americans was a clear instance of excess) in order to think that, given his specific goals, he found apt strategies to meet them in this speech.

Urban Architecture in Delhi and Hyde Park: How to Create Fear and How to Begin to Combat It

Cities bring people together from different ethnic, racial, economic, and religious backgrounds. Entrenched suspicions often divide them, and these suspicions can be either diminished or augmented by the layout of urban space. Urban architecture creates ways of living, sometimes fostering friendship, sometimes reinforcing fear. There are always grounds for fear in cities: crime, the volatility of employment, the diversity of groups and languages. But architecture can do a great deal to exacerbate fear into open hostility or to assuage it, encouraging problem solving in a spirit of fellowship.

The sad story of India's old and new Delhi shows us how easy it is to sow the seeds of fear and division, how difficult to restore Whitmanian "companionship" once it has been lost. We can begin with the fact that virtually all contemporary Indian writing about Delhi's architecture and layout is either hostile or nostalgic. The hostile predominates in tales of people from elsewhere forced to learn to live there. A paradigmatic instance is Aravind Adiga's *The White Tiger.* Adiga's hero, Balram, a rural man from Bihar, becomes a driver for a wealthy landlord; he spends much of his time lost in the endless maze of roundabouts with high-flown names, with no reference to daily life, chosen from the British imaginary of world history, which give New Delhi its virtually unintelligible structure. Surrounded by other people's prosperity on all sides, Balram feels simply lost and alienated, and he never can figure out what direction he is going in, an almost inevitable Delhi experience. To him the opulent white dwellings offer no beauty, only sadness and alienation. New Delhi seems like a place that is all about plan and not at all about people, a place where people, apart from the very affluent, have a hard time having a daily life. No place to walk to the market, to chat, to run into people of all trades, castes, and classes. Only endless roads seemingly going nowhere, people with nowhere to play cards, even, but in the center of a highway roundabout, cut off from other people and daily activities and surrounded by whizzing traffic:

> Every road in Delhi has a name, like Aurangazeb Road, or Humayun Road, or Archbishop Makarios Road. And no one, masters or servants, knows the name of the road. You ask someone, "Where's Nikolai Copernicus Marg?"
>
> And he could be a man who lived on Nikolai Copernicus Marg his whole life, and he'll open his mouth and say, *"Hahn?"* . . .
>
> And all the roads look the same, all of them go around and around grassy circles in which men are sleeping or eating or playing cards, and then four roads shoot off from that grassy circle, and then you go down one road, and you hit another grassy circle where men are sleeping or playing cards, and then four more roads go off from it. So you just keep getting lost, and lost, and lost in Delhi.[12]

By contrast, old Delhi is loved by virtually all who write her story, from the poets of the eighteenth and nineteenth centuries who peopled her streets to modern historians and architects. "Who would want to leave the streets of Delhi?" wrote the Urdu poet Zauq in the midnineteenth century, and modern authors, from the British historian of India William Dalrymple to Mushirul Hasan, current director of India's National Archives, agree with Zauq in judgment and emotion.[13] This love, however, is nostalgic, adoring something that has not existed in reality since 1857, although it still exists in painting and poetry.

Old Delhi was the sort of city that iconoclastic architecture critic Jane Jacobs would have loved: that is, the opposite of a planned city, a city that grew organically around people's daily lives and interactions.[14] It exemplified as well as any city ever has (or so the tale is told) the idea of human freedom expressed by Jacobs when she wrote of cities, "Their intricate order—a manifestation of the freedom of countless numbers of people to make and carry out countless plans—is in many ways a great wonder."[15] The many surviving artistic renderings of the Delhi of the eighteenth and nineteenth centuries[16] show its architectural splendor and its uniquely eclectic style, in which Hindu and Islamic cultures met to create a hybrid style all its own. Narrative history, based on letters and journals, tells the same tale: Hindu, Muslim, and Christian, tradespeople and Mughal royalty, all interacted in a web of connections, in which even the British occupants played a cooperative role.

Delhi was no stranger to military conquest, and even in the eighteenth century the poetry of Delhi expresses a sense of fracture, and corresponding nostalgia. The great eighteenth-century Urdu poet Mir Taqi Mir wrote, "The custom is now quite extinct—and yet in days gone by/Friends would sit down and talk to one another night and day."[17] After a particularly savage battle, Mir exclaimed: "Delhi, which was the city select of the world where the elite of the times lived;/Has been robbed and destroyed by circumstance./I belong to that very desolate city."[18] Still, by the mid-nineteenth century the old city was basically intact, as activities of all sorts—from the bustle of shopping to all-night poetry parties—brought people together. As Dalrymple's marvelously detailed narrative shows, the British and Indian inhabitants had comically different conceptions of what daytime was, the British rising at 4:00 AM and ending the day by 8:00 PM, Indians rising around 2:00 PM and going to bed at dawn. Still, there was enough interaction to produce many borrowings in dress and art, and even quite a few Anglo-Indian marriages, before the sad era of division to which we shall shortly turn.[19] To be fully included in that city, you didn't have to profess any particular creed—although you did perhaps have to love poetry and music.

When the British invaded the city in 1857, at the end of the Sepoy Rebellion, it would have been enough to capture the last Mughal emperor and take control of the Red Fort. Instead, however, in an act of savagery deplored on all sides ever since, they decided to lay waste to it in truly Homeric fashion, extinguishing the embers of its former greatness, lest the Mughals rise again to power. We know what Delhi was from a few surviving bits—part of the Red Fort, and the Jama Masjid—but also, and far more, by the pictures and narratives of what it was before 1857. As Dalrymple shows, the new British style of rule was militant, evangelical, intolerant of both Hindu and Muslim cultures. Rather than respecting Delhi's cultural heritage, as prior generations had done, they aimed at cultural genocide. No rebuilding was undertaken; Delhi became a city of ruins. And in order to put an end to the Mughal dynasty, all Muslim citizens were simply exiled for years—thus creating a division between religions that had not existed previously and which the British continued to encourage until their departure. "For a whole generation," writes historian Salman Kurshid, "Delhi became a city of distant nostalgia mixed with bitter and sad memories, shattered monuments and ruins of its imperial days."[20]

The deliberate aim of the British was thus to create fear and to fracture fellowship. But of course they could not rule from a pile of rubble, and so their next task was to create a Delhi from which they might rule: imperial Delhi. For this purpose they turned to the architect Edward Lutyens, who, with his colleague Herbert Baker, created New Delhi— very much as we now know it.[21] Their aim was to express superiority and inspire awe—and awe, unlike wonder, is an inherently hierarchical emotion, expressing submission to a greater power.[22] New Delhi, accordingly, was about as far removed from old Delhi as could be imagined: in a remote spot in a far southern area, rather than in the city itself; pristine white instead of intricately laid out in mosaics of color; impenetrable to daily life, so that ordinary people would be afraid to go there; and partly on the lofty Raisina hill, so the rulers could look down on the inhabitants they ruled. Lutyens was in his own way a gifted architect, and his attempts to infuse Indian motifs into the basically European buildings do lead to some interesting results. Teen Murti, which later became famous as Nehru's house and now houses the Nehru Museum and Library, is impressive in its classical simplicity. Nonetheless, the new city is massive, weighty, and untouchable, rather than active and lived-in. It creates a feeling that one should not go near, and its very whiteness, together with its maze of geometrical but still barely intelligible streets, inspires fear. The American is less troubled, because of its distant resemblance to Washington, D.C. and the preservation of open green spaces for (today) some public park land, as well as for private polo and cricket grounds, is a reassuring touch to the non-Indian eye—though not to Delhi's poor, who live too far away to use the relatively few beautiful public areas.

From a city of poetry, Delhi quickly became a city of fear. As historian Malvika Singh writes, "It became 'them' and 'us,' the insular seat of government and the active, ever growing, rooted cultural hub."[23] But this hub experienced itself from the start as wounded. Mirza Ghalib, court poet of that last Mughal court (whose flight from the city Dalrymple chronicles in detail, using diaries and letters), summed it all up: "Four things kept Delhi alive: the fort, the daily crowds at the Jama Masjid, the weekly walk to the Yamuna bridge, and the annual fair of the flower people. None of these survives, so how does Delhi survive? Yes, there once was a city of the name of Delhi in this land of India."[24] When Jane Jacobs describes the "death" of great American cities, she is referring to the inadvertent destruction of patterns of living by zealous yet well-intentioned urban planners. The destruction of Delhi was not just a death; it was a murder.

Today nothing can be done to recover what was lost. A new indigenous elite now rules from New Delhi, but the "hub" is nothing like what it was once. Much of it commercialized and uglified, it inspires even more fear, perhaps, than Lutyens's gracious if remote and weighty constructions—although the area around Delhi University gives some sense of the old days. A tiny beginning of memory further south is the new project of a group of architects, who have been authorized to restore the sixteenth- and seventeenth-century Mughal tombs in Lodhi Garden, one part of old Delhi that was geographically far enough from the cataclysm to have escaped erasure. Other restoration projects are also in progress, but too much is gone to reestablish anything like the old city. In terms of group relations, the Hindu-Muslim coexistence of the nineteenth century has never been fully re-created, except at a very upper-class level; specific quarters of the city are now "Muslim neighborhoods," vulnerable to police harassment when there's a terrorism scare.[25] And the gulf between elites and everybody else that New Delhi and the British created persists, albeit with a new cast of characters.

The story of Delhi does not show that planning is a bad thing. Jane Jacobs is wrong to oppose it in a general way. Especially as urban populations grow rapidly, centralized planning is essential if cities are to work for people, as the story of Central Park shows. Many cities in the developing world (Bangalore, Dhaka, Jakarta) have become unlivable not because of deliberate malice but simply because of unplanned chaotic sprawl. What the Delhi story shows is that the deliberate plan to create fear can ruin urban life for centuries, especially when accompanied by planning that deliberately creates a hub of power that is unlivable for all but elites.

Delhi's sad story shows us how intimately urban architecture is bound up with fellowship between groups—how easy it is to sow the seeds of fear, how difficult it is to change fear's architecture once destruction is accomplished. Fear feeds on separation and is augmented by images of force; no sense of fellowship can easily encompass the fissures such architecture creates.

But architecturally created fear can sometimes be reversed. I now turn to a story very close to home, in fact in my home. Since the middle 1990s, the University of Chicago, often in partnership with the city, has taken some creative steps to address racial fear on Chicago's often-tense South Side—reversing a policy of fear-ridden separation that had persisted for decades.

The "university-school out there on the Midway," as Richard Wright's character Bigger Thomas calls it in *Native Son*,[26] long saw itself, and was seen by others, as a bastion of white privilege in the middle of alarming and degrading dangers. The university's self-conception in the early days was that of an inward-looking scholarly community. Architecturally, this idea expressed itself in the Gothic revival buildings arranged around enclosed courtyards. The choice of Gothic over other styles was deliberately intended to create an impression of age, and the quadrangles to convey the idea of quasi-monastic inwardness. (Romanesque architecture was rejected as not sounding the right monastic note.) As former president Don Randel writes, "The Gothic impulse created a community turned inward and away from an outside world that, in the

Middle Ages and in some parts of the twentieth century, was seen as dangerous."[27] In 1915, John D. Rockefeller, who was a major donor, wrote an editorial entitled "A Wonderful Campus," in which he approved of these choices. He noted that Harvard does not as successfully convey the impression of "antique dignity": "There are many red-brick buildings on the Harvard campus. Red brick may grow old, but it is hard for it to acquire an air antique and dignified."[28] So strong was the desire to emphasize age that President William Rainey Harper actually proposed not holding any inaugural ceremony, declaring that the university's first day, October 1, 1892, should appear to be "a continuation of a work that had been conducted for a thousand years."[29]

The university's pursuit of antique dignity became strongly associated with racism and class exclusion as time went on. There were liberal voices in the community: for example, Alderman Leon Despres (1908–2009) and his wife, Marian Alschuler Despres (1909–2007), who promoted integration—and were leading forces in the racial integration of the university's Laboratory School, which first admitted African Americans in 1942.[30] A letter written by the Despreses and two others at the time read, "Under the present practice, we are denying our children the benefits of democracy by ingraining into their school life and personalities an old prejudice. How can we effectively urge our children to consider the superiority of democracy when we ourselves reject it for them?"[31]

Despite this progress, however, the situation Wright's novel of 1940 describes was very much the way things were for decades, both before and after: a person with a black skin (unless a carefully cultivated middle-class exception) was seen as out of place and, like Bigger, experienced himself as out of place, on the wrong side of an implicit color "line" that ran around the perimeter of Hyde Park. (Bigger lived at 37th and Indiana.) Journalist Brent Staples recalls in a 1986 essay that in 1972 his appearance at midnight on a Hyde Park street (he was then a graduate student at the University of Chicago) caused a young well-dressed white woman to start running. This woman, he writes with sad irony, was his first "victim," and his first experience of his own "ability to alter public space in ugly ways."[32] Such reactions to the presence of a black man in white space were of course not uncommon, but in Hyde Park they were virtually guaranteed by the invisible color line that, by the deliberate design of the university's leaders, cordoned off the university community from the surrounding neighborhoods.

There was a lot of crime in Hyde Park in those days—so much so that the university once considered a move to some "less exigent environment."[33] (Alternative sites mentioned included Wisconsin, suburban DuPage County, and Aspen, Colorado.)[34] But its own spatial and architectural choices helped create an atmosphere of mutual suspicion and furthered opportunities for crime. The university was said to have influenced the city to design the elevated public transportation system so that it did not come into Hyde Park, which the Green Line once had—thus keeping foreign elements away from the virtually gated community, but also keeping the community more solitary and isolated from the bustle of activity, and making it harder for its members to move freely into the city.[35] Through traffic was also discouraged by the large number of one-way streets and frequent dead ends. A typical sign of those times was a tall chain link fence behind the Law School parking lot (right on the "line" between Hyde Park and the Woodlawn neighborhood), which was not removed until 1998. Intended presumably to protect professors' cars from vandals intruding from 61st Street, the fence stood as a symbol of hostility and an inward-looking mentality—not malevolent, as were the British in Delhi, but disdainful toward the neighborhoods in a culpably obtuse manner. The university community might sing the words of the alma mater, "We praise her breadth of charity," and yet charity both began and ended at home.[36]

Beyond the symbolic and emotional significance of these separations, what all this meant was that no bustle of activity made the open spaces lighter and safer at night, and that the surrounding neighborhoods, left to be zones of lower-class rather than mixed-income housing, became breeding grounds of crime, almost as much so as the notorious Robert Taylor Homes further north. The looming university quadrangles, besides being pompous and derivative as architecture, created opportunities for acts of stealth, rather than invitations to mingle. The empty cavernous Midway Plaisance (the wide grassy strip running between 59th and 60th Streets, where the first Ferris wheel and Buffalo Bill's Wild

West Show entertained the world in connection with the Columbian Exposition in 1893),[37] was now a dark no-man's-land that invited crime rather than fellowship, and discouraged further southward expansion of the University. As *Chicago Tribune* architecture critic Blair Kamin writes, "For years, the greensward has formed a kind of demilitarized zone between the U. of C.'s cloistered, neo-Gothic quadrangles to the Midway's north and the hard-edged, sometimes-dangerous Woodlawn neighborhood to its south."[38] New faculty were warned to let fear rule: "Don't go into Woodlawn, don't cross the Midway after 5:00 PM, don't even walk alone on the lakeshore."

The strategy of separation was shortsighted and ineffectual; it was not thoroughly ill-intentioned. Some advocates for the poor in those days did hold that separate housing projects were more effective ways to show respect for the poor and for minorities.[39] Nonetheless, the university's version of the separation strategy was not especially respectful, but infected by contempt for its neighbors.

Gradually, at the beginning of the twenty-first century, all of this began to change. A change of spirit in the university administration came first: from now on, the university should think of itself as a partner of the neighborhoods, pursuing interaction and associated living, not to mention the mutual advantage of safety. President Don Randel was particularly aggressive in emphasizing the change of direction, contrasting the old idea of "the university in retreat" with a newer idea of cooperation and partnership.[40] While operating two charter schools on the north side of Hyde Park in partnership with the city, the university focused especially on the revival of the Woodlawn neighborhood to its south, adjacent to those parts of the university that had located south of the Midway (the Law School, the School of Public Policy, the School of Social Administration). The university police force began to patrol the Woodlawn neighborhood in partnership with the city police, while university officials encouraged neighborhood restoration and the increasing movement of graduate students and faculty into housing south of 60th Street. While the city was spending $11 million to revive the southern part of the lakeshore, with four new bicycle underpasses beneath Lakeshore Drive on the south side, renovating both the South Shore Cultural

Center at 71st Street and the beautiful 65th Street beach house (both splendid Art Deco buildings once in disrepair) and inaugurating plans to extend the drive itself further southward, the university was investing in several partnership projects closer to campus.

First, in 2002, was the Midway Plaisance Ice Rink, an Olympic-size skating rink that offers free skating for those who bring their own skates (by contrast to the hefty fees downtown), skate rental for only six dollars, a warming house with a roof observation platform, and food to purchase. This simple idea meant not only that the city now welcomed neighbors and tourists alike to Hyde Park, but also that the once-dark Midway became flooded with light more or less throughout the academic year, and full of people. I had been mugged right in that block at 5:00 PM in 1996; this would be virtually impossible today. Friendship and safety go hand in hand.

More recently, the university decided to locate its new Reva and David Logan Arts Center—itself an idea that departs from the ideology of those Gothic courts, where the arts were once frowned on as not seriously intellectual—on Ingleside between 60th and 61st, thus at the very southern and western end of Hyde Park.[41] From the start, the plan involved the neighborhoods. The new center plans many activities in cooperation with Woodlawn groups; it is also accompanied by retail development in the Woodlawn neighborhood, and is one more visible sign of the revival of the neighborhood as a racially and economically mixed neighborhood. The soaring, exuberant glass and stone building (designed by Tod Williams and Billie Tsien) does not exactly repudiate the Gothic—indeed, in its lofty ascent it pays homage to the past. But it sends a message of hope and dynamism. Its design exemplifies a change in architectural spirit in the university as a whole, from the backward-looking to the forward-looking (and, we might say, from the worship of the past associated with the era of Presidents Harper and Robert Maynard Hutchins[42] to the forward movement of Dewey's pragmatism).[43]

Finally, in connection with the new Arts Center, the university undertook a massive upgrade of the streets and crosswalks around the Midway, of which the centerpieces are the Light Bridges designed by James Carpenter[44] on Woodlawn and Ellis Avenues, and later added on

Dorchester as well. Huge stainless-steel masts that emit dramatic shafts of white light—and reflect the sun's rays during the day—the lights (known as "light sabers" to students) really do create a bridge from south to north, their arcing light a gesture of invitation. As Kamin approvingly notes, they form an aesthetic link between the modernist buildings south of the Midway (Mies van der Rohe's School of Social Administration, Eero Saarinen's Law School, the new Arts Center) and the Gothic buildings on the north side. They also fulfill metaphorically one of Frederick Law Olmsted's original plans for the Midway: he wanted water there, and literal bridges over it. The lighting itself was designed with an eye to safety as well as beauty. One of the designers says of the bridges, "They provide greater lighting on the vertical surface of people's faces. If the lights goes straight down, only to the pavement, you don't feel as safe."[45]

This story tells us a lot about fear and fellowship. When fear dominated university thinking, impeding inclusive sympathy, steps were taken that made things less safe as well as less hospitable. At the same time, the fearfulness of Hyde Park (genuine as well as fantasized) was augmented by the inward-looking exclusionary attitude that denied fellowship. Fear and exclusion fed on each other. It took bold decisions to break out of that vicious spiral, creating at least some trust. Bold thinking will continue to be required in our era of ongoing racial tension. Because this solution is of local rather than national or even citywide significance (unlike the Vietnam Veterans Memorial, Millennium Park, or the Burnham plan for the lakeshore), its larger effects, both in Chicago and in the nation, are difficult to assess. But good solutions are typically local, rooted in a deep understanding of local histories and problems, so progress is likely to be the product of many small experiments rather than one grand plan. In this case, the fact of the university's worldwide fame made it capable of creating a widely publicized paradigm that can encourage other efforts.

These are only a few examples of the good and bad management of fear. They suffice, however, to show that governments make decisions all the time that affect the level and nature of people's fear, and its relationship to common effort. They should ponder these emotions and make their decisions well.

IV. Envy and Fairness: A Common Project

Envy has threatened democracies ever since they began to exist. Under absolute monarchy, people's possibilities were fixed, and they might come to believe that fate, or divine justice, had placed them where they were. But a society that eschews fixed orders and destinies in favor of mobility and competition opens the door to envy for the prosperity of others. If envy is sufficiently widespread, it can eventually threaten justice, particularly when a society (like our hypothetical society) has committed itself to substantial redistribution in order to protect a threshold of well-being for all.

Envy is a painful emotion that focuses on the good fortune or advantages of others, comparing one's own situation unfavorably to theirs. It involves a rival, and a good or goods appraised as important; the envier is pained because the rival possesses those good things and she does not. The good things must be seen as important not in some abstract or detached way, but for the self and the self's core sense of well-being.[46] Typically, envy involves some type of hostility toward the fortunate rival: the envier wants what the rival has, and feels ill will toward the rival in consequence. Envy thus creates animosity and tension at the heart of society, and this may ultimately prevent society from achieving some of its goals. Because it is intuitively clear and experimentally confirmed that judgments of well-being are highly positional, and that this is true in a wide range of societies, envy is bound to remain a common experience and a likely cause of social distress.

Envy is similar to jealousy, in that both involve hostility toward a rival with respect to the possession or enjoyment of a valued good. Jealousy, however, is typically about the fear of a specific loss (usually, though not always, a loss of personal attention or love), and thus about protection of the most cherished goods and relationships of the self. Its focus is on the rival, seen as a threat to the self. It is basically about protecting the self from damage.[47] Its prototype, and perhaps its origin, is competition with one parent for the attention and love of the other; sibling rivalry is another ubiquitous prototype. Envy, by contrast, revolves around nonpossession of a desired status or possessions. Its focus is on the absent goods, and its hostility toward their possessors is indirect.[48] The rival is less central than the goods themselves; indeed, the rival is seen in a hostile light because she enjoys advantages that the envier lacks.

Jealousy can often be satisfied, as when it becomes clear that the rival is no longer a competitor for the affections of the loved person, or was never a real competitor. Only pathological jealousy keeps inventing new and often imaginary rivals, and jealousy is not always pathological. The psychology of Proust's hero—jealous of an indefinite number of imagined rivals for the affection of Albertine, and free from jealousy only when Albertine is asleep and thus unable to exercise independent will—is utterly doomed and unfortunate. Marcel has never managed to move beyond his obsessive childhood desire to monopolize the affections of his mother and convince her to spend the night in his room. One may have a type of jealousy that does not have this all-devouring nature and that responds to evidence. Given the uncertainty of human life, the position of Proust's hero, for whom no evidence ever counts for enough, is all too easy to occupy, but trust and generosity can help a more fortunate person avoid that doomed and loveless condition.

Envy, by contrast, is rarely satisfied, because the goods on which it typically focuses (status, wealth, other advantages) are unevenly distributed in all societies, and no position is utterly secure from invidious comparison. Iago's relationship to Othello is poisonous and murderous because it is primarily one of envy, not jealousy. Othello is hated not as a rival for some specific advantage, but as someone who eclipses Iago and looms above him. There is nothing Iago can do to be a hero, so he has to destroy the hero. The difficulty of satisfying envy is put succinctly by psychologists Maria Miceli and Cristiano Castelfranchi when they conclude, "The object of envy is 'superiority,' or 'non-inferiority' to a reference group or individual."[49] And that, of course, is rarely achieved in any society, so long as one cares about the material goods that are unequally distributed within it. Even when one already possess preeminence, it is continually under threat from competitors, so one may be "on top" and still be driven by envy, since future superiority is never ensured.

The Stoics therefore recommended not caring about such things, but this recommendation is rarely heeded, and probably would not make for a good world if it were. We may agree with the Stoics that people will live better and societies will go better if people attach more importance to nonhierarchical goods such as virtue and friendship, and rather less importance to positional goods such as money and status. Still, even nonpositional goods invite comparison; furthermore, society will go badly if we encourage people to be utterly indifferent to money and status. (Stoicism supplies some valuable features of Cicero's character, but his stubborn attachment to political causes, to his daughter, and even to money and glory form a large part of his human appeal.) If we are not to undertake the Stoic project of extirpating envy, however, we need to say more about how it can be contained.

Envy has three constructive cousins from which it is important to distinguish it. Emulation, like envy, focuses on a comparison between one's own situation and that of the better-off. But in emulation the good situation is seen as achievable by some type of effort, and the good is not understood as a zero-sum game, so emulation doesn't involve hostile thoughts toward the more fortunate person. If A, a high-school student, sees that B gets good grades in school, and A is moved to emulation, she typically says to herself, "I can achieve that too if I work hard." Envy is different, because, as psychologists have often concluded, it involves a feeling of hopelessness and helplessness.[50] Thus the envious high school student says, "Those popular kids. I hate them. I can never be like them." (Notice that I've shifted the example from getting good grades, which is often achievable by effort, to popularity, which usually isn't.) So, while emulation is compatible with wishing the competitor well, envy involves bitterness and hostility. Envy needn't involve a specific hostile wish. (In this sense it is distinct from hostile gloating at another's loss of good things, or the related emotion of *Schadenfreude*.) In my imagined case the envier doesn't necessarily picture the popular kids losing their popularity, though she might. But she will view them with animosity of some type, and will certainly not wish for a common good that includes them (such as success of the high school cheerleading squad or football team).

Envy is also distinct from resentment, a moral emotion that involves a sense of injustice.[51] The person who feels resentment at the advantages of others believes that things have gone morally wrong: some injustice is at work in placing them above her. Correcting this injustice would satisfy resentment and remove the pain of the resenter. By contrast, envy requires no such moral thought. As Rawls puts it, "It is sufficient to say that the better situation of others catches our attention."[52] Resentment is expressed by social critique, and it can often be constructive, leading to change that removes the injustice (if the resenter has analyzed things correctly). Envy is just "a form of rancor that tends to harm both its object and its subject."[53] To return to high school: the student who feels resentment might make a variety of complaints, such as "I wrote the best essay, but didn't get the best grade because I was daring and unconventional," "Sports are valued much too highly by comparison to academic achievement," or "I was not cast as Hamlet, although I am the best actor, because of my race." In all of these cases, whether the student is right or wrong, there is a moral grievance, and the emotion expresses that complaint. The envious student, by contrast, just feels bad about the superiority of others, without a moral grievance. (Of course, envy may often masquerade as resentment through manufactured grievances,[54] but that does not alter the conceptual point.)

Emulation and resentment are both healthy emotions in a decent society: the former encourages the individual to be better, and the latter encourages the society to be better. Envy has no such constructive function, and while it can spur individuals on to hard work and personal achievement, its rancor can indeed prove harmful.

Because envy of others can exist even when "their being more fortunate than we are does not detract from our advantages,"[55] it remains a potential problem in even the most decent and just society.

Finally, envy has a harmless, and often helpful, species in which one is temporarily pained by another's possession of a longed-for good—but, because one's desire for the good is fleeting and not seriously endorsed, the pain does not involve hostile wishing. Visiting my relatives, I briefly think, "Life in Ithaca is so peaceful and lovely," and feel a pang of longing for their life. But since I absolutely do not want to live there, and would hate it if I did, my fleeting envy is more like an empathetic appreciation of the goods that my relatives cherish. It involves friendship and participatory imagination, rather than hostility, and thus contributes to toleration. If I couldn't see why on earth someone would even for a moment want to live there, to that extent there would be a gap in our friendship. But there's no rivalry. What makes the difference, it seems, is my all-things-considered valuation. If they lived in Chicago and I was stuck for some reason in Ithaca, my visit to their home could produce a much more problematic emotion. That's a clear-cut case, but some cases of empathetic envy are more wistful and less clear, a record of the "road not taken" in one's own life. In all such cases, one wishes the other party well rather than ill, and envy contributes to understanding.

Under what conditions are hostile outbreaks of envy especially likely? Rawls mentions three.[56] First, there is a psychological condition: people lack secure confidence "in their own value and in their ability to do anything worthwhile." Second, there is a social condition: many circumstances arise when this psychological condition is experienced as painful and humiliating, because the conditions of social life make the discrepancies that give rise to envy highly visible. Third, the envious see their position as offering them no constructive alternative to mere hostility. The only relief they can envisage is to inflict pain on others.

We can now see that some social structures fulfill these conditions to a far greater degree than others. The average high school is a veritable cauldron of envy. Adolescents are especially likely to be in a psychological condition of insecurity about their worth and their future. Everything that happens makes rankings salient: grading, the competition for college entrance, the visibility of sports in most places, the frequently cruel formation of cliques and groups and the related ranking of people by attractiveness. And the low-ranked often do feel hopeless about their situation.

How might a high school be somewhat less like that, or contain that hostility to a greater degree? First, it would offer support for students thinking about their future and trying to develop self-esteem in an uncertain world. Parents are key here, but teachers and counselors can also play a part. Each student can come to feel that a basic level of attainment is within her grasp, and this will at least diminish the pain of thinking about the superior achievements of others. The social condition is tricky, since a good high school will encourage emulation by making achievement salient to some degree, but it can also find ways of rewarding other talents that students have, suggesting multiple paths to excellence; certainly it can inhibit the excessive dominance of competitive sports and the social prestige associated with it. The third condition is perhaps the most important: by offering a wide range of constructive paths to achievement (noncompetitive fitness activities, theater and other creative arts, social service), the school can encourage students to do something worthwhile that will make them feel good about themselves, rather than just sitting around hating the popular kids. Two things my daughter's middle school did that were useful were to create an "arts Olympics" side by side with a sports Olympics, so that a far wider range of students (often in groups) could win recognition, and simply offering things such as yoga, Pilates, and fitness running as athletic alternatives.

Let us now turn to society. Rawls argues that a society modeled on his two principles of justice will still have hostile envy, but that its damages will not be intolerably great.[57] With regard to the psychological condition, people know that their basic entitlements are guaranteed independently of merit, and this removes at least some insecurity. In addition, people have a "common sense of justice" and are "bound by ties of civic friendship"—factors that once again remove at least some painful feelings of insecurity.[58] With regard to the social condition, the economic structure of Rawls's society has located people closer to one another than is the case in many societies, and this makes positional differences somewhat less salient. The visibility of distinctions is also diminished by the sheer variety of organizations and occupations in society: no single scale is relevant for all. Finally, the existence of competition along a number of dimensions offers many constructive alternatives to envy, at least as many as in other societies.[59]

Rawls's account seems basically right, and the society we are imagining, though not identical to his in all respects, seems able to give basically the same reply to the challenge of envy. Much, then, will have to be done by laws and institutions that make basic entitlements secure for all, and by educational and economic systems that make people feel they have constructive alternatives. Society's institutional structure supports emulation by leaving room for competition, without creating the sense of hopelessness and helplessness that can paralyze effort (and, we might add, the economy). Robust political and legal institutions also support constructive indignation and resentment, as citizens are encouraged to bring forward real grievances.

An important part is played by the fact that the society we imagine does not value money alone. Its political culture sends the message that many types of human achievement have worth: friendship, literary and artistic expression, work for social justice, and much more. Consider a high school reunion in a society that values money alone: there will be a great deal of hostile envy at that reunion, because people will be very unequally placed with regard to money, and the reunion makes these inequalities evident, as such occasions always do. The rich will feel the preemptive envy that guards their position against future insecurity, and the not-rich will envy the position of the rich. In a society that values a range of types of constructive achievement, there will be no linear ranking, and people can take pride in a variety of lives. To that extent, hostile envy is diminished.

Still, such a culture remains prone to hostile envy, and therefore we need to ask what more can be done to support a culture of civic friendship that makes people less likely, at least, to be at odds with one another in this way. Envy attacks compassion in two ways: by narrowing the circle of concern and thus encouraging the "eudaimonistic thought" to focus on the self, or one's own group, and by inhibiting the sense of similar possibilities and the empathy that usefully accompanies it, suggesting that the envied are "other" or "the enemy."

What we need as an antidote, then, is a sense of a common fate, and a friendship that draws the advantaged and less advantaged into a single group, with a common task before it. Such friends should sense that the different groups are allies in the struggle, rather than adversaries. In a small homogeneous society, this sense of common fate can develop on its own, as a result of networks of connection and personal knowledge. I've asked people in Finland, where I've spent a lot of time, and which has a robust and utterly unopposed set of social insurance policies, why there is so little opposition on the part of the more privileged to policies that benefit the less advantaged.[60] The answer I typically hear is that the absence of interclass envy derives in large part from the sense that this small society (5 million inhabitants) is like a family, with the prospects of all citizens intertwined. That good feature of Finnish society, however, is closely linked to a more problematic one: its extreme homogeneity and reluctance to admit immigrants or asylum seekers.

In a larger and more diverse society, how might one create such a sense of common fate, or, in Whitman's terms, "plant companionship thick as trees"? An external enemy often has this effect, whether a rival high school or an attacking nation. People forget their differences in rising to a hostile challenge. Similarly, in young nations, citizens frequently construct friendship from their history of oppression: the memory of common suffering gives them a united purpose. Still, one would like to have some strategies for civic friendship that do not depend on the existence of George III or the British Raj, much less Hitler and Hirohito.

To illustrate the wide range of more peaceful devices a nation may use, I shall choose two examples from political theater/rhetoric—Franklin Delano Roosevelt's "Second Bill of Rights" speech and Gandhi's use of his personal lifestyle to alter the behavior of elites. I then turn to a very different type of case, the creation of New York's Central Park by Frederick Law Olmsted as a "People's Park" that can shape people's sense of their interactions with others.

Roosevelt and the "Second Bill of Rights"

Despite the achievements of the New Deal, emotional and legal, America during the years of World War II was not an emotionally unified nation. The war supplied emotional solidarity and cohesion. But as the war effort succeeded and the postwar era was in sight, thought had to be given once again to issues of class and economic security. Roosevelt understood that the war had to some extent put class envy on the back burner—not entirely, as those Bill Mauldin cartoons depicting the contrast between enlisted men and officers movingly show[61]—but had not solved the problem of creating emotional solidarity around economic issues. As so often in earlier times, he devoted a great deal of thought to the emotional underpinnings of social insurance. The State of the Union speech of January 11, 1944, often known as the "Second Bill of Rights" speech, was the result. It set some important policy goals, but it also, and more importantly, gave people a metaphorical and symbolic language in which to talk about economic justice—and which, if persuasive, might limit the role of hostile envy in the new era.[62]

An essential precursor to the "Second Bill of Rights" speech, crafting its language connecting economic security to liberty, was the "Four Freedoms" speech, his State of the Union address on January 6, 1941. Speaking at a time when the future of the "free world" hung in the balance, Roosevelt emphasized the obvious, insisting on the human importance of the freedom of speech (the first freedom), the freedom of religion (the second freedom), and the freedom from fear (the fourth freedom, by which he meant a future set of arms agreements that would make the aggression of the Germans and the Japanese impossible in the future). Against his advisors' advice, he insisted that these freedoms were not just for Americans, but should obtain "anywhere in the world."[63] But the third freedom on the list was the surprise: the "freedom from want—which, translated into world terms, means economic understandings which will secure to every nation a healthy peacetime life for its inhabitants—everywhere in the world." Roosevelt daringly appropriates the language of freedom for a purpose that would have been familiar to Aristotle or to British neo-Aristotelian philosopher T. H. Green, but perhaps not so familiar to the American public. By holding that the war is about freedom (which everyone would have agreed) and by then insisting that freedom from want is part of freedom, he positions the war effort itself as in part an effort on behalf of economic justice. The rhetorical success of this move was enormous: the idea of "Four Freedoms" quickly became a household word, and Norman Rockwell's famous series of paintings, first published in the *Saturday Evening Post*, carried the influence still further. Roosevelt had created a new picture of what the quintessential American is and strives for.

For Roosevelt, "freedom from want" addresses above all what we have called the first, psychological condition of envy. Security, he said, means "a kind of feeling within our individual selves that we have lacked through all the course of history."[64] But he did not think of insecurity as a pathological condition: it was a reasonable response to deficient political guarantees. He thought, plausibly, that decent political conditions would create a psychology that was robustly resistant to envy.

The "Second Bill of Rights" speech carries the rhetoric of the "Four Freedoms" much further. It addresses a family of emotions, but envy is central, as we shall see. The entire speech is about the war, which, of course, was ongoing—D-Day was still six months off. It begins with the observation that Americans have just been engaged for two years in "the world's greatest war against human slavery." Mere survival, Roosevelt now announces, cannot be the country's highest goal. Instead, America must aim at "security." What American, in 1944, could fail to attach the most intense emotions to that idea? Roosevelt thus moves the heart directly into the area of its greatest ferment and anxiety. Roosevelt now continues, "And that means not only physical security which provides safety from attacks by aggressors. It means also economic security, social security, moral security—in a family of nations." All the Allies agree that we must promote economic development, and that this means building industry, but also building education and individual opportunity, and raising standards of living. He now says that everyone can see that military security is henceforth essential; well, so too is social and economic security. "[A]n equally basic essential to peace is a decent standard of living for all individual men and women and children in all Nations. Freedom from fear is eternally linked with freedom from want." (With "eternally" he returns to the lofty biblical language of his First Inaugural Address.)

Roosevelt now turns to the enemies of his economic programs, arguing that they are forces of division that create danger and confusion in wartime. Once again, as in his First Inaugural Address, he characterizes them in language of derision rather than fear. These "pests who swarm through the lobbies of the Congress and the cocktail bars of Washington" want to advance the interests of special groups rather than those of the nation as a whole. The humorous comparison of his enemies to insects and the comical picture of those (petty and annoying) insects swarming through cocktail bars give the ensuing praise of the dignity of our fighting men particular force. Such imagery is slippery: minorities have all too often been denigrated by being compared to insects or other "low" animals, and we have seen that Roosevelt likes to disparage serious opposition without directly engaging it. This is a flaw, even if an understandable one. Still, the fact that the speech affirms the dignity of the vast majority of Americans and ridicules a few powerful people who seem to be enemies of that dignity—combined with the fact that the imagery is comic rather than disgust-laden, puncturing the pretensions of these selfish elites—frees it, I think, from that ethical problem.

In wartime, Roosevelt now continues, we must understand "how interdependent upon each other are all groups and sections of the population of America . . . If ever there was a time to subordinate individual or group selfishness to the national good, that time is now." The fellow feeling with people in difficulties that was a hallmark of Roosevelt's approach to life after his illness permeates the speech. Repeatedly he expressed impatience with those who blame the poor for their poverty, and here he will be suggesting that the nation itself has a responsibility to prevent extreme want.[65]

Roosevelt thus positions the war itself as a war against selfishness, and directs the urgent emotions of his hearers toward the goal of economic security. After making a number of concrete proposals—for new taxes, for agricultural subsidies and a ceiling on food prices, and, especially, for compulsory national service, Roosevelt then sets out a new understanding of basic rights:[66]

> We have come to a clear realization of the fact that true individual freedom cannot exist without economic security and independence. "Necessitous men are not free men."[67]
>
> People who are hungry and out of a job are the stuff of which dictatorships are made.
>
> In our day these economic truths have become accepted as self-evident. We have accepted, so to speak, a second Bill of Rights under which a new basis of security and prosperity can be established for all regardless of station, race, or creed.
>
> Among these are:
>
> The right to a useful and remunerative job in the industries or shops or farms or mines of the Nation;
>
> The right to earn enough to provide adequate food and clothing and recreation;
>
> The right of every farmer to raise and sell his products at a return which will give him and his family a decent living;
>
> The right of every businessman, large and small, to trade in an atmosphere of freedom from unfair competition and domination by monopolies at home or abroad;
>
> The right of every family to a decent home;

The right to adequate medical care and the opportunity to enjoy good health;

The right to adequate protection from the economic fears of old age, sickness, accident, and unemployment;

The right to a good education.

All of these rights spell security. And after this war is won we must be prepared to move forward, in the implementation of these rights, to new goals of human happiness and well-being.

Roosevelt alludes to an emerging international consensus that was shortly to be formalized in the Universal Declaration of Human Rights. The United States, however, has never accepted such a "second Bill of Rights" as a constitutional matter. Although many state constitutions do contain ingredients of this program,[68] and although a minority of the Supreme Court in the early 1970s held that the right to education was implicit in the Constitution, this never became doctrine and remains enshrined in dissent.[69] So Roosevelt knew that he was speaking metaphorically and wishfully; any move in that direction would have to be accomplished through legislation. By hitching the movement for social and economic rights to the war effort, and by using the resonant language of self-evident truth and a "second Bill of Rights," he is attempting to create the psychological and emotional conditions for such legislation.

Roosevelt takes aim squarely at the problem of envy. Repeatedly he depicts America as riven by self-interested factions, contrasting our economic disunity with the unity of America's fighting men and implying that this bickering subverts their courageous efforts. His audience includes the "have-nots" who might be moved by envy to support radical causes; to those people he offers reassurance that their essential needs are viewed by the nation as fundamental entitlements, for which we will fight. And it also includes well-intentioned "haves," to whom he also offers reassurance: they can keep what their efforts have won in the American capitalist system (and thus allow themselves to be motivated even by hostile envy, up to a point), while still supporting a decent social minimum that guarantees the basic entitlements of all. Only culpably greedy people would resent the social safety net and claim that all people who need welfare assistance are "chiselers and cheats."[70] The image of war is used metaphorically in two distinct ways, then: as a way of thinking about the struggle against want, and as a model of the desirable sort of common effort and goodwill. In effect, he is following Mazzini in trying to goad people out of their selfishness and narrowness toward a type of common effort that he sees exemplified in the war effort. The issue is not so much whether Roosevelt's policies are right or wrong (although our hypothetical society has adopted a similar account of basic entitlements). What is important is that the speech shows how one might forge a memorable and strongly emotive language to reposition social and economic issues in the American imaginary: the language of freedom, the language of war, and the language of a new Bill of Rights. All these ways of thinking and speaking reconfigure the political landscape. Instead of the feared and foreign "socialism," he gives us cherished and familiar American liberty. Clearly it worked for a time, getting Americans to understand their heritage and their future in a new way.

The heart of the political problem of envy is the intergroup hostility and factionalism it encourages and strengthens. No politician can hope to remove personal envy, since differences will remain and they will inspire at least some hostility; indeed, no capitalist politician should even want to remove envy. But the class-based envy with which Roosevelt grappled was disabling, and his speech was one of many rhetorical efforts on his part to produce a spirit of civic friendship and common work, convincing the disadvantaged that the nation will support their aspirations and attempting to convince the advantaged that narrow self-interest is un-American.

Gandhi and the Conduct of Leaders

India of the 1930s and 1940s contained astonishing inequalities—educational, cultural, political, bodily. That is still true today, although the gap has narrowed. What is not so true today was that the lives of the vast majority of India's people were utterly invisible to indigenous elites, who lived a cloistered existence. Frequently highly westernized, they encountered members of other classes only as domestic servants. Even though Indians were themselves treated with racial discrimination by the British, their own society was profoundly hierarchical, based on a quasi-feudal system of land tenure. Such a society could hardly have become a successful democracy without building a sense of common purpose that crossed lines of caste, region, religion, and especially of economic class, thus dissipating class hostility. But how could a sense of common fate be engendered when people's very bodies were utterly different (nutritional differences affecting height, and indoor versus outdoor lifestyles affecting skin color) and when patterns of life were so utterly different, upper castes eschewing manual labor of any kind, lower castes and classes more or less completely excluded from education and social advancement? Resentment could perhaps be satisfied by a wise set of institutions and laws that would guarantee to all their legal rights. But envy would remain as a cancer, infecting common efforts. The fact that India today is a highly successful democracy—not without grave problems, but not torn apart by class warfare, nor a failed state like Pakistan—owes a great deal to the way in which Gandhi tackled the problem of envy, convincing elites to adopt a simple lifestyle and to make common cause with laborers and peasants. It is no accident, but a profound tribute to Gandhi's influence, that Nehru entitled one of his most important books (written in a British jail) *The Discovery of India:* for a Kashmiri Brahmin like Nehru, his own (future) nation was unknown territory, in both historical and human terms, and his career thenceforth was a voyage of mental and psychological exploration.

Gandhi's decision to travel in many rural areas of India and to get directly involved with peasants' demands was not unique: Rabindranath Tagore and other progressive landlords had long taken a keenly personal interest in rural development, and Tagore's Santiniketan school had a rural development sister project at nearby Sriniketan. What was unique, however, was the way in which Gandhi insisted on, and achieved, behavioral changes that brought elites closer to the vast majority of the future citizens of India. Already in 1917, in helping the labor struggle of the peasants in Champaran, Bihar, he formed a supportive group of Bihari lawyers, but insisted that they had to give up caste rules and eat from a common kitchen. Since all were "engaged in rendering service," he said, eating separately made no sense.[71]

This became his strategy everywhere. His moral authority and his own example, as he transformed his own personal appearance in the direction of greater and greater simplicity, led his most influential followers to emulate his sacrifice of position—and to see it as not sacrifice but virtue. Motilal Nehru used to be one of India's best-dressed men, in fine British style. His son, Jawaharlal, describes himself as having the views and lifestyle, while at Cambridge, of a Cyrenaic hedonist, in the manner of Oscar Wilde and Walter Pater.[72] Within a short time of joining with Gandhi in the independence movement, however, both father and son utterly changed their attire, wearing homespun cloth and the simple cap that became the hallmark of Congress politicians. They also changed their lifestyle, working closely with rural peasants. "The whole look of the Congress changed," Nehru writes. "European clothes vanished and soon only khadi was to be seen."[73] During his long periods of imprisonment, Nehru was often at the spinning wheel. When, later, he organized the wedding of his daughter Indira, he urged her to wear a homespun sari—a particularly important statement, given the lavishness with which weddings are traditionally celebrated in India.[74]

A crucial turning point in Jawaharlal Nehru's career—one that seemed to bring a change in the "very core of his understanding of India and of the meaning of politics," as biographer Judith Brown puts it—was his experience of a peasant struggle in 1920, in which he worked side by side with rural peasants and came to understand their lifestyle and their thoughts.[75] He now saw India in terms of "such men and women as those who confronted him with their poverty and their hope . . . The casually intellectual parlour socialism he had toyed with in Cambridge paled before this human evidence."[76] In the corresponding passage of the *Autobiography*, Nehru reports listening to the peasants' "innumerable tales of sorrow," and concludes, "I was filled with shame and sorrow, shame at my own easy-going and comfortable life . . . sorrow at the degradation and overwhelming poverty of India."[77] He began to speak with them as individuals, rather than to remain in the posture of distant orator.[78]

Nehru had many profound disagreements with Gandhi, particularly about poverty and asceticism. "Personally," he writes, "I dislike the praise of poverty and suffering. I do not think they are at all desirable, and they ought to be abolished. . . . I understand and appreciate simplicity, equality, self-control, but not the mortification of the flesh. Nor do I appreciate in the least the idealization of the 'simple peasant life.' I have almost a horror of it, and instead of submitting to it myself I want to drag out even the peasantry from it, not to urbanization, but to the spread of urban cultural facilities to rural areas."[79] This winning down-to-earth humanity (entirely correct!), which comes as a relief after Gandhi's stern saintliness, would, however, not by itself have made Nehru a good leader for India. Given his cultural background, he would not have arrived at the spirit of "simplicity, equality, self-control" without Gandhi's almost dictatorial example. It was from Gandhi that he learned simplicity of dress and manner, directness of language and style, even the habit of speaking Hindi so that peasants could relate to him directly.[80] And an account he gives of Gandhi's force of character leaves no doubt of the man's uncanny power to inspire personal change:

> He spoke well in his best dictatorial vein. He was humble but also clear-cut and hard as a diamond, pleasant and soft-spoken but inflexible and terribly earnest. His eyes were mild and deep, yet out of them blazed out a fierce energy and determination. This is going to be a great struggle, he said, with a very powerful adversary. If you want to take it up, you must be prepared to lose everything, and you must subject yourself to the strictest non-violence and discipline. . . . [S]o long as you choose to keep me as your leader you must accept my conditions, you must accept dictatorship and the discipline of martial law. But that dictatorship will always be subject to your goodwill and to your acceptance and to your co-operation. The moment you have had enough of me, throw me out, trample upon me, and I shall not complain.
>
> Something to this effect he said and these military analogies and the unyielding earnestness of the man made the flesh of most of his hearers creep.[81]

This passage reveals the intense fascination, indeed passionate love, that Gandhi inspired in Nehru, and of course in many others. To Nehru, with his common sense, his embrace of bodily passion, and his realistic sense of people and life, Gandhi was a presence strange and wondrous, at times almost repellent in his fierce inflexibility. And yet what kept Nehru fascinated was the way in which this discipline was linked to high goals that the two men shared, and the inflexibility to a remarkable power of empathetic understanding. This understanding compelled change because it included the capacity for truly personal friendship with individuals.[82]

How did Gandhi's transformation of Congress elites alter the future of envy in the nation? First, it simply made distinctions of status and rank less salient. Rather than flaunting luxury goods, elites were now ashamed of them. That this never happened in Pakistan says much about the divergent histories of the two nations. I have heard Indian friends comment on excessive ostentation in dress or home furnishings, "Ugh. That looks like something you'd see in Pakistan." (Because of visa restrictions, most of them have never been there, so this is a stereotype based on report, but one with a basis in reality.) Second, it did away with the sense of hostile competition for social advantage: elites were now seen to be enduring hard work and sacrifice to secure benefits for everyone. This sense of service could have degenerated into a top-down noblesse oblige had Gandhi not carefully chosen to be the poorest of the poor and at the same time to encourage the voices of the oppressed. So there was a single community, united in a common work—a theme that Nehru picks up and continues even after the "work" of ending the Raj was complete. (We recall its prominence in his "tryst with destiny" speech.)[83] To the extent that the poor see elites as their loyal agents and trust them, they want them to succeed rather than to fail. To the extent that the idea of a common work catches on, to that extent envy's hopelessness and helplessness are transcended in favor of constructive and useful activity.

Had Gandhi engaged in brilliant symbolism and rhetoric and then done nothing, he would have made things no better, or perhaps worse. So the emotions and behavior patterns he engendered did not take the place of political deeds, and, ultimately, of political structures and policies. They did, however, provide crucial ingredients in forging a unified nation with a common work.

In one sense this story is bad news, for so much seems to depend on one extraordinary person. Nonetheless, although in times of crisis it is extremely helpful to have such a person to chart a course, once a direction is taken it can be sustained without charismatic authority, as the aftermath of both Gandhi and George Washington shows. For all the evidence of rich-poor divisions in today's India, and of increasing flaunting of luxury in the newly rich middle classes, it is still the case that leading politicians cultivate simplicity of style and an identification with the struggles of common people, something that is true even of the Hindu Right, where an ideology of discipline and selfless sacrifice is one of the movement's most attractive characteristics. Meanwhile, on the Congress side, the visitor to Congress president Sonia Gandhi today sits with other visitors from all social classes (and clearly she is eager to speak with the poor, with NGO leaders, etc.) in a plain room with only cane mats on the floor, and a handful of simple cane chairs. On the wall hang black-and-white photos of family members—and of Mohandas Gandhi. These things hang in the balance, clearly, in an age of increasing materialism and competition for goods. But even that market competition, which Gandhi would have despised and Nehru would have mistrusted, has something equalizing in it, in that it replaces the sense of fixed fate and immutable occupation assigned by caste that was so long the lifestyle of virtually all of India's people.

Central Park

Life in America's great cities was long an experience of unrelieved noise and clutter. Elites could escape inside their spacious dwellings. Equally important, they could escape to the seashore or the mountains, where many had weekend homes. Working-class people, however, seldom had these opportunities, except perhaps in the form of a trip to a crowded summer resort. In the mid-nineteenth century it had not yet occurred to city planners in the United States to create green spaces within the city for people to enjoy—largely because the elites had these opportunities anyway, and the needs of others were not taken into account. Or, perhaps worse, they were seen as mere working bodies, to whom elites did not attribute the wish for clean air, flowing water, woods, and grass.

This asymmetry was an obvious occasion for envy. Up to a point the preference for rural green space is cultural. (A Finnish/Bengali couple I knew had a very difficult time agreeing on a place to live for that reason: one values solitude in the forest, the other the noise and bustle of large cities.) Still, there is a threshold. People don't like living entirely without clean air, green spaces, room to play and walk. And they like dirty, crowded conditions much less when they are in a culture (strongly influenced by Romanticism) that valorizes green space and they know that elites have access to these culturally valuable goods and they do not. Moreover, since most new immigrants found work opportunities in the cities rather than in rural areas, one could not assume that their choice to live in a city reflects a preference for urban life conditions.

Europe had already begun to address this problem. The garden of the Palace of the Tuileries was initially private, but became a public park directly after the French Revolution. London's Hyde Park was created for the Exposition of 1851, and the earlier Kensington Gardens (again, originally private palace grounds) had already been opened to the public. John Nash designed Regent's Park as a public park, and it was opened to the public in 1835, though at first only on two days a week.[84] Other English cities followed suit, and perhaps went further, in that the London parks just mentioned were in fashionable areas and thus attracted a predominantly elite crowd, at least at first. By contrast, Birkenhead Park in Liverpool, opened in 1841, caught the eye of young American landscape architect Frederick Law Olmsted, then visiting England, because of the fact that all classes of society seemed to use it equally.[85] Olmsted observed that it was ironic that in democratic America there was nothing comparable to the "People's Park" that he found in Birkenhead.[86]

Having made a name for himself by his articles, which demonstrated his knowledge of the public parks of Europe, Olmsted was a leading candidate to undertake the novel task of designing such a park for New York, an idea that had gradually become a reality despite the political bickering that New York politics typically involved. The city had acquired more than eight hundred acres of land, and now a supervisor—ideally above partisan rivalries—needed to be found. After some aggressive lobbying by his supporters, Olmsted got the job. That, however, was only the beginning of his struggle, since the supervisor was permitted to submit a design to the competition, but so were many others. In the end there were thirty-three entries. Teaming up with architect Calvert Vaux, Olmsted eventually managed to win.

The competition was inspired by some general ideas put forward by the famous landscape gardener Andrew Jackson Downing. The park was to capture what Downing called "a real feeling of the breadth and beauty of green fields, the perfume and freshness of nature."[87] There also were some specific requirements: three playing fields, a parade ground, a skating pond, a fountain, a flower garden, a lookout tower, and a music hall. Vaux and Olmsted decided to take their inspiration from one particular remark of Downing's: "Pedestrians would find quiet and secluded walks when they wished to be solitary, and broad alleys filled with thousands of happy faces when they wished to be gay."[88] Singling out that one aspect of Downing's vision, the architects made the Mall their centerpiece, a broad, tree-lined boulevard leading to a formal terrace and a fountain. The avenue led to Vista Rock, a lookout point on top of a rocky bluff covered with dense bushes; thus the geological irregularity of the park was used rather than circumnavigated, and the design combined elements of European formality with native wildness. Throughout their design, they deemphasized buildings, and even fountains and gardens, remarking that none of these are "necessary" elements of a park. The essentials, rather, are "dry walks and drives, greensward and shade."[89]

Fending off objections that would have diminished the plan's use of the existing natural features of the landscape, Olmsted made the following astute prediction:

> The time will come when New York will be built up, when all the grading and filling will be done, and when the picturesquely-varied, rocky formations of the Island will have been converted into foundations for rows of monotonous straight streets, and piles of erect, angular buildings. There will be no suggestion left of its present varied surface, with the single exception of the Park. Then the priceless value of the present picturesque outlines of the ground will be more distinctly perceived, and its adaptability for its purpose more fully recognized. It therefore seems desirable to interfere with its easy, undulating outlines, and picturesque, rocky scenery as little as possible, and, on the other hand, to endeavor rapidly and by every legitimate means, to increase and judiciously develop these particularly individual and characteristic sources of landscape effects.[90]

As documents make plain, Olmsted was not suggesting doing nothing: preserving natural features required putting in a complex drainage system, removing boulders where roads needed to cross the park, and doing a lot of seeding and planting. But Olmsted made a case that was powerful at the time, and which is extraordinarily prescient seen in hindsight. What he was able to imagine was that the geology and topography that made Manhattan a specific place would ultimately be lost utterly to city life—and thus to the "people"—unless the park preserved them. Repeatedly, as the work went forward, Olmsted insisted that the real goal was not aesthetic, but public and human:

> It is one great purpose of the park to supply to the hundreds of thousands of tired workers, who have no opportunity to spend their summers in the country, a specimen of God's handiwork that shall be to them, inexpensively, what a month or two in the White Mountains or the Adirondacks is, at great cost, to those in easier circumstances.[91]

New York today is hardly a city of equal advantages for rich and poor. Given the cost of housing in Manhattan, even the park's vast north-south extent does not bring it close to as many "tired workers" (apart from doctors, lawyers, and other professionals) as Olmsted envisaged. Prospect Park in Brooklyn, another Olmsted gem, does somewhat better in outreach. Chicago's Burnham plan, which preserved sixteen miles of lakefront property as public parkland, with numerous bicycle access routes, also does better, moving through neighborhoods that are not entirely gentrified. And of course creating equal opportunity is a matter far more complicated and multifaceted than the creation of a single park. Still, public space is of real importance. And we can easily see that New York without Central Park would have been a much poorer and more envy-ridden place. Envy is hardly removed by such generous public gestures, but perhaps they supply an escape valve that preserves the possibility of friendship.

V. Shame and Stigma

Shame is a powerful and ubiquitous emotion in social life.[92] We all have weaknesses that we try to hide from others. When those weaknesses are uncovered, shame is the painful emotion that results; the blushing face is its sign. Shame is, then, a painful emotion responding to one's own failure to exhibit some desirable characteristic. Because nobody has all the characteristics that society values as desirable, shame is the daily companion of every one of us. As sociologist Erving Goffman acutely observed in his classic book *Stigma:*

> [I]n an important sense there is only one complete unblushing male in America: a young, married, white, urban, northern, heterosexual Protestant father of college education, fully employed, of good complexion, weight and height, and a recent record in sports.[93]

Some items on Goffman's list have become less salient: being southern and nonurban are less stigmatized today than when he wrote, in 1963, and being Catholic is somewhat less stigmatized, so long as one is not Latino. But we can quickly add other traits, such as impeccable English, and of course the valorized trait of maleness itself. Few people have all these traits, and nobody has them for long, since the stigmatized category of aging awaits us all.

Although shame is in that way a universal human experience, some people and groups are more marked out for shame than others. Every society contains its own list of stigmatized groups, and to some extent these vary across societies, but racial, ethnic, and religious minorities, sexual minorities, lower-class workers, the unemployed, and people with disabilities are fairly constant members of all lists. Typically, in each of these cases, the dominant group characterizes itself as "normal" and the divergent group as shameful, asking them to blush for who and what they are. Given that members of the dominant group are themselves usually concealing something about themselves that society considers shameful, or are anxious about the possibility of coming to have such a trait, the infliction of shame on others conveys a feeling of psychological relief, keeping shame at bay and reinforcing the sense that one is "all right."

Shame resembles guilt in some ways: both are painful emotions directed at the self. Sometimes we use the words interchangeably. There is, however, an important conceptual difference to be drawn between them.[94] Guilt is retrospective, and it pertains to an act (or intended act); shame is directed at the present state of the self, and it pertains (usually) to a trait. In guilt, one typically acknowledges that one has done (or intended) something wrong. In shame, one acknowledges that one is something inferior, falling short of some desired ideal. The natural reflex of guilt is apology and reparation; the natural reflex of shame is hiding. And while guilt typically suggests a constructive future—making reparations, not doing that sort of bad thing again—shame often offers no constructive advice. Sometimes one can resolve to correct a perceived inadequacy, but often what one is asked to blush for is an ineradicable part of what and who one is.[95]

Because shame pertains to any ideal, social or personal, it is a mistake to think that it is entirely a public or social emotion.[96] One may have a set of personal ideals that are shared by few others, and feel a powerful shame when one has not lived up to them. (This sort of shame played a large role in the emotional life of Gandhi.) On the other hand, few people fail to internalize their society's sense of what is good, and few, therefore, fail to experience shame about things deemed shameful by society— even if their own personal scheme of values does not rank those things as bad. Thus stigmatized minorities often feel keenly the shame that dominant groups inflict on them—even if they at the same time believe that there is actually nothing shameful about being themselves. In part this transfer of shame results from the sheer power of culture; in part it results from the fact that the dominant group creates for minorities conditions that are truly humiliating and an offense to their dignity, so they feel a shame about those conditions that can easily spread to include the identity itself. Even when it does not—even when justified anger against injustice and an inner sense of their dignity preserves minorities from self-hatred—their lives may still be full of shame directed at the outer conditions of their lives with others.

We can now see that humiliation is the active public face of shame: it is the hostile infliction of shame on others. When people are ashamed of their failure to meet personal standards, they do not experience humiliation; nor does humiliation ensue if the invitation to shame is made in a loving and constructive manner, as when a parent (in a generous spirit) urges a child to feel shame about selfishness or laziness. So it is the combination of publicity with hostility that makes an invitation to feel shame into humiliation.[97]

Why is hostile shaming so ubiquitous? Probably because shame itself is ubiquitous, and it gives rise to protective strategies. Just as the disgust people feel about their own bodily fluids is diverted by projection onto the bodies of others—*they*, not *we*, are the ones who smell bad, who resemble animals—so too with shame. If the dominant group can successfully establish a social norm of the "normal" and brand other, less powerful groups as shameful, they are thereby protected from the painful experience of facing their own inadequacies.

Psychologists find the origins of shame very early in infancy: along with fear, it is one of the earliest emotions.[98] It appears to respond to the overwhelming pain of helplessness—as contrasted with periods of omnipotence or completeness, similar to the symbiosis of the infant with the mother's body prior to birth. Infants sometimes experience a kind of blissful fullness or completeness that recapitulates prebirth experience; much of the time, however, they experience its absence, and have no skills to supply what they need. On the one hand, infants are encouraged by the life cycle and by parental attention to feel that they are omnipotent and the center of the universe, "His Majesty the Baby," to use Freud's phrase. But at the same time they are keenly aware (and the cognitive maturity of very young infants is increasingly understood) that they are physically helpless to bring about the bliss that they desire. Shame at the very condition of being a helpless baby is the result. It is a result of what one might call "narcissistic defeat."[99]

Some people continue to demand throughout life the type of narcissistic control of and specialness to another or others that babies typically demand for a while. They are not satisfied unless they are absolutely the center of the universe. (Proust's narrator is one sad example of this atrophied infantile condition.) Some people, by contrast, relinquish this demand in favor of concern and reciprocity—together with personal competence, since competence reduces the motivation to make slaves of others.[100] But because even the most competent human being is still helpless in so many respects, and, being mortal, remains helpless in the most important respect of all, infantile shame never entirely departs. Shame about the reality of human life is an emotion that never completely leaves anyone who is not stupid—unless such a person can resign herself to the reality of human life, which is perhaps a bit too much resignation. While "anthropodenial" is the source of many ills, one can acknowledge one's own animal humanity while still not wanting to die or suffer, and this means that ongoing shame about helplessness is not simply a product of defective social teachings, but, up to a point at least, a rational response to things as they are.

How does this underlying shame (which we can call "primitive shame") affect social shaming? We do not have to have a view about this question in order to notice and deplore the ubiquitous social shaming of minorities, which we can explain along Goffmanesque lines as an outgrowth of social anxiety. But it is useful to think about the question. If, as seems true, we are all to some degree longing for an ideal condition of nonhelplessness that we never attain, and are consequently ashamed of our vulnerability, this does help explain why most societies stigmatize the aging and people with mental and physical disabilities, and why the stigmatization of other minorities frequently involves the imputation to them of a hyperanimal nature.

Shame impedes inclusive compassion in several ways. First and most obviously, it divides people into mutually hostile groups. But hostility is not the end of the story: shaming is not like a feud between two factions, because it strikes at the very core of people's sense of self. If I'm a Whig, and Whigs and Tories are fiercely at odds with one another, both may continue to regard themselves—and the opposition—as equal and useful citizens. Shaming, however, confers on the shamed what Goffman calls a "spoiled identity," a diminished status that is very likely to be felt psychologically as a lack of full self-esteem. But even when the psyche of the shamed person can protect itself, there is no doubt that the person's social identity is a base humiliated status. On the side of the shamer, given the volatility of shaming, there is likely to be much anxiety and instability, and this may also inhibit full self-esteem.

In terms of our analysis of compassion: shame and shaming fracture the eudaimonistic judgment, putting some people in one "circle of concern" and others in a different one—and in a particularly lasting way, which is unlikely to yield easily to social healing. For related reasons, it infects the judgment of similar possibilities and the experience of empathy. And it can even infect the judgments of seriousness and nonfault: when something bad happens to the shamed group, it seems less bad to the dominant group if they already see these people as base, quasi-animals, and they are more likely to believe that this bad fate is exactly what those low people deserve. Thus many horrible and grotesque exclusions and crimes against minorities are not even recognized as crimes (lynching, marital rape, the exclusion of people with disabilities from schooling), because it is believed that the treatment is just right for the base nature of that group, or even that they "asked for it" by being who they are.

There is a healthy role for shame in social life when it does not divide or stigmatize but spurs people on to higher achievements. Recall Nehru's shame, as he worked with the peasants, about the luxuries he had previously enjoyed. Constructive shame is likely to be directed at the self, and to be part of a project of self-improvement; thus Nehru, expressing shame about his hedonism, is at the same time expressing a certain distance from it, and a new set of values. Shame is particularly likely to be healthy when it is collective, as when a society feels shame about some of its worst traits, such as sexism and racism (and, not coincidentally, its tendency to shame and degrade others, and to be indifferent to their suffering). Far more often, though, shame fractures social unity, causing society to lose the full contribution of the shamed.

Law is obviously of crucial importance in curbing the damages of shame. When society defines the rights and privileges of all citizens as equal and really puts energy into enforcing that equality, shame's pernicious effects are undercut. And all societies can do a great deal to open spaces in which previously shamed groups can appear in public with full dignity. Still, the baneful dynamics of social shaming are likely to persist even in a world of equal rights, threatening good political principles and their emotional underpinning. Now, therefore, we need to ask what steps the public culture can take to mitigate shame and impede hostile shaming. Among the countless examples, I shall focus on India's incomplete struggle against the stigmatization of people on grounds of caste, and the progress of people with disabilities in the United States.

Ambedkar and the Struggle against Caste

The chief architect of India's Constitution was B. R. Ambedkar (1891–1956), a *dalit* (formerly called "untouchable") from the Mahar community, a caste treated as untouchable in the Bombay Presidency, where he lived. The group was and is large, comprising some 10 percent of the population in that region. In ancient times the Mahars were Buddhists, and by now, following Ambedkar's own conversion to Buddhism, large numbers have become Buddhist again, ceasing to identify as Mahars. During the time of Ambedkar's youth, the group was forced to life on the outskirts of villages, performing a variety of menial occupations such as sweeping and wall mending, but also including the removal of corpses.

Ambedkar's own childhood was comparatively untouched by stigma, because his father was employed in the army of the British East India Company, rising to a high rank. With whatever blame we rightly attach to that company, we should mention as well this positive contribution, which made possible a remarkable legal and political career. Through his father's position, Ambedkar was able to study at good schools throughout his childhood, including Elphinstone High School, Elphinstone College of the University of Bombay, and the London School of Economics. He owed most, as he often said, to his years in the United States: he received a law degree, an M.A., and a Ph.D. from Columbia University, where he became a protégé of John Dewey.[101] Dewey's outlook had a formative influence on him: he continued to insist that society cannot progress if it allows itself to be encumbered by mere dead wood from the past. In other respects too Ambedkar remained a fan of America, consulting leading jurists (Frankfurter, for example) during the framing of India's constitution. He liked to point out that the U.S. Constitution showed that one may have democracy without crass majoritarianism, protecting fundamental rights beyond the whim of majority vote, and he modeled India's constitution on this achievement. In some respects he was starry-eyed about America, since he denied that the treatment of African Americans had the social features of stigma and separation that were present in the Indian caste system.[102]

Very early in his education, however, Ambedkar experienced the stigma of untouchability. In a posthumously published autobiographical fragment, *Waiting for a Visa*,[103] after narrating an extremely traumatic incident that happened to him and his siblings when they were traveling to be reunited with their father and were denied lodging all along the way (despite being well-dressed, well-behaved middle-class children with lots of money), he steps back and describes his schooling prior to that time:

> Before this incident occurred, I knew that I was an untouchable and that untouchables were subjected to certain indignities and discriminations. For instance, I knew that in the school I could not sit in the midst of my class students according to my rank but that I was to sit in a corner by myself. I knew that in the school I was to have a separate piece of gunny cloth for me to squat on in the class room and that the servant employed to clean the school would not touch the gunny cloth used by me. I was required to carry the gunny cloth home in the evening and bring it back the next day. While in the school I knew that children of the touchable classes, when they felt thirsty, could go out to the water tap, open it and quench their thirst. All that was necessary was the permission of the teacher. But my position was separate. I could not touch the tap and unless it was opened for me by a touchable person, it was not possible for me to quench my thirst. In my case the permission of the teacher was not enough. The presence of the school peon was necessary, for, he was the only person whom the class teacher could use for such a purpose. If the peon was not available I had to go without water. The situation can be summed up in the statement—no peon, no water.[104]

Ambedkar tells this story in order to convey the iron grip of caste: not even the most privileged can escape stigma. Ambedkar managed to rise above this shamed condition to a position of rare preeminence. But he never let people forget the daily reality of caste, and his political speeches were always filled with similar examples of social reality.[105] In the middle of a major statement on the constitution, for example, he cites in its entirety a petition from an untouchable group in the Punjab, saying that he does so in order to dispel any impression that abuses are in the past. A key section of the petition states:

They even do not allow our cattle to drink water in the village pool and have prevented the sweepers from cleaning the streets where we live so that heaps of dust and dirt are lying there which may cause some disease if left unattended to. We are forced to lead a shameful life and they are always ready to beat us and to tear down our honour by behaving indecently towards our wives, sisters, and daughters. We are experiencing a lot of trouble of the worst type. While going to the school, the children were even beaten severely and in a merciless manner.[106]

Ambedkar was a lawyer and a constitution maker. Most of the remedies he advocated for shame and stigma were legal, and he emphasized the importance of aggressive legal intervention with the harmful aspects of Hindu religion. The fact that the practice of untouchability—a central aspect of Hinduism historically—is outlawed in the fundamental-rights section of the constitution can certainly be traced to his influence, although Gandhi and Nehru supported him in this regard. But he boldly insisted on strong affirmative action measures for the scheduled castes, including quotas in public employment, the civil service, and the legislature, and he was careful to write the constitution in such a way as to leave no doubt about the constitutionality of such affirmative action—shrewdly forestalling debates the U.S. Constitution has engendered.

Despite the fact that Ambedkar saw such an aggressive role for law, however, he was in no way indifferent to our question about the crafting of public sentiment. He would have been extremely shortsighted had he thought law self-sufficient. People can get jobs, or educational places, on the basis of strong affirmative action measures, and their very presence sends a signal of inclusion and dignity to those who continue to face exclusion. But if the majority is unremittingly hostile to them once they are in such posts, and determined to keep throwing sand in the wounds of humiliation, and if government does nothing further to support them, they are unlikely to achieve their full potential, and their lack of success will reinforce hostile stereotypes. Public servants cannot be controlled by law in all details of their functioning; so long as social attitudes remain unchanged, it will continue to be the case, as Ambedkar observed, that "much of the suffering and harassment of the Scheduled Caste population arises from the fact that the discretion vested in public servants is in almost all cases exercised against the interests of the Scheduled Castes and with the object of keeping them down."[107] He went yet further: "It goes without saying that it is the mind of the Official which is, to a large degree, responsible for determining the direction which the affairs of the State will take."[108]

What measures might a benevolent government take to alter such minds? In a long 1942 memorandum, "Grievances of the Scheduled Castes,"[109] Ambedkar includes a fascinating section entitled "Neglect in the Matter of Publicity."[110] Taking as his starting point an official report produced by the Bureau of Public Information, entitled *The Trend of Indian Opinion between 1935–40,* Ambedkar observes that this report, 940 pages long, claims inclusiveness and exhaustiveness, and yet "the most annoying part of this volume is the complete neglect of the sayings and doings of the Scheduled Castes." To be clear: the scheduled castes today comprise 15 percent of India's population, and if we add the scheduled tribes, that figure rises to almost 25 percent. In Ambedkar's day reliable data were not available, on account of the pervasive Hindu custom of lying about the numbers, a custom he excoriates.[111] So this is no trivial minority. And yet, their concerns and opinions are dealt with in a mere three pages, and the material in those pages is of a "trifling character," omitting major social movements such as the movement for religious conversion. (Ambedkar notes that a leading Christian college managed to fill a report of 507 pages with the views and activities of the scheduled castes covering the same period.) Important intellectuals from the scheduled castes are totally omitted, their views not quoted, their names not even mentioned (including Ambedkar's own). This neglect, he argues, influences the minds of officials, conveying the impression that "the Government of India regards the Scheduled Castes as a negligible force not worth bothering about." We can see how this sort of thing reinforces stigma, by suggesting that these people are nonpeople. Government, like it or not, Ambedkar concludes, is a publicist, and so it ought to use its publicity apparatus shrewdly, acknowledging the achievements of previously despised groups.

Ambedkar's simple observation has wide applicability. Government's publicity machine has many aspects: reports like the one he criticizes, but also awards of a wide range of types, official invitations, official films, holidays and festivities. On the whole, India's national parties and the governments they have formed have not taken Ambedkar's message fully to heart. No national holiday honors him or, more generally, the *dalit* contribution to India's identity. By comparison to Australia, which has made huge efforts to publicize the achievements of Aboriginal people in the arts and to foreground their creative contribution to Australia's identity (as well as emphatically apologizing for the long injustices they have suffered), India has done relatively little. One cannot fly on Australia's Qantas Airlines without seeing Aboriginal art on the side of the plane. Nor can one attend any academic conference or public meeting in Australia without hearing a solemn public acknowledgment of the Aboriginal people and their rights. (Much the same is true in Canada of Native peoples.) *Dalit* contributions to culture receive no similar public acknowledgment in India. Admittedly, the fact that the scheduled castes have no common culture, but form a historically heterogeneous set of occupation-based groups, makes the problem a challenging one, but imagination could solve it. To take just one example, Ambedkar's life has been chronicled more by foreign than by indigenous writers and filmmakers. The leading parties' lack of warmth and celebration toward the scheduled castes[112] has contributed in no small measure to the formation of caste-based parties, and thus to the balkanization of politics along lines of caste rather than policy. Suitable attention to a group's "sayings and doings" creates an emotional climate of friendship and solidarity, undermining shame and laying the basis for compassion.

Another area in which Ambedkar persistently sought to create a spirit of friendship and reciprocity was education: he devoted much emphasis to inclusionary affirmative action projects. Here, however, his thought, focused on such legal strategies as government scholarships in higher and technical education, remains incomplete, leading us to ask for ourselves what further measures should be taken to produce a climate of full educational inclusion in a spirit of reciprocity.

His autobiography points to the first condition: adequate inclusion in primary education, meaning that schools must do their job in general (as is not the case at present) and that teachers must focus on creating a socially inclusive environment that encourages children to come to school and develop their potential. Social inclusion is understood to be part of a teacher's job in the United States, however unevenly it is practiced. Teachers whose classrooms are racially mixed or include students with disabilities, have thought long and well about how (through drama and art, through readings that foreground the "sayings and doings" of the vulnerable group, and so forth) a greater degree of inclusion may be achieved. Stopping hostile bullying is understood to be the teacher's job—again, however unevenly performed. This is all far less true in India, where teachers focus on rote learning. So the first thing that will need to happen, if shame is to be adequately addressed, is a new and more psychologically astute conception of teaching, particularly in the crucial early years.

Let us, however, leap ahead to technical education, Ambedkar's central focus, since he saw it as an avenue to employment opportunities. Here we have the advantage of detailed empirical research, and we can see clearly that reserving places for the scheduled castes in prestigious government technical institutes does little for them in the absence of a supportive social and emotional climate. In an excellent recent essay, D. Parthasarathy, a humanities instructor at the Indian Institute of Technology Mumbai, has discussed the problems *dalit* students encounter when they arrive at such a prestigious institution, for which competition is intense.[113] The basic story is this: institutions operate with a set of routines, techniques, and procedures that are assumed to be neutral, but which really disadvantage strongly the lower-caste student. "A particularly perverse form of self-fulfilling prophecy" pervades these institutions: unwilling to engage in serious reflection about their procedures, they admit the lower-caste students, and then when these students fail, it seems to confirm the prediction of the opponents of affirmative action. Among the non-neutral features of the system are the lack of remedial or preparatory training, particularly in the English language; the refusal of instructors to give extra help to students with weak preparation; and instructors' unwillingness to offer exams in a vernacular language, even though by law they are required to do so. Worse still, instructors look the other way when students choose their lab partners on the basis of caste and even when they shame and bully lower-caste students. Nor does any institutional discussion or reflection challenge majority students' belief that the lower-caste students are "free riders" who do not belong. Much learning at the Indian Institute of Technology is collective, so exclusion from the social group is crippling. Instructors can't be bothered with social formation, and most of them are hardened opponents of affirmative action anyway. When Parthasarathy presented his paper at a conference in 2008, he added in oral remarks that most students have had no cultivation of their imaginative capacities in prior education, where rote learning rules the roost. Intensely competitive and technically proficient, they display little capacity for empathy. Required humanities courses, though better than nothing, and though increasingly focused on addressing such problems, can't change hearts overnight.

In short, educational inclusion is a matter of changing hearts and minds. Good policies will wither and fail if social measures do not support them by shaping an emotional climate hostile to shaming and supportive of compassion. India falls far short of Ambedkar's goal—less because of legal failure than because of failure in the social/emotional support structure of government institutions.

Disability and Dignity: The Franklin Delano Roosevelt Memorial

People with cognitive and physical disabilities have been stigmatized at least as much as any minority in history.[114] Often they have been literally hidden from public view in institutions or in special education classrooms far from other children. They have been denied inclusion in public education. They have been unable to enter many buildings, which have been constructed with the needs of the "normal" in view, although they might easily have been constructed to accommodate a wider range of bodily abilities. They have been unable to board public buses or, in many cases, even to cross the street because of the absence of sidewalk cuts. Some people with disabilities were forbidden by city "ugly laws" to appear in public places at all.[115] In other, more subtle ways as well, they have been denied the right to "be in the world," as Jacobus tenBroek, the well-known constitutional scholar, puts it, discussing his own blindness and its implications. TenBroek points out that the tort law of his day was written in such a way as to infantilize a person with his disability: if he went out in the street without a sighted person and had an accident, he could not recover—although the public norm could easily have encouraged inclusion and raised the standard for maintenance of streets and other public facilities.[116]

Such hostile shaming inflicted psychological damage. It also cut society into two artificially segmented groups, the "normal" and the "handicapped," even though everyone has periods and areas of disability, and even though people with disabilities are often "handicapped" at least in part by social conditions. The talents and contributions of people with disabilities were often lost. Society, furthermore, told itself lies about the bodies of the majority, thus depriving many "normal" people of help they would have liked to have. (Thus sidewalk cuts are extremely popular with parents pushing strollers, people wheeling luggage, and many others.) Aging was stigmatized along with disability, and thus all citizens were demeaned, at least if they lived long enough. A realistic conception of the continuum of human abilities is important for solving a wide range of social problems, from education to health care.

This vast topic is one on which societies have made some progress over the past fifty years, so it is a useful one to study to see how emotion and law interact. Law, obviously, is a huge part of the process of removing stigma in this case. It was only through laws mandating transformation in public facilities and public education that people with disabilities were enabled to "be in the world" in the first place, making their contributions evident and getting people to see that they really were full human beings rather than monsters or subhuman creatures of some type. Educational mainstreaming has probably been the single most effective device in minimizing stigma. Nonetheless, such laws had to be passed, and this meant that people with disabilities had to come forward and tell the stories of their exclusion, showing their humanity vividly and changing hearts and minds. The hearings prior to passage of the Americans with Disabilities Act and the Individuals with Disabilities Education Act contained hours of such testimony.

Following the lead given by Ambedkar's reference to "sayings and doings," we might recognize the outstanding contributions by people with disabilities, with its subtle influence on social attitudes of inclusion and common purpose. This topic is itself immense, since people with disabilities have achievements across the human spectrum. The Special Olympics, the inclusion and recognition of people with disabilities in academic life and in the professions—all these are part of the public project of constructing emotions of sympathy and an egalitarian compassion rather than a derogatory pity tinged with shaming. But let us consider only one example, the public depiction of Franklin Delano Roosevelt, one of America's most famous leaders with severe disabilities.

Roosevelt's polio changed his life. Most now agree that it deepened his understanding and made him greater. The daily struggle to move did not decrease but only strengthened his famous serenity and optimism. He once said, "If you had spent two years in bed trying to wiggle your big toe, after that anything else would seem easy!"[117] And yet, during his lifetime Roosevelt always tried to conceal his disability from the public. He did not appear publicly in a wheelchair, and he contrived to appear to stand and even move forward by the canny use of helpers. In his time, acknowledgment of his disability would clearly have stigmatized him and undercut his work.

How, then, to memorialize him? Roosevelt himself mentioned his interest in a memorial, and even chose the site. Landscape architect Lawrence Halprin was selected as the designer in a 1974 competition, but funds were not appropriated until more than twenty years later; the memorial was finally dedicated in 1997.[118] The first decision relevant to our interest in disability was to focus on Roosevelt's achievements rather than on disability. Of course this is fitting, indeed crucial (and in keeping with Ambedkar's reminder to focus on "sayings and doings"). Each of the memorial's four outdoor rooms is dedicated to one term of Roosevelt's presidency. A connecting motif is water, arranged in ways that symbolize crucial aspects of his time in office (a single large drop represents the crash of the economy; chaotic falls at various angles represent World War II; a still pool represents Roosevelt's death). The site also includes a variety of sculptures, including a statue by sculptor George Segal depicting a breadline. Halprin's aim was characterized by architecture critic Benjamin Forgey as reflecting a "passion to give people as many options as possible to go this way or that, to reverse directions, to pause, to start over, to be alone, to meet others, and to experience as many different sights, smells and sounds as the site permits."[119]

This invitation to deliberate and rethink is an apt metaphor for what happened concerning the issue of disability. At first, although the memorial was carefully designed to be accessible to people with a wide range of impairments,[120] the president's own disability was hidden, as it was in his life. Halprin defended this choice: "He didn't want people to see him in a wheelchair. . . . This isn't a memorial to disabledness."[121] Roosevelt is shown sitting in a chair, which in real-life would have been a wheelchair, with his dog Fala at his side. But he wears a long cloak that hides the chair. At this point, deliberation began. People with disabilities and others complained that the cloaking of Roosevelt's (widely known) wheelchair reinforced the shame attached to his disability. They wanted to show the wheelchair both for historical accuracy and to allude to what many biographers saw as a major source of his human understanding.

What was needed was a solution that responded to these concerns without violating Roosevelt's own sense of decorum or making the memorial focus unduly on disability rather than achievement. Halprin eventually added casters to the back of the chair, making it in effect a wheelchair, although the casters are visible only from the back of the statue. Meanwhile, the National Organization on Disability raised a large sum of money to fund a second statue of the president, which clearly shows him in a wheelchair. In 2001, this statue was placed near the entrance to the memorial. Halprin said that the debate showed the success of his design: "The most important thing about designing is to generate creativity in others, and to be inclusive—to include the needs and experiences of people interacting with the environment, and to let them be part of its creation."[122]

The Roosevelt Memorial, then, is a deliberative work, comparable to the Vietnam Veterans Memorial for the way in which it invites participation by the spectator. It addresses the topic of shame in an understated and fitting way, negating shame while keeping the accent squarely on achievement and on Roosevelt's own inclusive compassion (toward which both the sculptures and the use of water and stone gesture metaphorically). In that way, it questions the shame that disability has long evoked while showing clearly that in Roosevelt's own life disability was secondary and compassion primary. Above all, it invites each visitor to ponder the meaning of these issues personally and to think about stigma in an open-ended way.

VI. Planting Companionship

Whitman's speaker announces that he will "plant companionship thick as trees" in the cities and open spaces of America. He does not mean literal personal friendship of each with all; instead, he means a spirit of civic love that carries people beyond suspicion and division to pursue common projects with heartfelt enthusiasm. But "love of comrades" it must be, no mere pallid sympathy, or it will not have the power to unite people who in daily life are divided by self-interest, traditional stigma, and fear. It is this same idea that we find realized (or by its absence confirmed) in all the protagonists of this chapter: by FDR, cultivating a surge of emotion for America's shared struggle; by Frederick Law Olmsted, envisaging places where people can wander and play on a basis of equality; by Gandhi, inspiring his friends to make human dignity and equality a practice of daily life rather than a set of noble words; by B. R. Ambedkar, searching for ways in which the inclusion of scheduled castes might be a human reality and not simply a set of inert legal requirements; even by a succession of leaders of the University of Chicago, searching for ways of turning exclusion into partnership.

In all these cases, political leaders are using emotions that a very different type of leader, with different goals, might also use—at the level of the large generic categories. They will, however, call forth different species of these generic emotions, in keeping with their specific goals. The shame that marginalized Ambedkar on grounds of his caste is no part of a just society, even though that society will cultivate shame at the failure to show concern for others, or at excessive greed. The fear that discouraged people from trusting and working for American institutions was strongly discouraged by Roosevelt, but he, like Churchill, certainly thought Americans should have a rational fear of the Axis powers. Envy is the most subtle of all: Roosevelt in effect tells people that because capitalism is good they may continue to feel hostile envy (not just emulation or resentment or wistful envy), only not so much that they fail to acknowledge the fundamental entitlements of others that are inherent in the New Deal's social safety net.

In all cases, we see that something of the spirit of Whitman and the Bauls—a poetic spirit, at times inspirational, at times playful—is required if problems of division and suspicion are to be solved. Sometimes this poetic element takes the form of stirring political rhetoric—the words of FDR, in their biblical and poetic resonance, go well beyond their literal meaning. Sometimes it takes the form of an imagined place, a garden of delight, where people come together through enjoyment of sports and of beauty, walk under arcs of light, or skate alongside their neighbors. Sometimes it takes the form of a transformative ennobling of the previously hidden and stigmatized. Sometimes it simply takes the form of leaving alone what has happened organically through daily life: *not* destroying Delhi's syncretistic art and its integrative ways of living, *not* sending Ghalib into exile.

Mazzini, Comte, and the other proponents of a "civil religion" saw their task in oversimple terms. As they saw it, they merely had to engender extended sympathy for all humanity, and selfishness would drop away. Mill and Tagore saw more deeply, seeing that we must deal with people as they are, and with the "very imperfect state of the world's arrangements" that pits one person's utility against another's. For Tagore, perhaps seeing most deeply of all, the "imperfect" situation was itself normatively valuable: all love has its roots in particular love of individuals, and thus a decent society will always contain uneven attachments, and a competition to promote the good of one's own loved ones that makes people rightly hesitate to support a common good with all their hearts. My argument, agreeing with Tagore, concludes that we cannot uproot particularism without uprooting love itself and depriving society of much of its energy for good. But if particularism remains, and is even valued and celebrated in some respects by the institutions of a decent society, it follows that people will always have reasons to feel emotions, such as fear and envy, that undermine their commitment to the common good. Society may be able to do largely without disgust, because that emotion seems unconnected to sources of positive good; it may even be able to do without the type of shame that pillories certain categories of people, because that type of shame (closely linked to disgust) does not seem intrinsic to the more constructive shame that spurs people on to achieve the highest ideals of which they, and their society, are capable. But fear for the safety of one's loved ones is something we don't want to get rid of—and yet, in a dangerous world, it does divide people and undermine many constructive projects. Envy too, as we have argued, should remain (not just its good cousin, emulation), because competition and an interest in competitive goods is something that a good society cannot discourage without losing energy for good.

The institutions of a decent society do keep fear and envy within bounds, and they do protect citizens against hostile shaming. But there is more to be done, and this chapter has given examples of the many ways in which a society can create an emotional climate that limits self-interested fear and envy and undermines the type of shame that stigmatizes classes of citizens. These are but examples. Few politicians think comprehensively about the political emotions (FDR being a salient and remarkable exception). Far more often, thought about creating fellowship and limiting harmful passions takes place piecemeal—sometimes with deliberate intent and public deliberation (as in the case of Central Park), sometimes incrementally in the way people live together (as in old Delhi), which political actors then need to value and protect, lest it be destroyed. But thinking about the emotions is always good at some point, since good things lapse or are destroyed if one does not value them, and it is sometimes hard to remember that political equality is not just a matter of good laws and policies. Often it is at least as much a matter of the buildings one inhabits, the streets on which one walks, the way the light arcs down upon a neighbor's face, and a glimpse of the green spaces that beckon down the block.

CHAPTER ELEVEN

How Love Matters for Justice

O I see flashing that this America is only you and me,
Its power, weapons, testimony, are you and me, . . .
Freedom, language, poems, employments, are you and me,
Past, present, future, are you and me.

—Walt Whitman, "By Blue Ontario's Shore"

I. Reinventing the "Civil Religion"

After the French Revolution, politics changed in Europe. Fraternity came to the fore. No longer held together by fear of a monarch and obedience to his arbitrary will, citizens had to imagine new ways to live with one another. Because any successful nation needs to be able to demand sacrifice for a common good, they had to ask how sacrifice and common effort would be possible in the absence of monarchical coercion. Hence arose many proposals for a "civil religion" or a "religion of humanity," a public cultivation of sympathy, love, and concern that could motivate a range of valuable actions, from military defense to philanthropy (and, as time went on, tax compliance). As new nations arose around the world, the thought of non-Europeans contributed to the enrichment of these ideas.

Part I examined this history, which reveals so much about the promises and pitfalls of such an enterprise. Thought about civic emotion quickly split into two branches. Both traditions sought extended sympathy and opposed narrow egoism and greed. But one strand, represented by Rousseau and by Comte, whose ideas had great influence around the world, held that emotional efficacy requires coercive homogeneity.

Partisans of this tradition advanced proposals for emotional solidarity without creating spaces for critical freedom. This lack of concern for dissent and critique affected, naturally, the type of political love to which they aspired. Rousseauian/Comtean love was not quirky, personal, like the love of one individual for another; instead, everything was engineered so as to produce people who loved and thought alike and experienced mass emotions.

On the other side, Mozart and Da Ponte, Mill, and Tagore agreed with Rousseau and Comte about the need for extended sympathy, but they conceived of this sympathy in a far more variegated and even antinomian way. It is not surprising that their metaphors for the new political love were drawn from lyric poetry, dissident music, and even comedy.

These two traditions, in conversation with each other and with political leaders thinking about these questions, provide us with rich resources for contemporary thought. Our argument strongly defended the Mozart/Mill/Tagore tradition against its rivals, as capable of creating and sustaining a more attractive type of society.

The Mozart/Mill/Tagore tradition, however attractive, still stood in need of further development: above all, it needed a richer account of human psychology. We can hardly solve social problems without understanding both the resources on which we may draw and the problems that lie in our way. Part II turned to that issue, laying the foundation for contemporary proposals in the spirit of Mozart, Mill, and Tagore by taking account of recent research in psychology, anthropology, and primatology. In particular, Part II argued that narrowness of sympathy is not society's only challenge. Ubiquitous problems of discrimination and group subordination require us to think about the role played in human development by disgust and shame at the human body itself, a problem that no other species seems to have. Promoting social justice, as Walt Whitman saw, requires addressing the roots of human self-disgust by forging a healthier relationship to the human body. Part II argued, further, in a Millian spirit, that a healthy society needs to counteract the tendencies all human beings share toward submissiveness to authority and peer pressure.

The account of development presented in Part II made it clear that respect is not the public emotion good societies require, or at least not the only one. Respect on its own is cold and inert, insufficient to over-come the bad tendencies that lead human beings to tyrannize over one another. Disgust denies fundamental human dignity to groups of people, portraying them instead as animals. Consequently respect grounded in the idea of human dignity will prove impotent to include all citizens on terms of equality unless it is nourished by imaginative engagement with the lives of others and by an inner grasp of their full and equal humanity. Imaginative empathy, however, can be deployed by sadists. The type of imaginative engagement society needs, Part II argued, is nourished by love. Love, then, matters for justice—especially when justice is incom-plete and an aspiration (as in all real nations), but even in an achieved society of human beings, were such to exist.

But if we agree that love matters for justice, we still do not have an ac-count of *how* it matters, how a decent society might arrange, compatibly with liberal freedom, to invite citizens to have emotional experiences of the sort that the theory imagines. Part III therefore turned to history, albeit with further theoretical arguments, showing a variety of ways in which this ideal theory might be and has been real. Through detailed reflection on the cultivation of patriotism, the use of public festivals of both the comic and the tragic sort, and a range of public strategies to undermine several pernicious emotions, we saw a variety of different ways to approach our problems, and we saw how powerful they can be in promoting emotional experience, within a context protective of liberty.

The examples in Part III yield at least three general lessons. First, our hunch was confirmed that good proposals for the cultivation of public emotion must be attentive to their place, their time, and the specific cul-tures of the variety of citizens who are their intended audience. One way of seeing this is to consider the relationship between two of this book's "heroes," Mohandas Gandhi and Martin Luther King Jr. King emulated Gandhi, and he studied his career very closely. But he did not use the same strategies, or even the same type of self-fashioning. He understood that some very general Gandhian norms might possibly be realized in the U.S. context, but only through the adoption of some very American and un-Gandhian modes of rhetorical self-presentation. In so judging, he again followed Gandhi; for Gandhi, having lived a large part of his life outside India, saw India comparatively, with both immersion and detachment. In consequence, he saw that a good strategy for India has to be keenly sensitive to a range of Indian traditions and cultures. The same is true with all of our proposals for public rhetoric and public art: they must be situated in their place and time, although parks and monuments, perhaps speeches too, also need to consider future as well as present time. To the extent that artists of international stature and residence are involved (for example, Frank Gehry and Anish Kapoor in Millennium Park), it is extremely important that their work be coordinated by someone who really knows the city and nation.

One interesting aspect of this contextualism is the question of cynicism. Some nations are ready for an appeal to strong public emotion, but in others events have made people disgusted with the public sphere. The Vietnam War made a whole generation of Americans shrink from appeals to patriotic emotion. The artist who would bring such people together needs to grapple with this, as Maya Lin so brilliantly did, creating an artwork that initially appeals to personal grief and detached critical reflection—both stances that remained available after the war—and, through those experiences, leads people toward an experience of reconciliation and shared grief.

I have just alluded to Walt Whitman's challenge to forge a less disgusted and healthier relationship with the body. The second general insight of the material before us lies here. From the very start of Part I we explored the danger posed by rigid gender roles to the possibilities of social cooperation, and Part II argued that some very common (and particularly male) gender conceptions are linked to "projective disgust" and social stratification. Through the normative analysis of emotions in the book as a whole, and ubiquitously in the examples considered in Part III, runs the invitation to think less rigidly about masculinity and femininity. Cherubino's male with a female voice, Gandhi's androgynous maternal self, Whitman's creation of a poetic persona who expresses the emotions of women, gay men, and racial minorities—all these ask us to think creatively and flexibly about the self and its embodiment, not discarding more traditional ways of being a male or a female, but understanding that culture is richer when these traditions are challenged and supplemented.

The third general insight yielded by Part III is that political love is and should be polymorphous. The love of parents for children, the love of comrades, and romantic love all are capable of inspiring a public culture in different ways, and we should not be surprised or disappointed if different groups of citizens react to the same public speech or artwork in different emotional ways. A sports fan might think of her beloved team as her children, in whom she takes pride and whom she wants to protect from harm; a different fan might identify with the athletes and imagine being them, loving what they love; yet another fan might have a romantic attitude toward the athletes; another might think of them as friends or comrades. These attitudes will naturally vary with age, gender, and personality. How much greater is this variety in a nation—and yet all are forms of love, and all efficacious, in different ways, in prompting cooperative and unselfish behavior. The loves that prompt good behavior are likely to have some common features: a concern for the beloved as an end rather than a mere instrument; respect for the human dignity of the beloved; a willingness to limit one's own greedy desires in favor of the beloved. But many types and instances of love can have these features, as we have seen from the very beginning: Cherubino's love for the Countess is very different from the friendly love of the Countess and Susanna, and both of these are different, again, from the reciprocal romantic love at which Figaro and Susanna arrive at the opera's end. All, however, are altruistic, and all repudiate the obsessive search for personal status and honor in favor of reciprocity and vulnerability.

In short, while the goals and ideals of the society we have imagined do place constraints on the emotions that citizens should be encouraged to feel, they permit and actively encourage different citizens to inhabit the public sphere differently, as best suits each person's age, gender, goals, values, and personality. Even the most normatively charged works have this sort of space. The Vietnam Veterans Memorial does invite some type of respectful and contemplative attitude, and it would be an inappropriate response to gambol and play there as one does in Millennium Park's Crown Fountain. But the emotions that visitors have, responding appropriately to the work, include personal mourning, communal or national mourning, detached contemplation, personal self-examination, and no doubt many others. Political emotions are the real emotions of real people; because people are heterogeneous, having different opinions, histories, and personalities, they can be expected to love, mourn, laugh, and strive for justice in specific and personal ways—particularly if their freedom of expression is protected and valued, as it is here. And some of them simply won't like Cherubino or wish to emulate his gentleness; they may prefer to play baseball, or cricket. Even so, they can find their own ways to respect and reciprocity. Cherubino and his descendants (the Bauls, Walt Whitman) are suggestive ideas, not a dictatorial program.

This, then, is the path we have traveled. Several general theoretical questions, however, still demand fuller comment.

II. Ideal and Real

We began with political ideals, imagining a nation that has made some taxing commitments to the freedom and well-being of all its citizens. Our examples, however, were drawn from history, and therefore from the flawed reality of real nations. Are we, then, developing an "ideal theory," or dealing with people and institutions as they really are? This dichotomy, common enough in philosophy, is oversimple and misleading. Ideals are real: they direct our striving, our plans, our legal processes. Constitutions are ideal documents in the sense that they are not always perfectly implemented all the time, and also in the sense that they typically embody a nation's deepest aspirations. But they are also real, supplying a basis for legal action when the rights they guarantee are not delivered to a particular individual or group. The "freedom of speech," the "free exercise of religion," and the "equal protection of the laws" are all lofty ideals, yet they provide the basis for action and adjudication in the real world, for the education of real people, and for progress toward the amelioration of vexing social problems.

The ideal is real in another way: if it is a good ideal, it acknowledges human life as it is, and expresses a sense of how real people are. Real people are bodily and needy; they have a variety of human frailties and excellences; they are, quite simply, human beings, neither machines nor angels. Who can say what constitution a nation of angels would make? Who can say what constitution would be best suited to a nation of elephants or tigers or whales? The nation we imagine is a nation of, and for, human beings (albeit in complex interrelationships with other species), and its constitution is a good one only to the extent that it incorporates an understanding of human life as it really is. (John Rawls understood this clearly, and that is why my project, although focused on aspiration rather than achieved justice, lies close to and complements his.)

The ideal, then, is real. At the same time, the real also contains the ideal. Real people aspire. They imagine possibilities better than the world they know, and they try to actualize them. At times their pursuit of the ideal can go astray, as people try to transcend the limits of human-ness itself. We saw that a lot of difficulties for political life come from that type of self-repudiating aspiration. But not all pursuits of the idea have this doomed and counterproductive character. People who strive for this-worldly justice typically aspire to distant goals—prominently in-cluding theoretical goals—and are moved by them. That's a large part of human reality, so any political thinker who rejects ideal theory rejects a lot of reality.

Our project is about just such real ideals and real striving. It is moti-vated by the difficulty of attaining and stabilizing lofty goals, but it un-derstands those goals as parts of real-life human politics. The emotions on which it draws are real human emotions, and its psychology a noni-deal and realistic human psychology. Like the speeches of Lincoln, King, and Nehru, it depicts a difficult task and a beautiful, distant goal—but in ways designed to move real people, who are moved by (realistically) ideal images of themselves and their world, as well as by the comedy of real bodies and their idiosyncrasies. So it is not distant from the real world, and it is entirely fitting that its examples come from real politics, though from a kind of politics in which leaders are trying to make things a lot better than they have previously been, correcting deep problems and moving forward to new achievements.

To put it another way, all love has aspects of the ideal, and political love no less than parental or personal love. When we love people, we want to be good to them, and this typically means being better than we sometimes, even usually, are. Personal love, like political love, is threat-ened by narrowness, partiality, and narcissism, and love therefore in-volves a continual struggle. There are certainly many ways in which ideals can deform love—if, for example, one's love for a child is condi-tional on the child not having the flaws that are typical of children, or if one's love for an adult is conditional on that person's being somehow beyond the human, an angel or disembodied spirit. So ideals can often endanger reality, or express a refusal of reality. To make love conditional on a human being's not being human and mortal is bad. To want to extend the life span and to think that death is a tragedy is humanly aspirational. (Tragic festivals remind us of the finality and deep sadness of death; they do not express a refusal of the basic lot of human beings.) The ideals that we are imagining are anchored in the reality of the human body and human psychology, so they simply reflect the undeniable fact that human beings want progress, beauty, and goodness. Any picture of the real that omits striving for something better brings an ugly and unhelpful kind of cynicism to political life, as it also does to adult love or the love between parents and children.

This has not been a cynical book, but it has been a realistic book. It has tried to face squarely the problems that a realistic human psychology shows us, and its "heroes" are real people, not dreams. Martin Luther King Jr., Jawaharlal Nehru, Mohandas Gandhi, Abraham Lincoln, Franklin Delano Roosevelt—these people certainly could be called dreamers, and this is a partial truth. All, however, were also highly strategic and skilled leaders who turned dreams into workable realities, in part by using the beauty of ideals to motivate real people. Like them, this book is not pretending that we have already reached the promised land: it is a book of motion and struggle, and it is rooted in history. But history does contain surprising instances of productive dreaming, from the birth of the United States and of the Indian democracy to a wide range of struggles against prejudice and hate. So there is no need to apologize for the fact that beautiful dreams are central to this book, and there would be no reason, short of an ugly cynicism that is false to the complexity of history, to think that beauty spells unreality. Indeed, part of what this book is saying is that the real is more beautiful than the lofty unreal.

III. Particular and General

Throughout this book, and especially in Part III, we have grappled with the problem that any appeal to love in the context of politics makes vivid: how to balance love's inherent particularism and partiality with the need to create and sustain policies that are fair to all. If purely abstract and principle-dependent sentiments are too tepid and empty of motivating content, as we have argued, and if a deeper and more powerful altruism has its roots in and is modeled on personal particular love, then we have to think hard about how this love can support justice, not subvert it. (Rawls left this project unelaborated, and that is how I believe my project complements his.)

One important fact about the conception of political emotion defended here is that it is not totalizing: it leaves spaces for citizens to have particular relationships with people and causes they love, in the part of their lives that is carried out apart from politics, under the aegis of whatever comprehensive view of life they favor, since the society I imagine is a form of political liberalism. The political is in that sense narrow, merely one part of what people are asked to care about.

But we have argued that the political too should be particularistic, in the sense that it takes its cue from the Bauls and their way of approaching general ideals through deep personal attachments. In the developmental process, children learn to love symbolic surrogates for their nation before they understand its abstract ideals, and the particular leads them to the general. But adults too, through the tragic and comic festivals that a good society offers, are also led, as on that long bridge in Millennium Park, from particular experiences of joy or grief to more general and inclusive sentiments. Both tragedy and comedy themselves create many such bridges. Political love exists in an uneasy oscillation between the particular and the general, in which the particular is never repudiated, but is seen in a way that promotes inclusiveness, and in which the general becomes motivationally powerful through its link to particular symbols and songs and sculptures. Principle-dependent emotions such as those envisaged by Rawls are thus reached by a route that tethers them to the particularistic imagination and to personal love, and these deep roots continue to infuse the principles even when we achieve them.

The dangers of bias inherent in particularistic emotion are kept in check through the rule of law and through a strong critical culture. But they are also checked by the specific way in which political ideals are realized particularistically. Some works of art encourage us to see common human predicaments and to reach out to others who are not like ourselves, and those are among the ones that a wise society will value most. Since I agree with Rawls in valuing sentiments directed to core political commitments, I have devoted particular attention to these "bridges" and to the works of art that construct them.

IV. Civic Culture and "Political Liberalism"

The society we have imagined is heterogeneous. It contains different religions, different ethnic, racial, and sexual groups, and a wide range of political views. Respecting this heterogeneity, we have insisted, requires practicing politics in the spirit of Rawlsian "political liberalism," not building institutions or the shape of the public culture around a single dominant group and its ideas.[1] This commitment has raised tough questions throughout: How can the public culture of a nation that repudiates all religious and ideological establishments have enough substance and texture to be capable of the type of poetry, oratory, and art that moves real people?

Political liberalism requires the public culture to be both narrow and thin: narrow in that it does not comment on every single aspect of human life, but only those of most pertinence to politics (including, however, basic social and economic rights); thin, in that it makes no commitments on divisive metaphysical matters, such as eternal life or the nature of the soul. It must be such as to become, over time, the object of an "overlapping consensus" among the many reasonable overall views of life that the society contains. We certainly do not need to show that an overlapping consensus currently exists: neither Rawls's conception nor mine requires this. We do, however, need to show that in time one might evolve, and in order to show that, we need to show that the imagined public culture does not create a hierarchy of religions or other views of life, and does not demote or marginalize any at the expense of others.

This is indeed a challenging restriction, but it does not doom our project. Symbols that are resonant sometimes come out of a religious tradition, but they can be appropriated into the general language of a society without being exclusionary, if they are advanced in connection with a robust pluralism. Thus King draws a lot of his imagery from the prophets (though also from Shakespeare and popular music); he uses those references, however, as a kind of civic poetry, and he makes it very clear that he looks to a future that includes everyone on a basis of equality. Gandhi, similarly, uses Hindu symbolism, but surrounds it with careful ritual gestures that emphasize the equality of Muslims and Christians. Other examples in Part III—Central Park, Millennium Park, the Vietnam Veterans Memorial, and many more—are free from even the appearance of establishment. So political liberalism reminds us to remain vigilant about the problem of pluralism and the dangers of hierarchy and establishment, but it does not doom the public culture to banality or silence.

In one way, the project attempted in this book is distinctly helpful to the goals of political liberalism, for it shows over and over again that, and how, real people of many different religions and other identities may be brought together around a common set of values through the power of art and symbol. Poetry, music, and art are great uniters: they take people out of themselves and forge a shared community. When people laugh together, whether at Bill Mauldin's cartoons or at the reflected images of their own bodies in the curved surfaces of Anish Kapoor's Cloud Gate, they share something they did not share before, and their differences become smaller. Shared grief—whether on the Gettysburg battlefield or at the Vietnam Veterans Memorial—has a similar uniting, and even healing, power. Songs of national pride and aspiration have a similar capacity to forge or reforge a national identity. *"Jana Gana Mana"* announces explicitly that Indians from different regions and different religions come together around a shared set of political ideals, but countless examples of public art and rhetoric perform this same task implicitly. How could the idea of *e pluribus unum* ever be real? The arts provide a large part of the answer. Their allure invites real people to join together, where without public poetry they might have remained apart.

V. Content and Freedom

Invite, not coerce. The society this book imagines, and its entire argument, gives a large place to critical freedom. It is to be expected, then, that some people will go to the Vietnam Veterans Memorial and others will stay away, that some people will hate and criticize the artworks of

Millennium Park while others will find them moving and playful, that some will think King's speech a shopworn set of clichés while others will continue to find it inspiring. That disagreement is actually part of the ideal. As we've seen, real public artists have many ways of dramatizing the dignity and beauty of the critical spirit. Indeed, they often help a society keep that spirit strong in a time of stress, by portraying it in an attractive poetic light. The fact that India is a highly successful democracy, in which critical freedom is real, owes much to Gandhi's choice of Tagore's *"Ekla Cholo Re"* as anthem of the freedom movement. Chicago's choice of *To Kill a Mockingbird* as the first book read in the One Book, One Chicago program reminds everyone that the capacity for risk-taking dissent is a core value of American public culture, needed to solve society's problems.

But isn't society jeopardizing critical freedom every time it urges citizens to have strong emotions of one sort rather than the other? Surely not. First of all, as I just said, the critical spirit itself is one thing toward which it is important to cultivate emotional attachment, urging people to care about it and fight to clear away the obstacles to it. Since critical freedom is always under threat, it's a good idea to bring children up to think of Atticus Finch as a hero, or to sing *"Ekla Cholo Re."*

Second, it is just wrong to think that an invitation to strong emotion must be coercive. It all depends on what becomes of the person who refuses the invitation, and that is why robust protection for freedoms of speech, assembly, and religion must be a key part of the institutional backdrop of this project. A prominent part of these protections, as we saw in Chapter 8, must be protection for young dissenters in schools, where peer pressure is particularly likely to be coercive even when law is not. Teaching patriotism in the schools invites, but we are allowed to rebel.

Most important, it is just mistaken to think that a society that protects the critical spirit should be neutral or halfhearted about its own core values. Any good society has definite ideas of what is good and bad: for example, that racism is bad and equal respect is good. There is nothing illiberal about that definiteness—so long as the free speech of dissenters is protected. The freedom of dissent is not jeopardized by passionate rhetoric directed at society's most cherished goals and aims; dissenters remain free to contest those goals. Meanwhile, there is nothing illiberal about the society trying hard to realize its goals, drawing on whatever emotional support it can muster. It would be simply bizarre to suppose that Martin Luther King Jr. was against the freedom of speech because he passionately opposed racism and did not include a proracism argument along with his antiracism arguments. And it would be equally bizarre to suppose that it is illiberal mind control to ask children to hear King's speech on a solemn holiday and not to hear, on that same day, with equal enthusiasm, speeches by racial bigots.

As for public artworks, monuments, and parks, it's not even possible for them to be emotionally neutral: they have to be organized in one way rather than some other way, and if they have any emotional impact at all, it must be of some definite type. So if you come near them, you make yourself vulnerable to the invitation they offer. Even this, however, is not an objectionable type of paternalism, because it does not remove critique or choice. As the story of the Roosevelt Memorial showed, critique can often even reshape the work itself; only time will tell. At most, then, the invitation offered by a park or a monument is like the "nudge" depicted in Richard Thaler and Cass Sunstein's "libertarian paternalism": it sets a default option, but it doesn't prevent you from doing, saying, or thinking otherwise.[2] Most people who walk through the Vietnam Veterans Memorial will find their emotions challenged in certain specific ways. That's how the artist has constructed the work. But one can always simply not go there, or go there steeled against the work's invitation. Public artworks have to set a default option; the only alternative to that is to have no public art at all, or only art of such stunning mediocrity that it communicates nothing.

When art is not mediocre, it is in fact all the more unlikely that it will impose a snoozy conformity and homogeneity. When we think of totalitarian regimes that attempted to impose their vision through art, we always find bad art: Soviet realism and its many soporific cousins. Real artists are dissenters, like Tagore's "madcap" Bauls. This book has sided from the beginning with the unpredictable and idiosyncratic in art: with the Crown Fountain and Cloud Gate, with Tagore's Baul-inspired poetry. Comte's desire to control the artists and prescribe their content to them was misguided.

In short, there is nothing wrong with a nation's taking a stand, including an emotional stand, and a stand made vivid through the arts. Nations should stand for something—indeed, for many things. And they should impart this vision in many ways. The only thing that would endanger freedom would be the suppression of divergent opinions.

VI. Intrinsic and Instrumental

But, we still must ask, *how* does love matter for justice? Are the public emotions we have imagined simply instruments, tools that a just society uses to achieve its goals and stabilize them once achieved? Or are they, as realized in the real lives of citizens, part of the goal toward which society is striving? To put it another way: If we once achieved our political goals, and had well-grounded confidence that they would be stably sustained into the future, would we have no further need of political love? Even though our argument has been that stability is not in fact possible without an emotional involvement that contains particularistic as well as principle-dependent elements, we still need to pose this question, because it goes to the very heart of what we are seeking. Do we want something that is simply very useful, like a Swiss army knife (and let's suppose that there's no other tool that can do various important jobs as well as this knife can), or is it something with its own distinctive value and beauty, without which our public lives would be incomplete? At the end of *Figaro,* the chorus says that "only love" made their day end in happiness. But is love like a ladder that might be thrown over once happiness is achieved? Or is it part of any (public) happiness that we should acknowledge as such?

Much of the tradition discussing a "civil religion" is ambiguous on this point. Mazzini, for example, imagines patriotism in ways that suggest the instrumental conception, even using tool metaphors (it is a "lever"), although he does not deny that patriotic emotion might also be part and parcel of the good society once achieved. Daniel Batson's research on compassion, to which we have frequently turned to illuminate motivational questions, values emotional experience to the extent that it promotes altruistic behavior, and not to the extent that it leads to partiality and unevenness—although, like Mazzini, Batson does not deny that there might be a type of compassion that is part and parcel of a good person, without which a person who behaves very altruistically might be judged to be incomplete. John Stuart Mill and Rabindranath Tagore, our two primary theoretical guides, incline strongly toward giving emotion a more intrinsic role, though both also acknowledge its usefulness. Mill's "religion of humanity" is not just a handy device for reconciling individual and general utility; it is, he strongly suggests, an appropriate way to relate to others, and Mill's *Autobiography* insists on the importance of emotional development for a meaningful life. Tagore's contempt for deadness and his evident love for richness of emotion leave little doubt that he would judge any society that achieved distributive goals without an inner enlivening of the heart not only impossible, but very unattractive. Rawls's treatment of political emotion in *A Theory of Justice* strongly suggests the intrinsic conception: the emotions of love and gratitude he describes are valuable parts of an ideal of the citizen. In *Political Liberalism,* however, he appears to bracket this claim, and he offers no argument that addresses the point.

What does this book itself say? The question of political liberalism makes this a hard rather than easy question. If we want a political conception that can ultimately become the object of an overlapping consensus among people who have many different religious and secular views of life, it had better be thin in certain ways, not making too many controversial claims about what is ultimately worthwhile in life. When we enter the contested terrain of emotions such as compassion and love, when we talk of tragic grief and comic celebration, we have an easier time bringing everyone on board if we say that these forms of public observance, and the emotions they cultivate, are like that Swiss army knife, useful for getting a job done, but not necessarily valuable in and of themselves. As to that deeper question, each person must judge for him- or herself, in accordance with his or her overall conception. There is a lot of evidence that public emotions are instrumentally useful in this way, and that they are not dispensable so long as stability is a problem to be grappled with—which is to say, so long as nations are governed by fallible human beings, and most certainly in nations where the aspiration to justice is as yet incomplete. So it is easy to be tempted to quit while we are ahead, saying something thin and uncontroversial rather than something deeper and more potentially contentious.

Is it, however, more contentious, when we are thinking of nonideal societies arguing about and aspiring to justice? So often people are not satisfied at all with their nation as it is, and yet they are bound to it deep in their hearts. That's the sort of love this book has tried to describe, embracing imperfection while striving for justice. Just as personal love and friendship are at their best when they are directed not at ideal images of the person, but, instead, at the whole person with flaws and faults (not, of course, without criticizing or arguing), so too with love of a city or country: it gets under one's skin, is undeterred by imperfection, and thus enables diverse people, most of them dissatisfied with reality, but in many different and incompatible ways, to embrace one another and enter a common future.

And now we see something that might not have been evident before: this project's demand for love, rather than ratcheting up the demands imposed by the political conception in a way that makes "overlapping consensus" more difficult to achieve, actually ratchets the demands down, by imagining emotions that do not presuppose full agreement on principles and institutions or even agreement that these lack major flaws. Just as two people can be friends and even lovers when their religions, their political views, and their ultimate goals in life differ, so citizens in the society we are imagining, or many of them at least, can share the heterogeneous experiences we have described—at least some of those experiences, and some of the time. So what we're asking, when we ask whether these emotions are intrinsically valuable, is not as threatening to political liberalism as it might at first have seemed.

What, then, are we asking? Let's put the question this way. Suppose we had a society of liberal New Deal–ish body snatchers: people do all the altruistic things that we hope for, and sustain the nation's institutions by exactly the same sorts of actions that might have been done out of real feeling—only they are not really feeling anything. They are just shells of people, feeling nothing in their hearts. It's telling, in the movies on that theme, that the body snatchers betray their nonhumanness by an inability to appreciate music, and particularly jazz, which demands a responsiveness to improvisation and eroticism that both Whitman and Tagore would have understood as hallmarks of the passionate citizen. In our experiment things are made more complicated by the fact that we have to concede that these people may be feeling many things in their personal lives—they are not body snatchers all the way through—but it's just a range of civic emotions that are mere form and show on their part, not sustained by real feeling.

Now of course the first thing we want to say is that the approach taken in this book does not require real feeling all the time. It just wants enough people to feel enough, enough of the time, and that is not even supposed to be a precise metric. But it is totally to be expected that some, even many, people will not be moved by the Vietnam Veterans Memorial, will never enjoy their trips to Millennium Park, et cetera. Some people are more like body snatchers (just going through the motions) than others, particularly in their civic lives. And even emotionally responsive people are fickle, with pockets of deadness and inattention. Moreover, there are many types of love, and we are therefore imagining a family of sentiments, not a single emotion.

Next we can say that in fact such a body-snatcher conception of public emotion will not work. We don't need to get to intrinsic value to have strong reasons for wanting a culture in which people are not just going through the motions of caring about one another. What holds people together must be more real than that or the power of self-interest will take over. Our question, then, is more theoretical than practical.

Still, it seems important. Ideals are real. Even if we don't attain them, they direct our search. So, what is our ideal of the good citizen? Do we imagine a good citizen as an impeccably right-acting sort of body snatcher, or as someone who really has love? The question Iris Murdoch asked long ago about personal virtue also has importance for political life. Murdoch imagined a mother-in-law, M, who resents her daughter-in-law, D.[3] She finds D pert, vulgar, and annoying. Being a very well-bred woman, M conceals these feelings and judgments, and Murdoch stipulates that this concealment is totally successful: so far as outward conduct is concerned, M behaves exactly as if she loved D. But she has no love in her heart. Nonetheless, realizing that her judgments are prompted by less-than-admirable facts about herself (class prejudice, personal envy), she sets herself the task of seeing D "justly and lovingly," so that over time she comes to have within the attitudes that she has successfully feigned without.

Murdoch's claim, which I endorse, is that this inner moral effort makes a difference: M has been active, has done something morally valuable, even if nothing out in the world of action is different as a result. It is this same contrast that I have in mind in the political case. In one case, citizens might be like empty automata, with no feelings at all, or they might, like the early M, be dutiful and self-controlled, feeling the wrong things but doing all the correct things. Contrasted with both of these is a picture in which citizens are emotionally alive, really reacting to one another with political love, at least sometimes and in some ways. Let us stipulate for the sake of the argument that the empty alternatives are stable, and that they successfully motivate altruistic action, although this is not likely to be the case.

Murdoch argued persuasively that the M with a rich inner life of imaginative and emotional effort is preferable to the dutiful M, for she has been morally active, trying to see D clearly and without prejudice. We can imagine many similar cases: for example, racists who behave impeccably, as contrasted with racists who sincerely engage in inner effort to see the world in a less biased way, even if they don't fully succeed. It seems clear that in the citizen case too, the citizen who really feels love of others is very different from the merely law-abiding dutiful citizen, in ways that make a difference to our analysis. Loving citizens are likely to be much more resourceful in action, but even if this is not the case—even if somehow or other the dutiful citizen were to do all the same things—we still should admire and prefer the citizen whose imagination and emotions are alive to the situation of the nation, and of its other citizens. As a political goal to strive for, the Tagorean/Whitmanian/Mozartian citizen is simply much more appealing than the inert dutiful citizen.

It would be surprising if we (I really mean, if I) found otherwise. After so much sympathetic discussion of love, imagination, and compassion, is it really likely that this book would have concluded that these parts of the personality are mere tools that could be deployed for limited ends by people who are content to be empty within, once their goals have been stably achieved? Still, even though this conclusion may have the air of a *parti pris,* the Murdochian argument is sound: the inner world is relevant to normative assessment, and it makes a difference to our conception of what we should be like as citizens, even where it doesn't make a difference to any actual conduct. In our other significant roles in life we readily grant this, granting that imaginative M is better than dutiful M, that the parent who really loves is better than the parent who simply does all the right things, that the racist colleague who is struggling to overcome racist perceptions and reactions is superior to the one who merely acts impeccably. Why, then, would we suppose that in one of our most important roles in life, that of citizen, an empty shell is all we need to be? We simply don't accept that picture as an attractive goal. Indeed the very success of *Invasion of the Body Snatchers* as political horror movie— whether its target is Communism or McCarthyism or both—testifies to the alarm and queasiness with which we contemplate the citizen who has become an empty shell. It also affirms our embrace of the quirky, unpredictable humanity of the citizen who really feels and imagines—in the movie, the citizen who responds to music.

To the extent that we are embarrassed by the idea of an emotion-driven politics (and Americans are more likely to be embarrassed than Indians, or indeed citizens in many other parts of the world), it is in part because of the legacy of post-Vietnam cynicism and alienation I have already mentioned, which has left its mark on all citizens of a certain age, at least to some extent. Other forms of alienation and cynicism also exist in the United States, in particular among racial minorities who have come to feel that politics offers them little hope. But this alienation— which at times in our history has given rise to a very passionate politics of dissent (both the civil rights movement and the anti–Vietnam War movement are such cases)—is not a cultural universal. And insofar as alienation is present in a given society, public artists and orators need, as we said, to take it into account, producing public artworks such as the Vietnam Veterans Memorial, which honors the critical and introspective stance and finds a remarkable way to turn this very stance into community.

It will be said, and frequently too, that the demand for love made in this book is a tall order, and unrealistic given the present state of politics in more or less every country. But think what this objection really says. The objector presumably thinks that nations need technical calculation:

economic thought, military thought, good use of computer science and technology. So, nations need those things, but they do not need the heart? They need expertise, but do not need the sort of daily emotion, the sympathy, tears, and laughter, that we require of ourselves as parents, lovers, and friends, or the wonder with which we contemplate beauty? If that's what nations are like, one might well want to live elsewhere.

Speaking of his imaginary republic, as yet not fully realized, Walt Whitman wrote that "America is only you and me." We should aspire to nothing less.

Emotion Theory, Emotions in Music:
Upheavals of Thought

The analysis of emotions in this book can be fully grasped without studying the emotion theory I developed in *Upheavals of Thought*. Nonetheless, for a deeper understanding of the theoretical background, some readers may be interested in a brief summary of the main contentions of that book. The chapter on Mozart, in particular, can be more richly understood by seeing how the earlier book developed the theme of emotional expression in music. This summary will therefore focus on that topic, giving only an extremely brief account of the general theory.

In the earlier chapters of *Upheavals,* I defend a conception of emotions according to which they all involve intentional thought or perception directed at an object and some type of evaluative appraisal of that object made from the agent's own personal viewpoint. This appraisal ascribes significance to the object in terms of the agent's scheme of goals and ends. Thus, we do not grieve for every death in the world, but only for deaths of people who appear to us to be important in our lives; we fear not all bad events, but only those that seem to pose some serious threat to our projects; and so on. These appraisals need not involve language or even complexity: most animals make at least some such appraisals of objects, and have emotions in consequence. All that is required is that the creatures see the object (a bit of food, say) as good from the point of view of the creature's own pursuits and goals.

In the balance of the first chapter, I then investigate the role of non-cognitive components (feelings, bodily states) in emotions. I argue that although some such elements are present in most of our emotional experience, and although, indeed, all emotions are embodied in some way, these noncognitive elements do not have the constancy and regular association with the emotion type in question that would be required if we were to include them in the definition of an emotion of a particular type. Even with an emotion as simple as fear, which is frequently associated with something like shivering or trembling, there are numerous counterexamples—including the very common case of the fear of death. Most of us have that fear most of the time, in a way that has psychological reality and motivational power, but (usually) we are not consciously aware of shivering or shaking. In this case, then, there is not only no single feeling, but sometimes no conscious feeling at all. With other, more complex emotions, for example grief and compassion, there are usually feelings of some sort involved (again, not always), but it is not easy even to begin to identify, in a general way, the bodily feelings that would belong to those emotions. And even when we think we have identified such elements (grief feels like a pain in the stomach, say), often we find, on closer inspection, that we may continue to have grief over time while these bodily manifestations change, sometimes greatly. (A grieving person may feel sometimes achy, sometimes exhausted, sometimes endowed with extra energy, and yet it would be wrong to say that she is not still grieving.)

We can still insist that emotions typically feel visceral and profoundly agitating (not the nonconscious ones, however), but we just do not, and should not, associate a given emotion type with any one particular feeling state. Furthermore, we should understand correctly what the agitation is. What feels wrenching and visceral about emotions is often not independent of their cognitive dimension. The death of a loved individual is unlike a stomach virus because it violently tears the fabric of attachment, hope, and expectation that we have built up around that person.

I do not rely on this relatively controversial aspect of my theory anywhere in the present book, although it still seems to me to be correct and important, and not even that controversial if all my qualifications are taken duly into account.

Next, investigating the emotions of nonhuman animals in Chapter 2, I argue that we should not understand the cognitive content of emotions to involve, in every case, anything like the acceptance of a linguistically formulable proposition. Many emotions, both nonhuman and human, involve only an evaluatively laden sort of seeing-as, where a creature sees an object as salient for its well-being. Where humans are concerned, such simpler emotions are particularly common in prelinguistic infants, but they can persist in adulthood as well.

In human societies, Chapter 3 then argues, the cognitive content of emotions is shaped by social norms and specific societal circumstances. General shared features of human life also exert a major influence, but even those shared circumstances (mortality, bodily illness) are differently shaped in different societies. Sometimes divergent social norms shape only people's views about the proper objects of a given emotion. But sometimes, in addition, they shape the emotional taxonomy itself, producing subtly different forms of anger, grief, and fear. Thus, anger is in a way a cultural universal, since in all societies people react to wrongful damages, but specific forms of anger are strongly shaped by social norms regarding what an insult is, what honor is, and so forth. Thus, for example, the emotions of the males in *Figaro* are shaped by the ancien régime's views and habits.

I then study (in Chapter 4) the developmental character of emotions: the fact that our earliest emotional experiences date from a time at which we cannot use language and are unable, even, securely to identify objects and individuate them one from another. Those archaic patterns frequently persist into adult life, underneath the often sophisticated structure of adult love and grief. This discussion parallels the account of human development provided in Chapter 7 of the present book, which, however, goes beyond it in many respects.

In Chapter 5, I then turn to music, asking how we can best account for the fact (which seems evident to most listeners) that music embodies and expresses emotions—in other words, the fact that we say, with good reason, that this passage is joyful, this one expressive of deep grief, and so forth. We ascribe these emotional properties to music with great specificity, indeed with no less specificity than we would find possible when talking about poetry. (For example, we can talk about the specific type of love embodied in the *Liebestod* of Wagner's *Tristan*, and contrast it with the very different type of love embodied in Cherubino's *Voi che sapete*—and we can do this concerning the music itself, not just the text.) In my view, this is not a question about the actual emotional experiences of the listener, since the listener might be distracted, musically ignorant, et cetera. But, following the lead of Wayne Booth's illuminating analysis of literary response, I connect the expressive properties of the music with the experience of the "implied listener," meaning a listener who follows, knowledgeably, attentively, and appropriately, the musical experience mapped out in the work.

I now point out that philosophers have had difficulty explaining how music could embody anything like an emotion. On the one hand, some theorists (e.g., Eduard Hanslick) have said, correctly, that emotions embody evaluative thought—but they have not been able to see how music, being nonlinguistic, could possibly embody such thought, so they have ended up denying that music can embody emotions. On the other hand, other theorists (e.g., Schopenhauer, Susanne Langer) have started from the observation that music does indeed embody emotions, but—agreeing with Hanslick that all thought is essentially linguistic in nature—they have concluded that emotions can't involve thought after all, but must be seen as stirrings or movements of the blood, without any intentionality or cognitive content.

The mistake made by both positions is to suppose that all thought is essentially linguistic. By this point, I have already argued that both non-human animals and small children have many nonlinguistic emotions, involving perceptions of what is salient for the individual's own well-being. What now needs to be added is the idea that these nonlinguistic experiences need not be archaic or primitive; language does not hold a monopoly on cognitive sophistication. Once we see that a nonlinguistic form of representation (auditory or visual) can contain as rich an array of possibilities as can language, we are ready to start thinking seriously about emotions in music.

Next, following the guidance of Mahler's letters, Proust's remarks on music, and Paul Hindemith's excellent book *A Composer's World*, I argue that music differs from language in one important way: it is not the shop-worn medium of our daily utilitarian communications, and thus it can often seem to have a superior power to illuminate the depths of the personality. In virtue of not being the language of habit, music possesses many properties in common with dreams.

Music, I argue, expresses emotions in ways shaped by culture and by the history of a particular type of musical art form—as well as, more specifically, by the particular composer's own expressive development. Listeners who hear music from a tradition unknown to them cannot identify securely its emotional content. The "implied listener," then, must be well educated in the specific musical tradition, including the composer's own way of expressing musical ideas. Thus, it is not possible to give an accurate account of a passage in a Mahler symphony, say, without being aware of how he typically uses the oboe, the harp, and so forth.

Finally, I discuss the vexed question of the relationship between music and text, arguing that although a verbal text may give a definiteness of reference to music that it would otherwise lack, the text often underdetermines the emotional trajectory of the music. Studying two songs from Mahler's *Kindertotenlieder,* I argue that the fact that these songs are about the deaths of two children is supplied by the text, yet the precise nature of the grief they express (as to whether it is consoled by religion or ultimately hopeless) is underdetermined by Rückert's text and is supplied by Mahler's music. This discussion is of obvious relevance to my account of Mozart and Da Ponte in Chapter 2 of the present book.

Notes

1. A Problem in the History of Liberalism

1. Locke ([1698] 1990, pp. 27, 32).
2. Kant ([1793] 1998). I discuss Kant's argument in detail in "Radical Evil in Liberal Democracies: The Neglect of the Political Emotions," Nussbaum (2007b), a shorter version of which was published under the title "Radical Evil in the Lockean State," Nussbaum (2006b).
3. Rousseau, however, does not use that term. Kant's psychology, while strikingly similar to that of Rousseau, is no doubt influenced, as well, by his own Pietist upbringing.
4. Rousseau ([1762] 1987).
5. Rawls (1986). I endorse this view in Nussbaum (2006a) and defend it at length in Nussbaum (2011b).
6. Rawls (1986, pp. 133–72).
7. Mill ([1874] 1998).
8. Rawls (1971).
9. See Rawls (1986, p. xlii and elsewhere).
10. The sophistication of Rawls's account of emotions is extremely impressive, since at the time he wrote the book almost no work was being done on this issue in Anglo-American philosophy. Here as elsewhere, Rawls has evidently learned from his deep study of the history of philosophy.
11. Rawls (1986, pp. 81–88).
12. For my arguments about this, see Nussbaum (2001, ch. 1), and the brief summary in the Appendix.
13. He made the translation, but as with most of his English versions of his work, it is rather stilted, and is generally agreed not to convey all the beauty of the original.

14. There are connections to Buddhism as well, in the choice of a simple mode of life and in views of universal human brotherhood.

15. Tagore ([1917] 1950).

16. "By Blue Ontario's Shore," lines 34–35, in Whitman ([1855] 1973).

17. Like Rawls, I use the term "nation" interchangeably with "nation-state" or "state," not as a way of designating an ethnic group within a state.

18. On India, see Nussbaum (2007a).

19. Nussbaum (2001). See also the Appendix for a summary of the argument of the first five chapters of *Upheavals of Thought* and discussion of the ways that theory is relevant to the present book.

20. For further explanation of my reasons for adopting a version of political liberalism, see Nussbaum (2011b).

2. Equality and Love

1. *"Già la speranza sola/Delle vendette mie/Quest'anima consola,/E giubilar mì fa,"* the end of his third-act aria. Throughout I rely on the edition of the libretto in Mozart ([1786] 1993).

2. The length of the pause is interpreted variously by different conductors, but both Solti and Karajan hold it for four seconds, which feels very long. In the score, the pause is designated by a quarter-note rest with a fermata. See Mozart ([1786] 1979, p. 422).

3. *Docile* is difficult to translate: one could also say "gentler," or "kinder." I've chosen "nicer," in order to convey the fact that this is an everyday word, not an exalted moral or philosophical one. It also connotes (to some extent in Da Ponte's time, even more so today) tractability and yielding, perhaps even submission. However, one cannot read even the libretto as saying that the Countess simply acquiesces in her subordinate role, for she says not "I am *docile*," but, rather, "I am more *docile*," suggesting that being *docile* is a virtue that all should possess, and that the Count possesses it to a deficient degree. I would think of it, then, as denoting yielding to life's complexities and imperfections, being pliant rather than rigid.

4. See also Joseph Kerman's (1956, p. 87) "half hymn-like." For related observations about Mahler's use of Bach in the Second Symphony, see Nussbaum (2001, ch. 15); Steinberg (2004); and Steinberg (2007). Michael P. Steinberg has drawn attention to the many ways in which the period's religious tensions are worked out in its musical culture, in such a way that Protestant and Jew are frequently aligned in a repudiation of a Catholic culture of representation, "idolatry," and hierarchy. Here, we needn't think of J. S. Bach in particular, since his music was rediscovered only later; the allusion is to the general culture of the Protestant chorale.

5. At this point the key changes from G major to D major, and the tempo is marked *allegro assai*.

6. Beaumarchais ([1785] 1992).

7. For an excellent treatment of the historical background of the opera that covers a wide range of issues, see Carter (1987). Wye Jamison Allanbrook (1983, pp. 13–194) has made an especially important contribution, very much in the spirit of this chapter (though

encountered only at the point of final revision). It is welcome to me that her insightful analysis, beginning from a very different starting point (Mozart's use of dance rhythms of his time), arrives at many of the same conclusions as my own account.

8. The received story has some foundation in Da Ponte's memoirs, which do at least tell us of what he said to try to persuade Joseph II. That hardly shows that the libretto's real intent was apolitical, however, and even if Da Ponte's intent had been utterly apolitical, that would hardly show us that the music that animates the libretto is apolitical.

9. See Kerman (1956, pp. 90–91), emphasizing Mozart's transformation of his material, especially at the end of the opera.

10. I see no reason to suppose that Mozart read Rousseau, but these ideas about civic sentiment were all around in the 1780s.

11. I shall be agreeing with Steinberg (2004) that the new political culture needs a new form of subjectivity, but I shall argue that, neglecting the opera's politics of gender, Steinberg cannot offer us a deep or precise enough account of what needs to change if the revolution is to be humanly possible. At the same time, engaging with Charles O. Nussbaum (2007), I shall argue that the opera's goal is to encourage not the transcendence of mere humanity but its joyful acceptance.

12. Bryn Terfel, for example, well known in performance for his Figaro, has also recorded the Count.

13. Allanbrook's (1983, p. 80) analysis of the aria emphasizes Figaro's refinement, and thus his similarity to the Count: he "cloak[s] his insolence in the noble *politesse* of the minuet."

14. The Countess understands that she too is a thing to him: later, when he addresses her as "Rosina," she replies, "I am no longer she, but the wretched *oggetto* of your abandonment." For a very similar account of the aria, with attention to its rhythmic aspects, see Allanbrook (1983, pp. 140–144).

15. I translate *audace* in this awkward way because to supply "man" or "person" would constitute an acknowledgment that Figaro is human, which is what the Count has just been denying.

16. Literally, the Count speaks of "revenges" in the plural—thinking, presumably, of the way in which he will both force Figaro to marry Marcellina and then humiliate him further by sleeping with Susanna.

17. For the general account of emotional expression in music on which I rely here, see Nussbaum (2001, ch. 5) (the main contentions of which are summarized in this book's Appendix). For more on the ability of music to go beyond a text, or to make more precise the emotional meaning of an indeterminate text, see the reading of Mahler's *Kindertotenlieder* in that chapter.

18. Steinberg (2004, p. 43).

19. Ibid.

20. "*La vendetta, oh la vendetta è un piacer serbato ai saggi. L'obliar l'onte, gli oltraggi, è bassezza, è ognor viltà.*"

21. "*Se tutto il codice dovessi volgere, se tutto l'indice dovessi leggere, Con unequivoco, con un sinonimo, qualche garbuglio si troverà. Tutta Siviglia conosce Bartolo: il birbo Figaro vinto sarà.*"

22. Because this aria is so commonly cut, it is not in the Dover edition of the libretto, and so I use the text from the libretto accompanying the 1983 Solti recording of the opera.

23. *"Cosi conoscere me fe'la sorte ch'onte, pericoli, vergogna e morte col cuoio d'asino fuggir si può."*

24. Allanbrook (1983, pp. 145–148) stresses that the musical interweaving of the two vocal lines created an "atmosphere of unanimity and intimacy." Ibid., p. 147. The music is in the genre of pastorale, and the "text and music figure the classless, timeless meadow where two women ordinarily separated by circumstance can meet and stroll quietly together." Ibid., p. 145.

25. For discussion of a similar moment in the final movement of Mahler's Second Symphony, the contralto and soprano voices wrapping around one another, see Nussbaum (2001, ch. 15). I now believe that Mahler, the lifelong opera conductor, may have derived the inspiration for this musical depiction of reciprocity from *Figaro*. It is also, as he makes clear, an image of freedom.

26. Allanbrook (1983, p. 148) sees in the music "the power of love to humble the arrogant and to elevate the humble." However, she sees its contribution as entirely personal, not recognizing its political side.

27. Where, if ever, in opera do men sing like that (in close-knit interweaving harmonies, each taking cues from the other)? The duet in Bizet's *The Pearl Fishers* comes to mind, but it is not nearly as complex: the men simply sing together in close harmony. Similar is the wonderful liberty duet *("Dio, che nell'alma infondere")* sung by Carlos and Roderigo in Verdi's *Don Carlo*—close harmony and, we might say, solidarity, but without responsiveness to the separate moves of the other. So it would seem that in opera, men can on occasion attain solidarity and unanimity, but perhaps not responsiveness or attunement.

28. Allanbrook (1983, pp. 100, 170) emphasizes that only the women's world can reveal and stand for universal humanity: the male world is too demarcated by hierarchy for human dignity and equality themselves to be visible.

29. This new world surely involves transformation on the part of real-life women as well—for although the world of males has its distinctive pathologies, it would be absurd to claim that the world of real-life women is a stranger to jealousy and rivalry. (We should not forget Susanna's sniping at Marcellina, and vice versa, in that Act I duet—although that rivalry is harmoniously resolved soon enough.) In this sense we ought to view Mozart's men and women as symbolic placeholders for types of human beings that one might be, or become. And Marcellina's Act IV aria *"Il capro e la capretta,"* like Bartolo's and Basilio's often cut in performance, tells us that the new world will also require change in the position of real-life women: men and women, she says, are at war with one another in a way unknown in the rest of nature—because "we poor women" are treated cruelly and subjected to all sorts of suspicions.

30. The Countess is eloquent about her husband's neglect and indifference. So much is made of the idea of Susanna's virginity at the time of marriage that it seems plausible to think that she and Figaro have not yet occupied the bed that he is so anxiously measuring at the opera's opening.

31. Da Ponte has altered Beaumarchais here in an interesting way. In Beaumarchais, the passage goes, "Finally, the need to say 'I love you' to someone has become so urgent for me that I say it when I'm all alone, when I'm running in the park, I say it to your mistress, to you, to the trees, to the clouds, to the wind that carries the clouds and my lost words away together." This comically confused utterance—he can hardly tell the difference between one woman and another, or between a woman and a tree—is subtly altered by Da Ponte into something much more delicate, a mood that the musical idea brings out more vividly still. Writing of the aria, Allanbrook (1983, pp. 84–88) draws attention to the movement into the country, thus the theme of the pastorale, which in her analysis figures equality and the absence of fixed ranks.

32. Allanbrook (1983, p. 96) sees Cherubino as a figure of Eros-Cupid.

33. See Allanbrook (1983, p. 97).

34. I say "leading character," because the various choruses saluting the Count for his wisdom and virtue—*"Giovani liete," "Ricevete, o padroncina,"* and *"Amanti costanti"*—are presumably to be imagined as real-life singing inside the plot: Figaro at one point says, "the music-makers are already here." I say "solo" because of the duet between Susanna and the Countess, the *"Canzonetta sull'aria,"* already discussed.

35. In Beaumarchais, he simply takes a traditional folk melody and writes his own words to it. The words themselves express love for the Countess, though they are far less interesting than the Da Ponte text; the music, however, is utterly banal, the tune of *"Malbrough s'en va-t-en guerre,"* a bouncy, somewhat aggressive war song.

36. See the musical and textual analysis in Allanbrook (1983, pp. 104–111). Plausibly, she hears in the text an echo of Dante's *"Donne ch'avete intelletto d'amore."*

37. Indeed, it is formally very different. The text is a repetitious strophic song, and each strophe is like the preceding, rather like a simple folk ditty. It is Mozart who supplies the contrasting middle section, with its more complex expressions of longing, fear, and delight.

38. *"... al concerto di tromboni, di bombarde, di cannoni, che le palle in tutti i tuoni all'orecchino fan fischiar."*

39. Allanbrook (1983, p. 115) suggests that the aria's objective is to exemplify a way of dealing with "the powers of Eros"—namely, through wit, play, reciprocity, and genuine vulnerability.

40. A possible allusion in the text is to the Christmas carol *"Venite Adoremus,"* "O Come Let Us Adore Him" (which would often be a prelude to kneeling). Here, Susanna says, "Come, kneel down"—but it is not adoration of the transcendent that she seeks, it is fun and play.

41. Here Da Ponte has made major alterations to Beaumarchais. The stage direction says that Cherubino kneels, but Susanna does not ask, so the inversion of feudal kneeling is not emphasized. Far more important, when Cherubino becomes a woman Susanna says that she, as a woman, is jealous of him. This not only puts rivalry and jealousy into the women's world, whereas Mozart and Da Ponte represent that world as a world of reciprocity; it also fails to state that a man is more attractive *as a man* for behaving in ways that we have heretofore associated with that world.

42. In a fascinating survey of the use of diminutives in the libretto (sent to me as a personal communication), scholar Marco Segala finds definite patterns in the use of different types of diminutives. The diminutives ending in -*etto/a* typically connote tenderness and playfulness, almost never sarcasm or irony; diminutives ending in -*ino/a* often have an ironic or sarcastic meaning. When diminutives (usually ending in -*etto/a*) connote affection or play, the speaker is always feminine—with the exception of Cherubino, who has learned to speak the women's language. The men of the opera mainly use diminutives (usually ending in -*ino/a*) to express sneering or sarcasm.

43. Hunt (1993, p. 44). Robert Darnton's (1997) earlier study of eighteenth-century pornography (and, in particular, of the anonymous novel *Thérèse Philosophe*) comes to a subtly different conclusion: the new idea is not one of intersubstitutability of bodies, but rather the idea of women's control and autonomy. Thus the relationships that are prized are personal and long-lasting, but include contraception.

44. Barshack (2008, pp. 47–67).

45. Rousseau ([1762] 1987). Parenthetical references are to this edition.

46. In a final paragraph Rousseau states that today there can be no exclusive national religion, so we should tolerate all religions that tolerate others—so long as their dogmas contain nothing contrary to the duties of citizenship. At first blush, this might be read as suggesting that he is suddenly backing off from his proposal of the unitary civil religion. However, that reading is incorrect. This paragraph immediately follows discussion of the important doctrine of theological toleration that is *a crucial element in* the civil religion, requiring that we do not believe that our fellow citizens who hold different theological beliefs are damned. So, Rousseau is just saying that we should endorse that theological doctrine rather than making the state intolerantly Catholic or intolerantly Protestant and then coercively imposing that doctrine, banishing or otherwise punishing dissenters. But that theological doctrine, of course, is one that no religion of his time accepted. All, then, did in fact contain dogmas contrary to the duties of citizenship (as Rousseau understands them). By requiring theological as well as political toleration, Rousseau forces them all into exile.

47. I owe this point to Daniel Brudney, who also points out that the *Letter to d'Alembert on the Theater* contains a rather different picture of the preferred types of social interaction.

48. Allanbrook (1983) plausibly proposes another: Bernardin de Saint-Pierre, whose novel *Paul et Virginie* of 1787 articulates similar sentiments.

49. Herder ([1792] 2002, p. 378).

50. Here Herder is apparently paraphrasing a writer named G. H. Loskiel (1740–1814), a priest of the United Brethren, who published an extensive account of Iroquois customs in 1794.

51. Again, Herder follows Loskiel's account. I am not in a position to say whether it is correct on this point—although the democratic customs of the Iroquois have by now attracted much attention. In similar fashion, thinker and political leader Roger Williams found in the Narragansett Indians valuable norms of reciprocity and hospitality—although in this case he had studied their culture and language in depth and written a book on the topic.

52. Steinberg (2004, p. 45). Steinberg writes of a pause in Susanna's aria *"Deh vieni, non tardar,"* which he discusses so nicely that I refrain from adding anything further.

53. Steinberg (2004, pp. 45–46) writes: "In his emotional maturity, Figaro is awarded by Mozart with a musical sensuality that departs from his earlier, metronomic ditties."

54. Here I think Barshack (2008, p. 51) is perceptive: "Affective intensity" (in Mozart) "does not result in a retreat from the play of variations and ambiguities which make up everyday existence . . . In the height of passion, Mozart often invokes the frivolous and the commonplace."

55. See Kerman (1956, p. 91). See also Tim Carter (1987, pp. 120–121), who writes that the text is "perfunctory to an extreme" and that the musical setting is "magnificent in its serenity and translucence."

56. I am grateful to Tim Carter for valuable correspondence on this point. For his interpretation of the opera, see Carter (1987). The same tension is even more evident in *Così Fan Tutte,* where the libretto is cynical and detached throughout, but the music achieves moments of deeply moving tenderness and reciprocity—all of which make the challenge of staging it well profoundly difficult.

57. C. Nussbaum (2007, p. 286) states that his intention is "to argue that the assuagement of the horror of the contingent came . . . to be one direct proper function (though by no means the only one) of the musical representations belonging to the musical style under consideration in this book." He refers to the analysis in the chapter as dealing with "certain central cases" of musical emotion. Ibid., p. 295.

58. Indeed, I'd be inclined to say that C. Nussbaum's characterization of religious experience is more at home in Christianity than in Judaism, with its emphasis on the earthly nature of our ethical duties.

59. And if I am right about the allusion to *Venite Adoremus* (see note 40), the aria quite directly pokes fun at the search for transcendence.

60. Here a comment made by Mollie Stone, Assistant Conductor of the Chicago Children's Choir, is illuminating. Describing the contribution the choir makes to the political and social development of children from a wide range of ethnic and racial backgrounds in an interview on June 5, 2008, she commented that the children become close to each other because they actually share their breath with one another, a kind of physical reciprocity that is much more intimate than anything that would be involved in orchestral performance. This comment fits well with the fine analysis of our physical engagement with music offered in Higgins (1990, esp. pp. 150–156).

61. A cover chosen by the author.

62. As was done in a remarkable concert version of *Fidelio* directed by Daniel Barenboim in Chicago several years ago, in close connection to his political activism in the Middle East, in partnership with the late Edward Said. The added text by Said expressed the message that *Fidelio* is unreal (just as unreal, Said suggests, as the idea of a decent Israel), and that we should all be both angry and pessimistic about the world as it is.

63. Because, after all, as I've said, the representation of female reciprocity in the opera does not by any means imply that real-life women are free from narcissism and the urge to control others.

3. Religions of Humanity I

1. A longer focus on Rousseau would also need to discuss the religion that Emile is taught in Book IV, in the Profession of Faith of the Savoyard Vicar, which is different both from the "civil religion" of the *Social Contract* and the type of natural religion advocated by Comte.

2. Fichte ([1808] 2009).

3. For an acute discussion of other contributions to the discussion of the new fraternity in the late eighteenth century, see Kleingeld (1999).

4. Mazzini ([1846] 2001, p. 3).

5. Ibid., p. 8.

6. Ibid., p. 67.

7. Ibid., p. 72.

8. Mill ([1865] 1891, p. 200).

9. Bagchi (2003, pp. 174–186).

10. On Comte and colonialism, see Bagchi (2003, pp. 176–177). Comte's pupil Richard Congreve explicitly urged British withdrawal from India after the Sepoy mutiny in 1856, citing "the interest of Indian independence and good government." Congreve ([1857] 1874, p. 76). Comte's racial views will be further discussed later in this section. See Comte ([1865] 1957, p. 427).

11. Comte wrote a great deal, but he viewed *A General Theory of Positivism* as a summary of his lengthier expositions of doctrine, and that work, combined with J. S. Mill's detailed, albeit critical, description, give us detail enough for our purposes.

12. For the role that Kant does assign to supportive emotions, see Sherman (1997).

13. Bernard Williams, "The Poverty of Humanism" (lecture, Cambridge, England, which I heard in the 1980s).

14. In the wonderful "Vatican Rag," Tom Lehrer certainly made comedy out of Catholic homogeneity, combined, as it was post–Vatican II, with a new emphasis on individual choice.

15. See Cohen (1999).

16. Mill ([1863] 1987, ch. 3). Parenthetical references are to this edition.

17. Mill ([1874] 1998).

18. See Schultz (2004).

19. For Mill's remarks about the family, see Mill ([1867] 1963, p. 31).

20. For the debate at the time, see West (1965).

21. Mill ([1859] 1956, p. 127). Parenthetical references are to this edition; the entire discussion occurs in ch. 5 of the work.

22. For a parallel discussion, see Mill ([1848] 1963).

23. I owe this information to Stephen Halliwell, Professor of Greek at St. Andrews, who draws these conclusions from university historical records.

4. Religions of Humanity II

1. See Bagchi (2003, p. 177). Bankimchandra's last name is also sometimes rendered as Chattopadhyay.

2. Tagore (1919) (translated by Surendranath Tagore). The translation by Tagore's nephew, though approved by Tagore, is generally agreed to be somewhat stilted by comparison to the original, and Tagore also approved various cuts that make it impossible for the English reader to study the novel in its entirety.

3. See Quayum (2007).

4. Here I am differing from Bagchi's (2003) interpretation; she suggests that Nikhil too embodies features of Comtean positivism, but I find her argument unconvincing.

5. Did Tagore know Mill's writings? I have found no evidence that he did, although there may be some. None of his English prose writings mentions Mill, nor does the leading biography, Dutta and Robinson (1995). The two thinkers were kindred spirits, certainly, and were linked through a shared, and similarly critical, interest in Comte. Tagore was acquainted with most major figures in English literature, and with some major philosophers (e.g., Rousseau), so the absence of Mill seems an unfortunate accident of history.

6. Tagore ([1931] 2004). Closely linked to *The Religion of Man* in spirit and time is a lecture Tagore delivered at Baroda in 1930 entitled "Man the Artist," Tagore ([1932] 2012). Parenthetical references within the text are to Tagore's *The Religion of Man*.

7. Amita Sen, who lived in Santiniketan until her death in 2006, is the mother of 1998 Nobel Laureate in economics Amartya Sen. Amartya Sen's given name, which means "immortal," was invented by Tagore. When his parents were stationed in Burma during the war, Amartya was raised by K. M. Sen, his maternal grandfather.

8. For representative examples of contemporary scholarship on the Bauls, see Openshaw (2002); M. Sen (2009); Capwell (1986); Dalrymple (2004); Dalrymple ([2009] 2011, ch. 9); Dimock (1959). A compelling portrait of one great Baul singer, Lalan Fakir, is given by the 2010 Bengali film *Moner Manush,* made by Goutam Ghose.

9. See particularly Openshaw (2002).

10. See Openshaw (2002, pp. 38–41), showing that Tagore omitted a section of K. M. Sen's article that dealt, very delicately, with sexual love. Capwell (1986, pp. 24–25) claims that Tagore has neglected the bodily reference of the term "man of my heart," *moner manush.*

11. M. Sen (2009, p. 108).

12. Capwell (1986, p. 27). For my own discussion of the Bauls' music, see Nussbaum (2012b).

13. Tagore's *Phalguni (Springtime)* of 1916, quoted and translated in Capwell (1986, p. 27).

14. I have written extensively about the school in Nussbaum (2007a, chs. 3 and 8) and Nussbaum (2010c, chs. 4 and 6). I shall therefore be brief here.

15. See Amartya Sen ([1997] 2005).

16. For more on this theme, see Mishra (2012, ch. 5).

17. For an excellent account of the school, see O'Connell (2002).

18. Amita Sen (1999, p. 35). Amita Sen (1912–2005) was the mother of economist Amartya Sen and the daughter of scholar K. M. Sen, who wrote the article on the Bauls that Tagore appended to *The Religion of Man*. (Thus, both her father and her husband had the last name Sen.)

19. For commentary on this theme I am indebted to an unpublished paper by Tista Bagchi, presented at a conference in memory of Amita Sen, in Kolkata in 2006.

20. Pratichi is still the home of the Sen family, and the Green Fairy was one of Amita's best-known dance roles.

21. See the photograph of Indira at Santiniketan in Hasan (2006). On Indira's unhappiness in the constrained atmosphere of a British girls' boarding school, see Frank (2002).

22. Tagore (2008), trans. Bardhan.

23. Even the vocal technique used to perform the songs is alien to Western classical practice: very little vibrato is used, and there is a frequent use of glissando that softens the approach to intervals.

24. I cite from Bardhan's translation of Tagore (2008, pp. 305–307). I have not followed all of Bardhan's use of spacing and indentation, which are valuable to give a sense of the rhythm of the original, but only if one is familiar with her system.

25. For the sheet music of both, see Tagore (2008, Appendix to Part I).

26. The only regions not listed are the former princely states, since it was not clear at that time that they would be included in the future nation. Since Sindh is now part of Pakistan, some politicians sought to change that word to "Kashmir," but the Supreme Court ruled against them, saying that "Sindh" can be understood metaphorically.

27. Notable too is Rahman's mixed Western-classical / Indian musical training. This shows up in his version of *"Jana Gana Mana,"* which at times shows Indians playing Western classical instruments in the middle of a dramatic Indian landscape. It is significant that this is the version of the national anthem that the government of India chose to put forward as its official birthday version for the fiftieth anniversary of the nation, with its message of interreligious and interethnic harmony. (August 1997 was during the period between two epochs of Bharatiya Janata Party control; they were a powerful minority, but a coalition led by the Janata Dal was governing.)

5. The Aspiring Society

1. This is Tagore's own English translation of his Bengali original, except that I have substituted "you" and "your" for "thee" and "thy." In general, the more literal translations by Kalpana Bardhan give a better idea of how the songs work, but her translation of this one is, I feel, somewhat awkward. Fortunately, Bardhan (2008, p. 289) also gives Rabindranath's own version.

2. See Devlin ([1959] 1965). I discuss his arguments at length in Nussbaum (2004a) and Nussbaum (2006c).

3. Tagore ([1932] 2012).

4. For Rawls's use of the idea of a family of liberal conceptions, see Rawls (1986, pp. xlvii, 6). For my own approach, see Nussbaum (2000b); Nussbaum (2006a); Nussbaum (2011b). Rawls never says that people with severe cognitive impairments are not fully equal human beings, so I feel it is not wrong to include him at this point, although, in my view, the principles he develops for dealing with issues of disability are inadequate.

5. My capabilities list:

The Central Human Capabilities

1. *Life.* Being able to live to the end of a human life of normal length; not dying prematurely, or before one's life is so reduced as to be not worth living.
2. *Bodily Health.* Being able to have good health, including reproductive health; to be adequately nourished; to have adequate shelter.
3. *Bodily Integrity.* Being able to move freely from place to place; to be secure against violent assault, including sexual assault and domestic violence; having opportunities for sexual satisfaction and for choice in matters of reproduction.
4. *Senses, Imagination, and Thought.* Being able to use the senses, to imagine, think, and reason—and to do these things in a "truly human" way, a way informed and cultivated by an adequate education, including, but by no means limited to, literacy and basic mathematical and scientific training. Being able to use imagination and thought in connection with experiencing and producing works and events of one's own choice, religious, literary, musical, and so forth. Being able to use one's mind in ways protected by guarantees of freedom of expression with respect to both political and artistic speech, and freedom of religious exercise. Being able to have pleasurable experiences and to avoid nonbeneficial pain.
5. *Emotions.* Being able to have attachments to things and people outside ourselves; to love those who love and care for us, to grieve at their absence; in general, to love, to grieve, to experience longing, gratitude, and justified anger. Not having one's emotional development blighted by fear and anxiety. (Supporting this capability means supporting forms of human association that can be shown to be crucial in their development.)
6. *Practical Reason.* Being able to form a conception of the good and to engage in critical reflection about the planning of one's life. (This entails protection for the liberty of conscience and religious observance.)
7. *Affiliation*
    A. Being able to live with and toward others, to recognize and show concern for other human beings, to engage in various forms of social interaction; to be able to imagine the situation of another. (Protecting this capability means protecting institutions that constitute and nourish such forms of affiliation, and also protecting the freedom of assembly and political speech.)
    B. Having the social bases of self-respect and nonhumiliation; being able to be treated as a dignified being whose worth is equal to that of others. This entails provisions of nondiscrimination on the basis of race, sex, sexual orientation, ethnicity, caste, religion, and national origin.
8. *Other Species.* Being able to live with concern for and in relation to animals, plants, and the world of nature.
9. *Play.* Being able to laugh, to play, to enjoy recreational activities.
10. *Control over One's Environment*
    A. *Political.* Being able to participate effectively in political choices that govern one's life; having the right of political participation, protections of free speech and association.
    B. *Material.* Being able to hold property (both land and movable goods), and having property rights on an equal basis with others; having the right to seek employment on an equal basis with others; having the freedom from unwarranted search and seizure. In work, being able to work as a human being, exercising practical reason and entering into meaningful relationships of mutual recognition with other workers.

6. Rawls (1971, p. 3).

7. For discussion of adaptive preferences, see Nussbaum (2000b, ch. 2).

8. By this I mean that they may not be capable of ranking and ordering ends, or even distinguishing between pursuing a goal for its own sake and pursuing it as an instrumental means to something else.

9. Rawls (1971, p. 586) has a similar view. For my own view, see Nussbaum (2008a).

10. I say something similar about nonhuman animals in Nussbaum (2006a): we have duties of justice to them because of their capacity for striving and activity. I don't think we have duties of justice to plants, though we may have duties of other types.

11. See Nussbaum (2006a).

12. For his different formulations of the difference principle, see the careful study by Philippe Van Parijs (2003).

13. Rawls (1986); Larmore (1996). For my own view, see Nussbaum (2011a); Nussbaum (2011b).

14. See Nussbaum (2011b, p. 35), where I discuss expressive subordination by the state as a form of religious establishment.

15. For details and the complex evolution of more specific doctrines, see Nussbaum (2008b).

16. Mill ([1863] 1987, ch. 5).

17. See Tocqueville ([1835] 1966, vol. 2, part 2, ch. 4).

6. Compassion

1. Earlier ideas on this topic are discussed in my "Compassion: Human and Animal," Nussbaum (2010a).

2. *Telegraph* (2010). See also NDTV (2010).

3. John Updike, *Rabbit at Rest,* quoted in Bloom (2004, p. 189).

4. For an excellent example of subtlety and caution, see Bloom (2004).

5. From now on I shall often write "animals" as a shorthand for "the other animals," although I am aware that the unqualified locution is often used as a device of distancing.

6. See Nussbaum (2001, pp. 304–335). The analysis here agrees with that proposed in *Upheavals,* but it adds new attention to the psychological literature, particularly to Batson's important work.

7. See ibid., pp. 301–304. For elaborations on the response to John Deigh, see Nussbaum (2004b); Nussbaum (2003). As for compassion's cousins: I avoid the term "pity" because, although used synonymously with "compassion" in translating Greek tragedies and Rousseau's French term *pitié,* in modern English it has acquired connotations of condescension and superiority that it did not have earlier, and I am focusing on an emotion that does not necessarily involve superiority. "Sympathy" is often used interchangeably with "compassion," though Adam Smith uses "compassion" only for fellow-feeling with another person's pain, and "sympathy" for a more general tendency to have fellow feeling with "any passion whatever." This distinction is immaterial in the present context, where we are focusing on painful events. "Empathy" will be discussed below.

8. See Appendix. We are, however, ascribing what the Stoics call "assent": people who experience a given emotion don't simply entertain the associated thoughts as imaginative possibilities, they accept them.

9. A case discussed by Adam Smith ([1759] 1976).

10. See Nussbaum (2001, ch. 6).

11. Clark (1997).

12. For my discussion of her findings, see Nussbaum (2001, pp. 313–314).

13. See ibid., pp. 315–321.

14. See ibid., ch. 1.

15. See ibid., pp. 31–33.

16. Batson (1991); Batson (2011).

17. Smith ([1759] 1976, p. 136): "Let us suppose that the great empire of China, with all its myriads of inhabitants, was suddenly swallowed up by an earthquake, and let us consider how a man of humanity in Europe, who had no sort of connexion with that part of the world, would be affected upon receiving intelligence of this dreadful calamity. He would, I imagine, first of all, express very strongly his sorrow for the misfortune of that unhappy people, he would make many melancholy reflections upon the precariousness of human life, and the vanity of all the labours of man, which could thus be annihilated in a moment. . . . And when all this fine philosophy was over, when all these humane sentiments had been once fairly expressed, he would pursue his business or his pleasure, take his repose or his diversion, with the same ease and tranquillity, as if no such accident had happened. The most frivolous disaster which could befal himself would occasion a more real disturbance. If he was to lose his little finger to-morrow, he would not sleep to-night; but, provided he never saw them, he will snore with the more profound security over the ruin of a hundred millions of his brethren, and the destruction of that immense multitude seems plainly an object less interesting to him, than this paltry misfortune of his own."

18. See Nussbaum (2001, pp. 327–334). For two edited anthologies on empathy, see Decety (2012); Decety and Ickes (2009).

19. See Batson (2009). Batson distinguishes eight things that are commonly called empathy: (1) knowing another person's internal state; (2) adopting the posture or matching the neural responses of an observed other; (3) coming to feel as another person feels; (4) intuiting or projecting oneself into another's situation; (5) imagining how another is thinking and feeling; (6) imagining how one would think and feel in another's place; (7) feeling distress at another's suffering; and (8) feeling for another person who is suffering. In my usage, empathy is clearly not 1, 6, 7, or 8; it is not 2, because 2 might be satisfied by mere contagion, as might 3; thus, 4 and 5 are the pertinent ones, and it is not clear that they are distinct. (Batson's reason for the distinction has to do with some earlier distinctions in the literature that may themselves be misguided.)

20. For a similar view, see de Waal (2006, pp. 26–27); Nussbaum (2001, pp. 327–28). See also Decety and Batson (2009, p. 109) (examining empathy considered as "a construct accounting for a sense of similarity in feelings experienced by the self and the other, without confusion between the two individuals").

21. For a similar argument, see de Waal (1996, p. 41); Nussbaum (2001, p. 329).

22. See Batson (1991); Batson (2011).

23. See Nussbaum (2001, p. 333) (in which I discuss Heinz Kohut's remarks about the Nazis and consider a variety of different types of psychopaths).

24. I did not recognize this in *Upheavals,* and was rightly criticized for this by John Deigh's (2004) excellent paper. See also Hatfield, Cacioppo, and Rapson (1994).

25. Rousseau ([1762] 1979, p. 224).

26. Ibid., p. 253. Rousseau puts the introduction of the idea of fault extremely late in the child's development: Emile is already going through puberty before he even experiences compassion (given Rousseau's belief that he will be turned toward others in the first place only by awakening sexual energy), and the thought of fault comes along considerably later than that. I think, by contrast, that children start to ask questions about fault as early as they are able to feel guilt about their own aggression, probably around the age of five or six, and it is only before then that their compassion is consistently of the simple Rollo variety.

27. See de Waal (1996, pp. 89–117). Marc Hauser (2000, pp. 249–253) argues for a thinner account of animal understanding of rules, denying any rich connection between rule following and moral agency.

28. Bloom (2004); de Waal (1996).

29. Langford et al. (2006).

30. Moss (2000, p. 73). See also Payne (2000).

31. Pitcher (1995). Pitcher is a philosopher; Cone (who died in 2004 at the age of eighty-seven) was a prominent composer and Pitcher's partner of many years. I discuss Pitcher's work in Nussbaum (2001) and Nussbaum (2004b).

32. Poole (1987).

33. See Plotnik, de Waal, and Reiss (2006).

34. Rousseau ([1762] 1979, p. 222), with a few revisions to the translation: "Human beings" is substituted for "Men," "rich people" for "rich men," and "the human being" for "man."

35. Bloom (2004, pp. 114–15). See also the extensive discussions in Hatfield, Cacioppo, and Rapson (1994).

36. See Bloom (2004, ch. 1); Bloom (2010).

37. Bloom (2004, p. 119).

38. Ibid., p. 121.

39. Some of the studies in this group measure preference by looking time, i.e., the time spent looking at the object. With older babies, the choice was established by bringing the two puppets to the baby and seeing which one it reached out for.

40. Bloom (2010).

41. Ibid.

42. Batson (2011, pp. 193–194).

43. Ibid., p. 194.

44. Ibid., p. 195.

45. Ibid., pp. 196–199.

46. See Batson (2011) for the research supporting the distinction in my text.

47. De Waal (1996).

48. Clark (1997) finds this attitude extremely common in the United States.

7. "Radical Evil"

1. In this chapter I develop ideas first broached in a different form in "Radical Evil in the Lockean State: The Neglect of the Political Emotions," Nussbaum (2006b), a longer version of which was published as "Radical Evil in Liberal Democracies: The Neglect of the Political Emotions," Nussbaum (2007b).

2. See Epstein (1992), assessing the Civil Rights Act of 1964, and arguing that it was necessary only because of artificial barriers to commerce erected by the Jim Crow regime.

3. On the Indian situation, see economist Prabhat Patnaik's (2012) consideration of the waste of human capital under the caste system.

4. He is not in favor of substantial material redistribution, apart from relief for widows and orphans, but this does not affect his suitability as a source for this part of our project.

5. Kant ([1793] 1998). Parenthetical references are to the Akademie edition, which are given in the margins of the translation.

6. Kant's views here are closely related to Rousseau's psychology, but Kant develops them in a powerful and original way.

7. Kant actually uses two different terms for the good and evil tendencies. The "propensity" to evil, for which Kant uses German *Hang* and Latin *propensio,* is defined as "the subjective ground of the possibility of an inclination"; it is distinguished from a "predisposition" *(Anlage),* the term Kant uses for the tendency to good, in that a propensity can be innate while yet being represented as not being such. See Kant ([1793] 1998, 6:29). This distinction, and the use Kant makes of it, are obscure, but what he clearly wants to achieve is to suggest that we naturally incline to evil and yet have a genuinely free will. I am grateful to Daniel Brudney for discussion on this point.

8. I discuss this evidence in Nussbaum (2001, ch. 5).

9. Stern (1990, pp. 31–32). Stern is a respected experimentalist and clinician, and his books document his research, which succeeds in bridging the gap between psychoanalytic and experimental approaches. See Stern (1977); Stern (1985).

10. Winnicott ([1971] 2005a).

11. See Lear (1990).

12. See Stern (1977).

13. See Nussbaum (2001, ch. 5).

14. Winnicott (1965).

15. Adorno's (1950) study of the German family argues that these traits really are particularly common in Germany, or were at the time.

16. Ibid.

17. Thompson (1987, p. 136).

18. See ibid., pp. 119, 137. There are many descriptions of these phenomena in the literature, and much is reported in Thompson's extensive bibliography.

19. Winnicott ([1971] 2005a, p. 7).

20. See my fuller treatment of this case in Nussbaum (2001, ch. 5) and Nussbaum (2004a, ch. 4).

21. Winnicott ([1971] 2005a, p. 18).
22. Winnicott ([1971] 2005b, p. 144).
23. Ibid., p. 143.
24. Rozin and Fallon (1987, p. 24n1).
25. Ibid., p. 25. See also ibid., p. 37 (reporting that participants in an experiment were averse to drinking a glass of juice in which a cockroach had previously been placed, even though the cockroach had been removed, the glass emptied, and the juice refilled).
26. For a discussion of research connecting disgust objects to animalness, see ibid., pp. 28–29. See also Rozin, Haidt, and McCauley (1999, p. 431) (observing that the core domains of disgust all deal with the essentials of animal life).
27. See Rozin, Haidt, and McCauley (1999, p. 437) (noting the ubiquity of disgust across cultures, as well as variations in disgust between cultures).
28. Ibid., p. 438.
29. See Rozin and Fallon (1987, p. 30).
30. See Mosse (1985).
31. Inbar, Pizzaro, and Bloom (2009).
32. See Chapter 5.
33. Conversation with historian Jane Dailey, who found this in a Reconstruction-era diary of a woman who had that experience. Genuine physical feelings of disgust are widespread in connection with disgust-hierarchies. For similar southern accounts of disgust arising from eating with African Americans, see Durr (1986, pp. 56–58, 122).
34. Lifton (1986, particularly ch. 19).
35. Tagore ([1910] 2002, p. 17).
36. Ibid., p. 567.
37. Ibid., p. 570.
38. "By Blue Ontario's Shore," sec. 10, line 153, in Whitman ([1855] 1973).
39. Ibid., sec. 10, line 157.
40. "Song of Myself," sec. 6, line 1, in Whitman ([1855] 1973).
41. However, de Waal's (1996) important work on bonobos establishes that their society is far less hierarchical than that of chimps, and they are as close to humans, genetically and historically, as are chimps.
42. Asch did his initial experiments at Swarthmore College, but they have been widely replicated.
43. Asch (1955). As he notes, the experiments build on a long history of work on social suggestibility.
44. Ibid.
45. See Milgram ([1975] 2009). Blass (2000a) has edited a valuable collection of essays reassessing Milgram's achievements. His article in that same volume, "The Milgram Paradigm after 35 Years: Some Things We Now Know about Obedience to Authority" (2000b), is especially useful.
46. See Milgram ([1975] 2009, p. 16).
47. Ibid., p. 3.
48. Ibid., p. 4.

49. Ibid., p. 21.
50. Ibid., p. 6.
51. Ibid., pp. 123–134.
52. Ibid., pp. 136–137.
53. Ibid., p. 137.
54. Adorno (1950).
55. For all this research, see Blass (2000b). The problem in the last case is that the questions used in the expected-obedience studies often described a more debilitating and dangerous procedure than the one described within the experiment, where, we recall, the "teacher" is assured that the "learner" will not be harmed.
56. Browning (1992).
57. See Glover's (1999) deeply impressive study of atrocity that ascribes central importance to the presence or absence of a critical culture.
58. See also Glover (1999); Hilberg ([1961] 1985, ch. 7).
59. See Zimbardo's (2008) discussion of his own research in the Stanford Prison Experiment and summarization of other related research.

Introduction to Part III

1. A remarkable story in this regard is that of Nelson Mandela's engagement with the Springboks, the Rugby Union team that symbolized apartheid to most black South Africans. By working with the team's captain, Francois Pienaar, he made the team a symbol of racial unity. This story is told in Carlin's (2008) *Playing the Enemy: Nelson Mandela and the Game That Made a Nation,* which is the basis for the Clint Eastwood film *Invictus,* starring Morgan Freeman as Mandela.

8. Teaching Patriotism

1. This poem was "written" by me at age six and a half, according to its label and date; it was typed up by my mother (I recognize her paper and font), and I found it in her family album. I am not sure what my contribution to its composition really was, or whether it had anything to do with a school assignment. But it was clearly a collaborative exercise, and one from which my mother thought that I would gain something. The general zeal for the Revolution was certainly my own. At that time I was obsessed with a children's book called *Ride for Freedom,* about a girl named Sybil Ludington (1761–1839), who, on April 26, 1777, rode out to warn colonial forces of the approach of British troops—riding forty miles over difficult, hilly terrain, a much longer distance than Paul Revere, and at the age of only sixteen. I remember requiring my parents to act out the story in our basement, using various objects stored down there as horses.
2. Because it celebrated the 400th anniversary of Columbus's discovery of the New World. The fairgrounds opened to the public in 1893.
3. This chapter draws on the following previously published papers of mine: Nussbaum (2012b); Nussbaum (2010b); Nussbaum (2008d).

4. All of this is extremely well portrayed in Erik Larson's (2003) novel *The Devil in the White City,* a work of popular semifiction that has, at the same time, a very serious historical thesis.

5. Quoted in Explore Chicago (2012).

6. The entire history of the pledge is exhaustively documented in Ellis's (2005) fine book. The words "under God" were added to the pledge in 1954, during the Cold War.

7. *Minersville Sch. Dist. v. Gobitis,* 310 U.S. 586 (1940) *overruled by W. Virginia State Bd. of Educ. v. Barnette,* 319 U.S. 624 (1943). See my discussion in Section III of this chapter.

8. Rousseau ([1762] 1987).

9. I mention this example as the result of a traumatic experience. In 1962, when I was the child relied on to play piano in school assemblies, I was told that the ambassador of Gabon was to visit my school in two days' time, and that I must learn to play the national anthem of this new (1960) nation in a ceremony welcoming him. But there was no sheet music—only a recording and a text of the words. I spent an anxious few days at that piano, terrified of giving offense, but helped by the fact that the anthem is abstract, boring, and short. (You can easily hear various versions on YouTube, by Googling "Gabon national anthem.") I've never forgotten it, which shows only that fear, as well as love, has the power to shape the mind. I note, however, that the optimistic words of the anthem have proven true, with or without a good anthem: Gabon has unusual political stability, and the highest Human Development Index in Sub-Saharan Africa. It has also become a recent leader in the struggle against the illegal ivory trade, setting fire to more than five tons of illegal ivory from elephant tusks in July 2012. And the anthem is good enough to have inspired some stirring interpretations by popular artists (available on YouTube).

10. Mazzini ([1846] 2001).

11. See Hobsbawm (1990).

12. Renan delivered his lecture "What Is a Nation?" at the Sorbonne in 1882. An English translation is printed in Renan ([1882] 1990).

13. Ibid., p. 19.

14. Ibid.

15. See Nussbaum (2006a, ch. 5).

16. For further details, see Nussbaum (2008b, ch. 5).

17. For an excellent history of the key role of Jehovah's Witnesses in this period, see Peters (2000).

18. The correct spelling of the name, misspelled as "Gobitis" in later court documents.

19. Lillian wrote out her points as a numbered list, mentioned the biblical texts by number only, and stressed the constitutional as well as religious arguments. William wrote a long discursive paragraph, quoted the relevant biblical texts, and mentioned his love of his country.

20. For the background and a detailed account of the case, see Nussbaum (2008b, ch. 5); Ellis (2005, pp. 92–101); Peters (2000, pp. 20–36); Irons (1988, pp. 15–35) (containing an interview with the adult Lillian).

21. 310 U.S. 586 (1940).

22. *W. Virginia State Bd. of Educ. v. Barnette,* 319 U.S. 624 (1943).

23. *Barnette,* 319 U.S. at 646. Despite his allusion to Judaism here, however, Frankfurter was never very Jewish-identified, in contrast to Louis Brandeis, an influential Zionist, and even to Benjamin Cardozo, who came from a highly observant Sephardic home. Despite his descent from a long line of rabbis, Frankfurter's autobiography makes no mention of his Jewish upbringing or of any prejudice he may have encountered.

24. He was known to whistle "The Stars and Stripes Forever" in the halls of the Court, and he told his biographer, on his deathbed, "Let people see . . . how much I loved my country." Quoted in Peters (2000, p. 52).

25. Quoted in Peters (2000, p. 53).

26. *Minersville,* 310 U.S. at 595.

27. Ibid.

28. Ibid., at 596.

29. Ibid., at 607.

30. See Nussbaum (2008b, ch. 5).

31. Justices Frank Murphy, Hugo Black, and William O. Douglas.

32. Charles Hughes and James McReynolds retired, and were replaced by James Byrnes and Robert Jackson; Jackson had already published a critique of *Minersville.*

33. 319 U.S. 624 (1943).

34. Ibid., at 642.

35. Ibid., at 641.

36. 505 U.S. 577 (1992).

37. Ibid., at 577, 592, 595. Justice Kennedy did not state that coercion is a necessary element of an Establishment Clause violation, but he did focus so intently on coercion that Justices Harry Blackmun, David Souter, Sandra Day O'Connor, and John Paul Stevens wrote or joined concurring opinions insisting that one may still violate the Establishment Clause without coercion. I support their view in Nussbaum (2008b, ch. 6). See also *Elk Grove Unified School District v. Newdow,* 542 U.S. 1 (2004), the abortive case involving the words "under God" in the pledge (which was not decided because the plaintiff was found not to have standing). Justice Clarence Thomas's opinion suggests that even a noncompulsory public recitation of the pledge in schools could be upheld only by denying the incorporation of the Establishment Clause and thus discarding this and numerous other precedents.

38. See Irons (1988, pp. 15–35).

39. Rawls (1971, p. 503).

40. Ibid., p. 494.

41. Ibid., p. 490.

42. Ibid., p. 494.

43. Habermas (1992, pp. 1–19).

44. In his particular case, he has described the way in which, as a member of the Hitler Jugend, though mocked by other boys because of his disability, he learned to separate himself from the group and to cultivate himself in isolation, reading the works of Kant.

45. For an account of the belated efforts of Weimar social democrats to mobilize public emotion around symbols of freedom and equality in 1932, see Evans (2003). As he tersely comments, "They should have started much much sooner."

46. For the best account of Marcus, see Hadot (1998).

47. Based on the Michael Chase translation in Hadot (1998), with some modifications.

48. It is significant that this adopted child did not, as the movie *Gladiator* shows us, make a principled rational choice of the best man to run the empire. In real life, Marcus chose his worthless son Commodus, tripped up yet once more by the love of the near.

49. Hadot (1998).

50. For further discussion of Stoicism in the context of political emotion, see Nussbaum (2003).

51. See also the valuable argument in Miller (1995).

52. This section of the paper is closely related to the argument in the last section of Nussbaum (2007b), which does not, however, focus on an idea of the nation; its reading of King consequently emphasizes different points.

53. Chernow (2010).

54. In her drama *The Adulateur,* written at the time of the Boston Tea Party, she represents the British as decadent monarchs, and the Americans as republican Romans; Brutus is her hero.

55. Chernow (2010, pp. 435–436).

56. Ibid.

57. Ibid., p. 549.

58. Ibid.

59. Ibid., p. 566.

60. Ibid., pp. 584–585.

61. See Griswold (1986). At the dedication, Robert Winthrop's oration mentioned both the theme of unity in diversity and the absence of "vainglorious" symbols. Quoted in ibid., p. 716n9.

62. For an excellent discussion, see Rybczynski (2012).

63. A panel that included Eisenhower's son David chose four leading architects to submit designs. Gehry's design was reviewed by the National Commission of Fine Arts (of which Rybczynski is a member).

64. The statue was dedicated on August 15, 1967, under the auspices of Mayor Richard J. Daley, and was commissioned in 1963 by the architects of the Richard J. Daley Center.

65. I cite the speech in what is known as the "Bliss Text," which has a good claim to be Lincoln's final version. For the different versions and their claims, see Wills (1992, pp. 18, 191–203, 261–263).

66. Wills (1992) provides an exhaustive study of Lincoln's rhetorical devices and his rhetorical learning. Lincoln's rhetoric is also well studied by the essays in Samuels (2012). For more on the Gettysburg Address and the Second Inaugural Address, see Cushman (2012).

67. Wills (1992, pp. 41–62, 148–175).

68. This is the overall thesis of Wills's book. For discussion of Lincoln's deployment of patterns of imagery of birth and death, see ibid., p. 62 (alluding to poet Robert Lowell's emphasis on these images). See also ibid., pp. 78, 86, 172.

69. See Cushman (2012, p. 62).
70. See Wills (1992, especially pp. 145–174); Cushman (2012, p. 63).
71. Cushman (2012, pp. 61, 65).
72. See Wills (1992, p. 145).
73. See Nussbaum (2012d).
74. See Cushman (2012, pp. 68–69).
75. See ibid., p. 70 (focusing particularly on a section I have not cited above: "Fondly do we hope—/fervently do we pray—/that this mighty scourge of war/may speedily pass away."
76. See Nussbaum (2007a, chs. 5–6).
77. The only regions not listed are the former princely states, since it was not clear at that time that they would be included in the future nation. Since Sindh is now part of Pakistan, some politicians sought to change that word to "Kashmir," but the Supreme Court ruled against them, saying that Sindh can be understood metaphorically.
78. See the discussion in Nussbaum (2007a, ch. 5). The documentary film *The Boy in a Branch* by Lalit Vachani shows how an exclusionary and submissive patriotism is taught to children in RSS *shakhas*. I return to this topic in the next section.
79. See the conversation with C. F. Andrews on this topic quoted in Mohandas Gandhi (1976, pp. 12–13), and quoted in Nussbaum (2007a, p. 105).
80. Rajmohan Gandhi (2007, pp. 556–557).
81. Ibid., p. 557.
82. Erikson (1969, p. 122).
83. Amita Sen (1999). The poem is cited only in the original Bengali edition.
84. See Rajmohan Gandhi (2007, pp. 303–311).
85. Quoted in ibid., p. 303.
86. Quoted in ibid., p. 308–309.
87. See ibid., pp. 313–316.
88. See Amita Sen (1999).
89. See the transcript in Wills (1992, p. 261), which mentions six occasions of applause in the very brief speech, the last being "Long continued applause."
90. The speech can be heard in recorded form on several CDs available at the Nehru Memorial Museum and Library.
91. See Brown (2003, p. 191).
92. Ibid.
93. Ibid., p. 192.
94. See Nussbaum (1997); Nussbaum (2010c); Nussbaum (2012b).
95. See Nussbaum (2010c).
96. "Smithsonian Alters Plans for Its Exhibit on Hiroshima," *New York Times*. August 30, 1994. Available online at www.nytimes.com/1994/08/30/us/smithsonian-alters -plans-for-its-exhibit-on-hiroshima-bomb.html.
97. Bird and Sherwin (1995).
98. See Nanda (2003). On the California schools controversy, see Nussbaum (2007a, ch. 9).
99. Sarkar (2003, p. 159).

9. Tragic and Comic Festivals

1. In this chapter, I draw on the following previously published papers of mine: "The 'Morality of Pity': Sophocles' *Philoctetes*," Nussbaum (2008c); "The Comic Soul: Or, This Phallus That Is Not One," Nussbaum (2005); "The Costs of Tragedy: Some Moral Limits of Cost-Benefit Analysis," Nussbaum (2000a); "Bernard Williams: Tragedies, Hope, Justice," Nussbaum (2009a); and "Radical Evil in the Lockean State," Nussbaum (2006b), a longer version of which was published as "Radical Evil in Liberal Democracies: The Neglect of the Political Emotions," Nussbaum (2007b).

2. All translations from the *Philoctetes* and *Acharnians* are my own, except where otherwise noted.

3. *Acharnians,* lines 1215–20. Cf. lines 1085 ff. (where Dikaiopolis prepares for a feast while Lamachus prepares for battle).

4. Thus Erich Segal (2001) goes badly wrong when he argues that the comic emphasis on erections signifies the victory of manly aggression. As I argue in Nussbaum (2005), for the Greeks a visible erection symbolizes lack of self-control and an over-indulgence in pleasure. The manly man is expected to have a clear plan of sexual control and release, so that he is never at the mercy of his appetites.

5. One famous vase shows chorus actors removing bearded masks to show beardless faces underneath.

6. One place to see this is in Aristophanes's *Frogs,* where Dionysus, the presiding deity of these festivals, goes to Hades to bring back one poet to advise the city. Even though this is comedy, it would not work as such if the idea of gaining advice were not itself serious.

7. Tagore translated Shakespeare's *Macbeth* into Bengali at the age of ten. I find wide familiarity with the well-known Greek tragedies in many developing nations, and one can see their structural influence in countless works of world literature.

8. See Chapter 5.

9. In Nussbaum (2008c), I discuss earlier philosophical reflections about the play in writings of Lessing and other Enlightenment thinkers.

10. See Clark (1997, p. 83); Nussbaum (2001, ch. 6).

11. This observation was made by Lessing ([1766] 1962) in his wonderful treatment of the play in *Laocoon.*

12. For similar reflections, see Rousseau ([1762] 1979, p. 224).

13. The type of generalization tragedy performs is thus extremely unlikely to trade in stereotypes that stigmatize groups on grounds of ethnicity, race, gender, or disability—although in a particular play this may of course happen. Still, the accent on universal human vulnerability helps most such works avoid that error, and it also contributes to undoing that error in the surrounding society.

14. Schopenhauer holds that tragedy, by showing us the horrors of existence, generates metaphysical resignation of the will to live; a surprisingly similar position is taken by Bernard Williams ([1996] 2006). For my critique, see Nussbaum (2009a).

15. I have written extensively about these predicaments in Nussbaum (1986, chs. 2–3), Nussbaum (1989), and Nussbaum (1990, especially the essay "Flawed Crystals").

For a detailed account of the tragic dilemmas in Aeschylus's *Agamemnon* and *Seven Against Thebes* and in Sophocles' *Antigone,* with many references both to scholarship on those works and to the contemporary philosophical literature on moral dilemmas, see Nussbaum (1986). For the contemporary philosophical literature that I have found most helpful, see Marcus (1980); Williams (1993a); Searle (1980); Stocker (1990); Walzer (1973).

16. *Mahabharata* (c. 3rd century BCE). This passage is quoted from the translation by Chakravarthi V. Narasimhan (New York: Columbia University Press, 1965), which translates only selections from the work, but renders fully those passages it does select (whereas many shortened translations are also reworkings). Van Buitenen's definitive unedited translation remains incomplete because of his death, and did not progress as far as this passage. The passage cited is from Book 6, ch. 23.

17. In the passage that has since become famous as the *Bhagavad-Gita,* Krishna advises Arjuna that he has "a right to action alone, but not to the fruits of action." Consequences should not be taken into account at all in choosing a course of conduct. "[M]en attain the highest good by doing work without attachment to its results."

18. The limitations of cost-benefit analysis in tragic contexts are discussed, in this connection, in Nussbaum (2000a).

19. Indeed, we might say that the main importance of reparations too is expressive. Obviously the fact that my grandmother-in-law received a regular income from the German government did nothing to bring back the family members who had perished during the Holocaust. Although the financial support was not negligible, its primary significance was as a public expression of wrongdoing and the determination to do things differently in the future.

20. My interpretation is defended with a lot of textual detail and full discussion of the scholarly literature in Nussbaum (1986, ch. 3).

21. Hegel (1975, pp. 68, 71).

22. For my own discussion of the cases, see Nussbaum (2008b, ch. 4).

23. The Greeks objected intensely to eating in public. The name Cynics, "doggy ones," was given to philosophers of that school because they ate their meals in the marketplace, something only a dog would do. Censoring the Cynic philosopher Diogenes, the ancient biographer says, "He used to do everything in public, the works of Demeter and of Aphrodite"—in other words, public eating and public sex. No mention is ever made of public urination or defecation in the stories told of the Cynics— very likely because that was not considered unacceptable in a culture with no indoor plumbing.

24. See my discussion of Plato's *Symposium* in Nussbaum (1986, ch. 6).

25. See my longer treatment of Aristophanes in Nussbaum (2005).

26. I once acted with the late Bert Lahr in Aristophanes' *Birds* in a professional repertory theater in Michigan. Lahr, worried about losing his TV commercial contracts for Lay's potato chips, bowdlerized the script.

27. The novel was compared to "secret sewers of vice," and much was made of its allegedly disgusting character. See Nussbaum (2004a, ch. 3).

28. All translations from the *Lysistrata* are my own.

29. The play was produced two years after the end of the disastrous Sicilian Expedition.

30. This is well argued by Foucault (1984).
31. See Jeffrey Henderson's (1987) commentary on line 1289.
32. *Lysistrata,* line 1321. Athena is named in a gloss in one of the manuscripts, and is a logical way of interpreting the periphrasis *tan pammachon sian.*
33. I am grateful to an unpublished paper by Bill Watson on this topic.
34. Dauber (1999); Dauber (2003). See also her major book on this topic, *The Sympathetic State: Disaster Relief and the Origins of the American Welfare State,* Dauber (2013).
35. See Dauber (2013, pp. 90 ff.).
36. See Clark (1997).
37. See Dauber (2013, ch. 4).
38. Dauber (2013, p. 90) ("The photographers were 'carefully self-censoring' and focused on subjects that depicted blameless victimization by larger forces and the potential for progressive social policy to aid society").
39. See Dauber (2013, p. 91).
40. All quotations are taken from Dauber (2003, ch. 4), unless otherwise noted. For a substantially similar discussion, see Dauber (2013, ch. 4).
41. I am grateful to unpublished work by Moran Sadeh on this issue.
42. My interpretation has been influenced by two excellent philosophical essays: Danto (1987) and Griswold (1986).
43. At the dedication ceremony, Robert Winthrop's oration mentioned both the theme of unity out of diversity and the absence of "vainglorious words." Quoted in Griswold (1986, p. 716n9).
44. See Danto (1987, p. 114).
45. *U.S. News and World Report,* November 21, 1983, p. 68, quoted in Griswold (1986, p. 718).
46. See Griswold (1986, p. 705).
47. See Danto (1987).
48. Here I agree with Griswold (1986, p. 711).
49. Griswold suggests that the questioning is fundamentally detached and nonemotional; that just seems wrong.
50. Danto (1987, p. 117). His article ends, fittingly, with two names of people unknown to him that caught his attention.
51. As Griswold (1986) notes, usually such a list of names would be on a memorial in the soldiers' hometown, not one at the heart of the nation's capital.
52. I owe my knowledge of these to Rachel Nussbaum Wichert.
53. Wright ([1940] 1991, pp. 79–80).
54. Translated from the Bengali in Tagore (1990).
55. See the discussion of this story in relation to Greek tragedy in Nussbaum (2009a).
56. "When Lilacs Last in the Dooryard Bloom'd," sec. 12, lines 89–90, in Whitman ([1855] 1973). Another great New York poem is "A Broadway Pageant," which depicts a parade celebrating a treaty between the United States and Japan, and, as the poet imagines himself blending into the dense and diverse crowd to watch the Japanese visitors, New York becomes a symbol of the whole nation: "Superb-faced Manhattan!/Comrade Americanos! To us, then at last the Orient came."

57. "Chicago," in Sandburg ([1916] 1994).
58. See Erik Larson's (2003) *The Devil in the White City,* a popular thriller that contains a very impressive amount of architectural history, and uses it to fine effect.
59. Daley crafted a public-private partnership to fund the park, using the appeal of Gehry's potential contribution to stimulate donors.
60. Actually to two Hindus: his first marriage, to Reena Dutta, ended in 2002, and he married Kiran Rao in 2005; Rao was an assistant director of *Lagaan.*
61. I owe this observation to Dipesh Chakrabarty.
62. For a wonderful collection of such materials in the context of World War I, see Fussell (1975, especially ch. 1).
63. My attention was drawn to Mauldin by an unpublished seminar paper by Jeffrey Israel, to whose ideas I am indebted (although the parallel to the ancient comic festivals is my own).
64. For many of the cartoons, see billmauldin.com, and the Library of Congress tribute at www.loc.gov/rr/print/swann/mauldin. Many other websites display the cartoons.
65. Mauldin (1972).
66. See Mauldin (1944).
67. Ibid., p. 209.
68. See the short biography of Mauldin, available online at www.spartacus.schoolnet .co.uk/ARTmauldin.htm.
69. Mauldin (1944, p. 303).
70. Ibid., p. 95.
71. Ibid., p. 133.
72. Ibid., p. 113.
73. Ibid., p. 114.
74. Ibid., p. 229.
75. Ibid., p. 232.
76. Ibid., p. 118.
77. Ibid., p. 376.
78. Ibid., p. 378.
79. Ibid., p. 374.
80. Available online at www.oldhickory30th.com/Photo%20Page%203.htm. The cartoon can also be found using a Google image search for "Mauldin."
81. Cohen (1999).
82. Bruce is the subject of a fine chapter in Jeff Israel's dissertation, unpublished.
83. See Rybczynski (2012) (arguing that it ought to remain rare).

10. Compassion's Enemies

1. See Arendt (1959). For a useful discussion of Arendt's work, see Allen (2004, ch. 3).
2. See my discussion of Batson in Chapter 6.
3. Consider the "availability heuristic." For a discussion about the heuristic and risk assessment, with references to the psychological literature, see Sunstein (2002, pp. 33–35).
4. See my discussion in Chapter 10.

5. See my discussion of these cases in Chapter 9 and Chapter 10.

6. See Sajó (2011, ch. 3).

7. For a longer account of fear research and Aristotle's analysis, see Nussbaum (2012a, ch. 2).

8. Is fear common to all vertebrates? I have made only the narrower claim that it is common to all mammals, for which there is experimental evidence; there is little evidence for fish, reptiles, and amphibians, though somewhat more for birds.

9. See LeDoux (1993); LeDoux (1994); LeDoux (1996).

10. Aristotle discusses fear in *Rhetoric* II.5; this is my own analytical summary of his discussion, adding the contemporary example of new ethnic groups. For more detail, see Nussbaum (2012a, ch. 2).

11. The speech was delivered on March 4, 1933, and is available online at www.bartleby .com/124/pres49.html.

12. Adiga (2008, p. 99). The street names are real, and they show that the British did attempt to show respect for Delhi's Mughal history, by naming streets after Aurangzeb and Humayoun, but when they ran out of Indian names they knew, they simply went for any other name they happened to know, even if it had no connection at all to India.

13. See Dalrymple (2006); Hasan (2011). For a terrific multiauthor collection on Delhi, see Losty (2012) (the Zauq verse is translated on p. 89).

14. Jacobs (1961). See also Rybczynski (2010, ch. 3).

15. Jacobs (1961, p. vii).

16. Quite a few can be seen in Losty (2012).

17. Quoted and translated in Hasan (2011).

18. Quoted in Losty (2012, p. 142).

19. See also Dalrymple (2002).

20. Quoted in Losty (2012, p. 143).

21. Irving (1981).

22. I am indebted here to the analysis of awe and wonder in a paper in progress by Bill Watson, J.D. candidate, University of Chicago.

23. Quoted in Losty (2012, p. 203).

24. Quoted in ibid., p. 139.

25. See Nussbaum (2009b).

26. Wright ([1940] 1991, p. 70). See also my discussion of *Native Son* in Chapter 10.

27. Quoted in Pridmore (2006, pp. x–xi).

28. Printed in the *Chicago Herald* and quoted in Goodspeed ([1916] 1972, p. 421).

29. Pridmore (2006, p. 2).

30. For a good account of the integration of the school, including the Despreses' role, see Harms and DePencier (1996).

31. Ibid.

32. Staples (1987).

33. University of Chicago Publications Office (1991, pp. 109–110).

34. For discussion of the proposed move to Wisconsin or suburban DuPage County, see ibid. For the proposed move to Aspen, see McHeill (1991, pp. 166–167). The reasons cited for moving were a drop in applications that occurred in the early 1950s and

difficulty in faculty recruitment. See University of Chicago Library (1992, p. 17). Even the decision to remain was expressed with an unbecoming air of superiority: President Lawrence Kimpton spoke of the university's duty "to act rationally and educate the community of which it is an integral part." Quoted in ibid.

35. Woodlawn leaders also supported the removal of the train that went along 63rd Street to the university, because the elevated tracks darkened the area beneath, so this issue is unclear. A cable car along Cottage Grove was also removed. The role of the university in these developments remains unclear and a matter of legend.

36. If one compares the words of the original alma mater with the version currently sung, one notes how unwelcome women too were in those monastic precincts, although they were present as students from the start: instead of "her whose daughters and whose sons," the original version reads, "her who owns us as her sons." See University of Chicago Undergraduate Council (1921).

37. The Ferris wheel, designed by Len Ferris, was 300 feet tall, and was at that time the largest structure in North America; individual cars were large enough to hold weddings inside them! Planned to be America's riposte to the Eiffel Tower, a highlight of the Paris World's Fair, the wheel was a central part of the exposition; the Wild West Show was a more informal adjunct, outside the fair's official parameters. See Larson (2003), a book in fictional form, but with accurate historical details.

38. Kamin (2011).

39. Sennett (2004). Richard Sennett, a white man who grew up in the infamous Cabrini Green housing project, describes with sympathy the complex thinking underlying the projects and the reasons for their failure.

40. For coverage in the *University of Chicago Chronicle,* see http://chronicle.uchicago .edu/040401/cityspace.shtml. For coverage in the *Hyde Park Herald,* see www.hyd epark.org/hpkcc/comrenewconf.htm#herald.

41. For an evaluation of the building and the plan, see Kent (2012).

42. I say "associated with" because the views of Hutchins and Dewey actually differ far less than their frequently heated rhetoric suggests: Hutchins too thought about contemporary events, and Dewey too thought that we could learn from the past.

43. This change can be seen in the Palevsky Commons dormitories (2003), by Ricardo Legorreta, with their use of brick and bright pastels; in the new Ratner Gym (2003) by César Pelli, with its off-center shape and soaring pylons, which playfully refer to Gothic towers, but in what we might call an off-center "Baul" spirit; and in the stunning glass and steel of Rafael Viñoly's Booth School building (2004), which refers to both the Gothic spire of nearby Rockefeller Chapel and to Frank Lloyd Wright's adjacent Robie House—a great but utterly non-Gothic building that was almost demolished twice at the initiative of the Chicago Theological Seminary, while the university conspicuously did nothing to prevent it. The demolition was foiled only by a combination of international protest and the intervention of the city. Wright himself, then ninety, commented, "It just shows the danger of entrusting anything spiritual to the clergy." Quoted in Hoffman (1984, p. 94).

44. See Kamin (2011).

45. Quoted in Kamin (2011). I note that Kamin's review made one criticism: a third bridge is needed at Dorchester. This bridge has now been built, another sign of dialogue.

46. See Lazarus (2001, p. 254).

47. And it often involves an idea of exclusivity. See Ortony, Clore, and Collins (1988, pp. 100–101).

48. See Lazarus (2001, pp. 254–255).

49. Miceli and Castelfranchi (2007).

50. See ibid., p. 456. For a valuable summary of the psychological literature, see Protasi (2012).

51. This distinction is drawn by many, including Miceli and Castelfranchi (2007, pp. 461–465), but the best discussion, which they follow, is in Rawls (1971, pp. 530–534).

52. Rawls (1971, p. 533).

53. Ibid.

54. See Miceli and Castelfranchi (2007, p. 464).

55. Rawls (1971, p. 532).

56. Ibid., pp. 534–537.

57. In a poignant passage shortly before the discussion of envy, he acknowledges that inequality is a natural outgrowth of the institution of the family. "Is the family to be abolished then? Taken by itself and given a certain primacy, the idea of equal opportunity inclines in this direction." Ibid., p. 511.

58. Ibid., p. 536.

59. Ibid., p. 537.

60. One can of course envy advantages that accrue to those generally less prosperous than oneself, if one sees them as things that would be one's own but for government policies.

61. See my discussion of Mauldin in Chapter 10. Eisenhower recognized the importance of Mauldin's affirmation of the work of ordinary soldiers, which helped to alleviate the military problem of envy.

62. For a fine treatment of the speech, its background, and the whole issue of social and economic rights in America, see Sunstein (2004).

63. For a discussion of the debate about this phrase and Roosevelt's insistence on it, see ibid., p. 83.

64. Quoted in ibid., pp. 90–91.

65. See ibid., pp. 94–95.

66. This view was not entirely new even in America: many elements of the program were part of the Free Soil movement, and had even been used against Roosevelt by the Left. Characteristically, he appropriates key aspects of the program of the opposition—in conjunction with a resonant reaffirmation of American liberalism.

67. This phrase is quoted from a 1762 English property case: *Vernon v. Bethell,* 28 Eng. Rep. 838 (1762). Roosevelt had used it before.

68. See Wood (2010).

69. *San Antonio Independent School District v. Rodriguez,* 411 U.S. 1 (1973). Justice Marshall wrote the famous dissent.

70. A statement by Roosevelt, quoted in Sunstein (2004, p. 94).

71. The Gandhi papers, vol. 94, p. 148, quoted in Rajmohan Gandhi (2007, p. 191).

72. Nehru ([1936] 1985, p. 20).

73. Ibid., p. 65. Congress is the political movement of which Gandhi and the Nehrus were leaders, the ancestor of today's Congress Party. *Khadi* means "homespun."

74. Gandhi was more constant in his attitude to class privilege than in his attitude to caste. Though always repudiating untouchability, he sometimes defended caste separations as a valuable occupation-based division of labor that need not be stigmatizing, and he differed sharply from Ambedkar, who wanted a much more radical transformation of Hinduism and would not have been unhappy to have seen the end of Hinduism (see later in this chapter). For one good treatment of Gandhi and caste, see Lelyveld (2011).

75. Brown (2003, p. 59).

76. Ibid., p. 60.

77. Nehru ([1936] 1985, p. 52).

78. Brown (2003, p. 60).

79. Nehru ([1936] 1985, pp. 510–511).

80. See Brown (2003, p. 60). Of course this was useful only in some regions—the initial peasant movement being in Uttar Pradesh. So far as I am aware, Nehru did not learn Gandhi's native language (Gujarati), although he probably knew some Bengali, since he sent Indira to school in Santiniketan, where education was primarily in that language. All three languages are closely related, but no more mutually intelligible than the diverse Romance languages.

81. Nehru ([1936] 1985, p. 46).

82. Nehru so trusted Gandhi in personal matters that he even suggested (from prison) that his daughter Indira consult Gandhi on her impending marriage to Feroze Gandhi—evidently feeling that his capacity for empathy extended to a passionate young woman's deliberation about marital life. (Feroze Gandhi was not related in any way to Mohandas Gandhi; in fact, he was a Parsi from Mumbai. The marriage was not happy, although it lasted until his death in 1960. For an excellent treatment of it, see Frank (2002).)

83. See my discussion in Chapter 9.

84. Although easy accessibility for many of the poor would await the construction of suitable public transportation, we should not forget how far people routinely walked in a day. David Copperfield thinks nothing of a walk from Covent Garden to Steerforth's home in Highgate, a distance of five miles each way, and Bob Crachit walks back and forth each day from Camden Town to Scrooge's office in the City, a distance of around four miles each way. These are unremarkable walks. Bob would have reached Regent's Park in under one mile.

85. Olmsted, "The People's Park at Birkenhead, near Liverpool," *The Horticulturalist,* May 1851, p. 225, quoted in Rybczynski (1999, p. 93). During the same period, Olmsted spent time in the American South, writing articles that were later published in book form as *The Cotton Kingdom;* he thought the South primitive and less civilized because of slavery and the lack of a common public culture.

86. Olmsted, "The People's Park at Birkenhead, near Liverpool," *The Horticulturalist,* May 1851, p. 225, quoted in Rybczynski (1999, p. 93).

87. Rybczynski (1999, p. 165).

88. Ibid.

89. Ibid., p. 167.

90. Letter to the Board of Commissioners, May 31, 1858, quoted in Rybczynski (1999, p. 174).

91. Ibid.

92. For a much longer discussion of shame, with references to both psychological and philosophical discussions, see Nussbaum (2004a, ch. 6).

93. Goffman (1963, p. 128). Notice that he omits income, another source of stigma that might have made his case stronger still: if the "fully employed" college graduate is working as a dishwasher, he is blushing.

94. See Taylor (1985, ch. 4); Piers and Singer (1953, chs. 1–2).

95. This distinction is not always sharp: I can say, "I'm ashamed of what I did." But where that is not just a loose use of words, it is likely to be an expression of the fact that I see what I did as betraying a weakness that is unworthy of my ideals.

96. For a powerful argument on this subject, see Williams (1993b).

97. For the relationship between shame and embarrassment, see Nussbaum (2004a, pp. 204–206). I argue that embarrassment is always social, as shame is not; it is a lighter matter than shame, and is often felt simply because something is out of place, even when there is no serious failure involved (as, for example, when one feels embarrassment when someone points out that a label in one's garment is hanging out); and it may be felt about something good, if one is not comfortable with other people pointing it out.

98. See Tomkins (1962–1963).

99. For an excellent discussion, see Morrison (1989, pp. 48–49).

100. This is a central theme of Rousseau's *Emile* ([1762] 1979): aristocrats are like big babies, who can't do anything for themselves, and therefore have to make slaves of others; young Emile will learn to fend for himself.

101. In 2012, the university dedicated a statue of Ambedkar on the campus and inaugurated the Dr. B. R. Ambedkar Chair in Indian Constitutional Law at the Law School. The first such lectures were given in 2012 by Ramachandra Guha, certainly an interesting thinker, but definitely upper-caste, which is a choice that seems problematic in the light of Ambedkar's own views about "sayings and doings."

102. See Ambedkar's (1993b) fascinating if quixotic essay, "Which Is Worse? Slavery or Untouchability?" The essay includes extended comparisons between untouchability and both Roman and U.S. slavery.

103. Ambedkar (1993a).

104. Ibid., pp. 670–671.

105. For a fine collection of the most important statements of this extremely prolific writer, see Ambedkar (2008). One of the editors of this volume, Sukhadeo Thorat, is a *dalit* who has written eloquently of the stigma and exclusion he himself suffered and is the former head of the University Grants Commission and a professor of economics at Jawaharlal Nehru University.

106. Quoted in Ambedkar (2008, pp. 319–320).

107. Ambedkar (2008, p. 217).

108. Ibid., p. 229.

109. Ibid., pp. 206–234.

110. Ibid., pp. 228–231.

111. See ibid., p. 176, quoting a report of 1932: "To the question what is the population of the Untouchables the replies received were enough to stagger anybody. Witness after witness came forward to say that the Untouchables in his Province were infinitesimally small. There were not wanting witnesses who said that there were no Untouchables at all!! It was a most extraordinary sight to see Hindu witnesses perjuring themselves regardless of truth by denying the existence of the Untouchables or by reducing their number to a negligible figure. The members of the Provincial Franchise Committee were also a party to this plan."

112. This is true even of the Communist parties: the West Bengal Communists are run by a very elite upper-caste group.

113. Parthasarathy (2012).

114. I have addressed these questions at greater length in Nussbaum (2006a, chs. 2–3) and Nussbaum (2004a, ch. 5).

115. Several U.S. cities had such laws. Chicago's 1911 ordinance, which forbade people "deformed so as to be an unsightly or disgusting object" from appearing "in or on the public ways or other public places in the city," was not repealed until 1974. (The maximum penalty was fifty dollars for each offense.)

116. TenBroek (1966).

117. Quoted in Sunstein (2004, p. 93) (Sunstein is, in turn, quoting Schlesinger 2003, p. 406).

118. See Martin (2009).

119. Ibid.

120. This project was initially not well executed: some of the Braille was mounted too high for people of average height to reach it!

121. Martin (2009) (quoting a 1997 NPR interview with Halprin).

122. Quoted in Sullivan (2009).

11. How Love Matters for Justice

1. See my discussion of political liberalism in Chapter 5. See also Nussbaum (2011b).

2. See Thaler and Sunstein (2009).

3. Murdoch (1970, pp. 17–23).

References

Adiga, Aravind. 2008. *The White Tiger.* New York: Free Press.

Adorno, Theodor. 1950. *The Authoritarian Personality.* New York: Harper and Row.

Allanbrook, Wye Jamison. 1983. *Rhythmic Gesture in Mozart:* Le Nozze di Figaro *and* Don Giovanni. Chicago: University of Chicago Press.

Allen, Danielle. 2004. *Talking to Strangers: Anxieties of Citizenship since* Brown v. Board of Education. Chicago: University of Chicago Press.

Ambedkar, B. R. 1993a. "Waiting for a Visa." In *Dr. Babasaheb Ambedkar, Writings and Speeches,* vol. 12. Bombay: Education Department, Government of Maharashtra, 664–691.

———. 1993b. "Which Is Worse? Slavery or Untouchability?" In Ambedkar, *Writings and Speeches,* vol. 12, 741–759.

———. 2008. *Perspectives on Social Exclusion and Inclusive Policies.* Edited by Sukhadeo Thorat and Narender Kumar. Delhi: Oxford University Press.

Arendt, Hannah. 1959. "Reflections on Little Rock." *Dissent,* Winter, 47–58.

Asch, Solomon. 1955. "Opinions and Social Pressure." Panarchy. Accessed October 2, 2012. http://panarchy.org/asch/social.pressure.1955.html.

Bagchi, Jasodhara. 2003. "*Anandamath* and *The Home and the World:* Positivism Reconfigured." In *Rabindranath Tagore's The Home and the World: A Critical Companion,* edited by P. K. Datta. Delhi: Permanent Black, 174–186.

Bardhan, Kalpana, ed. and trans. 1990. *Of Women, Outcastes, Peasants, and Rebels: A Selection of Bengali Short Stories.* Berkeley: University of California Press.

Barshack, Lior. 2008. "The Sovereignty of Pleasure: Sexual and Political Freedom in the Operas of Mozart and Da Ponte." *Law and Literature* 20, 47–67.

Batson, Daniel C. 1991. *The Altruism Question: Toward a Social-Psychological Answer.* Hillsdale, NJ: Lawrence Erlbaum.

———. 2009. "These Things Called Empathy." In *The Social Neuroscience of Empathy,* edited by Jean Decety and William Ickes. Cambridge, MA: MIT Press, 3–16.

———. 2011. *Altruism in Humans.* New York: Oxford University Press.

Beaumarchais, Pierre. (1785) 1992. *Le Mariage de Figaro.* Edited by Malcolm Cook. Reprint, Bristol: Bristol Classical Press.

Bird, Kai, and Martin Sherwin. 1995. "The Historians' Letter to the Smithsonian." www .doug-long.com.

Blass, Thomas, ed. 2000a. *Obedience to Authority: Current Perspectives on the Milgram Paradigm.* Mahwah, NJ: Lawrence Erlbaum Associates.

———. 2000b. "The Milgram Paradigm after 35 Years: Some Things We Now Know about Obedience to Authority." In *Obedience to Authority,* edited by Thomas Blass, 35–59.

Bloom, Paul. 2004. *Descartes' Baby: How the Science of Child Development Explains What Makes Us Human.* New York: Basic Books.

———. 2010. "The Moral Life of Babies." *New York Times Magazine.* May 5.

Brown, Judith. 2003. *Nehru: A Political Life.* New Haven, CT: Yale University Press.

Browning, Christopher. 1992. *Ordinary Men: Reserve Police Battalion 101 and the Final Solution in Poland.* New York: HarperPerennial.

Capwell, Charles. 1986. *The Music of the Bauls of West Bengal.* Kent, OH: Kent State University Press.

Carlin, John. 2008. *Playing the Enemy: Nelson Mandela and the Game That Made a Nation.* New York: Penguin.

Carter, Tim. 1987. *W. A. Mozart:* Le Nozze di Figaro. New York: Cambridge University Press.

Chernow, Ron. 2010. *Washington: A Life.* New York: Penguin.

Clark, Candace. 1997. *Misery and Company: Sympathy in Everyday Life.* Chicago: University of Chicago Press.

Cohen, Ted. 1999. *Jokes: Philosophical Thoughts on Joking Matters.* Chicago: University of Chicago Press.

Comte, Auguste. (1865) 1957. *A General View of Positivism.* Translated by J. H. Bridges. Reprint, New York: Robert Speller.

Congreve, Richard. (1857) 1874. "India." In *Essays: Political, Social, Religious,* vol. 1. London: Longmans, Green and Co., 67–106.

Cushman, Stephen. 2012. "Lincoln's Gettysburg Address and Second Inaugural Address." In *The Cambridge Companion to Abraham Lincoln,* edited by Shirley Samuels. New York: Cambridge University Press, 59–71.

Dalrymple, William. 2002. *White Mughals.* London: Penguin.

———. 2004. "The Song of the Holy Fool." *Guardian.* February 7.

———. 2006. *The Last Mughal: The Fall of a Dynasty, Delhi 1857.* London: Bloomsbury.

———. (2009) 2011. *Nine Lives: In Search of the Sacred in Modern India.* Reprint, New York: Vintage.

Danto, Arthur. 1987. "The Vietnam Veterans Memorial." In *The State of the Art.* New York: Prentice Hall, 112–117.

Darnton, Robert. 1997. *The Forbidden Best-Sellers of Pre-Revolutionary France.* New York: Harper Collins.

Dauber, Michele Landis. 1999. "Fate, Responsibility, and 'Natural' Disaster Relief: Narrating the American Welfare State." *Law and Society Review* 33, 257–318.

———. 2003. *Helping Ourselves: Disaster Relief and the Origins of the American Welfare State.* Ph.D. dissertation, Northwestern University.

———. 2013. *The Sympathetic State: Disaster Relief and the Origins of the American Welfare State.* Chicago: University of Chicago Press.

Decety, Jean, ed. 2012. *Empathy: From Bench to Bedside.* Cambridge, MA: MIT Press.

Decety, Jean, and Daniel C. Batson. 2009. "Empathy and Morality: Integrating Social and Neuroscience Approaches." In *The Moral Brain: Essays on the Evolution and Neuroscientific Aspects of Morality,* edited by Jan Verplaetse, Jelle De Schrijver, Sven Vanneste, and Johan Braeckman. Berlin: Springer Verlag, 109–127.

Decety, Jean, and William Ickes, eds. 2009. *The Social Neuroscience of Empathy.* Cambridge, MA: MIT Press.

de Waal, F. B. M. 1996. *Good Natured: The Origins of Right and Wrong in Humans and Other Animals.* Cambridge, MA: Harvard University Press.

———. 2006. *Primates and Philosophers: How Morality Evolved.* Princeton, NJ: Princeton University Press.

Deigh, John. 2004. "Nussbaum's Account of Compassion." *Philosophy and Phenomenological Research* 68, 465–472.

Devlin, Patrick. (1959) 1965. *The Enforcement of Morals.* Reprint, London and New York: Oxford University Press.

Dimock, Edward C., Jr. 1959. "Rabindranath Tagore— 'The Greatest of the Bauls of Bengal.'" *Journal of Asian Studies* 19, 33–51.

Durr, Virginia Foster. 1986. *Outside the Magic Circle: The Autobiography of Virginia Foster Durr.* Edited by Hollinger F. Barnard. Tuscaloosa: University of Alabama Press.

Dutta, Krishna, and Andrew Robinson. 1995. *Rabindranath Tagore: The Myriad-Minded Man.* London: Bloomsbury.

Ellis, Richard J. 2005. *To the Flag: The Unlikely History of the Pledge of Allegiance.* Lawrence: University Press of Kansas.

Epstein, Richard. 1992. *Forbidden Grounds: The Case against Employment Discrimination Laws.* Cambridge, MA: Harvard University Press.

———. 2010. "Rand Paul's Wrong Answer." *Forbes.* May 24.

Erikson, Erik H. 1969. *Gandhi's Truth: On the Origins of Militant Nonviolence.* New York: Norton.

Evans, Richard. 2003. *The Coming of the Third Reich.* London: Allen Lane.

Explore Chicago. 2012. "The Statue of the Republic." Accessed November 1, 2012. www .explorechicago.org/city/en/things_see_do/attractions/park_district/statue_of_the _republic.html.

Fichte, Johann Gottlieb. (1808) 2009. *Addresses to the German Nation.* Edited by Gregory Moore. Reprint, New York and Cambridge: Cambridge University Press.

Foucault, Michel. 1984. "The Use of Pleasures." In *History of Sexuality,* translated by Robert Hurley, vol. 2. New York: Pantheon.

Frank, Katherine. 2002. *Indira: The Life of Indira Nehru Gandhi.* Boston: Houghton Mifflin.

Fussell, Paul. 1975. *The Great War and Modern Memory*. New York and Oxford: Oxford University Press.

Gandhi, Mohandas. (1925) 1993. *An Autobiography: The Story of My Experiments with Truth*. Translated by Mahadev Desai. Reprint, Boston: Beacon Press.

———. 1956. *The Gandhi Reader: A Sourcebook of His Life and Writings*, edited by Homer A. Jack. New York: AMS Press. For "Mrs. Sanger's Version," see 306–307.

———. 1976. *Romain Rolland and Gandhi Correspondence*. New Delhi: Government of India.

Gandhi, Rajmohan. 2007. *Gandhi: The Man, His People, and the Empire*. Berkeley: University of California Press.

Glover, Jonathan. 1999. *Humanity: A Moral History of the Twentieth Century*. London: Jonathan Cape.

Goffman, Erving. 1963. *Stigma: Notes on the Management of Spoiled Identity*. New York: Simon and Schuster.

Goodspeed, Thomas Wakefield. (1916) 1972. *A History of the University of Chicago: The First Quarter-Century*. Reprint, Chicago: University of Chicago Press.

Griswold, Charles. 1986. "The Vietnam Veterans Memorial and the Washington Mall: Philosophical Reflections on Political Iconography." *Critical Inquiry* 12, 688–719.

Habermas, Jürgen. 1992. "Citizenship and National Identity: Some Reflections on the Future of Europe." *Praxis International* 12, 1–19.

Hadot, Pierre. 1998. *The Inner Citadel*. Translated by Michael Chase. Cambridge, MA: Harvard University Press.

Harms, William, and Ida DePencier. 1996. *Experiencing Education: 100 Years of Learning at the University of Chicago Laboratory Schools*. Chicago: University of Chicago Laboratory Schools. Available online at www.ucls.uchicago.edu/about-lab /history/index.aspx.

Hasan, Mushirul, ed. 2006. *The Nehrus: Personal Histories*. London: Mercury Books.

———. 2011. "The Polyphony of the Past." *Tehelka*. Accessed October 4, 2012. www .tehelka.com/story_main51.asp?filename=hub311211Polyphony.asp.

Hatfield, Elaine, John T. Cacioppo, and Richard L. Rapson, eds. 1994. *Emotional Contagion*. Cambridge: Cambridge University Press.

Hauser, Marc. 2000. *Wild Minds: What Animals Really Think*. New York: Henry Holt.

Hegel, G. W. F. 1975. "The Philosophy of Fine Art." Translated by P. B. Osmaston. In *Hegel on Tragedy*, edited by Anne Paolucci and Henry Paolucci, vol. 4. New York: Dover.

Henderson, Jeffrey, ed. 1987. *Aristophanes: Lysistrata*. Oxford: Clarendon Press.

Herder, Johann Gottfried. (1792) 2002. "Letters for the Progress of Humanity." Reprinted in *Herder: Philosophical Writings*, edited and translated by Michael N. Forster. Cambridge: Cambridge University Press, 361–369.

Higgins, Kathleen M. 1990. *The Music of Our Lives*. Philadelphia, PA: Temple University Press.

Hilberg, Raul. (1961) 1985. *The Destruction of the European Jews*. New York: Holmes and Meier.

Hobsbawm, Eric. 1990. *Nations and Nationalism since 1780: Programme, Myth, Reality*. Cambridge: Cambridge University Press.

Hoffman, Donald. 1984. *Frank Lloyd Wright's Robie House: The Illustrated Story of an Architectural Masterpiece.* New York: Dover Publications.

Hunt, Lynn, ed. 1993. *The Invention of Pornography: Obscenity and the Origins of Modernity, 1500–1800.* Cambridge: Zone Books.

Inbar, Y., D. A. Pizarro, and P. Bloom. 2009. "Conservatives Are More Easily Disgusted than Liberals." *Cognition and Emotion* 23, 714–725.

Irons, Peter. 1988. *The Courage of Their Convictions.* New York: Free Press.

Irving, Robert Grant. 1981. *Indian Summer: Lutyens, Baker, and Imperial Delhi.* New Haven, CT: Yale University Press.

Jacobs, Jane. 1961. *The Death and Life of Great American Cities.* New York: Random House.

Kant, Immanuel. (1793) 1998. *Religion within the Boundaries of Mere Reason.* Translated by Allen Wood and George Di Giovanni. Reprint, New York and Cambridge: Cambridge University Press.

Kamin, Blair. 2011. "Right Out of 'Star Wars,' a New Way to Light a Path at U of C." *Chicago Tribune.* March 8.

Kent, Cheryl. 2012. "Logan Center for the Arts Serving Varied Uses with Ease." *Chicago Tribune.* October 17.

Kerman, Joseph. 1956. *Opera as Drama.* Berkeley and Los Angeles: University of California Press.

Kleingeld, Pauline. 1999. "Six Varieties of Cosmopolitanism in Late Eighteenth-Century Germany." *Journal of the History of Ideas* 60, 505–524.

Langford, Dale J., Sara E. Crager, Zarrar Shehzad, et al. 2006. "Social Modulation of Pain as Evidence for Empathy in Mice." *Science* 312, 1967–70.

Larmore, Charles E. 1996. *The Morals of Modernity.* New York: Cambridge University Press.

Larson, Erik. 2003. *The Devil in the White City.* New York: Crown Publishers.

Lazarus, Richard S. 2001. *Emotion and Adaptation.* New York: Oxford University Press.

Lear, Jonathan. 1990. *Love and Its Place in Nature: A Philosophical Interpretation of Freudian Psychoanalysis.* New Haven, CT: Yale University Press.

LeDoux, Joseph E. 1993. "Emotional Memory Systems in the Brain." *Behavioural Brain Research* 58, 69–79.

———. 1994. "Emotion, Memory, and the Brain." *Scientific American* 270, 50–57.

———. 1996. *The Emotional Brain: The Mysterious Underpinnings of Emotional Life.* New York: Simon and Schuster.

Lelyveld, Joseph. 2011. *Great Soul: Mahatma Gandhi and his Struggle with India.* New York: Knopf.

Lessing, Gotthold Ephraim. (1766) 1962. *Laokoon: oder über die grenzen der malerei und poesie.* Reprint, Paderborn: F. Schoeningh.

Lifton, Robert Jay. 1986. *The Nazi Doctors.* New York: Basic Books.

Locke, John. (1698) 1990. *A Letter Concerning Toleration.* Reprint, Amherst, NY: Prometheus Books.

Losty, J. P., ed. 2012. *Delhi: From Red Fort to Raisina.* Delhi: Roli Books.

Marcus, Ruth Barcan. 1980. "Moral Dilemmas and Consistency." *Journal of Philosophy* 77, 121–136.

Martin, Douglas. 2009. "Lawrence Halprin, Landscape Architect, Dies at 93." *New York Times.* October 28.

Mauldin, Bill. 1944. *Bill Mauldin's Army.* New York: Random House.

———. 1972. *The Brass Ring.* New York: Norton.

Mazzini, Giuseppe. (1846) 2001. *Thoughts upon Democracy in Europe.* Edited and translated by S. Mastellone. Reprint, Florence: Centro Editoriale Toscano.

McHeill, William H. 1991. *Hutchins's University: A Memoir of the University of Chicago, 1929–1950.* Chicago: University of Chicago Press.

Miceli, Maria, and Cristiano Castelfranchi. 2007. "The Envious Mind." *Cognition and Emotion* 21, 449–479.

Milgram, Stanley. (1975) 2009. *Obedience to Authority.* Reprint, New York: HarperPerennial.

Mill, John Stuart. (1848) 1963. "Principles of Political Economy." Reprinted in *The Collected Works of John Stuart Mill,* edited by J. M. Robson, vol. 21. Toronto: University of Toronto Press.

———. (1859) 1956. *On Liberty.* Reprint, Indianapolis: Library of Liberal Arts.

———. (1863) 1987. "Utilitarianism." Reprinted in *Utilitarianism and Other Essays,* edited by Alan Ryan. New York and London: Penguin.

———. (1865) 1891. *Auguste Comte and Positivism.* Reprint, London: Kegan Paul.

———. (1867) 1963. "Inaugural Address Delivered to the University of St. Andrews." Reprinted in Robson, *The Collected Works,* vol. 21. Also available online at http://oll .libertyfund.org/index/php?option=com_staticxt&staticfile=show.php%3Ftitle=255 &chapter=21681&layout=html.

———. (1869) 1988. *The Subjection of Women.* Edited by Susan Moller Okin. Reprint, Indianapolis, IN: Hackett.

———. (1874) 1998. "The Utility of Religion." Reprinted in *Three Essays on Religion: Nature, the Utility of Religion, Theism.* Amherst, NY: Prometheus Books.

Miller, David. 1995. *On Nationality.* Oxford: Clarendon Press.

Mishra, Pankaj. 2012. *From the Ruins of Empire: The Intellectuals Who Remade Asia.* New York: Farrar, Straus, and Giroux.

Morrison, Andrew. 1989. *Shame: The Underside of Narcissism.* Hillsdale, NJ: The Analytic Press.

Moss, Cynthia. 2000. *Elephant Memories: Thirteen Years in the Life of an Elephant Family.* 2nd ed. Chicago: University of Chicago Press.

Mosse, George L. 1985. *Nationalism and Sexuality: Middle-Class Morality and Sexual Norms in Modern Europe.* Madison: University of Wisconsin Press.

Mozart, Wolfgang Amadeus. (1786) 1979. The Marriage of Figaro (Le Nozze di Figaro) *in Full Score.* Reprint, New York: Dover.

———. (1786) 1993. "The Marriage of Figaro." Reprinted in *Three Mozart Libretti:* The Marriage of Figaro, Don Giovanni *and* Cosi Fan Tutte. Complete in Italian and English. New York: Dover Publications.

Murdoch, Iris. 1970. "The Idea of Perfection." In *The Sovereignty of Good.* London: Routledge.

Nanda, Meera. 2003. *Prophets Facing Backwards.* New Brunswick, NJ: Rutgers University Press.

NDTV. 2010. "West Bengal: Seven Elephants Killed by Speeding Train." September 23. Accessed October 2, 2012. www.ndtv.com/article/india/west-bengal-seven-elephants -killed-by-speeding-train-54181.

Nehru, Jawaharlal. (1936) 1985. *Autobiography*. Centenary edition. Reprint, Delhi: Oxford University Press.

Nussbaum, Charles O. 2007. *The Musical Representation: Meaning, Ontology, and Emotion*. Cambridge, MA: MIT Press.

Nussbaum, Martha C. 1986. *The Fragility of Goodness: Luck and Ethics in Greek Tragedy and Philosophy*. Cambridge: Cambridge University Press.

———. 1989. "Tragic Conflicts." *Radcliffe Quarterly*, March.

———. 1990. *Love's Knowledge: Essays on Philosophy and Literature*. New York: Oxford University Press.

———. 1997. *Cultivating Humanity: A Socratic Defense of Reform in Liberal Education*. Cambridge, MA: Harvard University Press.

———. 2000a. "The Costs of Tragedy: Some Moral Limits of Cost-Benefit Analysis." In *Cost-Benefit Analysis: Legal, Economic and Philosophical Perspectives*, edited by Matthew D. Adler and Eric A. Posner. Chicago: University of Chicago Press, 169–200.

———. 2000b. *Women and Human Development: The Capabilities Approach*. Cambridge and New York: Cambridge University Press.

———. 2001. *Upheavals of Thought: The Intelligence of Emotions*. New York and Cambridge: Cambridge University Press.

———. 2003. "Compassion and Terror." *Daedalus* 132, 10–26.

———. 2004a. *Hiding from Humanity: Disgust, Shame, and the Law*. Princeton, NJ: Princeton University Press.

———. 2004b. "Responses." *Philosophy and Phenomenological Research* 68, 473–486.

———. 2005. "The Comic Soul: Or, This Phallus That Is Not One." In *The Soul of Tragedy: Essays on Athenian Drama*, edited by Victoria Pedrick and Steven M. Oberhelman. Chicago: University of Chicago Press, 155–180.

———. 2006a. *Frontiers of Justice: Disability, Nationality, Species Membership*. Cambridge, MA: Harvard University Press.

———. 2006b. "Radical Evil in the Lockean State." *Journal of Moral Philosophy* 3, 159–178.

———. 2006c. "Replies." *The Journal of Ethics* 10, 463–506.

———. 2007a. *The Clash Within: Democracy, Religious Violence, and India's Future*. Cambridge, MA: Harvard University Press.

———. 2007b. "Radical Evil in Liberal Democracies: The Neglect of the Political Emotions." In *Democracy and the New Religious Pluralism*, edited by Thomas Banchoff. New York: Oxford University Press, 171–202.

———. 2008a. "Human Dignity and Political Entitlements." In *Human Dignity and Bioethics: Essays Commissioned by the President's Council on Bioethics*, edited by Adam Schulman. Washington, DC: Government Printing Office, 351–380.

———. 2008b. *Liberty of Conscience: In Defense of America's Tradition of Religious Equality*. New York: Basic Books.

———. 2008c. "The 'Morality of Pity': Sophocles' *Philoctetes*." In *Rethinking Tragedy*, edited by Rita Felski. Baltimore: Johns Hopkins University Press, 148–169.

———. 2008d. "Toward a Globally Sensitive Patriotism." *Daedalus* 137, 78–93.

———. 2009a. "Bernard Williams: Tragedies, Hope, Justice." In *Reading Bernard Williams,* edited by Daniel Callcut. New York: Routledge, 213–241.

———. 2009b. "Land of My Dreams: Islamic Liberalism under Fire in India." *Boston Review* 34, 10–14.

———. 2010a. "Compassion: Human and Animal." In *Ethics and Humanity: Themes from the Philosophy of Jonathan Glover,* edited by N. Ann Davis, Richard Keshen, and Jeff McMahan, 202–226. New York: Oxford University Press.

———. 2010b. "Kann es einen 'gereinigten Patriotismus' geben? Ein Pladoyer für globale Gerechtigkeit." In *Kosmopolitanismus: Zur Geschichte und Zukunft eines umstrittenen Ideals,* edited by Matthias Lutz-Bachmann, Andreas Niederberger, and Philipp Schink. Göttingen: Velbrück, 242–276.

———. 2010c. *Not for Profit: Why Democracy Needs the Humanities.* Princeton, NJ: Princeton University Press.

———. 2011a. *Creating Capabilities: The Human Development Approach.* Cambridge, MA: Harvard University Press.

———. 2011b. "Perfectionist Liberalism and Political Liberalism." *Philosophy and Public Affairs* 39, 3–45.

———. 2012a. *The New Religious Intolerance.* Cambridge, MA: Harvard University Press.

———. 2012b. "Teaching Patriotism: Love and Critical Freedom." *University of Chicago Law Review* 79, 213–250.

———. 2012c. "Rabindranath Tagore: Subversive Songs for a Transcultural 'Religion of Humanity.'" *Acta Musicologica* 84, 147–160.

———. 2012d. "When Is Forgiveness Right?" *Indian Express.* October 9. www.indianex press.com/news/when-is-forgiveness-right-/1013768/0/.

O'Connell, Kathleen M. 2002. *Rabindranath Tagore: The Poet as Educator.* Kolkata: Visva-Bharati.

Openshaw, Jeanne. 2002. *Seeking Bauls of Bengal.* Cambridge: Cambridge University Press.

Ortony, Andres, Gerald L. Clore, and Allan Collins. 1988. *The Cognitive Structure of Emotions.* Cambridge: Cambridge University Press.

Parthasarathy, D. 2012. "After Reservations: Caste, Institutional Isomorphism, and Affirmative Acton in the IIT's." In *Equalizing Access: Affirmative Action in Higher Education in India, United States, and South Africa,* edited by Zoya Hasan and Martha C. Nussbaum. Delhi: Oxford University Press, 256–271.

Patnaik, Prabhat. 2012. "Affirmative Action and the 'Efficiency Argument.'" In Hasan and Nussbaum, *Equalizing Access.*

Payne, Katy. 2000. "Sources of Social Complexity in the Three Elephant Species." In *Animal Social Complexity: Intelligence, Culture, and Individualized Societies,* edited by F. B. M. de Waal and Peter L. Tyack. Cambridge, MA: Harvard University Press, 57–86.

Peters, Shawn Francis. 2000. *Judging Jehovah's Witnesses: Religious Persecution and the Dawn of the Rights Revolution.* Lawrence: University Press of Kansas.

Piers, Gerhardt, and Milton B. Singer. 1953. *Shame and Guilt: A Psychoanalytic and a Cultural Study.* Springfield, IL: Charles C. Thomas.

Pitcher, George. 1995. *The Dogs Who Came to Stay.* New York: Dutton.

Plotnik, Joshua, F. M. B. de Waal, and Diana Reiss. 2006. "Self-Recognition in an Asian Elephant." *Proceedings of the National Academy of Sciences.* September 13. Accessed October 2, 2012. www.pnas.org/content/103/45/17053.abstract.

Poole, Joyce. 1987. *Coming of Age with Elephants: A Memoir.* New York: Hyperion.

Pridmore, Jay. 2006. *The University of Chicago: The Campus Guide.* New York: Princeton Architectural Press.

Protasi, Sara. 2012. "Envy: Why It's Bad, Why It's (Potentially) Good, and Why We Care about It." Dissertation proposal, Philosophy Department, Yale University.

Quayum, Mohammad. 2007. "Review of Rabindranath Tagore: *Ghare Baire [The Home and the World].*" Freethinker. Accessed October 2, 2012. http://mukto-mona.net /Articles/rabindra_probondho/Quayum_on_tagore.htm.

Rawls, John. 1971. *A Theory of Justice.* Cambridge, MA: Harvard University Press.

———. 1986. *Political Liberalism.* Expanded edition. New York: Columbia University Press.

Renan, Ernst. (1882) 1990. "What Is a Nation?" Translated by Martin Thom. In *Nation and Narration,* edited by Homi Bhabha. New York: Routledge, 8–21.

Rousseau, Jean-Jacques. (1762) 1979. *Emile: or, On Education.* Translated by Allan Bloom. Reprint, New York: Basic Books.

———. (1762) 1987. "On Civil Religion." Reprinted in *Basic Political Writings,* edited and translated by Donald A. Cress, vol. 4. Indianapolis, IN: Hackett, 220–227.

Rozin, Paul, and April E. Fallon. 1987. "A Perspective on Disgust." *Psychological Review* 94: 23–41.

Rozin, Paul, Jonathan Haidt, and Clark R. McCauley. 1999. "Disgust: The Body and Soul Emotion." In *Handbook of Cognition and Emotion,* edited by Tim Dalgleish and Mick J. Power. Hoboken, NJ: John Wiley and Sons, 429–445.

Rybczynski, Witold. 1999. *A Clearing in the Distance: Frederick Law Olmsted and America in the 19th Century.* New York: Scribner.

———. 2010. *Makeshift Metropolis: Ideas about Cities.* New York: Simon and Schuster.

———. 2012. "I Like Ike (and His Memorial)." *New York Times.* March 23.

Sajó, András. 2011. *Constitutional Sentiments.* New Haven: Yale University Press.

Samuels, Shirley, ed. 2012. *The Cambridge Companion to Abraham Lincoln.* New York: Cambridge University Press.

Sandburg, Carl. (1916) 1994. *Chicago Poems.* Reprint, New York: Dover.

Sarkar, Tanika. 2003. "Semiotics of Terror: Muslim Children and Women in Hindu Rashtra." In *Fascism in India: Faces, Fangs, and Facts,* edited by Chaitanya Krishna. Delhi: Manak.

Schlesinger, Arthur M., Jr. 2003. *Crisis of the Old Order: 1919–1933, the Age of Roosevelt.* Boston: Mariner Books.

Schultz, Bart. 2004. *Henry Sidgwick: Eye of the Universe, An Intellectual Biography.* New York: Cambridge University Press.

Searle, John. 1980. "*Prima Facie* Obligations." In *Philosophical Subjects: Essays Presented to P. F. Strawson,* edited by Z. van Straaten. Oxford: Clarendon Press, 238–259.

Segal, Erich. 2001. *The Death of Comedy.* Cambridge, MA: Harvard University Press.

Sen, Amartya. (1997) 2005. "Tagore and His India." Original publication in *New York Review of Books*, June 26, 55–63. Reprinted in Sen, *The Argumentative Indian*, 3–33.

———. 2005. *The Argumentative Indian: Writings on Indian History, Culture, and Identity*. New York: Farrar, Straus, and Giroux.

Sen, Amita. 1999. *Joy in All Work*. Kolkata: Bookfront Publications.

Sen, Mimlu. 2009. *The Honey Gatherers: Travels with the Bauls: The Wandering Minstrels of Rural India*. London: Rider. Originally published as *Baulsphere*. Uttar Pradesh, India: Random House India.

Sennett, Richard. 2004. *Respect in a World of Inequality*. New York: W. W. Norton.

Sherman, Nancy. 1997. *Making a Necessity of Virtue*. New York: Cambridge University Press.

Smith, Adam. (1759) 1976. *The Theory of Moral Sentiments*. Edited by D. D. Raphael and A. L. Macfie. Reprint, Indianapolis: Liberty Classics.

Staples, Brent. 1987. "Just Walk on By: Black Men and Public Space." *Harper's Magazine*. Previously published, in a slightly different form, in 1986 in *Ms. Magazine*.

Steinberg, Michael P. 2004. *Listening to Reason: Culture, Subjectivity, and Nineteenth-Century Music*. Princeton, NJ: Princeton University Press.

———. 2007. *Judaism: Musical and Unmusical*. Chicago: University of Chicago Press.

Stern, Daniel. 1977. *The First Relationship*. Cambridge, MA: Harvard University Press.

———. 1985. *The Interpersonal World of the Infant*. New York: Basic Books.

———. 1990. *Diary of a Baby*. New York: Basic Books.

Stocker, Michael. 1990. *Plural and Conflicting Values*. New York: Oxford University Press.

Sullivan, Patricia. 2009. "Landscape Architect Lawrence Halprin, 93." *Washington Post*. October 27.

Sunstein, Cass R. 2002. *Risk and Reason: Safety, Law, and the Environment*. Cambridge: Cambridge University Press.

———. 2004. *The Second Bill of Rights: FDR's Unfinished Revolution and Why We Need It More than Ever*. New York: Basic Books.

Tagore, Rabindranath. (1910) 2002. *Gora*. Translated by Surendranath Tagore. Reprint, Delhi: Rupa.

———. (1917) 1950. *Nationalism*. Delhi: Macmillan.

———. 1919 *The Home and the World*. Translated by Surendranath Tagore. New York and London: Penguin Books.

———. (1931) 2004. *The Religion of Man*. Reprint, Rhinebeck, NY: Monkfish Press.

———. (1932) 2012. "Man the Artist." Parabaas. Accessed October 2. Reprinted online at http://www.parabaas.com/rabindranath/articles/pRabindranath_MantheArtist.html.

———. 2008. *Of Love, Nature, and Devotion: Selected Songs of Rabindranath Tagore*. Trans. Kalpana Bardhan. Delhi: Oxford University Press.

Taylor, Gabriele. 1985. *Pride, Shame, and Guilt: Emotions of Self-Assessment*. Oxford: Clarendon Press.

Telegraph. 2010. "Seven Elephants Killed by Speeding Train in India." September 24.

tenBroek, Jacobus. 1966. "The Right to Live in the World: The Disabled in the Law of Torts." *California Law Review* 54, 841–919.

Tessman, Lisa. 2005. *Burdened Virtues: Virtue Ethics for Liberatory Struggles*. New York: Oxford University Press.

Thaler, Richard H., and Cass R. Sunstein. 2009. *Nudge: Improving Decisions about Health, Wealth, and Happiness.* Rev. ed. New York: Penguin.

Thompson, Ross A. 1987. "Empathy and Emotional Understanding." In *Empathy and Its Development,* edited by Nancy Eisenberg and Janet Strayer. Cambridge: Cambridge University Press, 119–145.

Tocqueville, Alexis de. (1835) 1966. *Democracy in America.* Edited by J. P. Mayer and Max Lerner, translated by George Lawrence. New York: Harper and Row.

Tomkins, Silvan. 1962–1963. *Affect/Imagery/Consciousness.* Vols. 1–2. New York: Springer.

University of Chicago Library. 1992. *The University and the City: A Centennial View of the University of Chicago.* Chicago: University of Chicago Press.

University of Chicago Publications Office. 1991. *One in Spirit.* Chicago: University of Chicago Press.

University of Chicago Undergraduate Council. 1921. *The University of Chicago Song Book.* Chicago: University of Chicago Press.

Van Parijs, Philippe. 2003. "Difference Principles." In *The Cambridge Companion to John Rawls,* edited by Samuel Freeman. New York and Cambridge: Cambridge University Press, 200–240.

Walzer, Michael. 1973. "Political Action: The Problem of Dirty Hands." *Philosophy and Public Affairs* 2, 160–180.

West, Edwin G. 1965. "Liberty and Education: John Stuart Mill's Dilemma." *Journal of the Royal Institute of Philosophy* 40, 129–142.

Whitman, Walt. (1855) 1973. *Leaves of Grass.* Edited by Sculley Bradley and Harold W. Blodgett. New York and London: W. W. Norton and Company.

Williams, Bernard. 1993a. "Ethical Consistency." In *Problems of the Self.* Cambridge: Cambridge University Press, 166–186.

———. 1993b. *Shame and Necessity.* Berkeley and Los Angeles: University of California Press.

———. (1996) 2006. *"The Women of Trachis:* Fictions, Pessimism, Ethics." Reprinted in *The Sense of the Past: Essays in the History of Philosophy.* Princeton, NJ: Princeton University Press, 49–59.

Wills, Garry. 1992. *Lincoln at Gettysburg: The Words That Remade America.* New York: Simon and Schuster.

Winnicott, Donald. 1965. "The Capacity for Concern." In *The Maturational Processes and the Facilitating Environment.* Madison, CT: International Universities Press, 73–82.

———. (1971) 2005a. "Transitional Objects and Transitional Phenomena." In *Playing and Reality.* Abingdon: Routledge, 1–34.

———. (1971) 2005b. "The Place Where We Live." In *Playing and Reality.* Abingdon: Routledge, 140–148.

Wood, Diane P. 2010. "Constitutions and Capabilities: A (Necessarily) Pragmatic Approach." *Chicago Journal of International Law* 10, 415–429.

Wright, Richard. (1940) 1991. *Native Son.* Restored text edition, edited by Arnold Rampersad. Reprint, New York: HarperPerennial.

Zimbardo, Philip. 2008. *The Lucifer Effect: Understanding How Good People Turn Evil.* New York: Random House.

Acknowledgments

This project was invented by the late Terence Moore, the brilliant philosophy editor at Cambridge University Press with whom I worked on several projects, especially *Upheavals of Thought: The Intelligence of Emotions* (2001). He said to me that I really ought to write a book connecting the moral psychology of compassion, as developed in that book, to the normative political philosophy of the capabilities approach. I thought and rethought this project for a number of years, and it has by now taken on a somewhat broader form, as I came to believe that any such book would have to talk about a wide range of emotions, and not compassion only. During that time, tragically, Terry Moore died of cancer in 2004, at the age of only fifty-one. He was as good as it gets in the business. He believed in philosophy, knew how to convince others to believe in it and to market it aggressively, and knew how to help authors do work that had integrity and scope, while still reaching a wide audience. In the current era of declining trust in the power of ideas and arguments, indeed of the power of books themselves, his loss is especially to be mourned. (His life and personality are well described in an obituary in the *Guardian,* November 10, 2004.) This book is dedicated to his memory.

As I began to map out the book, I found it useful to write a series of articles on related themes, and here I was lucky to have the encouragement of another series of editors: James Miller at *Daedalus,* who published "Compassion and

Terror" and "Toward a Globally Sensitive Patriotism"; Matthias Lutz-Bachmann and Philipp Schink, who invited me to Frankfurt to talk about my new view of patriotism and published a longer version of that same piece; Thom Brooks of the *Journal of Moral Philosophy,* who published "Radical Evil in the Lockean State," and Thomas Banchoff of Georgetown University, who published a longer version of it in an edited collection; John Deigh, who invited me to prepare the article on *The Marriage of Figaro* that appears as chapter 2, and Sami Pihlstrom and Henry Richardson, who published preliminary versions of that same paper; and Jeff McMahan, Ann Davis, and Richard Keshan, who invited me to contribute to a festschrift for Jonathan Glover the paper that later became "Compassion: Human and Animal."

I've also been lucky to have perspectives from a number of different nations, having presented the material on patriotism in Germany, Finland, and India, "Compassion: Human and Animal" in India and Korea, "Radical Evil in the Lockean State" in Greece and India, and the essay on *Figaro* in France, Finland, and Peru. So I'm hugely grateful to audiences in all these countries for telling me how the issues look from the viewpoint of their heterogeneous experiences (even more heterogeneous than this list suggests, since the meetings in Finland and Peru were multinational).

I also got a lot of help from teaching: particularly a class on Rabindranath Tagore cotaught with historian Tanika Sarkar in 2006, a seminar on education and moral psychology taught in 2007, a seminar on patriotism and cosmopolitanism taught in 2006, and a class on emotions, reason, and law taught in the spring of 2010 and 2012. I am grateful to all the students in those classes for helping me understand things.

Finally, I have presented the material in workshop form at the Stanford University Political Theory Workshop and the Columbia Law School, and the manuscript is greatly enriched by those discussions. Above all, I am grateful to my colleagues at the University of Chicago Law School, who discussed four separate parts of the book at work-in-progress workshops and offered invaluable help. Aziz Huq, Alison LaCroix, and Saul Levmore read almost every part at some point and gave me especially insightful criticisms.

For comments and conversations on these and other occasions, I'm also grateful to Daniel Abebe, Douglas Baird, Corey Brettschneicker, Daniel Brudney, Emily Buss, Tim Carter, Joshua Cohen, David Estlund, Rick Furtak, Chris Havasy, John Deigh, Steve Darwall, Richard Epstein, Bernard Harcourt, Jeffrey Israel, Sharon Krause, Charles Larmore, Brian Leiter, Christopher Maloney, Douglas MacLean, Jonathan Masur, Richard McAdams, Jeff McMahan, Alison McQueen, Jennifer Nou, Charles Nussbaum, Joshua Ober, Eric Posner, Henry Richardson, Adam Samaha, Geoffrey Sayre-McCord, Marco Segala, Michael Steinberg, Nicholas Stephanopoulos, Madhavi Sunder, Cass Sunstein, Miira Tuominen, Bill Watson, Laura Weinrib, Susan Wolf, and Diane Wood. In the final stages of revision, anonymous readers' reports were enormously helpful. And for invaluable research assistance I am grateful to Ryan Long, Chris Skene, and Bill Watson.

Index